W9-ADO-803

VIRGINIA

Harrisonburg
Bridgewater
McDowell
Cross Keys
Weyer's Cave
Piedmont
Staunton
Waynesboro
Port Republic
Afton
Charlottesville
Barboursville
Montpelier
Gordonsville
Liberty Mill
Barnett's Fd.
Madison
Orange C.H.
Morton's Fd.
Rapidan R.
Mitchell's Fd.
Culpeper
Kelly's Fd.
Gap

Louisa C.H.
Virginia Central R.R.
Pamunkey R.
Hanover Jct.
Hanover C.H.
Spotsylvania
Guinea Sta.
Fredericksburg
Rappahannock R.
Po
Rapidan R.
Orange Rd.
Swift Run Gap
Brown's Gap

Lexington
Lynchburg
Appomattox
Orange & Alexandria R.R.

James River
Appomattox River
Burkeville
Sayler's Cr.
Amelia C.H.
Mattoax Sta.
Drewry's Bluff
Richmond
Ft. Harrison
Petersburg & Lynchburg R.R.
Petersburg & Danville R.R.
Five Forks
Petersburg
City Point (Hopewell)
Harrison's Ldg.
Malvern Hill
Cold Harbor
Gaines's Mill
Chickahominy R.

Miles
0 10 20 30

BARBARA LONG

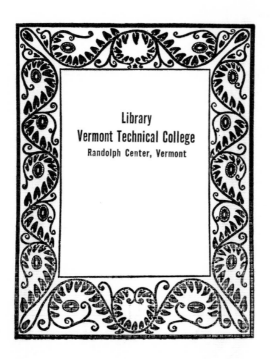

RECOLLECTIONS

OF A

MARYLAND CONFEDERATE SOLDIER AND STAFF OFFICER

UNDER

JOHNSTON, JACKSON AND LEE.

BY

M^C HENRY HOWARD

INTRODUCTION, CORRECTIONS AND NOTES By
James I. Robertson, Jr.
Head, Department of History
Virginia Polytechnic Institute and State University

ENDPAPER MAP By
Mrs. E. B. (Barbara) Long

Press of

Morningside Bookshop

1975

FACSIMILE
26

ISBN - 0-89029-019-9

Original printing by
Williams & Wilkins Company
Baltimore 1914

FOREWORD
to the Morningside Edition

Maryland during the Civil War was a border state in both geography and sentiment. It abutted Washington on the north and lay squarely between Union and Confederate territory. The eastern portion of the state was decidedly pro-Southern. The western region was just as avidly pro-Northern. The state contributed regiments and batteries to both sides. Marylanders of high rank were more prominent in Confederate service, even though more men served in the Federal armies. It is doubtful that as many as 21,000 sons from the state fought with the South, as has been asserted,[1] but those who did take their stand behind the Stars and Bars fought with unimpeachable gallantry.

It is therefore regrettable that so few memoirs by Maryland Confederate soldiers exist. Even those handful with a degree of fame and respectability leave something to be desired. Harry Gilmor, *Four Years in the Saddle* (New York, 1866), is well-known and dramatic, but a work unreliable and ghost-written. William W. Goldsborough, *The Maryland Line in the Confederate States Army* (Baltimore, 1869), lacks the depth of perspective and detail necessary for a sound unit history. Randolph H. McKim, *A Soldier's Recollections* (New York, 1910), is of limited usefulness as a Maryland narrative because much of the author's war service was as chaplain with a Virginia regiment. George W. Booth, *Personal Reminiscences of a Maryland Soldier in the War Between the States* (Baltimore, 1898), provides superb glimpses only, while Tunstall Smith (ed.), *Richard Snowden Andrews . . .* (Baltimore, 1910), is a deserved eulogy and little else.

[1]*Confederate Veteran,* XVII (1909), 266.

The premier Maryland book on the Civil War, and one of the scarcest of personal memoirs for the Army of Northern Virginia, is McHenry Howard, *Recollections of a Maryland Confederate Soldier and Staff Officer under Johnston, Jackson and Lee* (Baltimore, 1914). At its publication it was hailed as a work "with accuracy and fidelity to historic truth . . . a thrilling narrative, wholly reliable and most engaging in interest from beginning to end."[2] Time has only enriched this early judgment. Howard had the enviable ability to combine sweeping observations with personal insights. Moreover, his memoirs have a double importance in Civil War literature. They are the most voluminous recollections by a Maryland soldier, and they stand with the best of that small group of reminiscences prepared by Confederate staff officers—individuals whose position between officers and common soldiers enabled them to see war on both levels. Captain Howard acted as such an intermediary with both dedication and aplomb.

No participant in the Civil War had a more illustrious heritage. One of his earliest forebears was Sir John Howard (1430-1485), the first Duke of Norfolk.[3] McHenry Howard's great-great-grandfather, John Howard of Manchester, fought beside King James II during Monmouth's 1685 invasion. John Howard then emigrated to America and settled on a grant in the Baltimore area. Marriage to Joanna O'Carroll of a prominent colonial Maryland family produced a number of children. One of them was Cornelius Howard,

[2]*Southern Historical Society Papers*, XXXIX (1914), 220.
[3]McHenry Howard to Barnard C. Steiner, May 1, 1919, Howard Family Papers, Maryland Historical Society. Cited hereafter as Howard Papers.

who married Ruth Eager.

From this union came the most distinguished of the Howards. The eldest son (and McHenry Howard's grandfather) was John Eager Howard. He was one of the authentic heroes of the American Revolution. Shortly after hostilities began, he organized an infantry company for the Maryland Battalion. Heroism marked his conduct at White Plains, Germantown, Monmouth and Guilford. He was severely wounded in the fighting at Eutaw Springs. In the important battle of Cowpens, his superior reported, Col. Howard "seized the critical moment and turned the fortunes of the day." He was one of eleven officers awarded medals for extraordinary valor by the Continental Congress. So outstanding were this soldier's exploits that a verse in the Maryland state song calls on posterity to "remember Howard's warlike thrust."[4]

John Eager Howard served the new nation as state senator, governor and U. S. senator. His 1787 marriage to Margaret Chew, daughter of Pennsylvania's chief justice, attracted a host of dignitaries that included George Washington. Howard later declined the secretaryship of state but did accept a brigadier's commission when war with France seemed imminent.[5]

The youngest of John and Margaret Howard's six sons was Charles Howard. Born April 26, 1802, at "Belvidere," the family residence in Baltimore County, Charles Howard gave his life to civic affairs and com-

---

[4]Clement A. Evans (ed.), *Confederate Military History* (Atlanta, 1899), II, 313. See also Cary Howard, "John Eager Howard: Patriot and Public Servant," *Maryland Historical Magazine,* LXII (1967), 300-17.

[5]John Eager Howard headed a "committee of safety" in the War of 1812 while four of his sons served in the field. The old hero died in October, 1827, but his memory is perpetuated through an impressive monument in Baltimore.

iv

passion rather than to private concerns and commerce.
He served brief tenures as president of the Baltimore
and Susquehanna Railroad and as City Collector for
Baltimore. Yet, McHenry Howard later observed,
Charles Howard had "no private occupation but filled
many positions of public and semi-public character."[6]
He labored faithfully in a number of charitable organizations; he was at one time presiding judge of the
Orphans' Court in Baltimore; after his 1860 appointment to the Baltimore Board of Police Commissioners,
Howard became president of that agency. A biographical directory stated of him: "There was scarcely an
enterprise or an institution of public benevolence or
usefulness to which at some time or other he did not
give his personal aid and labor."[7]

Charles Howard followed the family tradition of
choosing a wife from solid stock. Elizabeth Phoebe Key
was the eldest daughter of Francis Scott Key and Mary
Tayloe Lloyd.[8] On November 9, 1825, Howard and the
daughter of the author of "The Star-Spangled Banner"
were married in the Washington suburb of Georgetown.
Six sons and three daughters eventually comprised their
large family. McHenry Howard was the youngest son.
He was born the day after Christmas, 1838, in the
family residence at the corner of Vernon Place and
Washington Place in Baltimore.[9]

[6]Biographical sheet, McHenry Howard file, Princeton University
Archives.
[7]The Biographical Cyclopedia of Representative Men of Maryland . . .
(Baltimore, 1879), 417.
[8]She was also the niece of Mrs. Roger B. Taney, whose husband pre-
sided over the U. S. Supreme Court at the time of the Dred Scott decision.
[9]Biographical sheet completed by Howard in 1913, Howard file, Princeton. An unidentified newspaper clipping in the same collection stated that
he was born "in an old colonial house that stood at Charles and Monument streets."

Most of his early education was at the highly respected academy of Everett M. Topping. In January, 1857, Howard entered Princeton University as a member of the junior class. He was a brilliant student. At the end of his junior year, he ranked second among his seventy-five classmates with a 99.26 grade average. He participated in a number of student activities and cemented a nickname, "Mac," that remained with him until his death. At his June, 1858, graduation from Princeton, he ranked second in a class of sixty-five. His academic average, however, had "slipped" to a 98.20 level.[10]

The legal profession seemed best suited for his talents, so Howard began studying law under noted Baltimore attorney Severn Teackle Wallis. It proved difficult to concentrate on law as storm clouds of sectional conflict steadily massed. John Brown's 1859 raid on Harper's Ferry was jolting proof that action was replacing discussion. Howard and several of his friends thereupon joined Capt. Harry D. G. Carroll's company in the prestigious Maryland Guard Battalion. In mid-April, 1861, the call to arms rang loud. Howard had just been admitted to the bar when Federal troops en route to Washington fought a bloody battle with citizens in the streets of Baltimore.

Twenty-two years old, unsettled, and filled with a Southern patriotism characteristic of most Baltimoreans, Howard hastened to Richmond and enlisted in a Maryland company being formed there. The company journeyed to the Shenandoah Valley to join Gen. Joseph E. Johnston's forces as part of the 1st Maryland Infan-

[10]Biographical sheet, *ibid.;* 1857-1858 autograph book, Howard Papers.

try, CSA. One officer, with obvious prejudice, described the regiment's members as "dandies of the army, better dressed, better shod, better drilled, and in gayer spirits than any in the whole army, and never one deserter."[11] Howard, who initially held the rank of acting orderly sergeant, refutes some of those compliments without distracting appreciably from the excellence of the 1st Maryland.

Howard always boasted that with the exceptions of Spotsylvania and Sayler's Creek (which, coincidentally, marked the two times he was captured), he "never was in a battle when our side was driven from the field." In July, 1861, he took part in both the rapid march to Manassas and the great battle that marked the beginning of full-scale civil war. His memoirs provide one of the best accounts of the late-afternoon Confederate attack that broke the Federal right flank and brought victory. Howard spent the quiet autumn months on picket duty in northern Virginia. Promotion to First Sergeant of his company came in December. A permanent transfer to staff level followed three months later. On March 26, 1862, Howard was named an aide on the staff of Brig. Gen. Charles S. Winder; and with the new assignment came a lieutenancy.[12]

Winder—like Albert Sidney Johnston and Turner Ashby—was a potentially superb field commander who did not live long enough to fulfill high expectations. Howard's narrative gives an intimate picture of the Maryland brigadier's service. Winder and Howard joined the Valley army of Maj. Gen. Thomas J. Jackson

[11]*Confederate Veteran*, XVII (1909), 266.
[12]The promotion to aide-de-camp is in the Howard Papers.

shortly after the battle of Kernstown. With Winder commanding the celebrated Stonewall Brigade, Howard was more than an eyewitness to all of the major battles of Jackson's now-famous 1862 Valley Campaign. Howard's performance of duty elicited repeated praise from Winder.[13]

Pressure on Richmond by Gen. George B. McClellan's Federal army led to a union there between the forces of Jackson and Robert E. Lee. A daring counterattack known as the Seven Days Campaign followed. Howard was in the thick of much of the fighting. At Gaines's Mill, the aide was "exposed to a heavy fire frequently and at great risk." The campaign ended with the battle of Malvern Hill. Howard and a fellow staff officer, wrote Winder, "particularly attracted my admiration by their coolness and untiring efforts to keep the men in their position. Their escape from injury is truly providential."[14] Yet the pleasure and self-satisfaction experienced by Howard was short-lived. On August 9, 1862, in a bitter fight at Cedar Run, Gen. Winder was killed.

This left Howard temporarily without a military assignment. He accompanied Winder's body to Richmond for burial. Overdue visits to friends in central and northern Virginia caused him to miss the Second Manassas and Antietam campaigns. Late in September, Howard joined the staff of Brig. Gen. George H. Steuart, a colorful Marylander commanding the Southern

[13]U. S. War Dept. (comp.), *War of the Rebellion: A Compilation of the Official Records of the Union and Confederate Armies* (Washington, 1880-1901), Ser. I, XII, Pt. 1, 737, 739, 742. Cited hereafter as *OR;* all references are to Ser. I.

[14]*Ibid.,* XI, Pt. 2, 571, 572.

forces in and around Winchester. Little of note occurred
during the three months that Howard spent in the
Valley. His recollections do attest to the extent to which
he enjoyed socializing. Not mentioned in his book was
a momentary infatuation with the daughter of Mrs.
Cornelia McDonald, one of Winchester's most prominent matrons.[15]

Late in December, 1862, sickness, boredom and the
absence from duty of Gen. Steuart induced Howard to
go to Richmond. He applied for a commission in the
line, and he somehow persuaded the usually tight-lipped
"Stonewall" Jackson to forward an endorsement.
Howard had performed staff duties "with marked
ability," the Confederate general stated, and he added:
"His patriotic course during the war, and the successful
manner in which he has discharged his duties, entitle
him to great praise and confidence."[16] Yet before
Howard's request could receive favorable action, his
health failed.

He journeyed first to Lynchburg and then to the
mountains of southwestern Virginia to recuperate.
Whatever the nature of his illness was, the change-of-
scenery worked well. On March 7, 1863, he accepted
an invitation to join the staff of another Marylander,
Brig. Gen. Isaac R. Trimble.[17] Unusual complications
then occurred. Trimble fell ill, and this caused a delay
in Howard reporting for duty. By the time the staff
officer started for the Confederate army, Gettysburg

[15]See Cornelia McDonald, *A Diary with Reminiscences of the War and
Refugee Life in the Shenandoah Valley, 1860-1865* (Nashville, 1934), 113.
[16]*Confederate Veteran,* XXXI (1923), 427.
[17]Howard's assignment was dated Mar. 12, 1863, to take rank from
Feb. 1. The original order is in the Howard Papers.

had been fought and Trimble (who had hobbled into battle) had been captured. Howard reached Lee's forces in time to take part in a brief fight at Greencastle, Pa. He then retreated with the army to Williamsport, Md., and served for a day on the staff of Gen. William E. "Grumble" Jones. Howard appears to have been one of the few officers who had real affection for that controversial Virginian. This may be attributed to his short tenure of service under Jones.

Howard then rejoined the staff of "Maryland" Steuart. He saw service in the Bristoe campaign, then went to Richmond and received confirmation into the Episcopal Church. He was back on duty for the Mine Run actions late in November. Steuart reported that the gallantry in action of Howard and another staff officer was "only equaled by their promptness and efficiency."[18]

The quiet winter of 1863-1864 ended in May with the collision of Lee and Grant in the Wilderness. Howard emerged unharmed from the May 5-6 holocaust in the woods west of Fredericksburg. Unknown to him, he was then an object of some concern. His older brother, army surgeon E. Lloyd Howard, wrote home in the midst of this new Federal advance: "I will keep my eyes upon him through the coming campaign as well as I can . . . I feel the most intolerable depression while the fight is going on, and he is in it. The suspense and anxiety is terrible. I am not prone to indulge in a display of feeling and Mac has never dreamed of the deep affection I bear for him. No one can know the utter wretchedness that comes over me at times when

[18]*OR,* XXIX, Pt. 1, 864.

x

I think of the peril in which he is placed, and watch
the point where his command is engaged."[19]

These fears for the baby brother in the family all
too quickly became reality. On May 12, at Spotsylvania,
droves of Federals charged through the rain and broke
the Confederate line at a point ever after known as
"The Bloody Angle." Never in the Civil War did more
vicious combat take place. The old Stonewall Brigade
ceased to exist. One entire Confederate division was
overrun and shattered. Howard was but one of hundreds of Southerners captured in the bitter fighting,
and he was in a contingent of 184 officers dispatched
shortly afterward to the Union prisoner-of-war camp
at Fort Delaware.[20] Howard was weary and dispirited
on his arrival at the prison. Yet he retained a sense of
humor. In his first letter home after being captured,
he commented: "I suppose you were much surprised
to hear of my being a prisoner. I certainly was surprised
myself."[21]

Howard's book presents one of the few extant memoirs of life inside Fort Delaware. He showed that while
the compound was lacking in luxuries, it was a far cry
from such other stockades of the Civil War as Elmira
and Andersonville. Fortunately for him, his incarceration was relatively brief. In November, he and several
score prisoners were shipped by boat to Savannah, Ga.
There they were exchanged under a system that represented one of the few niceties officially observed amid
the horrors of war. Howard leisurely made his way back

[19]E. Lloyd Howard to Mary Howard, May 8, 1864, Howard Papers.
[20]Isaac W. K. Handy, *United States Bonds* (Baltimore, 1874), 426.
[21]McHenry Howard to Elizabeth Key Howard, May 22, 1864, Howard
Papers.

to Lee's army by visiting acquaintances in Savannah, Charleston, Lynchburg and Louisa County, Va.

Late in January, 1865, with his exchange officially complete, now-Capt. Howard became a member of the staff of Maj. Gen. G. W. Custis Lee. This son of Robert E. Lee was in charge of the fragile, makeshift defenses of the James River line between Richmond and Petersburg. His command included landlocked sailors, artillerists without cannon, home guard units and such citizen-soldiers as Lee could scrape together. If Howard felt humiliated by the indignity of this last command, he made no mention of it. Indeed, he barely had time to become familiar with the heterogenuous units in Custis Lee's division before Grant launched the climactic assaults that broke the Confederate defense line south of Petersburg.

Howard served with the rear guard as the Army of Northern Virginia plodded westward in retreat. His war career ended abruptly on April 6 at Sayler's Creek. He was captured when Federal forces surrounded and hammered into submission no less than a third of the Southern army. In company with a brother, Lt. Col. James Howard, the staff officer was shipped to the Federal prison on Johnson's Island in Lake Erie. The two men reached the compound on April 19 (not April 20, as Howard mistakenly stated in his memoirs). On the following day, James Howard reassured his mother by writing: "We arrived here last evening and immediately found plenty of friends who showed us the attention and kindness which we so much needed."[22]

The Johnson's Island imprisonment lasted less than

---

[22]James Howard to Elizabeth Key Howard, Apr. 20, 1865, *ibid.*

a month. On May 26, Howard received his parole. The
trip to Baltimore ended on a cynical note. Howard
arrived home to find in his accumulated mail an 1862
conscription notice directing him to report for military
duty!

Only twenty-six at war's end, Howard still had ahead
of him a productive and prosperous life. He resumed
his law practice from an office at 41 Lexington Street.
For forty-five years he "was one of the most prominent
figures at the Baltimore bar, taking an active part in
many important cases."[23] However, his prompt successes
as an attorney did not curtail his personal life. On June
18, 1867, he married Julia Douglas Coleman at "Jerdone Castle," the bride's home in Louisa County, Va.
His family steadily increased thereafter with the addition of four children: Elizabeth Gray (1868), Charles
McHenry (1870), Mary (1874) and Julia McHenry
(1886).

Military matters and veterans' affairs also received
a large share of Howard's efforts. In 1867 he helped
organize the 5th Regiment, Maryland National Guard;
and for five years he commanded Company E. In 1871
he was instrumental in the establishment of the Society
of the Army and Navy of the Confederate States in
Maryland. He served both as secretary and as president
of that organization. He also became governor of the
Society of Colonial Wars in the State of Maryland,
vice president of the Society of Sons of the Revolution
in Maryland, and a long-time member of the Maryland
Historical Society's executive committee. Howard re-

[23]Unidentified newspaper clipping, Howard file, Princeton. A sizable
portion of his law practice was in acting as chief examiner of titles for the
Maryland Title Insurance Company. *Baltimore Sun,* Sept. 14, 1923.

turned briefly to active military duty in 1877, when he led a company of the 7th Maryland National Guard in combatting riots that swept through Baltimore. His role in quelling these disturbances doubtless played some part in his election to a two-year term on the Baltimore city council.

Throughout these busy decades, Howard remained tall and well-proportioned. The most noticeable change in his features was a huge mustache that he cultivated after the Civil War and wore for the remainder of his life.[24] His favorite pastime for many years was fishing. Yet the older Howard got, the more absorbed in history he became. Casual labors on his wartime reminiscences seemed only to whet his appetite for other historical undertakings. He began writing detailed accounts of his fishing trips; he meticulously organized and transcribed family letters of Revolutionary times; he worked for long stretches on a family genealogy (which was never completed). Years of research in local history resulted in a veritable outpouring of articles for the Maryland Historical Society's journal.[25] Yet the narrative of Civil War service was always his premier labor of love.

Howard spent over fifty years in the preparation of those memoirs. The project actually began in the autumn of 1861, when he recorded in a small notebook a summary of his first months in the Confederate army.

[24]A July, 1886, photograph of Howard is in the Howard Papers. So are some of the fishing journals and family documents subsequently mentioned.

[25]See *Maryland Historical Magazine*, IX (1914) 107-56; XIII (1918), 179-82; XIV (1919), 384-99; XV (1920), 65-71, 168-80, 292-303, 312-24; XVI (1921), 19-28, 178-89; XVII (1922), 20-33, 226; XVIII (1923), 1-22, 293-99.

Letters to his parents eventually became valuable reference sources. In January, 1863, Howard began keeping a diary too often interrupted by war. Nevertheless, armed with such materials, and with memories very fresh in his mind, Howard embarked on his narrative a few months after his 1865 parole.

Good intentions soon went awry. Progress was slow because of his varied postwar activities. In the preparation of his book, Howard spurned the traditional chronological approach. He began by writing the section on Lee's retreat from Petersburg to Sayler's Creek, This monograph originally appeared in an 1874 issue of *Southern Magazine*. It subsequently became Chapter XXXIV of his book.[26] Next came the memoir of the Wilderness-Spotsylvania campaigns. It was an April, 1883, address by Howard to the Military Historical Society of Massachusetts, which published it as part of its valuable Civil War series.[27] The address was republished without change as Chapters XXVII-XXIX of Howard's recollections. Howard bridged many gaps in his rough drafts by consulting with former comrades and by utilizing all available printed sources. He was one of the first Civil War soldier-authors to make extensive use of the *Official Records,* and his reliance on articles in the *Southern Historical Society Papers* is apparent throughout his work.

It is pathetic that Howard completed the memoirs under adversity. In 1908 Julia Coleman Howard, his beloved wife of forty-one years, died at the family

[26]Howard's first section was also published in *Southern Historical Society Papers,* XXXI (1903), 129-45.

[27]See *Papers of the Military Historical Society of Massachusetts,* IV (1905), 81-116.

summer home in Oakland, Md. Two years later, Howard "suffered a severe illness" that forced his retirement from active law practice.[28] He became increasingly confined to the family residence at 901 St. Paul Street in Baltimore. There he pursued historical projects and welcomed a steady stream of visitors. Howard spent the greater part of 1912-1913 in rewriting and polishing the narrative. The final manuscript, in longhand on legal-size paper, shows a small, precise script void of any hint of either haste or weariness.[29] Compatriots and friends who had waited long for its publication were rewarded early in 1914 when the Wilkins and Williams Company of Baltimore released *Recollections of a Maryland Confederate Soldier and Staff Officer under Johnston, Jackson and Lee.*

Howard continued to tinker with the book even after its publication. He seemed to relish preparing annotated copies for presentation to friends. Five copies with his extensive marginal notes are known to exist, and there may well be other such special volumes.[30] Meanwhile, Howard enjoyed quiet contentment in the twilight of his life. In January, 1922, a local newspaper ran a feature story on the white-haired veteran. Terming him "one of Baltimore's most prominent and venerable citizens," that paper added that he was "far from robust, but his charming personality is a thing that neither fades nor perishes, and there is still much about his bearing to recall the erect and gallant soldier."[31]

[28]Unidentified newspaper clipping, Howard file, Princeton.

[29]A few sections of the original manuscript are in the Howard Papers. The line maps are in black ink, with troop positions shown in red.

[30]For a summary of the known annotated volumes, see *Maryland Historical Magazine*, LXIV (1969), 295-96.

[31]*Baltimore News,* Jan. 19, 1922.

Outward appearances masked a waning of strength that accelerated in Howard's eighty-fifth year. In June, 1923, as was his custom in summertime, he journeyed to Oakland to be in the country surroundings he loved so well. The infirmities of old age suddenly became severe; and on September 11, "after a brief illness," he died at the summer home.[32] Funeral services were conducted two days later from the Baltimore residence. Private burial services followed at St. Thomas' Church Cemetery in Maryland's Green Spring Valley.

Howard secured a place in posterity largely because of his Civil War memoirs. *Recollections of a Maryland Confederate Soldier* has risen in value with the passage of each decade. It lacks such usual weaknesses as a rash of improbable details and anecdotes. It openly and authoritatively refutes statements in the long-respected recollections of W. W. Goldsborough, Robert L. Dabney and Henry Kyd Douglas. At the same time, it provides a broad, reliable vista of affairs inside the armies of Jackson and Lee. This explains why the book has been praised in recent years as "an excellent narrative," a memoir that is "among the most valuable of Confederate soldiers' reminiscences," and a work "possessed of both insight and interest."[33]

These are highly laudable evaluations, but a commendation that Howard must have prized deeply came in a letter he received a year before his death. A Northerner congratulated him on his book, then added: "The

[32]Mary Howard to "Mr. Collins," June 9, 1924, Howard file, Princeton. See also obituaries in *Baltimore Sun,* Sept. 12-14, 1923.

[33]Douglas S. Freeman, *R. E. Lee: A Biography* (New York, 1934-1935), IV, 564; E. Merton Coulter, *Travels in the Confederate States: A Bibliography* (Norman, Okla., 1948), 138; Allan Nevins *et al.* (eds.), *Civil War Books: A Critical Bibliography* (Baton Rouge, 1967-1969), I, 107.

cause for which you fought was lost, but the sincerity, gallantry and patriotic character of those who fought it will always remain a glorious American tradition."[34]

It is unfortunate that a large number of editorial slips marred the original printing of the Howard narrative. Yet most of these have been eliminated in this new edition. Fifty errors and omissions in the original text have been corrected with new type. Other misspellings and distortions of names are emended in the index compiled for this edition. Notes at the end of the narrative provide still more corrections, as well as clarifications on matters discussed by Howard. Throughout the preparation of this new edition, the overriding intent has been to improve a book justifiably regarded as a Confederate classic.

The Hon. C. A. Porter Hopkins of Glyndon, Md., first alerted me to the value of the Howard recollections. His friendly encouragement over a period of many years is deeply appreciated. I am also grateful to the following persons who helped in small but indispensable ways: Edward C. Campbell, Jr., Columbia, S. C.; Alexander P. Clark, Curator of Manuscripts, and Earle E. Coleman, University Archivist, Princeton University; Mrs. Lydia H. Davis, Maryland Historical Society; Richard B. Harwell, Librarian, Georgia Southern College; Mrs. Lilla M. Hawes, Director, Georgia Historical Society; Miss Mary E. Willey, Special Collections Librarian, Knox College; and W. Emerson Wilson, Wilmington, Delaware.

[34]George Gray to McHenry Howard, May 11, 1922, Howard Papers.

Mrs. Barbara Long's endpaper map again reflects the artistry that she lends to Civil War cartography.

A grant from Virginia Polytechnic Institute and State University paved the way for a necessary research trip. The Inter-Library Loan Department of Virginia Tech's Newman Library gave prompt attention to my every request. Robert J. Younger, proprietor of Morningside Bookshop, could not have been more helpful. His support and assistance truly lessened the complicated chores of editing.

James I. Robertson, Jr.

Blacksburg, Va.

PREFACE

In the Fall of 1865, when the details were fresh in my memory, I wrote out an account of the retreat from Richmond in April, 1865, of the command with which I was then serving in the Confederate Army. Some years afterwards it came into the possession of Dr. W. Hand Browne, Editor of the *Southern Magazine*, which was made the organ of the Southern Historical Society and gave to it a certain number of pages as a supplement to the *Magazine*, being page numbered separately. In 1874 Dr. Browne printed this account, under the title, "Retreat of Custis Lee's Division and Battle of Sailor's Creek," in these *Transactions of the Southern Historical Society*.

About 1883 I wrote for the Military Historical Society of Massachusetts an account of the capture of the salient at Spotsylvania Court House on May 12, 1864, and soon after elaborated it to "Notes and Recollections of the Opening of the Campaign of 1864," which completed paper I read to the Society April 16, 1883, and it has since appeared in Volume IV of its publications.

These two papers were referred to and quoted from by General A. A. Humphreys in his standard *Virginia Campaign of 1864 and 1865*—or rather the Spotsylvania part of the second paper was, for the completed paper had not been given to the Society when his history was written.

At different times since the war, from as far back as when my memory was much more distinct about details than now, I have put, roughly, in writing my recollection of other periods, selected as inclination led me or to which my attention would be drawn by something appearing in print or otherwise. And during the last two years I have been re-writing and connecting all these accounts until I now have a continuous narrative of the war as I saw it, from its beginning to the end. While so completing it now, I have often consulted authorities, and especially the War Records, but not for the purpose of introducing new matter in my own recollections, preferring to let them stand, generally, for what they were worth; I was willing, however, to look for corrections of plainly erroneous statements and to supply some exact dates or other such information; which I have for the most part put in notes. But several times when I was minded to at least modify some of my statements, I have unexpectedly come across confirmation of my recollection in minute particulars, and sometimes curiously.

At first I had no object in view but to make a record of my recollections and leave it behind me. But friends have advised me that what I have written is worth publication and would be interesting to a circle of readers; moreover, the use which General Humphreys made of my two early papers encourages me to hope even that I may be able to contribute something about the details of the war, and especially to the history of the Army of Northern Virginia, in which I served from Manassas to within two days of Appomattox. All accounts of eye-witnesses in such operations have some value, and one who was through the Valley Campaign of 1862 for instance, which will always be studied as a new chapter in military history, and was often close to the side of Stonewall Jackson and Ashby, and others, ought to be able to say something worth the telling.

My grandfather on my father's side was a Revolutionary soldier to whom Congress voted one of the only eleven

medals given by it in the war. He was Governor of
Maryland when the Federal Union of 1789 was put into
operation, and held other high offices, State and Federal.
In 1817 he received the complimentary vote of the 22
Massachusetts Electors for the office of Vice-President of
the United States. He died as late as 1827 and had between fifty and seventy-five descendants living when the
war broke out. They ought to have been attached to
the Union—and they were—but when the issue came in
1861 between North and South, every man, woman and
child was Southern.

On my mother's side, my great grandfather was a
Revolutionary soldier and his son, my grandfather, was
the author of "The Star Spangled Banner" and one of
the founders of the African Colonization Society. He
died as late as 1843 and in 1861 there were upwards of
sixty descendants living, and I think of them also every
man, woman and child was Southern. Of all these, on
both sides, I cannot recall that any owned slaves in 1861.

I mention this in illustration of the sentiment in Maryland, although many other families were not as happily
united. But if there was a division of feeling in Baltimore and other parts of the State, and a predominant
Union population in the Northern part, settled largely
from across Mason and Dixon's Line, yet I think there
is no doubt, and that it has become accepted history,
that if Maryland had had the opportunity, it would have
united itself with its sister States of the Confederacy.
Marylanders who went into the Southern army did so,
therefore, not merely to aid the cause of the Confederacy as it was constituted, but believing that they were
serving their own State—in subjection—in the only way
that was left to them.

CONTENTS

6 CONTENTS

ILLUSTRATIONS

SPECIAL PHOTOGRAPH SECTION

CHAPTER I

THE MARYLAND GUARD AND 19th APRIL, 1861

The Battalion known as the "Maryland Guard," in the 53d Regiment of Infantry, Maryland Militia, was organized in Baltimore in the winter of 1859-60, partly, and principally, for the purpose of being a reserve to aid the civil authorities in preserving law and order in the city, lately rescued by the Reform movement from the domination of a mob, and partly because of the feeling of insecurity and alarm that pervaded the Border and Southern States after the insurrectionary attempt of John Brown at Harper's Ferry. Shortly after its formation, or while it was organizing, I joined Company C, of which Langdon Erving was the first captain, but who was promoted to the lieutenant-colonelcy about that time and was succeeded by Harry Dorsey Gough Carroll. The French Zouave was the model soldier of that period according to American ideas, and the Maryland Guard uniform was patterned on his. The full dress was a dark blue jacket, short and close fitting and much embroidered with yellow; a blue flannel shirt with a close row of small round gilt buttons (for ornament merely,) down the front, between yellow trimming; blue pantaloons, very baggy and gathered below the knee and falling over the tops of long drab gaiters; a small blue cap, of the kepi kind, also trimmed with yellow; and, finally, a wide red sash, or band rather, kept wide by hooks and eyes on the ends, completed this gaudy dress, which made a very brilliant effect on street parade but was totally unsuitable for any active service. To fully adjust

9

it, a man almost required the services of a valet—or a
sister or sweetheart. The "fatigue" (undress) uniform
substituted a more generous blue jacket and ordinary
black pantaloons and left off the gaiters and sash, and
was therefore the more sensible or less absurd. But
there has never been a finer militia organization in this
country, and its schooling was of great service to the very
many of them who went South.

We drilled regularly and paraded on different occasions, notably at the reception of the Japanese am-
bassadors on 8th June, 1860—when we disgraced ourselves by presenting arms[1] on the march in passing in
review before the Gilmor House in Monument Square—
and at the opening of Druid Hill Park on 19th October,
1860, but nothing more eventful marked our history
until the 19th of April, 1861.

Of the affair on Pratt Street that day I saw nothing,
being engaged in my office writing a deed (I had been admitted to the Bar on the 4th of March), until Mr. John
H. Thomas hurried in and asked me "if I knew that they
were playing the mischief (in his excitement he used a
stronger word,) down town and that the militia had been
ordered out?" Leaving deed and office, neither of
which I saw again, I ran down to the Armory, at Carroll
Hall, southeast corner of Baltimore and Calvert Streets,
meeting my oldest brother, Frank Key Howard, on the
way, who went with me and asked Colonel Brush, standing at the door, if he wanted any volunteers. But the
offer was declined. I found the stairway guarded by a

---

[1] Guns are "presented," i.e., held in front of the body, only when at a halt and
in line. A marching salute is to bring the pieces to "shoulder arms" (afterwards
called "carry arms"), i e., along the right side, officers lowering the points of
their swords. But we consoled ourselves in our mortification by reflecting that
the heathen knew no better and probably thought it a very fine performance.
It made the men walk very wobbly.

double line of our men on the first landing up with fixed
bayonets, to keep out the crowd, every moment increasing and threatening to force an entrance to appropriate
the guns. The men of the battalion came hurrying in
and fell into line as fast as they arrived, many having,
like myself, not taken time to get their uniforms, and we
remained under arms the rest of the day, hearing all sorts
of rumors and expecting every moment to be led out,
either to drive back or to protect the Federal soldiers, or
preserve order in any way not involving a collision with
our fellow citizens. At night a strong guard was maintained, the rest of the command being dismissed with
orders to repair to the Armory at a moment's notice, a
signal for which would be a red flag or ball in the daytime
and a red light by night.

On the ensuing Sunday, April 21, news came of the approach of General Keim's force on the Northern Central
Railroad and the York Turnpike Road, which caused
another flurry of excitement almost equal to that of the
19th. From midday the battalion was held under arms
in the Armory and a detail was made from each company
to remain behind as a guard whenever the command
should move out. I was one of the detachment from
Company C, but succeeded, just as an order came to
march, in making an exchange with a man suffering with
heart disease. We joyfully descended the steps—our
Armory being the highest floor—but it was only to change
our quarters to the more commodious room of the gym-
nasium below. Here we remained cooped up, watching
the crowded street, along which furniture wagons and
other vehicles full of armed men were passing every now
and then, causing us to repine at our inglorious inactivity, instead of taking part in the conflict which we
surely believed was imminent, if not going on. Indeed,

some of us were so far carried away as to attempt to get out of the building, but could not flank the guard. I do not remember whether we remained under arms during the night, but from this time we were ordered to wear our uniforms and equipments habitually. About this time Colonel Brush was disabled by a wound in the hand from the accidental discharge of his pistol, and when Major Charles E. Phelps was summoned to take command—Lieutenant-Colonel Erving being ill with consumption, of which he soon after died—he replied that he had sent in his resignation, which step he followed up by leaving the city in a carriage by night. Major Phelps, a native of New Hampshire, afterwards served with distinction in the Union Army.[2] There were not more than a dozen, I think however, who failed to stand by the battalion to the last. On the other hand, very many joined us, and I presume we could have increased our ranks indefinitely if we had had uniforms and specially desired it. We did not long want an acceptable field officer, for, to our great satisfaction, Colonel Benjamin Huger,[3] of the regular army, then residing in Baltimore, was, on this Sunday I think, elected or appointed to command us. I was appointed by Captain Carroll a corporal, a promotion of which I was, perhaps, more proud than of any I ever received since.

We soon took possession of the spacious Maryland Institute, over the Centre Market, which we continued to occupy for some time, keeping a heavy guard by night, and having roll calls, drills, and at sunset dress parades which were attended by ladies and others, for after the memorable Sunday the city was very orderly and quiet.

[2] And later he was a very able Judge of the Baltimore Bench, Member of Congress, etc.

[3] Afterwards Major-General Huger of the Confederate Army

We had news of the approach of the Northern forces from different quarters but did not disturb ourselves over the situation, having confidence in our officers and the civil authorities. Business was little attended to, our minds were filled with high patriotic feelings, mingled with some enjoyment of the novelty of our half military life.

About eleven o'clock on the night of May 13, we were quietly summoned by our sergeants—having been previously divided into squads in view of such a contingency —to the Armory at Carroll Hall, to which we had gone back shortly before. We found the place dimly lighted and the guns being carried off, singly and by twos and threes or more, by any members of the Battalion who would undertake to hide them. The reason was that General Ben Butler had occupied, or was about occupying, Federal Hill with an overwhelming force and the city would certainly fall into his hands in the morning. I took and carried home three muskets, but did not attempt to hide them specially, for I apprehended that my father would be arrested, as President of the Board of Police, and his house, on Cathedral Street next to Emmanuel Church, would be searched, and it would not be well to have any concealed arms discovered there. These were found and seized when he was arrested afterwards, but I believe very few others were ever found, although diligently sought for. Many were taken South and did good service there, while some, no doubt, remain hidden away and forgotten to this day. The Armory was stripped by one or two o'clock. Several of us went up Charles Street, among them my cousin William Key Howard, who had the colors, the staff of which he broke and threw the pieces over the wall into the Archbishop's yard—there was then a high brick wall at the edge of the sidewalk.

The next morning not a uniform was seen on the streets which they had made so picturesque before, and General Butler took possession of the city; I saw him as he dismounted to establish his headquarters at the Gilmor House on Monument Square, and I walked over to Federal Hill and looked at the troops fixing their camps on that commanding eminence.

After this many of the Maryland Guard, with others, one or a few at a time, left for the South, while others remained longer, to be guided by the course of events. My own reasons for lingering after many of my friends and four of my five older brother had gone were partly because I was the youngest and as it was probable my father, and also my oldest brother (Editor of the *Exchange,*) would be arrested, I was not sure that my first duty was not at home, and partly because it was not clear that more could not be accomplished in Maryland than by leaving it. At that time W. Carvel Hall, Charles Goldsborough and Thomas Turner lived in bachelor style at No.——St. Paul Street, a few doors north of Mulberry, and here William Duncan McKim and others, with myself, held many secret consultations. One of our plans was to assist in raising a company of one hundred men under Captain William H. Murray, of the Maryland Guard, and to march, with our arms and uniforms, across the Potomac by way of Sykesville. Another was to form a secret organization at home and hold ourselves in readiness to act as occasion prompted. The first project was abandoned when Murray, being in danger of arrest, precipitately left for Virginia, and, moreover, the line of the river, or the Baltimore and Ohio Railroad, was guarded by the Northern forces.

The second was held under advisement a while longer, but in the meantime Carvel Hall was despatched to Richmond to ascertain what reception was given to Marylanders going over and whether their accession was at all desired. He went and returned secretly and safely, railroad communication not having been yet interrupted, and reported that our friends who had gone before were welcomed gladly. Finally, on the 31st of May, being tired of inactivity and doubt, Duncan McKim and I agreed that I should see Mr. S. Teackle Wallis and get his opinion of what would be the probable future in Maryland and that we would govern ourselves accordingly. His emphatic answer being "as quiet as the grave," we made our preparations to leave next morning.

CHAPTER II

BALTIMORE TO RICHMOND

Early in the morning of Saturday, June 1, 1861, William Duncan McKim, Clapham Murray and myself started for Virginia, taking what was called the lower route because we had received secret information the day before that on this morning the Baltimore and Ohio Railroad would be seized and the baggage of all passengers would be searched. As it was, we felt some uneasiness in driving down to the Patuxent River boat, half expecting to meet a guard there, and were relieved to find ourselves and our trunks—containing Maryland Guard uniforms—on board without hindrance or search and presently safely past Fort McHenry. We made a feeble pretense of visiting St. Mary's County to look at farms, but soon saw that our true character was more than suspected by all on board, for passengers, officers of the steamboat and servants marked us out for particular attentions. Arriving at Millstone Landing, just within the mouth of the Patuxent on the St. Mary's County side, we enquired on the wharf for George Thomas, at whose house, a couple of hundred yards off, we intended to spend the night and get information how to proceed further, and were referred to a gentleman wearing a broad brimmed hat as his brother; this was Richard Thomas, soon afterwards well known as Colonel "Zarvona."[1] George Thomas requested us to remain with him until Monday when he himself would accompany us, an offer we were glad to accept. The next morning,

[1] His romantic exploits made him well known in the first part of the war.

Sunday, we drove some distance to the Episcopal Church and were shown much attention by the congregation, there being no necessity of keeping up any disguise in this country.

On Monday morning, having put on our uniforms, we drove across the peninsula in an open wagon. Stopping for lunch at midday at the house of Dr. Sappington, early in the afternoon we came to the house of——————————on the east bank of St. Mary's River and near its head, where we were joined by several others who were also bound South—Edward Johnson of Baltimore and Thomas A. Hebb and his cousin Thomas W. Hebb Greenwell of St. Mary's County. After a short delay we sailed in a canoe directly down the river, landing in the evening at the place of Mr. Coad, near its mouth and on the west side. After dark George Thomas went in a boat to reconnoitre the Potomac and reported something like a gunboat as having passed, but we trusted the way would be clear by morning. In spite of Mr. Coad's hospitable protests, we lay down to sleep on the floor, thinking it time we should begin to accustom ourselves to the hardships of a soldier's life. At dawn, June 4, we started in a sail canoe for the southern bank of the Potomac, intending to make straight across for Westmoreland County, but a head wind compelled us to shape our course lower down. The inhabitants of St. George's Island, at the mouth of St. Mary's River, who are mostly pilots and their familes, were said to be, or many of them, favorable to the North, and the mysterious, as we thought, dipping of a United States flag on one of their boats, like a signal, gave us a deal of uneasiness. Without further adventure, however—except a drenching shower—the strong breeze, aided by some vigorous rowing, carried us swiftly over the broad water, and at 8 o'clock a.m. we entered the mouth of a beautiful creek, which turned out to be Cone River in Northumberland County, Virginia; we had therefore sailed about twenty miles. Upon a high hill a short distance above our landing place was the residence of Colonel James M. Smith, said to be the wealthiest man in the county, and George Thomas and I, leaving the rest of the party at the boat, went to ask hospitality. Doors and windows were wide open with a very inviting appearance, and George Thomas exclaimed confidently, "There's Virginia hospitality for you!" But when we reached the front door we perceived the Colonel rather hastily retreating out at the back, and when presently, in answer to our repeated knocks, a young lady made her appearance, she asked us defiantly, "what we wanted?" We requested to see Colonel Smith, who finally came, exhibiting an unaccountable want of ease, and although we informed him that we had been sailing since four o'clock, a part of the time in the rain, and had had no breakfast, he did not offer to supply us. Learning that his son, Dr. James Smith, lived but a mile off, who had married a lady of St. Mary's County, well known to George Thomas and also a distant cousin of mine, being a daughter of H. G. Sothoron Key, but whom I had never seen, we determined to go there, very much surprised and disgusted at our first experience of "Virginia hospitality." Leaving Colonel Smith, who seemed relieved to be rid of us, we soon arrived at the Doctor's and, although he was not at the house, we received a very cordial welcome from his wife. He, being sent for, soon came in and, first sending for our comrades at the boat, proceeded to refresh us after the manner of the country. Compounding a mixture in a large glass, he offered it to us with the remark, "I don't know whether you gentlemen are much acquainted with this liquor, but we drink a good deal of it in this part of the country." Such was my first introduction to an apple brandy julep. The rest of our party arrived soon and brought with them an explanation of our cold reception at the Colonel's. It appeared that our party, some of us being in Maryland Guard uniform which we had worn since starting from George Thomas's, had been taken for Yankees landing from a prowling gunboat. We received a message of warm apology from both the Colonel and the ladies of his family and an entreaty that we would remain long enough to give them an opportunity to make us some amends. But we were full of ardor to hasten on in order to be present at the first battle, expected to come off soon, and after partaking of breakfast and dinner, which were pressed on us in quick succession, Dr. Smith packed us in a carriage and wagon and drove us in to Heathsville, the county town, about two or three miles distant. Two companies of infantry were stationed or organizing here, having a picket thrown out on the road, whose sentinel brought his bayonet to a charge at sight of this formidable invasion of strange and very gaudy uniforms, but recognizing Dr. Smith, he allowed us to pass, with an expression of much doubt and astonishment. The companies were drilling on the village green, but broke ranks incontinently and fraternized. I suppose we were the most popular guests Heathsville had ever entertained and we had no small difficulty in persuading them to let us go on. Applejack flowed freely and I am sorry to record that enthusiasm led to much inebriation, although our party kept within the bounds of strict moderation, only avoiding the giving of offence. Bouquets were presented by the ladies, George Thomas as our spokesman making a suitable acknowledgment. Two wagons were at last

furnished for our transportation and we got into them before the horses were harnessed, thinking to hasten the
arrangements, whereupon some of our friends seized
hold and dragged us triumphantly around the place.
Being finally permitted to leave, we drove across Northumberland, perhaps a corner of Richmond, and Lancas-
ter Counties, and by 8 o'clock in the evening came to the
house of Mr. Richard H. Carter, a member of the Legislature, on the north bank of the Rappahannock, ten miles
above Urbana on the other side, by whom we were hospitably entertained.

Awakened before daylight in the morning, June 5, we
were first called upon to drain—perhaps twice—a large
two-storey tumbler of applejack julep, which our host
modestly informed us he had some reputation for mixing,
took breakfast and sailed in a flat bottomed boat down
and across the Rappahannock to Urbana, which is the
county seat of Middlesex County. This place also we
found occupied by two Companies and we were made to
give an account of ourselves in quite a formal way at
headquarters, but this stiffness was soon relaxed and a
reception was given us similar to that at Heathsville.
The soldiers were quartered in the principal church of
the village, and my feelings were for the first time shocked
by seeing a sacred building in military occupation; and I
never saw one abused as this was. A fiddle was soon
produced, as well as an abundance of applejack, and
dancing—among the men—drinking and card playing
offered for our entertainment, in which we declined to
join. After some delay vehicles were furnished and we
drove across Middlesex and "King and Queen" Counties
and shortly before dark were ferried over the Mattapony
branch of York River to West Point, in King William
County, at the junction of the Mattapony and Pamunkey,

forming the York. More troops were stationed here and, its situation at the head of the York River making it of more importance, better discipline was observed and there was a more business-like appearance in the arrangements. We were kindly received and treated, but our arrival did not create the same sensation as at the other two places. Wooden barracks, with bunks, had been erected, in which we were assigned quarters and we observed Tattoo and other regulations with the soldiers.

Next morning, we saw H. C. Dallam of Baltimore, whose wife, of the Braxton family, was from this neighborhood. He said that Judge John S. Caskie, of Richmond, wished to be introduced to us. Judge Caskie said, "You are Marylanders and I wish to call your attention to some stirring verses I have seen in the newspaper. I wish I could repeat them, but the refrain is, 'Maryland, my Maryland.'"

We presently took the cars to Richmond, about forty miles.

CHAPTER III

RICHMOND TO WINCHESTER

Upon our arrival at Richmond, June 6, 1861, we found that the two Maryland companies which had already been organized, commanded by Captains J. Lyle Clarke and Edward R. Dorsey, had, a day or two before, been sent off on an expedition to Chuckatuck in Nansemond County, towards Norfolk, and as William H. Murray, a captain of the Maryland Guard, for whom we proposed to raise a company, had gone with them as a volunteer, we waited for his return, most of our party staying at the Spotswood Hotel, southeast corner of Main and 7th Streets. We had all determined to go into service together. No good reason was assigned or appeared for this expedition, and it was said to have been the outcome of a dinner party at Governor Letcher's where Colonel Frank J. Thomas,[1] a Marylander and old army officer who hoped to command the future Maryland Regiment, was vaunting the spirit and readiness of the Maryland men. They came in a day or two from this bloodless foray into a peaceful community, full of stories of their first experience in campaigning; Jack Wamberzie was said, while on picket, to have challenged and then fired the first Maryland shot of the war—at a lightning bug. Our party now proceeded to assist in getting up the new Company, the rendezvous being the large boot and shoe store (wholesale) of J. Alden Weston, No 14 (?) Pearl Street, south of Main Street.

---

[1] He was killed at Manassas on July 21, acting as Chief of Ordnance on the staff of General Joseph E. Johnston and while rallying some disorganized troops.

While sitting at the Spotswood one evening, Captain Arnold Elzey, of Maryland, who had resigned from the United States Army, "desired to be introduced to me." He very civilly said that he understood I was aiding in getting up a Maryland company and he wished to say to me that some of his friends were recommending his appointment as colonel of the Maryland regiment and that, if he were so appointed, he would do all he could to promote the efficiency of the command and the comfort of the men. I was non-committal. My next interview with him was at Winchester, as will appear.

Having easily got together more than the number required by law for the formation of an infantry company, which I think was fifty, on the 12th of June we elected our commissioned officers: captain, William H. Murray; first lieutenant, George Thomas; second lieutenant, Frank X. Ward, and marched from Weston's to Capitol Square to be mustered into the Virginia service, for as yet the different States had their own troops, which a little later were turned over to the general government. Our expectation was to be enlisted, like most of the other commands, for the term of twelve months, and our indignation was great at being informed when drawn up in line, by Colonel Deas, the mustering officer, that we must enlist "for the war." Not one of us purposed serving for a less period somewhere, but we naturally wanted to be on an equal footing with almost all the other organizations and have some liberty of action at the end of one year; and having exiled ourselves from Maryland, it seemed to us that we were being imposed on in our necessities and treated with bad faith. But Colonel Deas was inexorable, and there being no help for it, we submitted, determining to appeal to the authorities. No non-commissioned officers had been appointed, but by Captain

Murray's direction I acted as orderly sergeant. The same afternoon (or was it the next?) we marched out Franklin Street to the "Old Fair Ground," afterwards called the Camp of Instruction, and Camp Lee, beyond the western end of the city, and were assigned quarters in one of the wooden buildings within the enclosure, hay or straw being issued for bedding.

The members of our company lost no time in taking steps to have the muster roll rectified, and to that end a joint committee of five was chosen from our company and one or both of the others—involved in the same trouble— to wait on President Davis and also on General Robert E. Lee, commanding all the Virginia forces. Richard C. Mackall and myself, of Murray's company, and Jim Sellman of Dorsey's company were three that I remember of this number, and we made Mackall our principal spokesman or chairman, he being the oldest, and especially because he was of more distinction, having been once a territorial judge in Kansas. Mr. Davis promptly gave us an audience, listened to our statement of grievances with great patience, and promised to interest himself in having them remedied. We had more difficulty in getting admitted to General Lee's presence but were importunate. He seemed not at all pleased at being interrupted and told us he did not see what could be done, adding sharply that the Maryland troops had already given more trouble than five times as many others. The committee replied and retired with dignity. General Lee at that time wore a heavy brown moustache, with no beard, and was a very handsome man, looking, of course, very much younger than as he was afterwards known and pictured. About the 18th of June we heard that the muster rolls were changed, but many doubters prophesied we would be held "for the war."

My note book—written up some months afterwards—
says that on this day, June 18, we were formally mustered
into service for twelve months, but we certainly were received, as before narrated, at an earlier date on Capitol
Square and by a regular mustering officer, in the usual
manner, (i e., the roll or list was called and each man
answered to his name, stepping a pace to the front,) and
my entry probably means that more formal muster rolls
were made out on this day, with the complete company
organization; for Captain Murray now appointed his
non-commissioned officers, who were: first or orderly sergeant, J. Harry Sullivan, second sergeant, McHenry
Howard; third sergeant, James W. Lyon; fourth sergeant, Chapman B. Briscoe; first corporal, Richard
Tilghman Gilmor; second corporal, Edward Johnson;
third corporal, Richard Covington Mackall; fourth corporal, William S. Lemmon.

We drilled very diligently—as often as four or five
times a day—the experience that some of us had had in
the Maryland Guard being now of great service. At
this time most of the troops, of whom there were probably several thousand in the Camp of Instruction, were
drilled by the young cadets from the Virginia Military
Institute at Lexington, but when one of these young
gentlemen presented himself to Captain Murray and reported that he was assigned for that service, he was
gruffly informed that "this company was drilled by its
own officers and sergeants," after which we were left to
our own training. The companies of Captains Clarke
and Dorsey, which had had several weeks drilling,
thought themselves proficient enough already to vie with
these cadets and imitated them in "double quicking"
from the ground after evening dress parade, which none
others were presumptious enough to do. Ladies drove

out from Richmond every evening and often brought or
sent provisions or dainties—sometimes beefsteaks on
silver dishes. One evening I remained in Richmond
until after dark and was sent out to camp by Mrs.
Robert F. Morriss in her carriage; when it stopped at the
gate, the officer on duty took me for some one of high
rank, an impression much strengthened when I stepped
out in the moonlight in blue and yellow Maryland Guard
uniform, turned out the guard and received me with
presented arms and the respect due to a general officer.

Within a week Dorsey's company and our own received
orders to proceed to Winchester to join the six Maryland
companies which had been formed at Harper's Ferry.
Lyle Clarke's company preferred to remain and attach
itself elsewhere. We left a new company forming under
Captain Michael Stone Robertson, of Charles County.[2]

On the evening of June 23, I was sent with a small detail to guard the baggage at the Virginia Central Railroad depot during the night, and next morning the two
companies marched in and took the cars, passing through
Gordonsville, Orange, Culpeper, Manassas Junction, and
Front Royal to Strasburg, where we arrived near dark
and were quartered in a church for the night. The short
march from the cars across one or two fields showed me
how I had overloaded myself with baggage—I could not
stagger under it even for that short distance—and I entrusted some of my Maryland Guard finery to a friend who
luckily passed (Alfred Hoffman of Baltimore), to be carried back to Richmond. The next morning Murray's
men were packed in a couple of omnibuses which
brought us the eighteen miles to Winchester after mid-

[2] Clarke took his company into the 21st Virginia which went to West Virginia
under General Loring. Robertson's Company joined us after the battle of
Manassas.

day. Having the excuse of being separated from all the officers and most of the men, I took dinner at Taylor's Hotel, and being introduced to Colonel A. P. Hill and one or two others afterwards well known, we had a bottle of champagne, the last I tasted for many a day. In the evening I strolled out to the camping ground on the Romney Road, across from and a little beyond the residences of Senator James M. Mason and Colonel Angus McDonald. Here in a grassy hollow I found tents going up and a very busy scene. While at Richmond, D. Giraud Wright, Duncan McKim, Wilson C. N. Carr, John M. Bolling, John M. Burke, myself, and I think two more, had formed ourselves into a mess and bought a wall tent, which we now started to put up. But Colonel Elzey—recently appointed—rode by and demanded to know "what that officers' tent was doing in the men's line?"—adding that we "must come out of those damned Baltimore notions." So we rolled up our investment and sat down disconsolately in a row upon it. Through some intercession, however, we presently received permission to pitch it at the side of the hollow, just outside the regular camp, so as not to spoil the symmetry of the bell tents, an arrangement with which we were well pleased, as we were thus a little apart from the crowd and on better ground. I think there were eight in our wall tent and we managed to pack in, four with heads up to one side and four to the other, the lower parts of our bodies and legs being sandwiched in the middle. Our first attempts at cooking were poor enough; in the way of bread we could only make "slapjacks," a sort of pancake out of flour and water. Campbell W. Pinkney[3] here joined the company and our mess as a volunteer, but, being of a delicate constitution his health soon gave way

[3] After the war a judge of the Baltimore City Bench.

under our cooking, and he was compelled to relinquish the idea of going into service.

On June 25, we heard Charley Inloes's voice from a little eminence, "Look out for your baggage, boys, the Plug Uglies[4] are coming," and lifting our eyes, there was to be seen winding over the hill one of the sorriest, raggedest crowds we had ever beheld, which turned out to be the six companies which had organized at Harper's Ferry and now, under Lieutenant Colonel George H. Steuart and Major Bradley T. Johnson, came to unite with us and form the 1st Maryland Infantry. Having seen what was thought at that time to be some rather rough service, they were poorly clad and presented an unkempt and unwashed appearance. That night, fearing lest such a necessitous set of poor relations might "Butlerize"—a word in common use then, the derivation and meaning of which are obvious—we secretly detailed a special guard in the street of our company, and kept it up a night or two. Two of my brothers, John Eager Howard and Charles Howard were in this command, and as another, Edward Lloyd Howard was in Dorsey's company, there were now four of us in the regiment; there were also three first cousins of the name, William Key Howard, John E. Howard of James (also of the "Plugs"), and James McHenry Howard of Dorsey's company; besides other relations, two as near—John and Murray Key. My brother James Howard, who had long since resigned from the United States Army, was now at Pensacola. About this time I heard of the arrest of my father, Charles Howard, in Baltimore, and to sum up this account, my remaining brother, Frank Key Howard, was also arrested in September. Only my mother and

---

[4] The name of the most notorious crowd of rowdies in the "Know Nothing" days in Baltimore.

sisters were left at home, spending their time in ministering to the Confederate prisoners.

Being entitled to a junior second lieutenant in our company, an election by the men was held at this place and Corporal Richard T. Gilmor was chosen over his competitor, Sergeant Sullivan. Little else occurred to vary the monotony of the camp life for some days, our time being taken up with drilling and other camp duties, with an occasional visit into Winchester. I went sometimes to Mr. James M. Mason's house, Mrs. Mason being my father's first cousin,[5] and was most kindly treated then as ever afterwards by the family—not in that house, however, for when I saw the place next year not one stone was upon another and the grounds were a barren waste.

About the 2d of July General Patterson crossed the Potomac into Virginia and we marched in that direction. On July 3 we turned off the Valley Turnpike Road at Darkesville to the right, about seventeen miles from Winchester, and General Joseph E. Johnston's whole army was drawn up in line of battle; our position was on or towards the right and, I should say from my recollection of the lay of the country, not far from the Opequon on the right. For four days we offered battle, and in our Regiment we confidently expected and were eager for it. I remember noticing many of our company lying about reading their Bibles, intending seriously to make a good fight of it.[6] In our regiment, at least, we suffered from insufficiency of rations and named the place "Camp Starvation." On Sunday the 7th of July we returned to Winchester. Many of us had no supper the evening before and no breakfast that morning and the march of

[5] She was Miss Eliza Chew, of Germantown, Pennsylvania.
[6] Randolph H. McKim, of Baltimore, here joined our Company.

seventeen miles was a very trying one. The hot sun and frequent vexatious halts, the road in front being filled with slow marching Virginia troops (Marylanders always had a short quick step), caused many to fall out of ranks, and our company, which started with over seventy men, reached Winchester with only twenty-two.

In the course of a few days we changed our camp to near the first toll gate on the Martinsburg road. Wednesday night, July 17th our company performed its first tour of picket duty, starting with two crackers apiece for supper. During the night W. E. Jones, formerly an officer of the United States Army (afterwards brigadier-general of cavalry,) was captured—I think by our men—passing the line without the countersign, and was carried in triumph to Colonel J. E. B. Stuart, as a spy attempting to pass over to the enemy.

While cooking breakfast after returning next morning, we were stopped by an order to strike tents and pack up everything immediately. By 7 a.m. (July 18), we were in line ready to move, but so remained at "in place rest," watching the long column of troops taking the road in advance through Winchester, and therefore it seemed in retreat, until 1 p.m. when we made a start and got as far as the town, but were three times halted in passing through; this enabled us, however, to refresh ourselves with some loaves of bread which we purchased. The porch of Taylor's Hotel and the windows of the houses were thronged with ladies of the place and surrounding country, who encouraged us by marks of sympathy and made the street present a very picturesque appearance. It was not until five o'clock that we got fairly under way, taking the Millwood road—to the east.

When about three miles out from Winchester, just as the sun was setting, we were halted and faced to the front in a narrow glen and our commander read an order from General Joseph E. Johnston that "General Beauregard was threatened by an overwhelming force at Manassas and called us by a forced march to his assistance." Cheer after cheer was taken up along the line, all discontent was forgotten, fatigue and hardship, past and to be undergone, unheeded, and exclamations of, "Lead us on," "We are on the road to Maryland and will march forever," were heard all down the line. The cheers, again and again repeated, of our regiment were taken up by the 10th Virginia and 3d Tennessee, in front and behind. I remember distinctly now the beautiful sunset, with some purple clouds floating in the soft sky, and the high hills between which the road ran, and the contrast of the enthusiasm of the men and the quiet, lovely scene. For some time we marched on with buoyant tread and the greatest animation. But as darkness came on, hunger and fatigue began to tell, the men became gradually silent and presently nothing was heard but the steady tramp on the stone road and the miscellaneous noises which accompany a body of troops in motion. The night so wore on, with only irregular and uncertain halts to let the way get clear in front. We passed through the village of Millwood, day broke, and at last, two hours after sunrise, we were gladdened by the sight of the Shenandoah River. Here we rested for a couple of hours. Coffee was made and some bread cooked, or the poor substitute for it which we called "putty cake," being of that consistency, made of flour and water and cooked in a frying pan, or sometimes in a griddle or "spider." Many sought to obtain a little sleep, while others chose instead a refreshing bath in the Shenandoah. The scene along the river was very picturesque and became more so when our companies were reformed and the order was given to cross by wading. The water was not more than waist deep, and by partially undressing and hanging shoes, clothes and accoutrements on our muskets, we managed in most cases to keep them dry, but some unfortunate would slip or stumble on the smooth round stones with which the bottom was covered and amid the laughter and jeers of his comrades, make his way dripping to the other side. Reforming on the shore, we took up the weary march through or over Ashby's Gap in the Blue Ridge. Shortly after midday we gained the summit and saw the country on the eastern side spread for many miles before us. Descending and passing through the village of Paris, where a basket of provisions presented by the country people to our company, or the regiment, was seized as if by a pack of wolves and in a few moments emptied, we shortly after—at about 4 o'clock—halted and broke ranks in a wheat stubble field, as we fondly supposed for the night. Our regiment seemed now to be alone, none others being in sight. Having failed to get anything from the Parisian basket, I and a comrade (Somerville Sollers) went out foraging and succeeded in obtaining some bread and buttermilk at a neighboring house. On returning I was surprised to find the regiment forming again and was told that an order had come from General Bee[7] stating that, owing to negligence in some quarter, we had wandered some miles from the route, and that if we were cut off the fault would be our leaders'. I believe the mistake came from our being under the impression that we were to march the whole way to Beauregard's army, whereas the other regiments had turned south some distance back to take the Manassas Gap Railroad at Piedmont, and ours was not

[7] General Bee was killed on the 21st after giving Jackson and his brigade the immortal Stonewall name.

I do not know that the order or message really came from him. I only state what I heard on getting back to the company from my foraging.

only alone, but getting too far to the north, especially if Patterson with his Union army were also moving down from the Valley. The column was now, therefore, kept well closed up, guards being thrown out in front and rear with orders to allow no one to fall out on any pretext, and we marched in quick time until we had passed through Upperville and turned sharp to the right, southward. The sun went down and night came, but, footsore, weary, hungry, thirsty and sleepy, we still pushed on. To add to our discomforts it began to rain about 8 p.m. and whenever we rested for a few minutes we had to lie down, wet on the wet ground, our first experience in that way, although several naps were enjoyed. At 8 or 9 o'clock Mr. Robert M. Bolling, who had a fine estate, called "Bollingbrook," in the neighborhood, and one of whose sons, John Minge Bolling, was of Murray's company and in my mess, sent some provisions in a wagon, which, divided up, gave us each a little. He also sent me, privately, two canteens of liquor, from which I gave every man in the company a small drink, but I unfortunately miscalculated in saving only a few drops for myself. Some of our men who were thoroughly exhausted, lay down behind the stone wall which fenced the road, and when the rear guard had passed, made their way to his house, where they spent the night, tantalizing us next day by an account of the comforts they had enjoyed. Continuing our weary march for an hour longer, we at length reached Piedmont and after some delay in line, were permitted to lie down on the wet ground and sleep for three or four hours. I promised to be one of a detail to cook some bread, but fell sound asleep.

In the morning, July 20, we cooked some rations, or half rations, of "putty cake" and coffee, and soon after moved to a wheat field near by, where we rested the remainder of the day.

CHAPTER IV

Battle of Manassas or Bull Run

At 2 a.m., Sunday, July 21, we were aroused by the shrill whistle of the locomotive and marched down from our somewhat elevated position to take the train, but delays ensued as usual and it was daybreak before we started. The cars were filled to their utmost capacity and I rode part of the way on the platform and part on top of a car. The engine made slow time and there were frequent stops. Having had scanty fare since leaving Winchester, indeed dating from before that in our company, the blackberries on the side of the embankment were an irresistible temptation during these stops. But while the side of the road was crowded with eager pickers on one of these occasions, I heard a voice exclaiming furiously, "If I had a sword I would cut you down where you stand," and raising my eyes I beheld the crowd scattering for the cars before an officer striding up from the rear. I stood still but felt very uncomfortable as he came up close and glared at me, thinking he was going to strike me and wondering what I would do, and when he turned off I was glad to regain my position on the car top. This was Brigadier-General E. Kirby Smith, but we did not know him, seeing him thus for the first time. So we straggled from the cars no more.

As we neared Manassas Junction we distinctly heard the booming of cannon at intervals and could even see the smoke from some of the discharges a few miles to the left, but we had no idea that a general engagement was then actually going on. We arrived at the railroad

junction, a few hundred yards west of the station, about
1 p.m. and immediately disembarking, threw off our
knapsacks into a pile and formed in line.   Colonel Elzey
galloped down the front, his eyes sparkling, followed by
General Kirby Smith who with the back of his hand
raised to the front of his cap, exclaimed, "This is the
signal, men, the watchword is 'Sumter;' " this was to
distinguish friend from foe.   Enthusiastic cheers were
given in response, and I now suddenly realized that we
were going straight into our first battle—and without
the Bible preparation of Darkesville.

We were marched north, partly across the country,
towards the firing, which, cannon and musketry, became
more and more distinct and as of a real battle.   We took
a quick step at first, but presently in our excitement
broke into a double quick, with a cheer, and kept up that
gait for a considerable time, the whole distance passed
over being about five miles.   The dust was most distressing, so thick at times that it was impossible to see more
than a few feet ahead of one, and floating high above the
tree tops, so that, as is well known, the enemy were able
to trace the march of our column and mark its progress—
as we did theirs.   Once we halted for a few minutes and,
being parched with thirst, some of the men eagerly lapped
the muddy water which stood in the fresh deep prints of
horses' feet in the road—a little miry at that point—
while others picked a few huckleberries on the right and
left.   As we neared the front the signs were very discouraging—would have been so to older troops and were
particularly calculated to try the nerves of raw soldiers.
We passed a great many wounded, and still more un-
wounded, going to the rear, many of whom assured us
that "we were getting cut to pieces this time," "we were
catching hell," "we were sure to be whipped, but to go

in," etc. Sometimes a man with no greater injury than a finger hurt would be supported by a comrade or two on either side. Wagons and ambulances with wounded and dead also drove by. Twice we passed directly over regiments lying as flat as they could get to the ground, some of the men raising their heads and feebly exhorting us to "go in," to which our fellows responded with an invitation, in strong language, to come in with us themselves. Marching steadily, we presently came out into an open field, the ground rising to a low crest in front, behind (this side of) which was drawn up a small body of horse, which I understood to be the Black Horse Troop. This was a little way to our right. Here a shell exploded seventy or eighty yards to the right, our first shot from an enemy.[1] After halting for a few minutes we again moved forward and some shots began to fall closer; I saw one shell strike in a ravine fifteen yards to the right which burst with what I thought was a tremendous explosion. Soon after the head of the column (we had been all the time marching in the usual formation of fours,) passed a low thicket which had screened us in front, when there was a succession of sharp reports like a pack of fire crackers and many bullets whistled around. A shell also exploded quite close to the side of the column. I saw General Kirby Smith, who was riding a little on my right, fall from his horse and two men (John Berryman and W. H. Codd) of Dorsey's company, C, which was leading, also fell to the ground not more than fifteen or twenty feet in front of me; for although, as second sergeant, the left or rear file closer of my company H, which came next, I had insensibly gotten ahead and was

[1] Shortly after leaving the railroad we must have got into the road which goes by Newmarket on to the Sudley Springs and were approaching the Henry house, around which the heaviest fighting had been, and perhaps was going on.

then with the file closers of Company C. Only these two companies had got well out into the open ground. Looking around I saw that the file closers had crossed over to the other (left) side of the column under the impression that the firing came from our own men in rear, and that the last half of our company had squatted down to the ground looking about for the hidden enemy. The first half went on, however, and I with it, feeling as if in a dream, the whole thing was so sudden, unexpected and novel. I passed directly by the two men who had been shot, Berryman raising himself on his elbow with an expression of agony, having received a terrible wound in the groin, I did not soon forget.[2] The firing soon ceased and although the regiment was quickly ordered to form line forward on first company and the movement was executed with tolerable promptness under the circumstances, we encountered no further opposition, the enemy, a skirmish line of New York Zouaves, having hastily retreated. We therefore lay down just in rear of a slight eminence, some shells passing overhead, while Colonel Elzey, who succeeded General Smith in command of the brigade, rode off to reconnoitre. It must have been now about 3 o'clock.

Colonel Elzey soon returned and moved us first to the left oblique in column across open ground and then forward in line of battle through a wood, the Maryland regiment now in the centre, and when about twenty or thirty yards from its further edge we received an unexpected volley and saw a line drawn up on high ground in the middle of the field beyond.[3] Colonel Elzey, who

[2] A surviving member of Company C tells me that the other man of the company was not wounded but his canteen being struck by a piece of shell and the warm water (it was a hot day) pouring down his leg, he thought it was a stream of blood and fainted!

[3] Our position was, I suppose, half way between the Henry and Chinn houses.

happened to be immediately behind the left of our company, called out to his aide de camp, "My glass, Contee, quick, quick." His staff gathered around him and all peered anxiously through and under the foliage which partly obstructed the view. After looking through his glass for a few moments, Elzey dropped his hand, his eye lighted up—I was a few feet directly in front of him—and he hastily cried, "Stars and Stripes! Stars and Stripes! Give it to them, boys!" The words were scarcely out of his mouth, the men seeming to take the command from his eye, when a rolling volley was poured into the enemy. Once or twice we loaded and fired, or many did, and we had the satisfaction of seeing the line disappear behind the crest in confusion. I think it doubtful if we did much execution, and on our side we had only one man killed—Private Swisher of Company A—although the bullets cut off twigs and leaves overhead.[4] The order was now given to charge bayonets (only our two right companies, Dorsey's and Murray's, had bayonets), and we pressed forward with a cheer, not in a very regular line but each one striving to be foremost. But in passing over the stubble or pasture field we discovered it bore an abundant crop of blackberries, and being famished with hunger and our throats parched with thirst, the temptation was too strong to be resisted, the men stopped with one accord and the charging line of battle resolved itself into a crowd of blackberry pickers. Officers swore or exhorted, according to their different principles, and presently succeeded in getting the line to

---

[4] The left of our company had got crowded up, several deep, and Nick Watkins in firing shot through the cap of George Lemmon who was in his front. Taking off his damaged cap and looking at it, George turned slowly around and in his drawling tone said, reproachfully, "Nick Watkins, what did you do that for?"

move on.   Still, whenever an unusually attractive bush
was passed over, we reached down without stopping and
stripped off berries, leaves and briers, which we crammed
into our mouths; for days afterwards I was occupied
extracting the thorns from the palms of my hands.   Just
before reaching the top of the ridge we were halted and
Colonel Elzey ordered Lieutenant T. O. Chestney of his
staff to ride forward and see if there was any enemy on
the other side, a duty which he performed in a very gallant manner and to our great admiration.   No enemy
was to be seen and he waved us forward and we advanced
some distance over the open ground until near a pine
wood in front, or a little to the left oblique.   At this
moment an irregular fire was poured into this wood by a
part of our line, it being supposed that the enemy had
halted there and some asserting that from it a fire had
been first opened on us.   Our fire was presently stopped
by the exertions of the officers, but the entire line, consisting of the 1st Maryland, 10th Virginia and 3d Tennessee, was halted while the Newtown Battery, Captain
Beckham, attached to our brigade, from the extreme left
shelled the woods for some time.   When this ceased we
again advanced and had scarcely entered the woods
when we saw abundant evidence of the place having
been occupied by the enemy and of our execution, both
from artillery and small arms, for I do not think it had
been the scene of a conflict earlier in the day.   At one
spot I noticed five dead bodies (Federal) lying close together and their faces seemed to me to be already turning
dark in the intense heat of the weather.   Their guns,
Minie muskets, were lying near, but I hesitated to appropriate one in exchange for my smooth bore.   We
passed other dead but came to the edge of the open
ground without encountering a living enemy.   The line

having been a good deal disarranged in passing through the thick old field pines, we now halted to reform it. A little stream[5] ran along the front, but, in our inexperience, many of the men would not drink from it, being told there were or might be dead or wounded in it. Here a stranger was observed to take a place in our ranks who attempted to pass himself off as a stray South Carolinian, but on cross-examination he proved to be a Federal straggler and was taken into custody.

Repenting that I had not taken one of the Minie guns seen while passing through the woods, I now asked permission of Captain Murray to take advantage of the halt to run back for it. This being granted, a few steps carried me within the dense foliage which seemed to have the effect of shutting out all sound of conflict, and every other. It was literally as still as death, and a disagreeable feeling succeeded to excitement, tempting me to give up my enterprise and get back among my comrades. Besides, it struck me as not unlikely that I might fall in with some stray party of the enemy, especially as we did not know how the battle was going on our right and left. Cocking my piece, I walked cautiously on, looking about and listening. I presently stumbled against something which gave a metallic ring and looking down, perceived what I took to be a bright piece of lead pipe, bent in the shape of a siphon, and wondered how it got there. But a closer examination showed it was a gun barrel, which had probably been struck on the end by one of Beckham's shells. I had scarcely taken ten steps more when I was startled by

---

[5] Chinn's Branch I suppose, General Beauregard's topographical map of the battle-field will be found in *Atlas to Accompany the Official Records of the Union and Confederate Armies*, Part I, Plate III, No. 2; see also Plate V–I for map of battle at the Henry house, Youngs Branch, etc.

hearing a voice calling me and discovered a man lying with his head and shoulders propped against a tree. Walking over to him, I saw that he evidently had but a short time to live, an hour or two at most, being horribly torn about the waist by a shell. He belonged to a Maine regiment, was a fine looking man of middle age, having a heavy dark beard, and belonging to a respectable class in society. I told him I was sorry to see him in such a condition—was there anything I could do? "Yes," he replied in a perfectly composed manner, "you can do one thing for me, and I wish you to do it—for God's sake, take your bayonet and run me through, kill me at once and put an end to this." I replied that I could not do that, and remembering what I had read of the sufferings of wounded men on battlefields, asked if he did not want some water. He answered, yes, but that made no matter, and reiterated his request to be put out of misery. I told him he had but a few more hours to live, and recommended him to make his preparation for death. He said he was ready to die and earnestly, but without excitement, begged me to run my bayonet through his heart. Having no canteen, I ran back to the company where I found Thomas H. Levering with one full of water and got him to go back with me. He drank eagerly but still begged us to kill him and as we moved away his voice followed us until we were out of hearing.

Without much difficulty I found the place where I had before observed the five Minie guns and hastily selected one and a set of accoutrements which had evidently belonged to one of the dead men lying near by. While doing so I heard Levering's voice, who had gone in a slightly different direction, calling out that he had found a wounded man trying to cut his own throat. I told him to take away the knife, which, stooping down, he apparently did.[6] We rejoined the company just as the line was about to move forward.

We continued advancing (not all the time in line of battle, I think), until we came to the Warrenton and Centreville Turnpike Road[7] but did not overtake the enemy, now in full retreat along his whole front. We found here a lot of haversacks and other stuff and I made a good meal out of one, in spite of a comrade's earnest warning that the rations might be poisoned. It contained crackers, beef, and mixed ground coffee and sugar; from this mixture I sucked out the sugar and chewed the coffee.

About this time President Davis and Generals Johnston and Beauregard came on this part of the field and were greeted by us with enthusiastic cheers. We were presently moved back, or to the right, to the Henry house where we halted for half an hour.   Here there were some captured pieces of artillery and one of them was directed on the flying column of the enemy seen pressing confusedly along the Turnpike near the stone bridge over Bull Run. This plateau witnessed the hardest share of the fighting during the day and numbers of dead and wounded men and horses gave evidence of the stubbornness of the contest for it. Under one tree, in particular, had been collected many wounded, belonging to Ricketts' Battery (Federal) and other organi-

[6] I never had or heard of any such experiences afterwards. But I wrote this down many years ago and had often told the incidents before. I think the first man belonged to the 5th Maine.

[7] So far I had been carrying along my old gun in addition to the Minie I had got, but I now threw the former aside. It so happened that some two months afterwards while inspecting the arms of the company at Centreville or Fairfax, one of the pieces held up to me seemed to have a familiar appearance, and the owner seeing me examine it critically, announced that it was a "Yankee trophy taken at Manassas," and was chopfallen when I told him I knew it came from that field, for I had thrown it away there myself.

zations, with whom we talked freely, our ranks having been broken (dismissed) for awhile. (Visiting the battle-field later in the summer, a long trench marked the spot where these men had been lying and, no doubt, containing many of their bodies.)[8]

Our ranks were presently re-formed and I think we now marched forward and across the stone bridge, or perhaps only the bridge over Young's Branch of Bull Run; it may have been that we made this movement before going to the Henry house, but I am almost sure it was at this time. After going some hundred yards beyond it, however, we turned about and struck off towards the railroad—not, however, by the route we had come. I think it was near sunset when we had made the halt at the Henry house and now night had come and found us trudging wearily on, although the men were terribly exhausted from fatigue and want of sleep. At length, when the night was half over, we went into bivouac in an open field, somewhere between Manassas and Bull Run and we sank down exhausted around blazing piles of fence rails.

Towards morning, July 22, it began to rain and a slow but steady drizzle fell nearly all day, making our condition a wretched one. We sought refuge under some flat bush shelters (oak and other branches), erected by troops which had previously occupied the ground, but they soon became dripping with rain and were worse than no shelter at all. Some crackers were issued to the men and were their only rations—except the ever-grateful blackberries.

[8] John Gill, a private of Murray's company, in his *Reminiscences of Four Years as a Private Soldier*, printed in 1904 for private circulation, says, "McHenry Howard and I tried to do something to alleviate the sufferings of the (Federal) wounded;" and I am pleased to be so recorded. . He also says that some of the wounded, apprehending—like my comrade before—poison, refused to drink from the canteen until he first drank out of it.

But Lieutenant Dick Gilmor found in one of the brush camps a sow with little pigs and he skilfully abstracted one of the sucklings without waking the slumbering mother (I witnessed the act from a safe position), and when cooked a morsel was given to me, than which nothing ever tasted more delicious. Towards evening our knapsacks which we had thrown off on leaving the railroad, were brought to us and with blankets we managed to keep off some of the rain. But it was a wretched night, and when reveille sounded some time before daybreak we were far from being rested after our continuous hardships since leaving Winchester. However, we folded our wet blankets and were soon in line.

CHAPTER V

By daylight, Tuesday July 23, we were on the Fairfax Court House road and, although it was at first ankle deep in mud, the sky presently cleared, to our great relief, and marching gradually got better. And after crossing Bull Run, by a wide and shallow ford,[1] listlessness and lassitude passed away in the excitement of noticing the abundant evidences of the enemy's hasty flight. Our regiment was having the honor of being the advance of the army, on this road at least, nothing, except possibly some cavalry, having gone over it since the disordered masses of the enemy. We began to realize the completeness of the victory and the extent of the panic although none had pursued. The road and adjoining fields were strewn with broken arms, knapsacks and other articles, and now and then one or more disabled wagons, loaded with crackers, sugar and luxuries of various sorts, excited, reasonably enough, our cupidity. I have no recollection of passing through Centreville and think we struck the Warrenton and Alexandria Turnpike Road just beyond or at it. When yet some distance from Fairfax Court House we deployed a line of skirmishers on either side who marched slightly in advance; they were rewarded by picking up pistols, etc. but saw no other signs of an enemy. Having started unrefreshed and in a bad condition in the very early morning, the men were now drooping as the excitement wore off, and were glad, by midday, to reach the village of Fairfax Court House.

[1] I suppose Blackburn's Ford.

With many of us pantaloons and shoes had suffered severely from the briars, mud and water, and stone road and presented a very sorry appearance as we marched through the main street. My own pantaloons hung in tatters from the knee down and my shoes were so dilapidated that it was with difficulty I could keep them on my feet as I shuffled along, and I noticed many of the citizens looking down at my legs and feet with mingled compassion and amusement. A short distance beyond the village, perhaps three or four hundred yards, we halted and went into camp on the right of the road in an open field beyond a skirt of thicket along the road. Two or three broken down wagons loaded with sugar happened to be where we halted and I ate handfuls from a barrel, which made me very sick for an hour or two.

Next morning, July 24, I went, by permission, to the tavern or a house in the village to breakfast and ate ravenously; and I don't think an Indian, of whose capacity we read so much, would have surpassed me. For half a dollar I bought a very good pair of boots, although not new and several sizes too large for me—which I suspect came from the feet of some fallen soldier—and having borrowed a pair of pantaloons, my appearance and comfort were considerably improved.

We remained here several weeks. We gradually became aware of the completeness of the victory we had gained—incomplete only in not having been followed up—and the conviction became settled in the minds of the men that a great and unfortunate error had been committed in that respect. We did not, however, exercise ourselves much with considerations of the past or future, having dropped into the dull routine of soldiers' lives and concerning ourselves with the occupations, comforts and discomforts of the present. We soon had tents pitched but I generally spread my blanket at night under the open sky. We drilled assiduously, beginning immediately after reveille. We had not yet learned to cook very well, but could always get an abundant and tolerable meal at any of the boarding houses in the village, or, indeed, at almost any of the neighboring houses, a privilege of which I availed myself about once every other day. It was said that many of the men, especially in Dorsey's company, were regular boarders at some of these places.

After several days our company went on picket down the Alexandria Turnpike Road to Annandale, six miles distant and therefore only seven miles from Alexandria. A part, if not the whole of the company was merely in reserve, but I spent the entire night awake with Captain Murray, mistaking bright rising stars for signal lights and otherwise anxious after the usual manner of green soldiers. We returned to camp next day but went on another tour shortly afterwards, when we were on outpost and had a somewhat more eventful time. I was instructed to take five men straight through the woods to the right oblique and establish a post. It being night when we started we had some difficulty in pushing through the brush but went the prescribed half mile and placed a sentinel or two out. Not knowing where we were or what was in front or around, I was a good deal startled after midnight to hear the approach of a body of horse which halted before reaching us and apparently settled themselves for the night. Thinking, under the circumstances it was as likely as not they were Federals, their coming having been from our right front, I went, alone, down the road (which I then discovered for the first time,) and after listening for a long time, having crept quite close, finally, to end the suspense, hailed them. They were, themselves, put in an equal state of alarm and I heard them in energetic but suppressed tones waking the sleepers and getting in order of battle. In answer to my repeated demands and claim of priority of hail, one presently advanced, with cocked revolver and mounted, when to our mutual relief, we found that we belonged to the same side. At daylight my party rejoined the company and I was just in time to make one of a volunteer scouting party towards the enemy's line. Ten of us under first Lieutenant George Thomas marched about two miles down the Turnpike Road and then crossed the field to the left where, in the misty light, we thought we saw a party of the enemy, who turned out to be a couple of old women digging potatoes. At the neighboring house we were taken for a party of Federals, an impression we did not care to remove, being, if not inside the enemy's line, certainly in his territory. Drums were beating reveille in several camps and at no great distance. The good people invited us to help ourselves in the orchard and gave us buttermilk, but we had to listen to a good deal of abuse of the "rebels." They were a little bewildered when William F. Smith tendered a Winchester note in payment for some honey but were pacified by his prompt assurance that, Winchester being on the border, its money passed in both armies. Without further adventure we returned to the company, which being relieved from picket, marched back to camp. That evening I had the hard luck to be detailed as sergeant of the guard and, a drenching rain having set in, I had to sleep my share of the night on a pile of rails.

We remained two or three weeks at Fairfax Court House and the regiment was then moved over, some three miles, to Fairfax Station on the Orange and Alexandria Railroad, our camp being near and on the north side of the Rail Road and three or four hundred yards east of the Station. A number of good men, recently from Maryland, here joined our company, among them George Williamson, Spencer France, Winder and William Laird and others. Company I, Captain Robertson, which we had left organizing in Richmond, was added to the regiment, which now presented a very handsome appearance on dress parade, numbering about 700, more than at any time before or afterwards. While here, Lieutenant Colonel Steuart became colonel by Elzey's promotion to brigadier-general (he had been in fact commanding the brigade, and Steuart the regiment, since Manassas) and Major Bradley T. Johnson became lieutenant colonel; the senior captain, Edward R. Dorsey of Company C, was promoted to the majority, and was succeeded in the command of the company by second Lieutenant Robert Carter Smith, he being elected over the first lieutenant.

The whole regiment now went on picket several times— times of hardship but also of some excitement. The first tour carried us to Mason's Hill, to the left of Annandale and about two miles further advanced. Here we were mixed up with other troops and had a very comfortless time, being without shelter in the rainy weather and, for some unexplained reason, with very scanty rations. Fortunately, I found an old colored servant at Captain Murray Mason's² house who years ago had known the family of my grandfather (Francis Scott Key,) in Georgetown, and I once or twice received from him some broken victuals from the table where some higher officers seemed to be dining sumptuously. But green corn, which was fairly fit for roasting, formed our princi-

---

² Brother of Senator James M. Mason, lieutenant in the U. S. Navy and captain in the C. S. Navy.

pal, and on some days our only food. From Mason's Hill the white dome of the Capitol with the Stars and Stripes floating from it was in plain view, and the Maryland men spent many hours lying on the grass looking at it and speculating when they would be able to return to their homes beyond it. Sellman Brogden declared that he would be a miserable man if he did not believe the war would be over by the 12th of September (anniversary of the British attack on Baltimore in 1814), and it was the expectation of many or most at this time that it would last only a short time, although the opinion seemed to be that Brogden's limit might be a little too short. There were many speculations, too, as to General Johnston's plan of operations and William H. Ryan, who was famous for confusing words which sounded alike, was confident that he would cross his army over the Potomac by a "vantoon" (vingt et un)—meaning pontoon-bridge; there was much gambling at this game about this time which put the sound in the "H" man's head.

I remember one day the curious phenomenon of our witnessing a skirmish, in the taking of Munson's Hill, a mile or more to our left and still farther advanced than Mason's, without hearing the guns, owing to some singular condition of the morning's atmosphere; officers and men were seen advancing and the smoke of the discharges was visible but with as much silence as if it were a pantomime—in these days we would say a moving picture.

We had several tours of picket, by regiment, to Mason's, Munson's and Upton's (a little to the left of Munson's) Hills, on each of which we enjoyed some little excitement, although we were never made comfortable. Once Colonel Charles S. Winder (of Maryland), then commanding the 6th South Carolina Regiment, sent over for a small force to aid him in expelling the enemy from Hall's

Hill, an eminence to the left of Upton's and still nearer Washington, and Company H and another were sent. There was a little shelling after which our infantry support went forward at a double quick, hoping to make some capture, but we did not. We did not fire at all and I am doubtful if we were really exposed to any, although there was a good deal of noise and excitement. As usual in those days, the enemy quickly sent up a balloon to see what the matter was and one of our two pieces took a long shot or two at it. At Upton's Hill I remember the fine peaches and an ugly looking hole through an oak tree or the house by which it stood, or both, made by a cannon ball in some former skirmish.

But our most exciting episode at this time was a skirmish which was recklessly provoked by two companies of our regiment. A Georgia lieutenant-colonel (Cumming) happened to be the senior officer of the small body of troops at Mason's Hill one day, who was an easy going, reckless fellow, sociable with privates as with his equals in rank, often entertaining us with his cock fighting reminiscences, and to him Captain W. W. Goldsborough, Company A, and Captain William H. Murray, Company H, made the request, which was readily granted, to be permitted to take their companies out on a reconnoissance. We marched some distance down the road[3] until we came to a trough or valley[4] crossing it at right angles and wooded on the further side where we apprehended the enemy's pickets might be posted. Halting, therefore, I was directed to take three or four men and go to the left, cross the bottom and examine the woods beyond. After advancing several hundred yards and hearing, or fancying that we heard,

[3] The "Columbia Road," I suppose.
[4] Holmes's Branch?

voices of a number of men in front, we turned to the right in order to explore the ground in front of the companies. We presently came out on the road and were near being shot by our own men, who, without waiting for our return, had been moved forward to that point. We then marched on some distance until we came on the enemy beyond a collection of several houses on the road[5] whereupon a brisk skirmish ensued. Between us was a large clearing, part of which—to our right and front—was covered with a growth of tall corn. I was presently ordered to take three men and occupy a ruined log house which stood on the further side of the corn and to the right, nearly midway between our line and the enemy, and so to guard our right flank. Taking Thomas H. Levering, William F. Smith and Burke Steuart, we passed through the strip of high corn and made a run across the 50 to 60 yards of clear ground to the cabin, receiving several shots in doing so. I had observed a road leading away to the right and had posted Burke Steuart a short distance down it, as the corn prevented our having any view in that direction and the enemy might get in on our flank and rear. The chinking had fallen out from between the logs of the one room house so that we had loopholes to look and fire through. We did not, however, take part in the shooting but confined ourselves to our duty of watching the flank and waited for an advance of the enemy. A peach tree loaded down with ripe fruit stood a few paces in front and Levering ran out and, with head bowed down under a sharp fire, gathered his hat full, on which we feasted leisurely during the rest of our stay. Once or twice I noticed a shot from some near point, the explanation of

[5] Bailey's Cross Roads?

which came soon afterwards. Presently Smith or
Levering called out to me that our men were about to go
back, and seeing that we were being forgotten, we decided
it was the part of wise discretion to rejoin them. We
therefore ran quickly, with heads down and receiving a
sharp but ineffective fire, across the open and got to the
standing corn, a place of safety we supposed. But just
as we reached the edge there was a loud report between
us and our comrades and a bullet whistled in close prox-
imity and a small cloud of smoke curled over the corn
tops. We dropped to the ground, supposing the enemy
had come upon our flank and that it was the explanation of the falling back. Luckily it occurred to me to
call out Burke Steuart's name, to which that individual
responded, and he reluctantly and apprehensively came
forward. "Why," said he, "I thought you were Yankees! Were you in that house? I have been firing at
you every time I could get a sight of you." He must
have got tired of his lonely post during the skirmishing
and come back from the right to our rear.

On overtaking the companies, which were already
moving back, we learned that orders had come from
Colonel Smith (of Georgia), Colonel Cumming's superior,
to come back instantly, and that he had severely reproved
Colonel Cumming for letting us make the expedition,
asking him "if he did not know that those Maryland
fellows would go to hell if they were permitted?" No one
was struck on our side in this skirmish, but there was
much talk, of course, of a number being seen to fall on
the other side. Chaplain Cameron, who had accompanied us, took a gun and fired once and was assured he
had killed his man through or around a haystack, and,
not doubting it, was filled with mixed feelings of triumph

and remorse. It was not the last of his uncanonical acts.[6]

While at Fairfax Station the efficiency of the regiment became presently much impaired by an increase of the sick, although not so seriously so as with the rest of the army. Our men were largely from Baltimore and other towns or thickly settled communities, where mumps, measles and the like are apt to be passed through in early life, and were not much affected by these diseases which now ran through most other regiments as in a nursery. I remember once we spent a night near a regiment from the far South (at Annandale), when it was distressing to hear the chorus of coughing which was kept up through the night. But camp fever was a more serious trouble, from which we did not escape, and from it and the other diseases I have mentioned many regiments were for a while so reduced as to be almost unfit for any service and in some, it was said, there were scarcely enough well men to nurse the sick and perform necessary duties around camp. Our own ground had much decayed or rank vegetation about it and the camp and its surroundings were not put or kept in a sanitary condition and we were careless about water, and so we paid the penalty by having more and more down with camp fever, which is like typhoid. Hospitals had been established at Culpeper Court House and other places in the rear and many of our sick were sent back there.

In October[7] the army was moved back for a better and more permanent line of occupation and the Maryland regiment was placed in camp on a bleak elevated ground

[6] This affair seems to be dignified by a Federal report in the *War of the Rebellion —Official Records of the Union and Confederate Armies*, Series 1, volume V, page 119, and if so, was on August 30.

[7] October 19.

near and south or southeast of the village of Centreville. Men had been joining Company H singly or by twos or threes and we here attained our maximum strength of 97 or 98 on the muster roll.

The Centreville camp was one of almost unmitigated discomfort, and my recollections of it are like a bad taste in the mouth. Being on a high ridge, with the country open for a long distance around, we were peculiarly exposed to the chill November winds, which sometimes came in blasts violent enough to blow down many tents. There were rains, too, in which the summit of the Bull Run Mountains, visible to the West, would generally appear white with snow and from which came a penetrating wind. We had not yet, in our company particularly, learned to warm our tents by properly constructed chimneys, but practised various contrivances, some of which we took from stray newspaper accounts of what our opponents were doing in that way, having a good opinion of their ingenuity in such matters. At this time D. Giraud Wright, W. Duncan McKim, John M. Burke and I, with perhaps others, were occupying a wall tent, possibly our old purchased one. After inspecting different heating arrangements and reading the available newspaper literature on the subject, we constructed one thus: just inside the tent door we dug a hole, about fifteen inches square and deep, covered with a stone slab and having a slanting opening at one side, like a coal shoot, large enough to receive chunks of fuel; a passage or flue led from outside of a corner of the tent into the bottom of the hole and another went out from the top of the hole at the opposite side, also across and outside the tent in the opposite direction, this last flue being barely under the surface of the ground. Theoretically, the deeper or lower flue was to conduct air into the bottom of the hole to supply oxygen to the fuel and the draught and smoke were to pass out by the upper passage. To put this furnace into operation we would empty a mass of hot coals (gotten from the kitchen fire, generally against the angry protest of the cook,) into the hole by the side slanting opening, pile in half a bushel of knots and chunks and seal up this entrance, and then await the result with mingled hopes and apprehensions; the hoped for result being that the draught of air would pass into the bottom of the mass of fuel and cause its slow combustion and the smoke would go out by its appointed exit and the tent be comfortably warmed for many hours. But what often happened was that either the

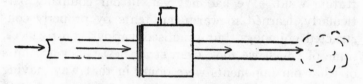

fire went out in the kindling or there would be suddenly a dire combustion, with loud roaring, causing us as much apprehension as warmth, and the furnace would then get cold in as short a time as it had taken us to get it started. T. Harry Oliver, who had joined us as a volunteer private,[8] left his knapsack one night on the fire and smoke escape flue, during one of these conflagrations, and a fine roll of white india rubber, which he had brought from Maryland, sufficient for many blankets, was scorched through and ruined. He adopted the plan of putting a bottle of hot water wrapped in woollen blanket at his feet, but was wakened one night by find-

[8] He served with us two or three months but his health giving way, spent a year in the mountains of North Carolina, but not being restored, finally went, via blockade, to Europe.

ing his feet and legs deluged with cold water, the bottle having cracked. He said he thought he heard something go "fick."

I think it was about the first of November that we— the Maryland regiment and perhaps other troops—made an expedition outside the lines to Pohick Church,[9] in which we had a severe day's march there and back and the usual want of sufficient rations. We crossed the Orange and Alexandria Railroad at Burke's Station (where I remember the fine appearance the command made, now at its best, stretched out in column), and then went many miles in a southerly or southeasterly direction until, as we were interested to be told, we were back of and not far from Mount Vernon. We bivouacked in the woods that night and Sergeant James W. Lyon and I wandered among the camp fires until a mess of another company, seeing our hungry condition, gave us a small part of their supper. Bewildered among the numberless blazing fires—nothing is more confusing—we had some difficulty in finding our way to our own company. We marched home again without adventure, the whole expedition being simply a hard march and hungry bivouac. Our understanding of the affair was that a brigade of Federal troops was in the habit of coming out to Pohick to cut wood, or protect wood cutters, and we were to try to cut them off, but, if so, we failed to meet them.

We performed several tours of picket duty from Centreville, generally on the Little River Turnpike Road over to the left. While on one of them, Charlie Grogan and one or two others besides myself determined to go outside the lines one morning to get a good breakfast. I think we asked for no permission, certainly we neither got nor could have gotten leave to go in that di-

[9] General Washington was a vestryman of this church.

rection. But we just marched straight on and when we crossed the Turnpike paid not the slightest attention to the hail of the sentinel posted some distance up the road. He hailed us a second time and then fired, but we never turned our heads and neither quickened nor slowed our gait. We went out about a mile and found a house where we got an excellent hot breakfast in the frosty morning, and after a leisurely stay of an hour went back to the company without interruption or question. I think the Grogans (James J. and Charles E. in our company and Kennedy O. in Company C) had as little sense of fear or danger as any men I ever saw.

Many expressive words which were current in the army for the rest of the war were coined at Centreville, or about that time, for it is not certain exactly when or where such expressions originate; they appear to come up like mushrooms and spread like epidemics. So, wild rumors of victories of the western army, the sinking of Federal fleets by the storms which blew our tents down, etc., which proved to be unfounded, were said to have come by the "grapevine" telegraph, that is, to have got twisted, and presently they were laconically called "grapevine messages," or, for still more economy of breath, simply "grapes." "Skedaddle," to run away in a panic, has even got a foothold in the dictionary, and some claim with plausibility that a scholarly soldier adapted it from the Greek skedannumi, but I doubt such a classic derivation.

I remember several mornings, while lying in my tent trying to keep warm, listening to conversations which illustrate traits of Irish character. There were many of that race in the company whose line of tents was back to back with ours and they were having animated discussions about generals in the Crimean and other wars.

Not only did they seem to know which of them were Irish by birth but details about them and their families in Ireland, nicknames and anecdotes, good and bad reports, were talked over for hours. These men, or many of them, were of little education and their information was traditional or clannish.

A question of natural philosophy was of passing interest. Some one discovered or proclaimed that the centre of the bottom of a kettle of boiling water was always cool to the touch, and for a day or two men were to be seen lifting their kitchen utensils from the fire and gingerly putting a finger tip on the right spot and arguing the explanation of the phenomenon. Such trivial matters go a long way to fill up the dull monotony of camp life.

But a soberer incident was the execution, by musketry, of two or three of Wheat's Louisiana Zouave "Tiger" Battalion for insubordination or rioting, a rough set of men who had to be ruled with a strong hand. I think the whole Division was drawn out to witness it.

Elzey's Brigade was composed of the 1st Maryland, the 10th and 13th Virginia and the 3d Tennessee. The men of the Tennessee regiment, while good material for soldiers, were a thrifty set and as appetites were much sharpened by the keen autumn air and the unaccustomed deprivation of sweet things in army fare caused a morbid craving for articles of that sort, they went largely into the business of making and selling molasses ginger cakes; also I am sorry to relate, the selling of liquor. It was a saying with us that all of that regiment who were not sutlers on this humble scale were runners for different rivals in the business, and that when any one visited their camp and was halted by one of the surrounding chain of sentinels, he was in the next breath directed where to go to get the best cakes or liquor. Its major, "Wash" Morgan, said to be of part Indian descent, had a great admiration for the Maryland regiment and was popular with our men. But he was not of the most temperate habits and used to ride up and down our front at dress parade, making most favorable but discomposing remarks on our appearance.

A Maryland organization, the Baltimore Light Artillery, came up from Richmond and camped near us—I think it was attached to our brigade. It had a short and light English rifled Blakeley gun which we admired and of which much was expected, but, besides kicking like a mule, these pieces were not found to have advantages and soon disappeared from the army, the long Parrott being much better.

Colonel Steuart, by his firm and able, if somewhat eccentric, handling had now brought our regiment to a fine state of discipline and efficiency, and whenever our drums were heard as we marched, with the Maryland short quick step, through Centreville on our way to picket, general and other officers turned out to see us.

CHAPTER VI

Winter Quarters at Manassas, 1861–1862

I think it was in the first week in December (1861) that the 1st Maryland Regiment moved from the bleak hill side at Centreville about five miles across (south) to a position on or very near to the Orange and Alexandria Railroad about two and one-half miles east of Manassas Junction and less than a mile West of the railroad bridge over Bull Run. The object was to construct huts for winter quarters and we occupied our tents while these were being built. The location selected was a hundred yards or so to the east of the camp and in a dense growth of old field pine, the trees so close together that lower branches could not spread, giving fine straight logs or poles for hut building. Each company constructed a row of cabins, fronting on a wide street between two companies, the officers' houses at the end of each street and facing down it. In my mess of about eleven there was not one who had done any manual work before the war and we felt rather helpless in our inexperience. But by watching others, at least half of whom were countrymen, and getting some help, we managed to get out the trimmed logs, notch them at the ends and set up the four walls of our residence, with slenderer poles running the length of the slanting roof up to the ridge pole on which to nail the clapboards. But to "get out" these rough shingles was too much for us and we hired comrades to do it. The method is to take a sawed out section, about two feet long, of a good sized oak log, quarter it, and from each quarter split off a number of clapboards. The splitting is done by driving in at the end a heavy knife blade with a side handle at right angles, and by alternate driving with a mallet and working the handle as a lever the clapboard is easily rived out. It takes only a few minutes to prize out quite a number. Each clapboard is thin along the inner edge and thick along the outer, so as to go under each other like exaggerated shingles, of which they are the prototype—only, sidewise instead of endwise. There was a low door and a small fixed window, for which we procured somewhere a frame with a pane of glass. We also got a stove, for economy both of fuel and labor in making a chimney and fireplace. The interstices between the logs were chinked with mud. We made bunks, I think a double tier. Our mess had the proud distinction of a hired cook, a colored man— "contraband," in army phrase—from Warrenton, and for him and his kitchen we built a small shebang (another army word), at the end of our house. I think we were established in our new quarters by the first of January (1862) and, with our servant to cook for us and wash up the things and a large mess chest, sumptuously furnished, which John Bolling's father had sent, we enjoyed them. Bolling was a descendant of Pocahontas[1]—like so many good Virginians—and his appearance and quiet taciturn manner indicated Indian descent.

Reveille was at dawn, at the unreasonableness of which I repined every morning. The first (orderly) sergeant of the company had gone away sick in the fall and never returned, and as second and acting orderly sergeant I had to turn out first, or with the first, to form the company and call the roll. I woke so instantaneously as to be roused by the first tap of the drum and to hear that first tap which so waked me. One morning when I was

---

[1] The granddaughter of Pocahontas married a Bolling.

about to dismiss the company after roll call, Captain Murray stopped me and read an order appointing me first sergeant. This added $1, in fact I think $3, to my pay and a further adornment on my sleeve. The pay of a Confederate infantry private soldier was $11 a month, of a sergeant $14, and the first or orderly sergeant got either $1 or $3 more. I don't think a corporal had more than a private. My duties preventing my sharing regularly in mess work, I turned over to the mess my excess of pay over the $11 as some compensation. The mark of rank of a corporal was two chevrons, I think of black braid, on the left sleeve of the jacket, at the el-

bow; a sergeant had three chevrons, and the first sergeant put a small square or diamond in the angle of the chevrons.

I may add that a lieutenant had on the sleeves of his coat a complicated figure of a single strand of gold lace, also a single bar of same on each side of the collar; a captain wore two strands and two bars; field officers wore three strands and in addition a major had one star on each side of the collar, a lieutenant-colonel, two stars, and colonel three stars. A brigadier-general had four strands and his three stars were in a wreath. The number of strands of gold lace could go no further, but the surrounding of the stars on the collar showed the rank of higher generals, besides the distinctive grouping of the row of buttons on the front of the coat. The cap had the same figuring of strands of gold lace.

Sergeants were entitled to wear a plain sword, and an iron one issued to me at Winchester, which would bend almost like lead, I clung to with affection for a long time although it was a nuisance.

My mess in winter quarters numbered about eleven, and I think its members and their subsequent careers deserve brief mention.

D. Giraud Wright, of Baltimore, was afterwards a lieutenant in the Irish Battalion (1st Virginia Regulars), and then a lieutenant in Mosby's command. Since the war he has been a judge of the Baltimore Bench.

William Duncan McKim, of Baltimore, became a major on the staff of Major-General Trimble and was killed at Chancellorsville, on 2d May, 1863, while behaving with the most conspicuous gallantry.

James William Lyon, of Baltimore County, became major and commissary on the staff of General Trimble and later of Major-General Hoke.

Randolph Harrison McKim, of Baltimore was aide de camp to Brigadier-General George H. Steuart and later a chaplain in the army.

George Williamson, of Baltimore, was captain and assistant adjutant-general of Steuart's Brigade, and was killed at Fisher's Hill, 22d September, 1864, serving on the staff of Major General John B. Gordon.

Charles Edward Grogan, of Baltimore, served on the staff of General Trimble and afterwards was a lieutenant in Mosby's command.

George J. Redmond was an Irish gentleman who had settled in Talbot County, Maryland. He was killed in Florida or South Carolina towards the last of the war, serving on some general's staff as I heard.

Wilson Cary Nicholas Carr, of Baltimore, became a captain and quartermaster.

John Minge Bolling, of Virginia and Baltimore. I do not know about him after the dissolution of the company.

John M. Burke, of Irish descent, was from the southeastern part of Ohio but was teaching in Virginia and a student of theology when the war broke out. After the disbandment of Company H in 1862 he was at the Episcopal Theological Seminary, temporarily removed from Alexandria to Halifax County. He turned out to defend the Staunton River bridge in the Wilson-Kautz raid of June, 1864, and, raising his head above the breastwork, was shot in the head and instantly killed.

McHenry Howard.

So eight or nine of the mess (including myself), became commissioned officers. Other messes had not such a record to show, but from this fine company might have been well officered a couple of regiments.

In January, 1862, as the term of service of most of the soldiers would soon expire, a furlough of thirty days was offered to anyone who would re-enlist for the war. Randolph McKim was the first to do so in the Maryland regiment, not for the sake of the furlough, but animated by high patriotic motives. Not many followed his example, it being claimed that most of the companies were in "for the war" already and others preferring to reserve an option—many intending to change to the cavalry or artillery.[2]

Colonel Steuart had organized a fine drum corps, under the peerless Hosea Pitt, and was getting up a band, under Bandmaster Hubbard. And all day was heard in the air the doleful practising of "Hark, I Hear An Angel Sing," the "Mocking Bird" and "Maryland, My Maryland"—now becoming known.

[2] Furlough was the proper term in connection with enlisted men, leave of absence with officers; but the distinction was not always observed.

CHAPTER VII

Opening of Campaign of 1862—Manassas to the Rappahannock

On the 9th of March, 1862, a part of the 1st Maryland Regiment—Company H, Captain William H. Murray, Company F, being Captain J. Louis Smith's company but then commanded by first Lieutenant William Dickinson Hough—if there were any others I do not remember them—under Lieutenant-Colonel Bradley T. Johnson, left winter quarters on the west side of Bull Run for picket duty. We marched east on the Orange and Alexandria Railroad about five miles to Sangster's Station,[1] where we relieved the 13th Virginia. These two companies established themselves in the woods beyond the station and on the north side of the railroad and Company F, or part of it, went forward a very short distance to the open ground and took the place of that part of the picket line which was directly in our front. But this had scarcely been effected when we of Murray's company who were proceeding to settle ourselves comfortably, being in reserve, heard a sharp firing break out, apparently not more than one or two hundred yards in advance, and, of course, the company sprang to arms. We learned that Hough's small party had been suddenly charged by a body of cavalry which captured second Lieutenant Joseph H. Stewart and about a dozen men.[3]

[1] Colonel Johnson says there were four companies, *Confederate Military History*, volume 2, page 65.

[2] Not Burke's Station as Colonel Johnson says, *ibidem*.

[3] But they made a stout resistance, killing Lieutenant Hidden who commanded the charging party. See *War of the Rebellion—Records of the Union and Con-*

66

The firing soon ceased, the enemy falling back. We stood under arms for some time and then our small battalion moved back along the railroad. We had gone but a short distance when we were first somewhat alarmed to see a regiment drawn up in line on a hill side on the south side of the railroad facing us as we were now marching. But we thought we recognized the flag (a Virginia one I think), and found it was the 13th Virginia, which we had just relieved and which had hardly started on its return to camp when it heard the firing and halted for our support. These two commands stood together in line facing the enemy, but no further advance was made by them and presently the 13th Virginia resumed its march back. Our little battalion waited in line for some hours, momentarily expecting an attack. Our position was half way or more up an open hillside, with woods at the bottom in front and a house behind us, on the south side of the railroad and either at or a short distance West of Sangster's Station. If there were or had been any of our cavalry between us and the enemy, we had not seen them. At some hour in the afternoon we also withdrew and marched leisurely back along the railroad track, burning the small bridges as we went, understanding that there was nothing back of us but the enemy; but we did not take the responsibility of destroying the large bridge over Bull Run.[4]

federate Armies, Series 1, volume V, page 537, et seq. Lieutenant Stewart was from Cambridge, Maryland, and a resigned West Point cadet. Lieutenant Hough exhibited one or more bullet holes through his coat.

[4] One of our drums was captured, or more likely thrown away by the drummer, in this affair, who made his way back to winter quarters. Assistant Surgeon Latimer told me that this drummer, on being asked what had happened, was going through a pantomime of running away and casting back a drum over his shoulder when Colonel Steuart grabbed him from behind and demanded in an awful voice, "Where is your drum?" He turned to Drum Major Hosea Pitt and said, "It's a good thing, Pitt, it's a good thing that I had not yet had the Maryland flag painted on those drums!"

My recollection is that on arriving at winter quarters we found them abandoned—at least by the mass of the citizens—and that after lingering there an hour or two we pushed on southwesterly on the railroad track, the crossties making an irregular step and tiresome marching. Strange to say, my memory does not preserve any distinct picture of passing Manassas, while I do remember a station some three miles still further on in the woods, by which time it was growing dark. And about here I saw for the last time our hired mess cook, Asbury, who was trudging along the railroad with pots and pans in his hands. No doubt he considered his contract broken by this moving and was striking for home, Warrenton, with as much of our kitchen furniture as he could carry. We were now getting very tired and I think we must have soon stopped for the night. We understood that the whole army was falling back and that on our line of retreat we were bringing up the rear.

The next morning we resumed the march, still along the Orange and Alexandria Railroad, and either on that day or the next—10th or 11th March—came to the Rappahannock River. Here we found General Joseph E. Johnston, the army commander, dismounted and directing in person the preparations, piling wood, etc., for the setting fire to the bridge at its northeast end.[5] We crossed and the Maryland regiment (I do not remember where it became united,) went into camp, or bivouac, about a mile back (southwest) of the river and half a mile or more south of the railroad, on top of a slightly wooded or brushy ridge. We had come out of Prince William County, passed over Fauquier and were now in Culpeper. We had no tents, but the weather was fine, requiring only light fires.

[5] It was not burned, however, until later.

I remember several amusing discussions and incidents here. Sergeant James W. Lyon and Private George Williamson, of my mess, were the best of soldiers but with some opposite characteristics. Williamson was conscientious to an extreme in all things and kept his uniform and accoutrements in the best possible condition; his gun looked as if it were new. Sergeant Lyon was not very particular in those matters. The outward appearance of Lyon's gun vexed Williamson's orderly soul and he often reproached him about it, to which Lyon would reply that his piece could always be relied on for service and the outside was of little importance. One day the company, or part of it in which were Lyon and Williamson, went a little way down the hill to fire off their pieces which had been loaded ever since the picket affair of March 9. The men were in line and in succession each one stepped to the front and fired at a mark. When his turn came Sergeant Lyon stepped briskly forward, raised his gun to his shoulder with a confident expression, aimed deliberately and pulled the trigger. But instead of the expected loud report, there was a faint fizzling sound and the ball came slowly out, described a short parabolic curve, all the while visible, and fell to the ground about ten paces in front. Williamson was decently jubilant and taunted him about his "always serviceable" gun. But a day or two afterwards the regiment was drawn up for inspection—probably the usual Sunday morning inspection. Although only orderly sergeant, I was in command of Murray's company for the occasion, and when the inspecting officer (Lieutenant-Colonel Bradley T. Johnson, Colonel Steuart having probably gone to Richmond on being made brigadier-general,) came to our company, I, as was customary, stepped out and went down our line at his elbow. When

we came to Williamson, Colonel Johnson, who knew him
well, smiled on him and Williamson smiled respectfully
back.   He handed his gun to the Colonel, who looked at
it and it was as clean and bright as could be.   But when
the Colonel.proceeded to give the gun the usual jerk to
make the ramrod, which was loosely in the barrel, spring
up to fall back with the expected ring against the bottom
showing that all was clean within, it came back with a
dull thud.   The Colonel's smile changed to an expression
of reproach at this fall from grace of a model soldier.
Williamson's face narrowed and took on a look of horror.
But still greater was the amazement of both when the
Colonel, after turning around the ramrod against the
bottom of the barrel drew it out and the end was coated
with sugar!   Colonel Johnson handed back the piece
and passed on without a word.   He knew Williamson's
feelings required no spoken reproach from him.   Now
the sugar ration was a small and irregular one at that
time and we accused Williamson—of course in jest—of
having abstracted a part of our mess allowance and hidden it in his gun.   The mystery was never explained, but
I believe that Williamson always thought that Lyon had
put the sugar in his gun and Lyon that Williamson had
poured water in his.

In fact the whole ration was uncertain, in quantity
and quality, and we occasionally went off to a house
down the south side of the hill to get a "square meal."
Like others similarly situated, when the appetite is
greater than the supply, we often sat around the fire recalling the good things we had had at home.   I once remarked on the incongruity of mixing on the same plate
at Christmas two such extreme things as plum pudding
which was brought in on fire and ice cream.   Sergeant
Lyon said he never heard of such an absurdity.   I main-

tained that it was a usage in good society and we had quite a heated controversy, Lyon finally intimating a doubt whether I knew what the habits of good society were

Such were some of my parting reminiscences of life in the ranks.

CHAPTER VIII

Appointment as Staff Officer—Rappahannock River to Richmond and the Valley

On the 24th or 25th of March (1862) being then in the camp or bivouac on the southwest side of the Rappahannock River, in Culpeper County, I received the following letter:

March 24.

My dear Mac:—

As perhaps you have heard, I've been appointed a Brig. Genl. and requested Jim to write you, asking if you w'd accept the position of A.D.C. on my Staff. I sh'd 've written myself but for want of material and place. Jim felt so sure of y'r acquiescing in my wishes, that I have applied for you to be ordered to report to me at once and also for yr. appointment as A.D.C. and Lieut. in the P.A.C.S. Genl. Johnston told me he w'd sanction the first and I think I can accomplish the last in Richmond. I regret the Regt. is so far off I can't see you at once.

I go to Richmond tomorrow to pass the week and get some clothes etc. If you get the order in time, join me at the Spottswood, if not, at Orange. Jim will be able to tell you of my whereabouts. You of course will wish to visit R. and I w'd like to have you there with me but there'll be no trouble about y'r going down later. I'm assigned to no Brigade yet or do I know where I'll go. I hope you are all well. My kind regards to John and all friends. I've heard nothing from home for a long time.

Our command camped a little beyond Orange on Saturday. Write to me at the Spottswood. Good bye,

Yrs truly

Chas. S. Winder.

The envelope was addressed:

Lt. Col. B. T. Johnson,
    1st Md. Regt.
        for Sergt. McH. Howard,
    Compy. H. Capt. Murray.
Will Col. J. cause this to be delivered.
    Oblige, C. S. Winder.

On receiving this letter from General Winder I made application for leave of absence, which had to pass through the regular channel of regimental and brigade headquarters:

Camp Hill, March 25th, 1862.

MAJOR GREEN,
    A. Adjutant General, 2nd Division, Army of the Potomac, C. S.

Sir:
    I have the honor to apply to you for leave of absence to go to Richmond for four days for reasons apparent in the enclosed copy of a letter.
Respectfully,

McHENRY HOWARD,
1st Sergeant Co. H., 1st Md. Regt.

And which application was endorsed as follows:

McHenry Howard
Ord. Sergt. Co. H, 1st Md. Regt.
Application for leave.
    Forwarded and respectfully recommended—Sergt. Howard having since the beginning of the War faithfully done his duty as a soldier and now well deserved this promotion.

BRADLEY T. JOHNSON,
Lt. Col. Comdg. 1st Md. Regt.,
March 25, 1862.

Hd. Qu. 4th Brigade   March 25, '62.
    Approved and respectfully forwarded.

ARNOLD ELZEY, Brig. Genl.

Head Quarters 3rd Division, March 26th, 1862.
    Approved.   By order of Maj. Gen'l Ewell.

G. CAMPBELL BROWN, A.A.A. Genl.

On the 26th of March, before reveille and without disturbing my comrades to say good-bye, I left the camp and walked over to Brandy Station, two miles westerly, to get the approval of General Ewell to my application, which it still then lacked.   William Duncan McKim, of my mess, went with me, he having received the appointment of aide de camp to Brigadier-General Isaac R.

Trimble. From Brandy we walked the railroad track four or five miles to Culpeper Court House, which was then the terminus of passenger travel. I do not remember at what hour the train started but I think it was about dark when we got to Richmond and went to the Spotswood Hotel, at the corner of Main and 7th Streets and from which I had gone into service nine and a half months before. Our jackets and other clothing were shabby and the clerk told us, superciliously, that he could not give us a room. But we presently met Colonel (or perhaps he had just been made brigadier-general,) George H. Steuart, who spoke to the clerk and we were allowed to register. The sensation of being in the midst of civilization again after nearly a year's living a soldier's life in the field was peculiar and most agreeable.

We soon met Columbus Baldwin, an intimate friend of Duncan KcKim in Baltimore, who had come over on a visit to settle or straighten out his firm's affairs in the South, and we sat in the upper parlor conversing. Presently another old friend of Duncan came in excitedly and said, "Baldwin, have you heard the news? Duncan McKim is here, I have seen his name on the registry." Baldwin said, "Hollingsworth, let me introduce you to Mr. Smith." They shook hands formally, Hollingsworth not recognizing his old intimate friend, who now wore a beard, having always had a smooth face before the war. We talked for some time, Hollingsworth declaring he would not go to bed until he had seen Duncan McKim and wondering where he was. He presently asked, "Mr. Smith, where are you serving?" when Duncan's hearty laugh at first offended and then made Hollingsworth recognize him.

I had been told that after lying on the ground, or in a bunk in winter quarters, and getting up at daybreak for so long, I would not be able to sleep in a comfortable bed with sheets and pillows, but I did sleep soundly and not waking until about nine o'clock next day, March 27 (or 28?).

I think I found a letter from General Winder, telling me that instead of being assigned to a brigade in General Longstreet's Division, as he had expected, he had been suddenly ordered in Richmond to report to General (Stonewall) Jackson in the Valley of Virginia, to command the 1st or Stonewall Brigade in the place of General Richard B. Garnett, whom Jackson had placed under arrest for withdrawing his men without orders at the battle of Kernstown on March 23. He directed me, therefore, to join him in the Valley by way of Gordonsville, his stay in Richmond having been cut short.

I remember that I found it difficult to get from Richmond to Gordonsville, the railroad transportation being all engaged in connection with the change of operations from northern Virginia to the Yorktown Peninsula. Some years after the war Lieutenant James B. Washington, of General Joseph E. Johnston's staff, an old schoolmate, reminded me that he met me in Richmond in this difficulty, and told me that General Johnston was about to return, with an engine and car, from a military consultation at Richmond back to Orange where his headquarters then were with part of the army, and invited me to use the opportunity to get to Gordonsville. And I think it was on Sunday the 30th of March that I so left Richmond after a stay there of only two or three days. I had bought a plain gray coat, without sign of rank, to replace my soldier's jacket. Arriving at Gordonsville (where there was some snow), I found I could get no further that day and spent the night at the house of a minister, Mr. Ewing, sleeping on the parlor floor. The next day I took the train for Staunton, where I spent the night at the hotel. And the following morning I took the stage for Mount Jackson, 50 miles, where I was told I would find General Jackson's army halted after its falling back from Kernstown, and where I found it in the afternoon. I think this was the 2d of April (1862).

CHAPTER IX

VALLEY CAMPAIGN—ASHBY AND JACKSON— REORGANIZATION

I found General Winder at a small house on the east side of the Valley Turnpike Road and I think he had, himself, arrived that morning, having ridden from Gordonsville or Orange across the Blue Ridge. He had reported to General Jackson on his arrival but had not assumed command of his brigade in any formal way.[1] Captain John F. O'Brien, a resigned West Point cadet, had accompanied him to be his assistant adjutant-general.[2]

We were almost immediately introduced to the activity of the "Valley Campaign." We were eating on the porch of this house, which was close by the side of the Turnpike, some time in the afternoon, when firing was heard down the road—to the north—and wagons and ambulances soon came hurrying past to the rear. With them there were a number of stragglers, and General Winder remarked, "That must be stopped." I think this must have been Jackson's final falling back to his position at Rude's Hill, a short distance south of Mount Jackson and with the north fork of the Shenandoah River crossing the Turnpike in his front, which position he held for two weeks.

[1] An order of General Jackson, dated April 4, announces the organization of his army and General Winder's assignment to the 1st brigade. Allan's *Jackson's Valley Campaign* page 60. But he had already assumed command.

[2] "Assistant" adjutant-general is misleading to a layman, but all adjutant-generals under General Samuel Cooper, adjutant and inspector-general of the Confederate Army, were "assistant," even the adjutant-generals of Johnston's and Lee's armies. So with the inspector-generals.

The next morning, April 3, the brigade was under arms and in column along the west side of the Turnpike, with its head towards the enemy, and the former adjutant-general, Captain Wingate (who immediately thereafter left,) introduced General Winder to the colonels at the head of their respective regiments, who were, Colonel James W. Allen, of the 2d Virginia; Lieutenant-Colonel Charles A. Ronald, of the 4th Virginia; Colonel William H. Harman, of the 5th Virginia; Lieutenant-Colonel Andrew Jackson Grigsby, of the 27th Virginia, and Colonel Arthur C. Cummings, of the 33d Virginia, and I suppose, also to Captain William McLaughlin of the Rockbridge Battery and Captain Joseph Carpenter, of the "Allegheny Roughs" or Carpenter's Battery, both of which were parts of the 1st or Stonewall Brigade. He also introduced him to Colonel Turner Ashby who with his cavalry and Chew's Battery was, as usual, guarding the rear, with the Stonewall Brigade that day in support.

My recollection of Ashby's appearance is not, of course, from my first impression at that time; I saw and was near him very often, sometimes day after day until he was killed two months later. I would describe him as of slender build and somewhat under medium height. His beard, thick and of a very dark brown color, covered the entire lower half of his face, from above the line of the moustache, and was so long as to come to his breast. His eyes were a dark hazel, perhaps some would call them brown, and his complexion also was brown—nothing being light in his appearance but the whites of his eyes. I thought he looked more like an Arab, or the common idea of one, than any man I ever saw. His manner was grave but courteous. Where there were many fine riders, no one was a better or more graceful horseman. Careless of the increased risk, he generally rode a beautiful milk white horse, which was said to be well known to the enemy, and certainly he was very often so close to them as to give them every opportunity of recognizing him.

He presently suggested to General Winder to ride forward and look at the enemy's picket line and we accordingly rode to our outposts a little way in front on the west side of the Turnpike road, and for some time we looked at them, not far off and plainly visible through the thin timber. As we stood there, a small group on horseback, one or more bullets came over to us and I thought it was a needless and foolish exposure. But Ashby paid not the slightest attention to the shots, nor did General Winder, and staff officers had, of course, to simulate a like indifference. I was relieved when we leisurely moved back. General Winder said to Ashby that he would not assume active command of the entire rear unless something occurred to require it, to which Ashby made no reply, but he looked surprised, not being used to receive orders from any except the commanding general.

Presently General Jackson—Stonewall—rode up with part of his staff (among whom I remember Captain "Sandy" (Alexander S.) Pendleton, well known afterwards), and I then saw him for the first time. But I saw him nearly every day after this and was very often close to his side, and the following sketch is now written from my general recollection, fixed in my mind by many conversations about him since the war. He was above middle height, compactly and strongly built but with no superfluous flesh. His eyes were a steel blue in color and well opened when he looked straight at one, which he did in addressing a direct remark. His hair was dark brown and the hair on both his head and beard was curly or wavy. The beard was thick and over the lower part of his face but was not long and luxuriant like Ashby's. His nose was well made, perhaps roman in shape, but not prominently large, and his mouth, half seen under the moustache was very firm and the lips usually compressed. The lower part of his face was tanned by exposure, but when his cap was off, the forehead, high and broad, was white. I remember a feature about his face, which I have never seen noticed by others, however, was an unusual fullness of the temples. He wore at this time, if not during the Valley campaign, a dark blue uniform, being, I understood, his dress as a professor and major at the Virginia Military Institute at Lexington. The cap was particularly noticeable, being of the kepi kind, high in make but the upper part not stiff and showing as you faced him the small round top falling over to the front and almost, if not quite, resting on the visor, which was well down over his eyes. He wore high boots, as did nearly all mounted officers.

I heard of his habit of raising his arm and hand at times while riding, which has been often told in books, and, among other theories, that it was to promote the circulation which he imagined to be defective on that side, also that it was to invoke a blessing; but I never remarked it as a frequent gesture, although with him often on battle fields, as well as on the march and in bivouac, and I believe the impression that it was a very frequent habit is much exaggerated. While very courteous, his words were few and to the point, the voice distinct but rather low and, sometimes at least, a little muffled—but that may be too strong a word—like that of many partially deaf persons; he once told me he was deaf in one ear and could not well tell the direction of sounds. The habitual expression of his face was that of one communing with his own thoughts and others seldom spoke to him without being first addressed. We heard that the colonel of one of the Stonewall regiments had vowed that he would never go to his headquarters again unless sent for, because, on making some remark, Jackson brusquely replied that he had no time to talk on other than military matters. In fact, all the field officers, certainly the colonels, were resenting strongly the arrest of General Garnett—Winder's predecessor—for withdrawing the brigade when out of ammunition at Kernstown on March 23, and I believe the feeling was shared largely by the men. The implicit confidence in and devotion to Jackson came later—after the experiences of the Valley campaign—if not indeed still later.

I return to my story.

The enemy showing no disposition to advance, towards evening the regiments of the Stonewall Brigade went to their nearby bivouacs.

I think it was the next day, April 4, that I walked over to see my friends in Clarke's company of the 21st Virginia Infantry, one of the regiments which had joined Jackson under General Loring and which were still sometimes distinguished as "Loring's men." This Maryland company was raised at Richmond at the same time that Dorsey's and Murray's companies were formed—May and June, 1861—but instead of going thence with those two companies to Winchester to unite with the six companies enlisted at Harper's Ferry to form the 1st Maryland Regiment, Clarke's company preferred, or its captain did, to go into this Virginia regiment under Colonel Gilham, a Virginia Military Institute professor, which went to West Virginia.[3] I think Captain J. Lyle Clarke

[3] When Jackson went in the Fal' of 1861 from Manassas to take command of the Valley District, his o'd Stonewall Brigade soon followed him, and this was all the force he had except cavalry and the called out militia. (The conscript

had been promoted and that Richard Curzon Hoffman was now captain and William Stuart Symington was first lieutenant. Like Murray's and Dorsey's, the company had in it a number of the old Maryland Guard Battalion, also some of the Baltimore City Guard Battalion and the Independent Greys Company.

I sat on a log and talked with my friends of this company for some time. They said they were glad to see me but were sorry for me to have come to serve under a crazy man. They told me much about Jackson's eccentricities, both personal and in his military operations and predicted that some dire disaster would one day befall him and his army.

Major G. Douglas Mercer, the brigade-quartermaster, a Marylander, had told General Winder that he would give him only a few weeks to hold his command, before the expiration of which, he predicted, Jackson would have him under arrest for some cause or other. All these forebodings were calculated to make a newcomer feel uncomfortable, but soldiers do not worry much over "mañana."

We remained in this position at Rude's Hill about two weeks, confronting the enemy, who did not seem inclined to attack us.

A citizen riding by one day, a large man with a heavy red beard, was pointed out to me as Abraham (?) Lincoln,

law, passed early in 1862, pretty much did away with Militia.) General Loring joined Jackson the last of December with three brigades from West Virginia, but having never gotten on harmoniously with Jackson, he was assigned to another command early in 1862 and all except the Virginia regiments in his three brigades were also sent elsewhere. These remaining Virginia regiments Jackson formed into two brigades, as the 2d and 3d brigades of his army (see Allan's *Jackson's Valley Campaign*) but for some time they were often called "Loring's men" as distinguished from the 1st or Stonewall Brigade. When Ewell's Division joined, these three brigades came to be called "Jackson's Old Division."

a cousin of the President. Major Mercer had procured for me a young half-broken horse in the neighborhood, before which I had ridden, when I had occasion to ride, one of General Winder's, he having two, one a strong young brown horse, dappled with darker spots, and the other a well bred sorrel of slender make, both rather small but active and serviceable. I had got a ready made plain grey coat in Richmond and picked up somewhere an artillery sabre, and so was sufficiently equipped as a staff officer, although without sign of rank. For some time the field officers showed their resentment at General Winder's assignment to the command of the brigade in Garnett's place by not coming to headquarters, but presently Colonel Harman, of the 5th Virginia, a gentleman of very courteous manners, and Lieutenant-Colonel Grigsby, of the 27th, a bluff soldier much given to swearing, came and the latter got into the habit of sitting around our camp fire. And I think it was Grigsby who told us that at a meeting of the field officers before Winder's coming it had been determined that they would show their feeling by not calling on the new brigade commander. One day when I was riding with General Winder past the encampment or bivouac of one of the regiments there was some faint hissing. I was not certain that the General heard it, but as soon as he reached his headquarters he sent for the colonel and told him it indicated a bad state of discipline in his regiment and if anything like it occurred again he would hold the colonel responsible.

After about two weeks we fell back from our position at Rude's Hill.[4] In the morning, but not very early, the sound of artillery, quite frequent and sharp and I thought

---

[4] Allan's *Jackson's Valley Campaign* says April 17.

alarmingly close, was heard down the Turnpike. The
enemy had developed a sudden activity and pressed
Ashby back through Mount Jackson and over the north
fork of the Shenandoah which crosses the Turnpike less
than a mile this side of that village. After getting over,
Ashby had attempted to burn the bridge but was too
closely pressed and had his horse shot and came near
being killed himself. The artillery firing was probably
from Chew's Battery, attached to his command. But
Jackson did not hurry himself and our Brigade stood for
some time in column along the roadside. Ashby's
beautiful white horse was led by to the rear, his left side
red with blood from a wound. He was moving well and
tossing his head and we all hoped—for all knew him—
that it was not a fatal wound, but when we had presently
taken up the march and gone a very short distance we saw
the noble animal lying dead near the west side of the
road and cavalrymen were cutting off hair from the long
white mane and tail for souvenirs.[5]

I do not remember that the enemy after forcing Ashby
across the Shenandoah pressed us at all, and we must
have gone into camp before getting to the town of Har-

[5] Captain John Esten Cooke, in the first edition, published in 1866, of his
Life of Stonewall Jackson, in the text makes the incident of the killing of Ashby's
white horse to have occurred at this time but in a note refers to the appendix,
where, on page 470, he makes a correction and says that it happened in Jackson's
second retreat up the Valley, six weeks later. In the reprint made by Rev. J.
William Jones in 1876, the text and note are the same, but I do not find the referred to appendix. Dabney's *Life of Jackson* seems to make it on the second
retreat, but he makes slight mention of it, and he was not present in the first
retreat, not having joined Jackson until afterwards. Allan in his *Jackson's
Valley Campaign* makes it on the first retreat. Avirett's *Ashby and his Com-
peers* also seems to make it on the first retreat. Unfortunately, a diary which I
kept in the Valley campaign was lent by me to Captain Cooke when I heard he
was about to publish a second edition and I never got it back. But on 1 November 1912 I wrote to Colonel R. Preston Chew, who during the Valley campaign was captain of Chew's Battery, serving with Ashby's command, asking

risonburg, County seat of Rockingham, which is about twenty miles south of Rude's Hill. And if so, it was the next morning, 18th of April, when, to our surprise, we left the familiar Valley Turnpike Road at Harrisonburg, on which we had supposed we would continue falling back towards Staunton, and took the road which went off easterly, passing around the south end of Massanutton Mountain to Swift Run Gap in the Blue Ridge.

The lofty Massanutton range is a very prominent feature in the territory of the great Valley and played an important part in Jackson's operations. Beginning abruptly in the middle of the Valley between Strasburg and Front Royal, it extends southwesterly forty or fifty miles to a point nearly opposite Harrisonburg, where it ends almost as abruptly. It has but a single "gap" or road over it in all this extent. It thus bisects the Valley for that distance, the Western part being considered to be "the Valley," although watered by the smaller fork of the river, the eastern part being commonly distinguished as the Luray Valley, and through which the larger south fork of the Shenandoah runs north to its junction with the other Fork at Front Royal.

him if he could tell me positively on which retreat the incident occurred and his answer settles the question:

"Charles Town, West Virginia, Nov. 4th, 1912.

MR. McHENRY HOWARD,
     901 St. Paul Street, Baltimore, Md.

DEAR SIR: Replying to your favor of Nov. 1st, I beg to say that Ashby was attacked at the bridge over the Shenandoah river after the battle of Kernstown. The enemy charged with unusual spirit and drove him back with a few cavalry, and came very near killing him. His horse was shot and died a little south of Rude's hill. I was there when the horse was shot, and rode with him as he came back, his horse bleeding from a wound in the side.

Yours very truly
R. P. CHEW."

Ashby will always be a romantic figure in the history of the Valley and this incident in his career should be accurately fixed, as on this first retreat.

If I remember right, it was either this day or the next, while going around the south end of the Massanutton that we passed, or there passed us, a large and rather rough looking man on horseback, with two or three others, at whom the men jeered, as infantry commonly did at anything on a horse, not recognizing Brigadier General Edward ("Allegheny") Johnson, who had ridden over from his command in the mountains west of Staunton to confer with Jackson—and whose visit we were soon to return.

We crossed the south (main) fork of the Shenandoah at Conrad's Store and went into camp on Elk Run, which comes out of Swift Run Gap of the Blue Ridge. Swift Run, which gives its name to the Gap, runs out on the eastern side and is one of the head streams of Mechum's River which empties into the James—through the Rivanna.[6]

This was a disagreeable camp, partly from the ground, or much of it, being stony or gravelly as the washing down from the mountain gap, more so from the weather which was snowy or sleety many days, and even still more from the unpleasant details of the military reorganization following the expiration of the year's enlistment of most of the men and the passage by the Confederate Congress of the conscript law, which put into active service "for the war" all between the ages of 18 and 35 (afterwards extended). My impression is that this reorganization was a new election of company officers

[6] According to Colonel William Allan and others we reached this camp on April 19. I think the modern town of Elkton must be built about on its site. Swift Run Gap is commonly supposed to be the pass to which (if they did not go beyond), the "Knights of the Golden Horseshoe" came in Governor Spotswood's romantic exploring expedition in 1716.

by the men—certainly there was a new election of regimental field officers, colonel, lieutenant-colonel and major, by the company officers of the respective regiments. In the 2d Virginia these field officers were, James W. Allen, colonel; Lawson Botts, lieutenant-colonel; and Frank B. Jones, major; and I believe there were here no changes. But I understood that Colonel Allen was dissatisfied, and that he soon, or at some time thereafter, sent in his resignation, not wishing to serve longer under Jackson. If he did, it was not accepted down to 27th June when he was killed at the head of his regiment in the Seven Days Battles around Richmond. He was a fine officer.

In the 4th Virginia we had found on our coming Charles A. Ronald, colonel or lieutenant-colonel commanding, and, at any rate, he now (or possibly soon afterwards,) became full colonel.[7] I do not remember the lieutenant-colonel, but I think William Terry was made major.

In the 5th Virginia Colonel William H. Harman now, possibly soon after, retired, and the new field officers were William H. S. Baylor, colonel; J. H. S. Funk, lieutenant-colonel, and H. J. Williams, major.

The 27th Virginia was, properly, a battalion, lacking one or two of the full ten companies which make a regiment. It came from the remoter parts of West Virginia, which were in possession of the enemy, Shriver's company being from Wheeling. It was not, therefore, as full as the other regiments. Its former colonel, John Echols, was disabled by a severe wound at Kernstown, and Lieutenant-Colonel Andrew Jackson Grigsby was commanding the regiment. I suppose Echols continued as colonel,

---

[7] He was lieutenant colonel at the battle of Kernstown, March 23, but signs his official report of the battle of Winchester, May 23–25, as colonel.

although absent, as Grigsby certainly did for a time as lieutenant-colonel.[8]   I think E. F. Paxton was major.

In the 33d Virginia Colonel Arthur C. Cummings, who was considered a very efficient officer, positively declined a re-election, to the great regret of all.   We understood it was for the same reasons of dissatisfaction as with Colonel Allen.[9]   The former adjutant of the regiment, John F. Neff, a young man but a graduate of the Virginia Military Institute, was made colonel.   He was a member of a Dunkard or Tunker family, a numerous sect around Mount Jackson, which like the Quakers, is principled against military service, and we heard that there was much displeasure in his family and community at his voluntarily going into the war.   I think Edmund G. Lee continued as lieutenant-colonel and Frederick W. M. Holliday either continued as or was now made major.

Captain William McLaughlin of the Rockbridge Battery also retired and first lieutenant William T. Poague became captain.   One of the lieutenants was Archibald Graham—I do not recall others.

Carpenter's Battery[10] remained unchanged, at any rate, the captain was Joseph Carpenter, first lieutenant (his

---

[8] Grigsby signs his official report of the battle of Winchester, May 23–25 as lieutenant-colonel commanding, but his report of the battle of Port Republic on June 8 as colonel.

[9] The dissatisfaction of the colonels of which I have spoken did not proceed merely from their resentment of General Garnett's arrest and the implied censure of the brigade; they thought Jackson had treated them with a want of consideration in several ways.   See page 16 of Allan's *Jackson's Valley Campaign* for an illustration—where they had written him a joint communication of complaint and received a tart reply.

[10] This was originally an infantry Company of the 27th Virginia until the Fall of 1861, when it was detached from the Regiment and converted into an artillery Company.   In 1911 C. A. Fonerden, a Member of the Company, published a history of it, printed by Henkel & Company, Newmarket, Va.

brother), John C. Carpenter; second lieutenant, George McKendree. I do not remember another lieutenant. The company was also known as the "Alleghany Roughs," many companies at the beginning of the war styling themselves by such names—some of which were very ferocious.

First Lieutenant James Mercer Garnett, of Virginia, was here assigned to the brigade as ordnance officer, so that General Winder's full staff was now made up as follows: Captain John F. O'Brien, assistant adjutant-general; Lieutenant James M. Garnett, ordnance officer; Lieutenant McHenry Howard, aide de camp; Major G. Douglas Mercer, of Maryland, was brigade quartermaster—the commissary I have forgotten. Dr. Black, of the 4th Virginia, was senior surgeon and may be called brigade surgeon or medical director.

About this time I received my commission, or notification of appointment, which I give as a sample of such Confederate documents:

CONFEDERATE STATES OF AMERICA

WAR DEPARTMENT

Richmond, April 16, 1862.

SIR:—You are hereby notified that the President has appointed you First Lieutenant and Aid de Camp. To take rank Mar. 31, 1862, in the Provisional Army in the service of the Confederate States. You are requested to signify your acceptance or non acceptance of said appointment: and should you accept you will sign before a magistrate the oath of office herewith, and forward the same with your letter of acceptance to this Department. You will report for duty to Gen. Chas. Winder.

GEO. W. RANDOLPH,

Secretary of War.

1st Lieut. Henry Howard, Aid de Camp.

—Md.———. J.E.J.

I accepted the commission, but not my abbreviated name.

In the latter part of this month, April, General Jackson issued an order partially breaking up Colonel Ashby's command. He had, and under a commission for the raising of an independent command, twenty-two companies of cavalry, but as fine a body of men as it was, they were said to be not well drilled or disciplined and held by Ashby in little restraint. General Jackson's order assigned ten of these companies to the 3d Brigade to be under Brigadier-General William B. Taliaferro, and directed Ashby himself with the other twelve companies to report to General Winder and be under his command. Ashby promptly wrote his resignation and sent it to General Winder to be forwarded. I remember very distinctly riding out with General Winder to the cavalry outpost at McGaheysville (pronounced McGackeysville), near the south end of the Massanutton, where he had a long talk with Ashby, who finally consented to Winder's retaining the resignation in his own hands for the present and trusted the forwarding of it to his judgment. The General then went to Jackson, and I think he had several conversations both with him and with Ashby. The result was that the order was rescinded or suspended, or was allowed to remain unexecuted, while the matter of Ashby's status was referred to Richmond.[11] To General Winder's offices was largely due the settlement or smoothing over of what at the time threatened serious trouble. And from that time there was a warm regard between Ashby and Winder. These particulars about Ashby's resignation have never been given before.

On one of the very last days of the month I heard that Ewell's Division had come over from the Rappahannock,

[11] A few weeks later Ashby was appointed brigadier-general and so his commission for an independent command was abrogated. Jackson tried other and more regular methods for disciplining the cavalry.

or the Rapidan, to join us and was in camp on the other side of the Blue Ridge, and the next morning I rode through the Gap (or rather over it, for the road, going up Elk Run mounts, sometimes zigzagging, to a high elevation and then descends Swift Run on the eastern side), to see my old comrades of the 1st Maryland. I found them encamped between the Gap and Stannardsville, and after some hours rode back, having enjoyed both the meeting and the picturesque ride across the mountain.

The enemy had not followed us in any force from Harrisonburg, nor did he venture to advance further up the Valley with Jackson on his flank, and so we had a quiet time in this Elk Run or Swift Run Gap camp—except for the weather and the internal troubles I have mentioned.

CHAPTER X

VALLEY CAMPAIGN—BATTLE OF McDOWELL

On April 30 or May 1, we broke camp at Swift Run Gap[1] and took the road which went southerly between the Blue Ridge and the Shenandoah River. This was one of the hardest and slowest marches I ever saw. The persistent wet weather had made almost a quagmire of the strip of country between the foot of the mountain and the river, although I remember noticing that the numerous small streams which came down from the clean mountain side, while swollen, were running clear. The dirt road was almost impassable for guns, caissons, wagons and even light ambulances, and if they tried to get on better by turning off into the woods—which extended nearly all the way—the ground there was found to be as soft. Wheels sank to their hubs, and deeper, and although the men lent their hands and shoulders, it seemed impossible sometimes to extricate them. I must here do a piece of justice, however, to Carpenter's Battery, the hardy men of which were from Allegheny and adjacent mountain counties. I once rode back finding the men of the brigade floundering through the mud and many guns and vehicles completely stalled, when I came to Captain Carpenter and asked him how he was getting on. "Very well," he replied cheerfully, and to my astonishment I saw that his battery was well closed up. But I think he had lighter pieces than some, at least, of the guns of the Rockbridge Battery. By nightfall the army had made

---

[1] Ewell came across the mountain in the evening and occupied our abandoned camp.

a very short distance and was strung out for miles back and I think much of it so bivouacked. It was nearly as bad next day, and I believe it took about 48 hours to make the dozen or so miles from Swift Run Gap to Brown's Gap. But I do not remember the exact division of time or camping places in these and the next few days, although my memory is distinct about the country we passed through and the principal incidents of the marches.[2]

On the day that we passed through, or over for it is very much like Swift Run Gap, the gloomy and depressing weather was gone and the sun shone brilliantly on a beautiful May day. We crossed the summit of the Blue Ridge in good order, being now on a hard road, and went down along the side of a branch of Moorman's River, here a small but gradually increasing stream from the eastern side of the Gap. We were now in the well cultivated Albemarle country, and I can call up in my mind now very distinctly the pleasing sight at the village of Whitehall of the large number of ladies in white or bright colored dresses who had gathered there from the neighborhood to see the soldiers go by, and also to bring them baskets of substantial refreshment. In the Valley they had worn a more sober attire, soldiers being no novelty to them.

I do not recall any intervening stop at night but, at any rate, either on that same day or the next we reached the Virginia Central Railroad[3] at Mechum's River   And I think our brigade must have spent a day here while the

[2] Dabney's *Life of Jackson* says we left Swift Run on *Thursday* Apr'l 30 and on *Saturday* May 2 crossed over to Whitehall, etc. Allan's *Jackson's Valley Campaign* says we left on *Wednesday*, April 30 and did not get to Brown's Gap until Friday May 2 and crossed over on Saturday, May 3. The 30th of April was Wednesday, as Allan says.

[3] Now the Chesapeake and Ohio Railroad.

rest of the army was being transported by rail back across the Blue Ridge to the Valley at Staunton. When it did move, whether on the 4th, 5th or 6th of May, it marched West to Afton Station, well in and up Rockfish Gap—within sight of its summit—where we too took the cars and were carried to Staunton or its vicinity. And the next day we were allowed to rest. I think our camp was west of the town.

I remember well that on the day of the battle of Mc-Dowell, which was on the 8th of May, our brigade had started a day behind the rest of the army and made an extraordinarily long day's march to catch up, and I think, therefore, that our day's rest near Staunton must have been on the 7th and that we left there on the morning of the 8th, following the road, westerly, by which we learned the army had gone the day before. We came to Buffalo Gap in the Alleghenies, and, entering it, I have a photograph in my mind of the railroad curving away to the left and our road turning, but not so much, to the right. I have no recollection of any very steep ascending, but we did go upward and then through a mountainous wooded country—unlike the descent on the other side of a Blue Ridge Gap.

Some time in the day we saw along the road two or three cadets of the Virginia Military Institute at Lexington and learned that its corps of students had been ordered out for temporary service and was somewhere ahead.[4] These young stragglers (but I do not apply the term with any sense of reproach,) seemed much exhausted and one of them asked General Winder, "Mister, won't you take

[4] I understood later in the day that this corps was put by Jackson under General Winder and I think it went into Camp with or near us that evening, but I do not recall his assuming any particular control and I th nk it must have gone back next day.

me up behind?" and the General helped him up. Presently he asked, "Mister, what cavalry company do you belong to?" "I don't belong to any," the General replied. "Well, to what battery?" "To none." "Well, to what regiment then?" "To none," said the General. "I am General Winder of the Stonewall Brigade." "O, General," said the young fellow, "I beg your pardon, I never would have asked you to take me up if I had known who you were," and he made a motion to slide off. But the General prevented and carried him a long way, the two soon getting into an easy chat. I had taken up another.

We passed a large house, with out-buildings, on the left (west) side of the road and with a signboard "Lebanon Sulphur Springs," and here a road went off to the right (east). This was at the foot of Shenandoah Mountain,[5] up which our road—the Staunton and Parkersburg Turnpike—now went on an ascent of perhaps two or three miles. Arriving at the top we had a far view in front over the valley of the Cowpasture River or one of its head streams and could descry the road, fully two miles or more distant, ascending the opposite mountain on a slant to the left. We were told that the day before General Johnson,[6] leading the advance, had en-

---

[5] Shenandoah Mountain, or this end of it, has nothing to do with Shenandoah River. Since leaving Buffalo Gap we had been on James River waters. The Cowpasture River some distance down to the southwest of where we were, unites with the Bullpasture, which comes down past McDowell, and the united stream continues to be called the Cowpasture until it empties into Jackson's River, an upper fork of the James. So the cow is here held in greater dignity than the bull. Another branch of the Cowpasture is the Calfpasture, which also forks into the Big and the Little Calfpasture. The region is well watered. I need hardly say that it is a grazing country.

[6] Brigadier-General Edward Johnson, of Chesterfie'd County, Virginia, called "Allegheny Johnson" from a battle he had fought on 13th December, had commanded the small army operating in these parts before our arrival, and naturally had the advance in this movement to McDowell.

countered and driven the enemy's picket here and that
in descending he had been fired on, ineffectually by
artillery on the further side of the valley.

We descended—zigzagging—the western side of Shenandoah Mountain, crossed the wide valley and the Cowpasture stream[7] (which ran close to its further side), and
went up the mountain side three or four hundred yards
when we met ambulances and artillery, and I think some
wagons, coming down. We also saw, coming back, two
or more of Jackson's staff officers, who said that the army
was about to go into camp. General Winder requested
them to inform Jackson that he had come up with the
army and that, having to make way for the vehicles and
artillery descending the narrow and steep road, he would
move back to the bottom and camp on the other side of
the stream, where it was level. We did so, and the men
made fires in the low sycamore and other bushes which
half covered the bottom and began cooking or heating
what little they had. It was now approaching dusk.
But a courier came in haste from General Jackson ordering the brigade to come quickly to the front where fighting was going on. By the time it was formed another
courier came with orders to hurry. And when we had
crossed the stream and had nearly reached the top of the
ascent on the other side but were still a long way—perhaps nearly two miles—from where the conflict was, we
met Jackson, himself coming back for his old brigade.[8]
But when we got to the front—or a point on the road

[7] It seems to be in my recollection that the first stream after descending
Shenandoah Mountain was a branch of the Cowpasture and that after crossing
it we passed over another ridge and then came to the Cowpasture.

[8] This seems almost incredible and as it was quite dark it is possible that it
was a staff officer whom I mistook for Jackson. But my recollection is distinct
that it was my impression at the time, and I have always, in conversations since,
repeated that it was Jackson himself who came riding back.

opposite the battle field, which was on the hill top
on the left (west), firing had about ceased, except that a
piece or two of the enemy's artillery continued for a
while to send shots from some high position, apparently
on the east side of the road; but it was now night and
they were only random shots. We had met two or more
ambulances going back, one with the body of Colonel
Gibbons, of the 10th Virginia, whose death was much regretted. Another may have carried General Edward
Johnson, for he was painfully wounded in the foot. The
brigade was halted in the road. A ravine led up from
its side at this point through the woods to the hilltop or
high plateau of the battle field, on the left (west), and
the practicability of dragging up by hand some pieces of
artillery was discussed, but the hollow was steep and
rough and the idea was abandoned. General Winder
and his staff rode up to the battle field where we found all
quiet but the men still under arms. To the front but
far below, and apparently less than a mile distant, we
saw a great many lights, which we were told were the
enemy's camp fires in and around the village of Mc-
Dowell.[9]

Early the next morning, May 9, I rode over the battle
field. This elevated piece of open ground was some
acres in extent, having evidently been cleared for pasture
like many such elevated places in West Virginia, but
numerous white-thorn bushes or small trees were scattered over it. I was astonished to observe, as I thought,
that these thorns were in bloom thus early in the season,
but on investigation found that this appearance of bloom
was the white wood of the branches and twigs splintered
by the enemy's bullets, many of the bushes being about
the height of a man. The ground in front descended

[9] In Highland County, having passed out of Augusta.

some hundreds of feet and two or three hollows came up from the wooded bottom for some distance. Up and out of these, darker in the evening twilight, the enemy had come and so often had our men exposed against the clear sky line. This accounted for the extraordinary splintered condition of the thorn bushes on the hill, which must have looked to them like men or groups of men. Up hill shooting, too, is more accurate than down, which is apt to overshoot the mark, as every sportsman knows. And I thought then, and always have believed, that in this battle we lost more than they did, although there were wild rumors of numbers of dead having been found or burned in houses in McDowell. Our dead, or most of them, had been collected and laid on the grass side by side, in a double row, and I counted 52 or 53—I know it was fifty odd.[10]

After some time we descended—by the winding road—to the village of McDowell, where we found the enemy's abandoned camp, or camp ground, covered with little conical sheet iron stoves, like inverted funnels, a pattern new to me and I thought a very simple and good one. I think there was no bottom. There were also cooking utensils and other such articles, but we did not capture any valuable "plunder" that I saw.

I believe we did not go much beyond McDowell that day and that it was next morning, May 10, when we took up the pursuit in earnest, the Stonewall Brigade being in the lead. At the distance of six or seven miles northwesterly from McDowell we came to a fork of the road, a signboard saying that the Staunton and Parkersburg Turnpike went off northwesterly to Monterey and

[10] Colonel Allan, in his work which I have often quoted, gives the losses as follows: Confederate, 71 killed and 390 wounded, total 461; Federal, 28 killed and 225 wounded, with 3 missing, total 256.

beyond, while the right-hand fork went northerly but had no sign. It was the left hand fork on which General Edward Johnson had fallen back. As General Winder had no instructions which one to take, he halted and sent back to General Jackson for directions. Arms were stacked along the road, which was a narrow one, with the ground descending on the right (east) side and rising quite steeply on the left. At this point, or shortly before getting to it, Major Mercer, the brigade quartermaster, came up from the rear and told General Winder that it was reported at Staunton that Jackson had put him under arrest for not having his brigade up at McDowell.[11] Presently a battery came from behind and the musket stacks had to be broken to give it room to pass, and soon after Jackson himself appeared. General Winder mounted his horse—I saw the color rise in his face—and when Jackson came up, told him the rumor he had heard and demanded to know if he, Jackson, had said anything to authorize it. Jackson replied that he had not. General Winder said "I have always obeyed your orders," when Jackson broke in and said, "But General Winder, you are not obeying my orders now, my order is that whenever there is a halt, the men shall stack arms." "I did obey your order" said General Winder, "but had to break the stacks to let a battery pass." He added that he intended to have his rank as second in command of the army respected by everybody. I was close by and heard the whole brief conversation, and I fully expected Jackson would put him under arrest then and there. Just then a courier came up—from Richmond I believe—with a despatch and after reading it Jackson

[11] It will be remembered that when General Winder first came to the army, Major Mercer told him that Jackson would have him in arrest before many weeks passed.

handed it to General Winder, at which I was greatly relieved, for I took it to be meant as a mark of amity and confidence.

I remember idly pulling a small pinkish white flower from the bank on the upper roadside and enjoying its fragrance and thinking that a botanist in peace time would find many new wild flowers in this wild country. But I know now that it was the common arbutus.

We took the right hand road, which went northerly down the valley of a small stream, which we were told was one of the headwaters of the South Branch of the Potomac, having thus left the Cowpasture or James River watershed, as we had before left that of the Shenandoah.

My recollection of the rest of this day and of the first half or more of the next does not bring to my mind any particular incidents, but it is very clear as to the general characteristics of the marching. The enemy, to cover his retreat better and delay the pursuit, had resorted to the novel but effective expedient of firing the woods all the way behind him, and the valley became more and more filled with smoke. I suppose we had some cavalry in front, or more probably scouts only, for Jackson had left nearly all his cavalry in the Valley to watch the enemy there and prevent information of our movement from leaking through. At any rate, the progress of our brigade was slow and interrupted by halts. The road continued down the stream (on its left—west—side), which gradually got larger and whose valley became wider. Being a fisherman from boyhood, I thought it must be a good trout country and was interested to hear that Harry Gilmor,[12] who had fished the same streams in

[12] Afterwards the well known Major Harry Gilmor, commanding a cavalry battalion in Northern Virginia and author of *Four Years in the Saddle*. He was a Baltimorean.

Baltimore County that I had, went out one of these evenings and caught a fine lot.

In the afternoon of the second day (May 11) there were signs that we were close on the enemy's rear, and there was now certainly no cavalry between our brigade and them. At a place where the road ahead went on a long curve a little towards the right, with the thickly wooded hillside rising up on the left (west), General Winder halted the brigade and sent the 4th Virginia, Colonel Ronald, off the road and up the hill, with orders to form in line at right angles with the road and move forward parallel with it and so sweep the woods in front. And presently he rode up there himself with his staff. But he almost immediately came on the line of this regiment in full but not disorderly retreat. He asked the Colonel, "What is the meaning of this?" "Why," said the colonel," we came on the enemy." "What did I put you here for but to come on the enemy," said the General. "Face your men about and move forward," which was done. The General also rode forward, at first with the regiment but presently losing it by inclining to the right and also getting ahead—which I thought was too reckless.   There was some firing, not at our particular group I think, but it was close and alarming enough to make the two mounted couriers we had with us vanish in the brush. But the General rode straight on. We came to burning brush and low timber, through which we had to pick our way, and saw some camp fires with cooking utensils and even half cooked food, which seemed to have been abandoned just before our approach. I know I was much relieved when we came out on the road, without misadventure, half a mile or more beyond where we had gone in. The General directed me to ride back to see if the road was clear of the enemy and to report to

Jackson where he was and also to say that his couriers
had deserted him and ask for others. I galloped back,
finding all clear and coming to Jackson waiting in the
road where we had left it. When I added the request
for new couriers, Jackson said, "General Winder's couriers have deserted him, have they?" and turning to
Harry Gilmor, who was near by, he asked, "Captain
Gilmor, can you send General Winder couriers who will
not desert him?" Harry Gilmor said he could. When
I was starting to go back, Jackson said, "Captain Howard, I will go with you," and we rode side by side followed
by Harry Gilmor's two warranted couriers. I don't
remember that Jackson's staff or any others went. Before we had gone far shells began coming up the valley,
bursting over the bottom between our road and the
stream, which was here on the far (eastern) side. When
one exploded nearer to us than the others, Jackson turned
to me—I was riding on his right side—and asked,
"Captain Howard, where did that shell come from?"
I looked at him with some surprise and he added, "I am
deaf in one ear and cannot well tell the direction of
sounds."

I do not remember very well what happened immediately after we came to General Winder, but I think that
we mounted the wooded hillside and that the General
arranged his men in position—probably only the 4th
Virginia. We found that we could not go any further
directly forward and Jackson did not order it.[13] For the
hill or mountain which had been running parallel with
and on the west side of the road, here came to an end in
front, this end descending steeply into a deep chasm,

[13] Franklin, the county seat of Pendleton, into which we had passed from
Highland, was only a mile ahead and so Jackson had pushed back the enemy
about seventy miles from Staunton which they had been threatening.

evidently the valley of a side stream breaking through
from the west, across which the hill or mountain abruptly
rose again. We saw that the enemy held this further
side in too strong a position to be assailed directly in
front. And I heard General Winder say to Jackson that
a force ought to be sent to turn their right flank. Either
now or later—for it was when it was getting dusk—
General Winder with his staff, and I think Jackson, went
forward and down to the extreme end of this knob or
shoulder we were on, to examine the enemy's position
across the chasm. After we had stood there for a while,
I heard a voice in the distance, but distinctly in the still
evening air, say, "Ready, Fire," and a shell came over
at our group and exploded near by. We retired. There
was a curious illustration here of how the imagination
will sometimes play a trick with a perfectly brave man.
As we were going back, O'Brien, our adjutant-general,
of both Irish and Spanish blood, I believe, said to me,
"Did you see that man who was struck?" I said, "No."
"Why," said he, "he was a horrible sight—shot all to
pieces." There was really no one struck I was told.
But it was dusk, if not dark, and small fires among the
trees here and there were giving fitful lights and shadows
and room for the imagination to work. We had a quiet
night.

The next morning (Monday, May 12,) General Jackson issued an order congratulating the army on the victory at McDowell, proclaiming a half day of rest and
directing that the chaplains should hold a thanksgiving
service in the regiments—all of which did not have chaplains, however. The men were accordingly formed in
the level bottom between the road and the north fork of
the south branch of the Potomac—for such the stream
was—and the services were held. As General Winder

appeared, the men spontaneously cheered him in all regiments of the brigade, which gave him evident gratification.[14]

I think it was in the afternoon of the same day the army took up its march back, but I do not remember the camps or the details of the march until we got to the Lebanon White Sulphur Springs again where we turned off on the road to the left (east), and after 9 or 10 miles came to the Stribbling Springs, out of the rough mountain country and on or near the western side of the well cultivated and beautiful "Valley of Virginia." We were now on the Shenandoah waters again. Here we rested one day (May 18, Sunday). I found the springs three in number, two being strong alum and the third pure water although near the other two, all issuing out of the side of a dark slate rock.

[14] From this time all coolness of the officers and men of the brigade towards him disappeared and always afterwards they cheered him the first time they were drawn up in line after a battle, and on other occasions.

CHAPTER XI

VALLEY CAMPAIGN—BATTLE OF WINCHESTER

The next day (May 19) we marched through a fine open country and at the village of Bridgewater crossed North River—one of the three upper branches of the south or main fork of the Shenandoah River. This crossing was effected on a Confederate pontoon bridge, made by putting planks on the running gear and beds of wagons in the stream. On that day or the next we came to the Valley Turnpike at Harrisonburg and marched down it seventeen or eighteen miles to Newmarket. Here (on May 21,) we turned off to the right (east)[1] and crossed the Massanutton Mountain by the only "gap" in, or over it, in its long extent, being the road from Newmarket to Luray and beyond across the Blue Ridge to eastern Virginia. When about a mile before coming to Luray—having crossed the south or main fork of the Shenandoah River—I noticed several small sunken places in the ground on the north side of the road, filled with briers, and I said I believed there were caves underneath.[2] At Luray we turned north on the Front Royal road and after going three miles on it camped.

We had now united with Ewell and Jackson had under him, therefore, two divisions of infantry, with batteries of artillery attached to the brigades, including "Alleghany" Johnson's men who were now constituted into

[1] We were now getting used to Jackson's divergences from the straight road ahead and they ceased to cause any surprise.

[2] I understand that the famous Luray cave, discovered just after the war, is at this place or near it.

two small brigades and made parts of Ewell's Division; also a large part of Ashby's Cavalry.

In the afternoon of May 23 we were approaching Front Royal and understood that it was occupied by the enemy. Our brigade was not in front and it went on slowly and haltingly while others in advance made the attack on the place.[3]   We soon heard the firing and presently moved forward to the town, which we learned, with interest, had been held by the Federal 1st Maryland under Colonel Kenly, an officer of the Mexican War.   And we presently knew that the enemy were driven out of the place and across the Shenandoah, the north and south forks of which unite about two miles north of the town.   I rode forward to and half way over the bridge[4] and found it in a damaged condition, the enemy having set fire to it after crossing; it was much charred but not impassable. I saw many members of our 1st Maryland, who were highly excited and jubilant over the encounter with the Federal 1st, of which latter regiment I saw a number of prisoners being brought in.   I remember meeting Hebb Greenwell (with whom I had crossed the Potomac when on our way to Richmond the year before,) on the bridge with one, and I heard several stories of meetings of relations and acquaintances in the two "Firsts."[5]

[3] The troops which made or began the attack were the Confederate 1st Maryland and Wheat's Battalion ("Louisiana Tigers") of Taylor's Brigade in Ewell's Division.   Meanwhile our cavalry had gone to the west of Front Royal and the south fork to ford the north fork of the Shenandoah and get on the enemy's flank or rear.

[4] This must have been over the north fork, which comes east from Strasburg. But I do not remember another bridge, over the south fork, and were it not for what the books and maps now show I should say there was a single bridge over the river, just below the junction of the two forks.

[5] The main body of the Federal 1st Maryland was captured by the cavalry, in Jackson's own presence, several miles on the Winchester road.

It was now nightfall and our brigade camped near Front Royal—I do not remember exactly where.

The next morning, May 24, we marched on the Winchester road, but after going a few miles, turned off at Cedarville and took the road which goes off to the left, northwesterly, to the Valley Turnpike Road at Middletown. Our brigade was not leading and our progress was slow. When we arrived at the Turnpike we found on it a long line of abandoned wagons, but all was quiet and no enemy was visible. I think when we first entered it the head of our column was turned to the left (south) towards Strasburg, for I remember there was some countermarching before we took the other direction, towards Winchester. The Stonewall Brigade was now in the advance. There were many sutlers' wagons in this abandoned train and some of the contents had been pulled out and were lying along the road, and I picked up an officer's broad red silk sash which helped to give to my plain dress evidence of my being a commissioned officer; I wore it almost through the rest of the war. After going five or six miles towards Winchester, our advance—I think it was at the south edge of Newtown[6]— was checked by a fire from one or two pieces of artillery, the shells from which seemed to come from a position in front on the west side of the Turnpike and to cross it diagonally or burst over it a little ahead. I thought they were using the rather new "Schenkel" shells, for which we had a dislike—shaped, somewhat like an old fashioned soda water bottle. I remember one falling on the stone face of the road with a crash and seeming to me to break into pieces like a bottle. But I don't think

[6] Newtown is a village seven miles south of Winchester. Middletown is half way between Newtown and Strasburg—about five and one-half miles from either place.

any part of our brigade—infantry at least—became engaged, and presently these guns withdrew and we moved on. Evening passed and night came and we went on, making slow progress and being several times checked by the infantry rear guard of the enemy which sometimes even stubbornly resisted our advance. At one point they delayed us by a show of force in our front, and at another where a rather deep stream crossed the Turnpike,[7] they even drove back the small force of cavalry, or scouts, in our front which rode back over the head of our column and put the leading regiment, or part of it, in such confusion that General Winder and his staff, and I think Jackson too, had some difficulty to resist being carried along towards the rear. I think this happened about ten o'clock at night. Here General Winder had two companies detailed—from the 2d and 5th Virginia—whose men were from that part of the country— and had them deployed on both sides of the road, to cross the stream and drive the enemy back. But I think they withdrew, having well accomplished their object of delaying our march. These two companies continued on, in skirmish line, and we had no more trouble, except in making slow progress, until we were only about a mile from Winchester, when, near or at daylight, General Jackson allowed the men to halt where they were in the road and take an hour's sleep or rest.[8]

Before sunrise (Sunday, May 25) we were under arms again and the brigade moved forward until the head of the column reached the line of skirmishers at Hollingsworth's Mill. There was a slight haze over the country which the risen sun was dispelling. Here General Win-

[7] The Opequon (Opàcon), at Bartonsville.
[8] It was the 2d Massachusetts, principally, which thus resisted our advance and it performed its duty well.

der, with his staff, rode forward to reconnoitre. On the north side of the Mill buildings a road went off up a hollow to the left (west), having a plank fence along its south side and open ground, rising rather steeply, on the north side. As we went on this road, the General in front, with a guide or some one, there suddenly came several shots down from a small hollow or break in the high ground on our right which rattled like stones against the plank fence. The General put spurs to his horse and got safely past the mouth of the hollow. Next came Captain O'Brien, assistant adjutant-general, and myself, O'Brien, who was riding a clay colored horse, leading. We too spurred our horses to get by the dangerous point as rapidly as possible. Two or three shots came and as I bent my head low to my horse's neck I was astonished to see the cream colored tail of O'Brien's horse—which was close to my own horse's head—suddenly turn red all over. A bullet had passed through the root. No other harm was done, but the horse went quicker!

I do not well recall the details of the movement, but we were soon in occupation of this high ground on the north of this side road, and my first precise recollection is that Poague's (Rockbridge) and Carpenter's Batteries of the brigade were in position on it and firing on the enemy who held some also elevated ground, almost on the south edge of Winchester. Our infantry regiments were supporting in rear, sheltered by the rising ground and somewhat apart. Our two batteries were exposed to a very sharp fire, both of art'llery and musketry, and lost severely, particularly in horses. They were much annoyed at first by a line of skirmishers behind a stone wall, not far in front, until the General ordered solid shot to be fired at the wall, which soon made them scam-

per back.[9] General Winder who before his promotion in
the United States Army to a captaincy in the 9th Infantry had been in the 3d Artillery, always had a liking for
that arm of the service, and now remained for the most
of the time on this part of the field, directing the fire of
our guns, and being much exposed. I remember a shot
or shell passing so close to my head and left shoulder
that it seemed to make the blood stir in the shoulder.

General Jackson presently came on the scene and asked
how the battle was going on. General Winder told him
the enemy ought to be attacked on his (the enemy's)
right flank. "Very well," said Jackson, "I will send you
up Taylor," and he rode off. General "Dick" Taylor
soon appeared at the head of his fine Louisiana Brigade,
moving in column across our rear towards the left, and
General Winder pointed out where he should go to get
on the enemy's right flank. I think there was a piece of
woods over there which Taylor reached unobserved and
from which we saw his brigade emerge in a fine line of
battle at right angles with the enemy's line. Their
coming was soon detected and we could see a sudden
commotion on that end of their line (the whole of which
was in our plain view on the high open ground opposite
to us and not far distant as battles go), and we saw them
making frantic efforts to turn one or two of their guns to
fire on Taylor's men as soon as they would come into
view at short range ascending the acclivity on that flank.
General Winder tried to move one or two of Poague's
guns to a position to open on them but the battery horses
had been much cut up and before it could be done, Taylor
went forward with such rapidity, but preserving a splendid line, that the enemy, as I remember, had not time to

[9] This was the only occasion during the war when I distinctly remember
seeing solid shot used.

fire a single round, and they broke in disorder and all were speedily in full flight. Meanwhile General Winder had brought forward his infantry brigade and formed it in line of battle and it moved in fine order over the battle ground to the town, which lay just behind it. But the enemy retired so quickly from Taylor's charge that we could not come up with them. In passing over where the Federal line had been I observed a fine officer's great coat—the long detachable cape lined with red flannel—lying on the ground, with a little dog on it. I dismounted, routed the dog and secured it.

We passed on through the town, the people of which were in a state of jubilant excitement, and continued on the Martinsburg road—Valley Turnpike—between four and five miles, when, there appearing no prospect of overtaking the enemy, we halted and went into camp[10] in some woods. And we remained there quietly the next two days.

[10] I have, in these pages, used the words camp and bivouac somewhat indiscriminately. But properly camp implies a more lengthened stay or with camp equipage, while a bivouac is a night's halt, or short time in campaigning, without such equipage. After the first part of the war the men generally had only little shelter tents which they carried—or india rubbers—two buttoned together making a shelter for two men; these were captured from the enemy.

CHAPTER XII

Valley Campaign—Charlestown and Retreat up the Valley

On the morning of May 28 General Winder marched with his brigade, except the 2d Virginia Regiment which had been detailed as provost guard in Winchester, on the road to Charlestown and Harper's Ferry, which goes off from the Valley Turnpike to the right (easterly) from near where we were camped.[1] His orders were to go to Harper's Ferry —at least those were the orders as I understood, and the manner of the march showed that the General was under the impression that he would find no obstacle on the way. But when a few miles this side of Charlestown, as I was riding carelessly a hundred yards ahead, I saw a horseman coming back at full speed, whom I recognized on his approach as Captain R. Preston Chew, of the Horse Artillery serving with Ashby's Cavalry. He reined up and on my asking what was the matter, said the Yankees were at Charlestown. "That cannot be," I said, "for our orders are to go to Harper's Ferry." He replied they were certainly there and he had just narrowly escaped being captured by them   He had gone there, being his home, to visit his family.   By this time General Winder, at the head of the brigade, had come up, to whom he repeated the information, with further details. General Winder immediately sent back Lieutenant James M. Garnett, of his staff with a dispatch to Jackson at Winchester, but determined to press on and attack the

[1] Charlestown is eighteen miles from Winchester and Harper's Ferry is six or seven miles beyond that.

enemy if not found too strong. One straggling cavalryman after another came along until there were about a
dozen and the General pressed them into service under
Captain Chew for an advance guard. After proceeding
a couple of miles or more these reported the enemy's
skirmishers ahead and General Winder deployed two
companies as skirmishers before whom those of the enemy
retired or were driven back through the woods to the
edge of the open ground, beyond which was their main
body drawn up in line of battle, just this side of Charlestown. The General formed his four regiments in line
and sent forward one or two guns which fired a few rounds
when the enemy retired. Our whole line advanced and
pursued through the town which was wild with excitement, the people thronging the streets with demonstra-
tions of joy at our coming, as we had seen at Winchester
three days before. We continued the pursuit four miles
to the village of Halltown, when we saw the enemy in
large force and occupying a strong position on Bolivar
Heights, a ridge which extends from the Shenandoah
River across the road to the Potomac, just beyond which
was Harper's Ferry with the unapproachable Maryland
Heights dominating it, on the other (north) side of the
Potomac. Seeing that he could accomplish nothing
more with his small force, General Winder returned to
the neighborhood of Charlestown, camping about a mile
in front of it. The General and his staff took dinner or
supper at the house of Mrs. Andrew Kennedy—"Cassilis"—on the east side of the road, who, having lately
been to Baltimore, gave me news of home, and who also
gave me and sewed on my shoulders a pair of first lieutenant's epaulets (though Federal), so that while not
in regulation Confederate uniform, I had now sufficient
marks of rank. We were also entertained by Mrs.

Mason, a sister of Major Frederick W. M. Holliday of our 33d Virginia.

There was small loss on either side in this day's affair, but I think General Winder's conduct in pressing forward and engaging the enemy in this unexpected encounter, instead of halting in the little knowledge he had of what force he would meet and waiting for further orders, was one of the things which were rapidly getting him Jackson's high opinion and confidence. It certainly added to the brigade's growing confidence in him.

The next day, May 29, Jackson came up with his whole army. That night General Winder received information from two separate sources (citizens,) of the size of the enemy's forces in Harper's Ferry and also that they had guns planted on the Maryland Heights, across the Potomac but completely commanding the town and its approach.

The next morning, May 30, Jackson had his army in the road to go, as I understood, into Harper's Ferry. He, himself, was at the head of the infantry column, and just in front—not over fifty yards—there was a barn, or some such building, on the east (right) side of the road and on its very edge and which to some extent shut out the view in front, particularly as the road here seemed to take a bend to the right. I know I thought that the moment we passed from under cover of this building we would come under fire. General Winder and General Elzey—who was commanding one of the two brigades which had been formed of "Alleghany" Johnson's men—here rode up to General Jackson. I was close by and heard what was said. General Winder told him what information he had gathered the day before from the people of Charlestown and others about the enemy's strength and that two citizens had come to him during the night with the further intelligence that large reinforcements had been received. General Elzey said that he had had information to the same effect and that "they had heavy guns on the Maryland Heights." Jackson said, "General Elzey, are you afraid of heavy guns?" at which I saw Elzey's cheek redden (he was an old artillery officer in the United States Army), but he made no reply. I understood that we were to move forward and I did not like the prospect. But just then a courier came up behind and handed a dispatch to Jackson who read it and, without giving any order to move forward, rode back towards the rear. In the light of the next two days I supposed the dispatch was about Shields and Fremont closing in on Front Royal and Strasburg nearly fifty miles in his rear.[2] Orders presently came from Jackson for the army to march back to Winchester except the Stonewall Brigade and the 1st Maryland Infantry, which was also put under General Winder.[3] Our 2d Virginia had rejoined the brigade when the army came up and had been sent forward and to the right across the Shenandoah to Loudon Heights, where it still remained. Our small force kept its position in quiet for the rest of the day, after the army had gone back in the morning.

Late that night I was roused by some one stumbling over the tent ropes and found it was a courier from General Jackson, who had lost his way and was several hours late in bringing his dispatch. This, when read, was alarming, and the more so for being thus belated. Jackson wrote that he was leaving Winchester and ordered

---

[2] If Jackson had not really intended to go further, certainly he effectually deceived, to the last moment, his own subordinate generals as well as his adversary and the authorities at Washington.

[3] Colonel Bradley T. Johnson says it received no orders to fall back with the army and that Winder took it under his command.

General Winder to fall back immediately and that if he found Winchester in possession of the enemy, he must make his escape by the Back Road. This is a road which goes up the Valley some distance to the west of the great Valley Turnpike. The 2d Virginia was immediately recalled from Loudon Heights and early in the morning, May 31, the brigade and the 1st Maryland started back on a forced day's march. When, late in the evening we got to Winchester, we found it deserted by all except a few stragglers and we pushed on through to Newtown where at night we went into a cheerless, rainy bivouac. We had marched over twenty-eight miles and the 2d Virginia several miles more.

The next morning, June 1, we resumed the march. Before we had gone many miles we heard artillery firing in our front, towards Strasburg, which made us apprehensive that we might be too late and find ourselves cut off at that place. But soldiers take things of that sort philosophically. At or near Middletown I was riding about a hundred yards ahead, as I was very apt to do, when I saw a group of cavalry men in front, standing in the mouth of the road which forks off to Front Royal[4], the same road by which we had come into the Valley Turnpike from that place eight days before. When I approached, one of them rode out from the mouth of the road to meet me and I recognized the brown face of Ashby. "Is that General Winder coming up?" he asked. I said it was. "Thank God for that," he exclaimed. When the General came up, Ashby shook his hand warmly and said,

[4] The picture in my mind of the entrance of the Front Royal road into the Turnpike, both when we came by it a week before and as we now passed it, is, distinctly, of a road coming over an open country, whereas maps now show it as entering the village of Middletown. The road may have been changed—or the village may have grown.

"General, I was never so relieved in my life. I thought that you would be cut off and had made up my mind to join you and advise you to make your escape over the mountain to Gordonsville." After passing this point there is a view from the Turnpike of the country in front (south), and to the right oblique and three or four miles, or less, distant can be seen the course of the low valley of Cedar Creek. This stream runs down from the northwest and, crossing the Turnpike, enters the north fork of the Shenandoah below Strasburg, and down its valley comes the road from Moorfield, by which it was understood Fremont was advancing to cut us off at Strasburg. And we could plainly see the smoke of the discharges of the guns we had heard, seeming to be almost in our front as the Turnpike was then running, and we knew that Jackson was holding back Fremont until we got by. To our relief, everything continued quiet on the Front Royal (east) side, where we looked for trouble from an advance by Shields or McDowell. We squeezed through and went on several miles beyond Strasburg on the Valley Turnpike and camped on the right hand side. In the night we were roused by a commotion on the road and cavalrymen came from the rear in confusion, having been attacked by the enemy with unusual boldness, but presently things quieted down again.

Next day, June 2, we resumed our march up the Valley, leisurely at first, but soon heard that our rear was being seriously pushed by the enemy and General Winder halted his brigade and formed it in line of battle across the Turnpike. The enemy was checked but kept such a threatening attitude that when it became time for us to withdraw and resume the march—the rest of the army having gained a sufficient distance—the operation seemed to be a delicate one. But General Winder effected this in a novel way which excited my admiration. He withdrew the regiments in echelon, that is, the one furthest from the road was faced about and marched, still keeping in line, some distance to the rear, the movement being taken up successively after a brief interval of time by the adjoining regiments, the show of force being thus kept up last at the Pike. Finally, when they had got a sufficient way back, the regiments moved by the flank and formed the brigade column of march on the Turnpike. All this was done with the precision of an evolution on a parade ground.[5] We had no more serious trouble

[5] Brigadier-General (as he then was), Richard Taylor, in his book *Destruction and Reconstruction*, gives the following account of this affair: After stating that his brigade had been bringing up the rear that morning and was being pressed by the enemy, he says, "A body of troops was reported in position to the south of my column. This proved to be Charles Winder with his (formerly Jackson's own) brigade. An accomplished soldier and true brother in arms, he had heard the enemy's guns during the night, and, knowing me to be in rear, halted and formed line to meet me. His men were fed and rested, and he insisted on taking my part in the rear. Passing through Winder's line, we moved slowly with frequent halts, so as to remain near, the enemy pressing hard during the morning. The day was oppressively hot, the sun like fire, and water scarce along the road, and our men suffered greatly. Just after midday my brisk young aide, Hamilton, whom I had left with Winder to bring early intelligence, came to report that officer in trouble and want of assistance. My men were so jaded as to make me unwilling to retrace ground if it could be avoided; so they were ordered to form line on the crest of the slope at hand, and I went to Winder, a mile in the rear. His brigade, renowned as the "Stonewall" was deployed on both sides of the pike, on which he had four guns. . . . The problem was to retire without g'ving the enemy, eager and persistent, an opportunity to charge. The situation looked so blue that I proposed to move back my command, but Winder thought he could pull through, and splendidly did he accomplish it. Regiment by regiment, gun by gun, the brigade was withdrawn, always checking the enemy, though boldly led. Winder, cool as a professor p!aying the new German game, directed every movement in person, and the men were worthy of him and of their first commander, Jackson. It was very close work in the vale before he reached the next crest, and heavy volleys were necessary to stay our plucky foes; but once there, my command showed so strong as to impress the enemy who halted to reconnoitre and the two brigades were united without further trouble." General Taylor further says that Ashby now came, having

on this day's march and, I think, in the evening passed over the Shenandoah (north fork), a mile south of Mount Jackson and where Ashby's white horse was shot a month and a half before, and bivouacked just beyond. I am not sure whether we stayed in this bivouac next day or not, but it seems to me that we did. At any rate, on June 3 or 4 we continued to fall back up the Valley and on either June 5 or 6 came to Harrisonburg, where we turned off to the left (east), not on the road to Swift Run Gap which we had taken in April, but one which went more southeasterly to Port Republic and Brown's Gap, higher up the South Fork.

The first distinct impression or picture in my mind after leaving the vicinity of Mount Jackson is that on the evening of June 6 we were camped somewhere along this Port Republic road, with our brigade headquarters in woods on its left (northeast) side. And this I remember

been, he thinks, over in the Luray Valley burning bridges, and took charge of the rear.

From this time General Taylor and General Winder appeared to entertain a warm mutual regard and often rode together at the head of the one brigade or the other. I do not preserve in my memory a very distinct impression of General Taylor's personal appearance, but as I recall him he was of strong make, although not stout, and fluent and agreeable in conversation, having seen much of the world. He was the son of President Zachary Taylor and brother-in-law of President Davis. He wore a black hat and overcoat (a mounted officer who could so conveniently carry his overcoat bundled up and strapped behind his saddle, wore it often even in summer for protection from chill or rain,) while Winder's overcoat was white or light drab, and riding just behind the two I used to think of them as the black and the white generals. General Winder's overcoat had nothing military about it, although he looked very soldierly in it, as in everything. Not long before the war, it had been suddenly discovered on the Eastern Shore of Maryland that the thick and strong white or light drab cloth which was bought in large quantities for the "servants" (they were seldom called slaves there), was excellent material for overcoats and nearly every young gentleman in Miles River Neck (Talbot County), had one made. A long cape came down to the wrists.

from several incidents—one a great misfortune for us. We had heard firing in the rear and understood that a Sir Percy Windham—an English soldier of fortune who commanded the advance cavalry which had been pressing us, and to whom we had been giving the credit of that unusual display of spirit—had been captured by Ashby, and he presently passed by on his way to the rear with some other prisoners. And later we heard to our great sorrow, that Ashby himself had been killed in an engagement with the Pennsylvania "Bucktail" Regiment, in which the 1st Maryland had suffered severely, but gained great credit. About dark Ashby's body was carried past in an ambulance. That evening there were brought to our headquarters two iron or steel breast plates, worn by Federal cavalrymen, which we inspected with much curiosity. I think one had a hole through it.[6] There was also some conversation that evening about explosive bullets, which it was reported the enemy was using—not loaded like a shell, but made so as to fly into several pieces on striking an object. I see no ground of objection to them if the purpose be that the fragments may have an increased chance of hitting a man, or even

[6] General Richard Taylor in his *Destruction and Reconstruction*, having mentioned that he saw breast plates from captured cavalrymen in this campaign, a Captain Judson, assistant adjutant-general of Hatch's Brigade of Federal Cavalry, in a communication to *The Nation*, published 10 July, 1879, declared that not only had General Taylor written what was not true, but that he knew it was a falsehood when he wrote it. Whereupon in *The Nation's* issue of 24 July, 1879, appeared a letter from Captain W. Stuart Symington, of Baltimore and another from Colonel LeRoy Brown, of the Richmond Arsenal, both testifying to having seen and handled such breastplates, and also a letter from a New England soldier, admitting their use. A plenty of other testimony might have been forthcoming, but *The Nation* declared the subject closed. But there is no reason why such defensive armor should not be used, and it ought to be if effectual; but it did not seem to be found so.

two or more, but if it be to mutilate beyond disabling, the humaner rules of modern war are against such use.[7]

This was the evening of June 6 and I think we must have moved next day, for certainly on the night of the 7th we were within a mile of Port Republic and I do not think we had been that close the night before.

[7] Dabney's *Life of Stonewall Jackson* says that after the battle of Port Republic on June 9 a soldier picked up one and handed it to the General.

CHAPTER XIII

Valley Campaign—Battles of Cross Keys and Port Republic

On the morning of June 8 we were expecting to have a quiet Sunday in camp. I had taken my little store of clothing out of my carpet bag and had it lying around me as I knelt, when, between 8 and 9 o'clock I heard a cannon shot in the direction of Port Republic and immediately began to put them back again. Some one of the staff, O'Brien or Garnett, asked me what I was doing. "Well," said I, "it's Sunday and you hear that shot."[1] I think a courier came with a message from Jackson to send forward a gun immediately, but at any rate Jackson himself rode hastily up and directed General Winder to double-quick a regiment to the Port Republic bridge. The General ordered Captain Poague to send the gun and have the whole battery fall in, and I remember that Captain Carpenter told me that, thinking as I did, he began of his own volition to harness up as soon as he heard the first gun. Our whole command was under arms and in motion in a short time, the General going with the first gun. It was open country and down hill to the bridge and we soon came in sight of it, with the village on the other side. From over there a gun—I think only one— of the enemy was firing, but wildly, the shots going overhead and to our right, and there only two or three rounds. As our batteries arrived, the guns were posted in a line from the road along the high commanding ground which

[1] The army fully believed that Jackson would rather fight on Sunday than on any other day.

extended like a terrace to the left, parallel with and down the main river. They opened fire and this advance party of the enemy soon fell back from the village. Presently a column appeared coming up the road on the other side of the level bottom of the Shenandoah and across the river, its flank directly exposed to the fire of our line of guns, and perhaps a thousand yards distant, and we opened on it vigorously from our high position along the crest. At first our infantry had been posted in line in front of our guns but lower down the declivity, but the sabots (wooden bottom shoeing,) of the shells fell among them and they were withdrawn to the rear of the guns; they were of no use anyway, as the enemy could not get at us across the river. We could see that our fire was inflicting some damage and the enemy's column soon wavered and retired in confusion. Our brigade, infantry and artillery, held this position during the rest of the day.[2]

At 10 or 11 o'clock we heard the sound of artillery apparently four or five miles back on the Harrisonburg road and learned that General Ewell, with several brigades, was having a battle with Fremont. Some time later, probably about midday, General Jackson, with his staff, came to where General Winder and his staff were, on the south side of the road and a short distance west of the Port Republic bridge, and remained several hours. I

[2] Three upper branches of this south fork or main Luray Valley branch of the Shenandoah come together near and at Port Republic. Two of these unite a mile or two above the village and then these two united streams join with the third (which flows down the west foot of the Blue Ridge), just at the north edge of Port Republic and so form the main river. The bridge here spoken of is over the united first two streams into the village, and the road by which the enemy had advanced from Luray comes up the bottom on the East side of the main river. These three streams are called North, Middle and South Rivers and they water the whole Valley south of Harrisonburg. We had crossed the upper part of North River three weeks before at Bridgewater, coming from McDowell.

was quite close to him all the time. He spoke to me about the Marylanders and said he liked to have them under him. I overheard him say in an undertone to his adjutant-general, Major Dabney (a Presbyterian minister, so appointed by him to the wonder of many and ridicule of some), "Major, wouldn't it be a blessed thing if God would give us a glorious victory today?" And I saw his face with an expression like that of a child hoping to receive some favor. But the most of the time he stood, on foot, silent, with his cap bent down over his eyes and looking towards the ground. Only two persons came from the distant battle field, a courier or cavalryman and the eccentric Chaplain Cameron of the Maryland Regiment, and each, on being asked, simply reported that the battle was going on without change. I was greatly astonished therefore, when Jackson presently said in his crisp, curt voice, "Pendleton!" "Well, Sir." "Write a note to General Ewell. Say that the enemy are defeated at all points, and to press them with cavalry, and, if necessary, with artillery and Wheat's Battalion." I was sitting on my horse at the time and Pendleton placed his paper against my horse's shoulder and, I supposed, wrote to that effect. I could perceive nothing whatever to give any justification for sending such a dispatch. Jackson had not been to the Cross Keys battle ground—four miles distant—certainly for several hours and had received no information from it but what I have stated. He could not have drawn any inference from the sound of the firing diminishing or receding for it did not diminish or recede; moreover, he had told me at Franklin, as I have narrated, that he was deaf in one ear and could not well tell about sounds. I waited the result with much curiosity. And about the time I calculated the message would reach General Ewell the firing certainly began to abate and after a while intelligence came, substantially, that the enemy had been driven back.[3]

On Cross Keys battle ground proper, General Ewell commanded without interference from Jackson. And Marylanders may justly be proud that the three infantry brigades which did the most of the fighting were commanded by Marylanders—Trimble, Elzey and George H. Steuart. And if our affair in driving and holding back Shields's column was a part of the battle—and it should undoubtedly be so considered—then General Winder was a fourth Maryland brigade commander in this day's battle. The 1st Maryland Infantry—which had distinguished itself two days before in the "Bucktail" fight, when Ashby was killed—and the Baltimore Light Artillery were also parts of Ewell's force. Elzey and Steuart were wounded. Maryland men, commanders and soldiers, bore a prominent part in Jackson's whole Valley campaign.[4]

All day our brigade remained in its position, our guns commanding the low grounds and road across the river, but Shields's army made no further effort to advance, and at nightfall we moved over the bridge and bivouacked just outside of Port Republic, which, as I have said, is on the point, or in the angle, between the united two streams and the third stream. Our 33d Virginia was

---

[3] I have often told this incident since. A year or two after the war I gave it in writing to Captain John Esten Cooke, Jackson's first biographer, who published it in some magazine. I think the *Lawyers' Green Bag*, or something of the kind—and I believe that what I have now written will be found to correspond closely with my account of that early date.

[4] General Trimble was ardently in favor of making a night attack on Fremont and would have done so with his Brigade alone if permitted. He reconnoitered close to the enemy's camp fires and then went to Ewell but he would not approve, referring him, however, to Jackson. He went to him but he would not consent without Ewell's approval, who finally refused permission.

left on picket, however, well down the west side of the river, to watch for a possible advance of the enemy on that side after crossing below.

We had orders to be in Port Republic[5] by dawn.

On Monday, June 9, our men were roused at a very early hour, while it was yet dark, and the head of the column (shortly after it was light I think), was at the side of the "third stream"—South River—where the road crosses going from Port Republic down the Shenandoah to Luray, and we now knew, therefore, that Jackson was aiming at Shields. Our brigade was in the lead. A rough bridge, on wagon running gear, was being constructed when we got there and we were delayed some time before we could begin to pass over. And it was slow work crossing on the narrow two or three insecure planks which made the top,[6] so that it was after sunrise when the four regiments (the 33d Virginia being on picket across the river,) were over, and with the two batteries, which forded just below, were moving in column down the road. We had gone only a few hundred yards when we came to several dead bodies by the roadside, one with the head missing, a few inches of the spinal column projecting above the shoulders, testifying to the effect of our fire yesterday, for we were passing reversely the way the enemy had attempted to come up. Passing the mouth of a road going in the woods to the right, towards the mountain, General Winder directed me to ride up it and look for an abandoned gun, for he thought he had seen one being taken up it from under our fire the day before. I went some distance but discovered none and

[5] Some years ago I received a Deed executed before a Notary Public of this place who signs himself as a "Note Republic!"

[6] General Taylor says his men found much difficulty in passing over it and that many fell into the water.

returned, not liking to remain long from the brigade which I knew was going into action; but the abandoned piece was afterwards found somewhere in that direction. When the head of our column had gone about a mile the enemy was reported to be in position in front and Jackson ordered General Winder to attack.

The 2d Virginia, Colonel Allen, was sent to the right of the road and forward, where the woods came down from the Blue Ridge to the road, and the other three regiments, 4th, 5th and 27th Virginia, were deployed in line of battle across the open bottom between the road and the river, the 4th being soon sent, however, to support the 2d. This open bottom, cultivated fields, several hundred yards in width, was a fine battle ground for straight forward fighting, but the advantage was with the enemy who occupied a strong position, being a slight ridge or rising ground extending across the bottom from the road (where it was wooded), to the river bank, and he had a number of guns posted along it with his infantry line; it was said that the colors of five regiments were counted. It appeared that this position should be turned by a force sent up through the woods on its left where our 2d and 4th Regiments had gone, but General Winder's orders were to attack in front[7] and he made his dispositions accordingly. He sent for two of Poague's guns (Rockbridge Battery), which he stationed in front of the infantry and the fire of which he directed in person. We were now under a severe shelling. A Louisiana Regiment[8] came to our assistance which the General disposed

[7] General Jackson's intention had been to drive back Shields's army early in the morning and, hastening back across the river at Port Republic, fall upon Fremont, but the delay in the construction of the bridge and the obstinate resistance of the enemy made him give up the latter part of the plan. If he had so won three victories in twenty-four hours it would have been unprecedented. But there was glory enough in the two.

[8] The 7th Louisiana, under Colonel Harry T. Hays.

with our front.   He now advanced his line, both infantry
and guns, to carry the enemy's position, but we soon
came under a most destructive fire of musketry as well
as artillery which checked our inadequate force.   The
General sent me back, either to Jackson for reinforcements or to tell Colonel Allen to press forward, I do not
remember which—perhaps both.   As I was going I saw
a regiment marching in column down the bottom to our
assistance which I found to be the 31st Virginia, Colonel
Hoffman.   I do not remember what I did and my first
recollection is of getting back and finding our line in much
confusion under the very severe fire and the enemy even
making a countercharge.   Not finding General Winder,
I remained with this centre and left part of the command
for some time, which was pressed back for a space.
Finally, General Richard Taylor's charge through the
woods on the enemy's left flank first relieved the pressure
on our left and then caused them to take to a hasty
retreat.   I went forward until I met General Winder
returning from the pursuit.

I have given a meagre relation of this battle, of which
a full account will be found in General Winder's Official
Report, the original of which is in my possession.[9]   It
gives one of the most vivid narratives of the details of
a hard fought battle that I know, and, I think, shows
General Winder's conduct on a battle field at its best—
his boldness in pushing forward in attack from an unfavorable against a superior position held by greater
numbers—his tenacity in resistance—turning alternately
to infantry and artillery, even sacrificing a piece when
necessary—rallying his men and pressing into service
any other commands within his reach, until his persist-

[9] It will be found in the *War of the Rebellion—Official Records of the Union and
Confederate Armies*, Series 1, Volume 12, Part 1, page 739.

ence under adverse circumstances contributed not a little to the success of the final attack on the enemy's flank and gave him a position to join promptly in the pursuit. The way he handled his artillery—his own and some of other commands—is particularly noticeable. No one can read his report without forming a high opinion of his ability.

It is but bare justice to say that the enemy on this field fought stubbornly and well.

It was evening—about sunset—when our troops came back to the battle field from the pursuit. Fremont had come up on the other (west) side of the river, and finding that Jackson had burned the bridge, ranged his guns along the high ground where ours had been the day before, and was firing across at the parties of our men who were removing the wounded and burying the dead. Our army, or at least part of it, was compelled therefore, to leave the road and strike into a woods road which passed through the forest along the mountain side to the Brown's Gap road. Reaching this, east of Port Republic, we went up the Gap and mountain and, about midnight, bivouacked on the very summit of the Blue Ridge.

I think we stayed in this elevated bivouac the next day and the day succeeding that and that we moved down and out of Brown's Gap on June 12 and went into camp in the level and more open Valley country near Mount Meridian and Weyer's Cave—in which the soldiers jestingly said Jackson intended to take refuge if hard pressed. Here we had, and thoroughly enjoyed, a rest for nearly a week.

Being so near to it, I went twice into the cave, although I have little inclination, in fact a strong disinclination, for underground exploration. The first time I had one companion; the next time I was induced to go with Colonel Bradley T. Johnson, of the Maryland regiment and a party of others. The entrance to this cave is very small—like an enlarged fox's hole, as in fact it was when discovered—and it goes down steeply and has several narrow passages through which one can hardly squeeze; but further in there are rooms and a large long, wide and high chamber. There are, of course, stalactites and stalagmites, a bridal veil, etc.

Our next move was the long march to Richmond and the Seven Days Battles.

The evening before we started I rode with General Winder to the headquarters of another brigade commander, I think it was General Trimble, and another or two others dropped in, so that there were either three or four brigade commanders in the tent—Winder, Trimble and, according to my recollection, General William B. Taliaferro of the 3d Brigade; a fourth I have forgotten, it may have been Taylor, for I think there were four. They discussed the campaign just ended and all were of the opinion that Jackson could not continue to take such risks without at some time meeting with a great disaster. They dwelt particularly on the situation in which he put himself when near Harper's Ferry with two armies closing in forty miles in his rear and his wonderful escape, passing between them at the last possible moment. I think their criticism and apprehensions at that point in Jackson's career were natural and justifiable. Later, when Jackson's operations in the second Manassas and Maryland campaign, not to speak of Chancellorsville and other battles, had given such evidence that "luck" was not such a factor in the Valley campaign as it then fairly appeared to have been, these generals, who had been his able coadjutors, would, I am sure, have had a more confident opinion of his ability to extricate himself in any emergency. I have not the slightest doubt now, nor have any of Stonewall's men, that if Fremont and Shields had closed his way at Strasburg, as they came so near doing, he would either have dealt them a crushing blow, as he did later at Cross Keys and Port Republic, or else have successfully passed around and out to their west or east.

Another criticism probably was—I know we thought and spoke of it after the battle—of Jackson's pressing his small advance against Shields's front in a strong position at Port Republic, with the result of our being checked with loss until others of our superior force came up on the enemy's flank. But it was not known at the time that Jackson's intention was to defeat Shields early in the morning and then recross the river and fall upon Fremont again with his whole army. If he could have carried out his whole plan it would have been almost, if not quite, without a precedent in military annals. It was prevented by the delay in the construction of the substitute for a bridge out of Port Republic across the South Fork, and, it is fair to add, the obstinate resistance of Shields's men (Shields himself was not up with them). If he had so defeated Fremont perhaps nothing but orders from Richmond would have prevented Jackson from clearing the Valley again to the Potomac. But Richmond might have fallen.

Dr. A. J. Volck, of Baltimore, made a pencil sketch of Jackson from life in September (probably the 3d or 4th) 1862, of which he afterwards made an etching. I have a letter in which he gives the following account of his making it:

The drawing from which this hasty etching was made is from life. It was on one of my blockade running trips not long after the second battle of Bull Run. I had crossed the Potomac above Ball's Bluff and, carrying important papers, was making my way across the country to get to a certain place the name of which I have forgotten, but where I knew of a person who would have me pushed forward. I came quite unexpectedly upon a camp and not meeting any picquets I walked right through it. On the other side of the tents and shelters I saw some officers talking together, amongst them Jackson. As I seemed unobserved I pulled out my sketchbook and made what can hardly [be] pronounced a speaking likeness of the Genl. I was almost done with it when one of the officers pointed me out and Genl. Jackson looked around at me with a pleasant smile and turned away. I had, however, to show what I had done for some officer and also prove myself to be a friend. I was sent on on horseback with a guide.

Balto., April 20, '98.   A. J. VOLCK.
   The etching was made immediately after my return home 3 or 4 days afterwards, one or two prints taken and for some reason now forgotten, probably one of my frequent arrests, the plate was mislaid. Some 5 or 6 years ago I saw an account of this print, said to be the only one in existence, described in one of the monthly magazines (I think the Century). This caused me to look through some old rubbish dating from war times and I found the plate, from which the prints were taken. I am sorry the plate has again disappeared   V.

I think Dr. Volck meant: "The hasty drawing from which this etching was made." The prints mentioned were presented by him to the Maryland Confederate Relief Bazaar, April, 1899, and were sold off rapidly.

Dr. Volck, a man of much accomplishment, in working in silver and other metals and ivory, in painting and drawing, and in other artistic work, and whose character had won him a large circle of friends, of whom the writer was not one of the least attached, died in Baltimore 26th March, 1912.

CHAPTER XIV

MARCH FROM THE VALLEY TO RICHMOND

I do not remember exactly on what day[1] we broke up our camp between South River and the Blue Ridge, near Mount Meridian and Weyer's Cave, and crossed over Brown's Gap to the east side of the Blue Ridge, as we had done about six weeks before. Nor have I in my memory an exact itinerary of the march to join Lee's army at Richmond. Whether it took us more than one day—a day and a half or two days—to reach the point on or near the Virginia Central[2] Railroad and turn east, I do not now recall. We had heard of the arrival at Staunton of large reinforcements—Lawton's Georgia Brigade and Hood's Brigade—and until we did turn east we did not know whether we would take the road or railroad west to Staunton, as we had done before, to unite and fall upon Fremont, or were bound for Richmond.

I recollect crossing one[3] or more streams on the road to Charlottesville, but have no recollection of passing through that town. The cherry trees along the way, loaded with ripe fruit, have, however, left a picture in my mind— through the stomach. And I remember passing, a couple of miles or so east of Charlottesville, what I was told was Shadwell, an old plantation of Thomas Jefferson, and two sycamore trees by gate posts were pointed out as having been planted by him. And General Winder and his staff turned in for some hours at Edge Hill,

---

[1] Dabney, Allan and others say Tuesday, June 17.
[2] Now the Chesapeake and Ohio.
[3] Mechum's River, etc.

the home of Miss Sarah Randolph and her sisters, Jefferson's grandchildren, and were shown many articles which had belonged to him, with several models of inventions, among which I remember an odometer—to be fastened on a carriage wheel and record the distance traveled. We finally reached Gordonsville and camped on its western edge.[4]

The next day, or perhaps the day after that, we marched on the Richmond road, and it was not until after passing this point that we felt sure where we were going, for some had still thought that Jackson might be having northern Virginia in his mind. It was either on this day's march or a day or two later that General Winder saw one or two of the other brigade commanders of the division (it will be remembered that there was no division commander between them and Jackson), who complained that they were receiving no orders and were stumbling along the road without directions. The General assumed control for the time being and they willingly took orders from him. I never knew anyone under whom stray commands were so ready to serve,[5] and it was his habit to annex any such that came within his reach, particularly on a battlefield. I am sure the whole division— officers and men—would have gladly welcomed his appointment as major-general, a position which Jackson seemed reluctant to fill.

I think it was at Louisa Court House that our brigade took to the cars and had the benefit of the equivalent of a days march. I suppose we rode eighteen or twenty

[4] Probably on June 20.
[5] After Winder's death Jackson wrote: "Richly endowed with those qualities of mind and person which fit an officer for command and which attract the admiration and excite the enthusiasm of troops," etc.

miles—probably to Beaverdam Station.[6] Wherever we did disembark, I remember vividly some features of our further march to Ashland—the slow progress over the bad roads through the forest—the halts while bridges were being repaired, etc.   In particular, one bridge, over Little River or Newfound River, I believe, delayed us until axemen felled two trees on opposite sides of the stream, so as to fall parallel across it, and many, if not most or all, of the men of our Brigade passed precariously and slowly over on these trunks.   I have no recollection of our crossing the larger South Anna River, as we must have done, but I seem to remember passing a little cross road place bearing the name of Negrofoot.   Nor do I remember coming to Ashland—15 miles North of Richmond—at or near which we turned east and crossed the Richmond and Fredericksburg Railroad and after an interval the Virginia Central Railroad.

We then bent Southeasterly and went into bivouac near Tottopotomoy Creek.   This was the evening of June 26.[7]

[6] The railroad beyond this point had been torn up by the enemy.   Perhaps we disembarked at Frederickshall.

[7] It was on this march, while passing through Albemarle County that Jackson is said to have seen a straggler getting over a fence to make for a cherry tree and to have demanded where he was going.   "Don't know."   "What command do you belong to?"   "Don't know."   "What State do you come from?"   "Don't know."   Jackson asked what was the meaning of this.   "Well," said the man, "Jackson has ordered us not to know anything until after the next fight."   Jackson turned off, not displeased.

CHAPTER XV

SEVEN DAYS BATTLES AROUND RICHMOND— GAINES'S MILL

On the morning of Friday June 27 (1862), Jackson's Division, as it was commonly called, moved at an early hour from its bivouac near Totopotomoy Creek, our 1st, or Stonewall, Brigade being the third in the line of march. The Georgia brigade, commanded by Brigadier-General Alexander R. Lawton and said to be 3500 strong, which had been sent to Staunton only to turn around and come back with us, had I think the day before, taken a place as the 4th Brigade in our division. I remember, while lying on two spread rails on top of a worm fence during one of the many halts from stoppages in front, listening to some talk in the ranks of that brigade, which showed what little idea they had of battle, of which they had had so far no experience. An order came down their line for reports of the number of rounds of ammunition in the cartridge boxes, and captains and orderly sergeants[1] accordingly made rather languid enquiries of their men. "Captain," replied one, "I have fifteen rounds, and I reckon it's all I kin shoot." "Captain, I have twenty," "I have ten," etc. I do not think they averaged twenty, and I saw none issued.[2]

Later in the morning we heard firing, gradually getting heavier, but some distance to our right, for we were now

[1] The orderly sergeant is simply the first sergeant of a company.

[2] A cartridge box would hold forty cartridges. It is no wonder that General Lawton and his regimental commanders say in their official reports of the evening's battle that the men got out of ammunition.

marching eastwardly, we supposed to get entirely around the enemy's right flank. We seemed to be moving parallel, or nearly so, with the line of battle, from which presently some shells came, passing over our heads into the woods which were on the left of the road. About 4 p.m. Captain W. Carvel Hall, of General Trimble's staff, Ewell's Division, came galloping rapidly across from the direction of the firing on our right and said to General Winder that General Ewell had sent him to order the brigades to break from column and move immediately to his assistance. (We were not in Ewell's Division or under his command, and, in fact, had no division commander as I have stated; in this instance Ewell either acted on the emergency or had received authority from Jackson.[3]) The head of the brigade was promptly turned out of the line of march to the right (south) and I saw that as Captain Hall passed up the column the next brigade did likewise. General Winder directed his march, in column of fours, across open ground, to the sound of the heaviest firing. As we approached, the artillery fire became more furious and while yet comparatively far in rear some shells fell quite close, although not meant

[3] In the *Confederate Military History*, volume III, Virginia, by Major Jed. Hotchkiss, General Jackson's very competent topographical engineer, it is stated, page 289, that Jackson sent an order for his divisions to come up by a staff officer whose duty was not to be on the field or carry such orders, and who failed to deliver the order properly, but that Major Dabney, adjutant-general, rectified the error after some delay. See also Dabney's *Life of Jackson*, page 448. That staff officer was, I am sure, Major John Harmon, Jackson's hard swearing but very efficient chief quartermaster. I saw Major Harmon sitting on his horse before we had moved out of the line of march, and wondered what he was doing there, for shells were doing considerable execution among the branches of the trees on the left of the road we were marching on and his proper place was with his wagon train. But I did not hear or see him giving any order to General Winder, and our first and only order that I know of was that brought by Captain Hall. I did not see Major Dabney.

for us and doing no damage, even passing by or over and crashing through the woods behind. We were presently delayed a while by one of the other brigades (Lawton's?) crossing our front diagonally from left to right, but soon moved on and found ourselves at or near the scene of action. The brigade was formed by regiments closed in mass behind (on the north side of) a road, which we called the Telegraph Road, running about east and west. Where we were so halted the ground was open and on the road, perhaps immediately to our left, was a small collection of houses;[4] a short distance to our right there was a wood which, I think extended to and across the road, and between us and this wood I saw General Trimble and his brigade. The enemy was not visible to us, his line being still apparently some distance off, at any rate a line of thicket on his (south) side of the road made a screen between us. But while we were not yet actually engaged, the battle was raging furiously, with much roar of artillery and musketry. From our front shells were bursting over the line of the road with much precision, but rather high up in the air; I remember noticing, and under other circumstances would have admired, the perfect ring of smoke that marked each explosion.

We presently formed line of battle a'ong the north side of the road. And in forming, I remember very vividly an incident that I have often told since, but the telling of which has been generally received with incredulity. The general and staff were riding at a gallop along the front from left to right, General Winder leading, I being next and Captain John F. O'Brien, assistant adjutant-general, just behind me, when, looking over my left shoulder towards the front, I saw a cannon ball ricocheting directly towards our party. I apprehended, on a very

4 Old Cold Harbor.

hasty calculation, that it would exactly take me or my horse and over my shoulder watched its course with considerable interest, but just passing the line of its path myself, I saw it bound up from the ground and strike O'Brien's horse in the flank. I expected to see horse and rider go down, but the horse merely gave a grunt and made a convulsive movement and went on.[5]

When he came on the field General Winder had met and conferred with Major-General A. P. Hill, the senior officer there present, by whose order he sent forward two regiments, the 2d and 5th Virginia, to support a battery.

Shortly before sunset an order came, in some way from Jackson I think,[6] to charge the enemy's position and our three remaining regiments, 3d, 27th and 4th Virginia, were accordingly dressed in line and moved forward, to which was soon added the "Irish Battalion,"[7] of the 2d Brigade, under Captain B. Watkins Leigh, which had become separated from its proper command and willingly put itself under General Winder's orders. After going a short distance in very good order, and picking up our 2d and 5th Virginia, which joined on our left, we came to the screening thicket I have mentioned, which proved to be a rather wide marshy bottom with trees and undergrowth, running parallel with the Telegraph Road, and in crossing it it was impossible to preserve this good alignment. I had some difficulty in getting through the

[5] The horse was a little crippled or stiff for a few days but was ridden by one of us at Malvern Hill on July 1. It was the same yellow clay colored horse which O'Brien was riding at Winchester on May 25 when it was shot through the tail. It will be supposed by many that my imagination deceived me in some way— for instance that it may have been a clod of earth which struck the horse but I tell the incident now as I have always told it and thought I saw it. And a ricocheting ball must at some time before it stops have little force.

[6] General Winder's official report says he was ordered to make the attack by A. P. Hill.

[7] The 1st Virginia Battalion of Regulars.

mire on horseback.   On the further side we found several regiments of different commands which General
Winder ordered to move forward with his line; I remember particularly one of General Lawton's Georgia regiments, which his brother and assistant adjutant-general,
Captain Lawton, in the absence of field officers perhaps,
led forward very gallantly.   And considerably further on
we came to the 1st Maryland, standing alone in perfect
order, which also promptly joined in the charge.[8]

The distance from the swamp thicket from which we
had emerged and the enemy's line was from a quarter to
a half of a mile and the ground was open and swept by
artillery and musketry, the latter being the heaviest and
most continuous all along the battle line I had ever heard;
the sound was like the roar of falling water or rising and
falling like the groaning of heavy machinery in motion
in an old building.   It was the only field I had seen on
which the smoke of battle rested, through which the setting sun shone red and dim.   I now saw only our 2d
and 5th Virginia, the other regiments having borne off
too far to the right, I think, and so not sustaining much
loss.   I had been busied for a while in getting forward
some Virginia regiment of another command, which
seemed to have no field officers and to be inclined to
falter, and after getting it well started (by carrying the
colors forward on horseback, which the color bearer gave
me with reluctance and which I was glad to hand back to
him as they seemed to draw a good deal of fire), I found

[8] Major W. W. Goldsborough, in his History of the Maryland Line and Colonel Bradley T. Johnson in the "Confederate Military History," volume 2,
Maryland, represent me as using some ceremonious language.   In fact, being
excited, I rode up and asked "Are you going to remain here like cowards while
the Stonewall Brigade is charging past?"   And Captain J. Louis Smith told me
afterwards that one of his men, in resentment, levelled his gun at me, but he
struck it up.

myself again with the 2d and 5th Virginia. These two
regiments here suffered severely and the 2d lost two field
officers—Colonel Allen[9] killed and Major Jones[10] mortally wounded. And about the same time and place
Mr. Samuel D. Mitchell, of Richmond, serving for the
day as volunteer Aide to General Winder was also killed.
I saw Colonel Allen's dead body, and also saw Major
Jones on the ground who was in a shattered nervous condition and did not wish me to come near him. At this
time I observed another regiment apparently inclined
to falter, at a road which ran diagonally across our front,[11]
and went over to it. Leaving it when it went forward,
rather hesitatingly, I went on but did not again see our
2d and 5th Virginia, which must have inclined to the left,
or else I myself obliqued to the right, probably to look
for a continuation of the brigade line. But I found no
troops, although just before crossing the diagonal road
I saw the flag of some regiment (Virginia, I think,) lying
abandoned on the ground. I did not stop for it, and,
doubting if there were any troops connecting with the
right of our charging line, continued to ride forward to
see what was there, until I came under such a close and
heavy fire (I do not suppose directed at me particularly,
but simply sweeping the field), that I was convinced I
was riding on the enemy's line and turned back a little
way. Seeing a large body of Confederates to the right
(west) and a short distance in rear, I rode over there and
found General Lawton with part of his brigade, General

[9] Colonel William Allen, born in Shenandoah County, afterward lived in
Bedford and finally when the war broke out in Jefferson County. He was one
of the best regimental commanders in the service.
[10] Major Frank Jones, of Frederick County, was a fine officer and most amiable
Christian gentleman. I have always since remembered him as reading his
Bible all or most of the way on the cars several days before.
[11] Southeasterly to the McGee house?

Garland[12] with his, and perhaps other scattered bodies, massed or crowded together in some confusion and seemingly uncertain what to do. I spoke to them and explained that General Winder was charging on the left and asked if they could not join with it. They said they must look for their own commanding officers. General Lawton asked, "Where are the enemy?" I said "In front," and that I had just ridden on them and that a movement to the front would connect with General

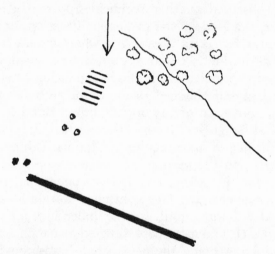

Winder. Nothing being immediately done, I was starting to go to look for General Winder when I came across several companies of our 33d Virginia in the crowd, under Major F. W. M. Holliday, and undertook to show them the way. But I proposed to Major Holliday that instead of going diagonally across to the left front (southeasterly) where I expected to find the General, we should move straight to the front and see what was there and

[12] Brigadier-General Samuel Garland, Jr., of Lynchburg, commanded a brigade in Major-General D. H. Hill's Division.

fill up a vacancy and so join on the right of the rest of the brigade. He assented and we moved forward in column of fours. We presently crossed a little branch or narrow bottom and began to go over a stubble field and I was just saying to the Major that I believed it was here I had ridden on the enemy, when in the twilight or later dusk, we saw ahead, on the crest of the rising ground, a shadowy line of men, its left about opposite to us and stretching away to its right and rear oblique. Major Holliday and I rode forward until we were near enough to see two (?) men, apparently officers, standing a little in advance of the end of the line and we called out, "What command is that?" The answer came back, "   .   .   .   .   New York, what do you belong to?" We made no reply and I looked anxiously back to see if our men were not coming up. But an inevitable straggler was trudging at our horses' heels who answered, "33d Virginia;" "Which side?" was quickly asked, and now I tried to turn my horse's head around as fast as I could, but the straggler said, "Confederate," whereupon the enemy fired. Fortunately only those on their left were in position to do so. I remember well the little ghostlike pillars of white dust which sprang up from the bullets striking the dry ground of the stubble field—at least one under my horse's nose and making him unmanageable for some moments. Before our men could form and return the fire the New York regiment had melted away.[13] More than ever convinced of the im-

[13] I either did not catch or do not remember the number of the regiment, but it was probably the 27th New York, whose commander, in his official report, *War of the Rebellion Records*, Series 1, Volume XII, Part II, page 454, says, "The appearance of a large force (apparently a brigade) on the left, marching as if to flank this brigade, who responded irregularly to the challenge of the color bearer," etc. Our meddlesome straggler was probably killed. See the report of Colonel Neff of the 33d Virginia in same volume, page 585.

portance of this gap being filled, I rode back to Generals Lawton and Garland and said I could now tell exactly and positively where the enemy were, for I had just ridden on and been fired at by them. General Garland said he had just received orders to rejoin his command, "but," said he, "Captain, I will see what I can do for you," and turning to Lawton he asked, "General Lawton, what is the date of your commission?" He replied, "Sir, I am the oldest brigadier-general in the service"— or "next to the oldest." "That settles it," said General Garland, "You see, Captain, I am sorry I can do nothing for you." General Garland began to move off and General Lawton busied himself very actively in organizing the troops around. But being anxious to get back to General Winder, from whom I had been separated so long, I did not wait further and pushed across to Mc-Gee's house, where I found him conferring with Major-General D. H. Hill.[14] It was now quite dark and the action had ceased everywhere and our men were resting beyond the McGee house, having driven the enemy from their last position and gone beyond it and darkness only preventing further pursuit. The house and yard were filled with their wounded and dead. The General directed me to ride back and bring up our Surgeons and ambulances. It was very dark and I was only prevented from trampling on or riding over wounded men many times by their suddenly crying out under my horse's head. After riding up and down the Telegraph Road and over the field for two hours or more, I could not find

[14] In an article or chapter written by Lieutenant-General D. H. Hill in *Battles and Leaders of the Civil War*, volume 2, page 347, he says: "General Winder thought that we ought to pursue into the woods on the right of the Grapevine Bridge road but . . . . I thought it advisable not to move on. General Lawton concurred with me . . . . Winder was right; even a show of pressure must have been attended with great results."

the ambulances and, making my way back with some difficulty, so reported. About midnight I lay down on a fallen section of the yard paling fence, among the dead and wounded, and fell asleep.

Such is my account of the battle of Gaines's Mill, or of part of it, in which I have not gone outside of my own personal experiences, and may have gone into them too diffusively. Apart from these little personal experiences, it was more like a great battle, such as I used to imagine one was, than any I had been in, not only our part in it but the sound of furious firing all along the line, the smoke hanging over it, and other signs of deadly conflict. There was a certain exhilaration in it, too, and I think that the charge over the open fields under a very severe fire was the only time I ever felt a sense of real enjoyment in the middle of a battle, a feeling generally postponed with me to the close when the enemy's line gives way or night puts an end to the struggle. For it happens that I never was in a battle when our side was finally driven from the field.[15]

The next morning, June 28, Saturday, I was wakened after sunrise by the pitying comments of a couple of civilians who were standing over me wondering where I was shot, and who walked off disconcerted at discovering I was not a corpse. This day we remained in position, advancing our skirmishers, however, and gathering the spoils of victory on the field. We got, at or near the McGee house, five pieces of artillery, counting as such two small revolving or repeating guns with hoppers on top of the breech, into which bullets were poured I suppose. Our pickets brought in from the Chickahominy swamp, or the woods extending back from it, Brigadier-

---

[15] Spotsylvania Court House and Sailor's Creek are not exceptions, in both of which I was captured on the field—on the firing line.

General John F. Reynolds, an old friend of General Winder in the United States Army. He asked General
Winder, "Have you seen Buchanan?"—meaning Colonel
Robert C. Buchanan, also of the old Army and General
Winder's brother-in-law. "No," said Winder, "was he
with you?" Reynolds hesitated a moment and said,
"He commanded a brigade[16] opposite to you yesterday
evening." General Winder immediately sent instructions to the picket to look for him but he was not found.

Some time before, the young horse which I had bought
in the Valley when I joined General Winder as his aide
had become run down in Jackson's hard marching and
Major Douglas Mercer, the brigade quartermaster, had
sent it off with the spent horses of his train to "run
afield" for a time. He told me that it had got mixed
somewhere with the government horses, and now proposed to me to take in its stead a captured horse which
had been turned over to him and which, it was said,
General Reynolds was riding when captured, and I did
so. It was rather small but well made and suitable for
my riding, and, although it had a fresh bullet wound in
its side, I think I was able to use it at once.[17]

The weather being very warm, the dead bodies which
lay around were becoming very offensive and next morning, June 29, Sunday, exertions were made to have them
buried. Some time during the day we moved forward
and down to the Chickahominy, with its wide wooded

[16] Of Regulars of the U. S. Army.

[17] This dark bay horse—or mare I should have said—I rode, habitually, to
the end of the war, that is to say, to the battle of Sailor's Creek on 6 April, 1865,
when she was struck again in the side, whether mortally or not, I do not know as
I was captured. Recollecting her former wound, she would turn black from
profuse sweat at the opening of every battle.

A curious dispute in the following Fall, at Winchester, about the ownership
of the mare will be told further on.

swamps, and rested near the Grapevine Bridge—about a mile, as the road wound, from the McGee house.   A few stray prisoners were brought in from time to time from the swamp, and I remember a drunken Irishman being interrogated in Jackson's presence, which way the enemy had gone?   "The last that I saw of them," said he, "they were skedaddling in that direction," and he flourished his hand towards the Chickahominy.[18]

After waiting a considerable time, the bridge not being completed, at sunset we returned to our former place.

[18] The coinage of the expressive word "skedaddle" in the Fall of 1861, I have mentioned.   It reminds me here of a letter written about this period from Baltimore by my mother to my father, Charles Howard, a "prisoner of State" in Fort Warren, Boston Harbor: "I heard lately why General McClellan left the Peninsula.   He said he was surrounded by four swamps and the frogs were constantly saying 'Bull Run, Bull Run, Bull Run,' 'Big Bethel, Big Bethel, Big Bethel,' 'Ball's Bluff, Ball's Bluff, Ball's Bluff,' and then the little frogs took it up, 'Skedaddle, Skedaddle, Skedaddle,' all the time and he could not stand it."

CHAPTER XVI

SEVEN DAYS BATTLES—WHITE OAK SWAMP AND MALVERN HILL

Early the next morning, Monday, June 30 (1862), we moved, with all the troops of Jackson's command, crossed the Chickahominy with its wide wooded swamp at Grapevine Bridge, and, marching south, soon struck and crossed the Richmond and York River Railroad.[1] We here saw some evidences of fighting and heard there had been an engagement the day before.[2] I do not remember that we had heard the sound of it while it was going on not half a dozen miles off. After crossing, we marched eastwardly parallel with and for a while near to the railroad, but presently diverged in a southerly direction. In the afternoon there was a more protracted halt than usual on the march and I rode ahead, or was sent, to see what caused the delay. It was not far—I suppose under a mile—when I came almost out of some woods and found Jackson's staff on the left side of the road who told me the General was lying asleep under a tree. The trees were large and not close together here and through them could be seen ahead the road descending over open ground, curving a little to the left in doing so, to where it appeared to cross a stream[3]—a few hundred yards distant. The place of the stream was marked by a line of alders or other bushes at the crossing and I think it had a wider thicket with trees above (west) if not also below.

[1] At Savage Station.
[2] Savage Station—By Gen'l Magruder, etc.
[3] White Oak Swamp.

At intervals a shell came from across the stream but not falling or passing near us, but Jackson's staff told me that one had gone through one of the oak trees and killed a man behind it. With the exception of this slow firing everything seemed to be quiet, and it looked to me as if on our side we were waiting for Jackson to wake up. There was no change in the situation while I remained

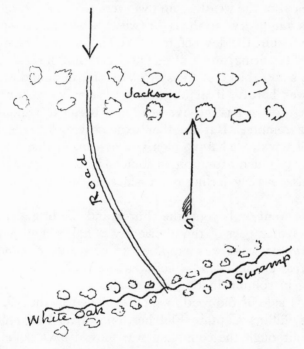

for a time talking with these staff officers. I know that while there and in riding back I wondered at the inactivity. We finally went into bivouac for the night.[4]

---

[4] There has been much discussion about Jackson's inactivity at White Oak Swamp. His devoted biographer Major Dabney says that he was suffering from physical exhaustion. Some think he was not at his best during the whole Richmond campaign. Jackson says in his official report that the marshy char-

The next morning, Tuesday, July 1, the army passed over this place—White Oak Swamp—without further opposition, at least none that I saw, and marched on south in pursuit of the enemy. Towards evening firing was heard in front, growing more and more heavy, and our division was halted near a church.[5] Dead bodies in blue uniform were lying about, already decaying in the heat of the weather, and we were told they were very thick a mile or so to the right (west), where an act on had been fought the day before.[6] We had not, as I recollect, heard the firing, and it often happened that in these dense woods and thickets of eastern Virginia the sound of battle was hardly, if at all, heard some miles distant, although often passing overhead and borne to regions far more remote. But another explanation may be that soldiers who are having plenty of fighting of their own do not pay much attention to somebody else's fighting beyond a passing feeling of satisfaction that they are not in it.

We went on beyond the church and the brigade, with the greater part of the division, was halted and held in reserve at what was supposed to be a safe distance in the rear of the battle, which was now raging. But while lying in column in the edge of the woods on the right (west) side of the road, a shell exploded in the 5th Virginia, killing Captain Fletcher, one of its best officers, and although the command was moved back some dis-

acter of the soil, the destruction of the bridge over the swamp and creek and the strong position of the enemy for defending the passage prevented his advancing until the following morning. And he curtly remarked afterwards that if General Lee had wanted him, he would have sent for him. See a full discussion of the matter in Henderson's *Life of Jackson*. I simply give my brief observation and my impression at the time.

[5] Willis's Church.
[6] Battle of Frazer's Farm or Glendale.

tance, another shell killed and wounded several more of the same regiment, making a second change necessary. We were under the impression that this fire, and part of that to which we were exposed afterwards, came from the enemy's gunboats on James River.[7]

A little before sunset General Winder was ,ordered to take his brigade to the front and report to Major-General D. H. Hill. After passing down the road a short distance we filed to the right into the woods a little way—perhaps a hundred yards—and then turned to the left and went forward through them, still in column of fours. We soon came under a very heavy artillery fire. We emerged from the woods into an open field across which streams of shells were passing which seemed to come from different directions and to cross each other's paths. The nearest point of conflict appearing to be to the left oblique, General Winder turned the head of the column in that direction and so diagonally over the field towards the road. But seeing a house[8] in the field between one and two hundred yards to the front and right, he ordered me to ride to it and see if General Hill was there. I think I can say that this was the most disagreeable duty I was ever called on as a staff officer to perform. As I approached the house it seemed to me that the fire of several batteries was converging on it or on that quarter of the field, and there was a constant hissing or other sound of heavy missiles from different directions and passing not high above the ground, although my recol-

[7] General McClellan, in his official report, *War of the Rebellion Records*, Series I, Volume XI, Part II, page 23, thanks Commodore John Rodgers for the valuable assistance by the fire of a portion of the flotilla, in James River, on the flank of the enemy attacking Malvern Hill on the 30th of June and 1st of July, which fire "was excellent and produced very beneficial results." James River appears to have been only about two miles distant or less.

[8] The Crewe house?

lection is there were few explosions. Several horses with military equipments were tied to the yard fence, but although I rode around the house twice, calling out, no one answered and the place was evidently deserted, as well it might be. I remember feeling a despairing conviction that I could not hope to get back through such a fire alive and how hard it was to be alone at such a time. Bending down to my horse's neck, I went back, or across, at full speed, while more than once it seemed to me that a missile passed within a few feet or inches.[9]

I found the head of our column just about striking the road at a point where towards the front it (the road) re-entered woods or a wooded swamp. We filed across the road and then attempted to move in line straight to the front across the wooded swamp, but it was now dark, in this bottom at least, and the ground was so thick with timber trees and underbrush, as well as deep with mire and water underneath that the brigade was much scattered. The General and staff found it necessary to dismount and leave their horses and pass through on foot. On the other (south) side of this strip we found open ground rising towards the enemy's position, a very short distance in front as we judged, for nothing could now be seen beyond a little way, except the flashing of the guns. But there was no cessation or diminution yet of the enemy's fire—musketry here—which swept the field to such an extent that it was difficult to believe anything could escape unhurt. But we found here some men of the 1st and 3d Regiments of North Carolina State Troops[10] holding their ground in

---

[9] We used to illustrate afterwards the severity of this fire over the open field by saying that even Colonel Grigsby, the gallant colonel of the 27th Virginia stopped swearing.

[10] I was to become very well acquainted later with these two fine regiments in General George H. Steuart's Brigade.

the most gallant manner, to whom were now added parts of our 33d and 4th Virginia as they came up behind us after struggling through the swamp, the rest of the brigade having lost the connection in the darkness. General Winder passed up and down animating the men and endeavoring to form a more regular and orderly line. A few were demoralized and were loading and firing their pieces without bringing them to the shoulder,

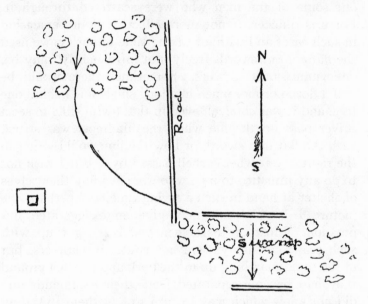

and the impression made on us at the time was that in some instances they shot down their comrades in front. I remember the General seizing a man by the shoulder and exclaiming, "Scoundrel, you have shot one of your own friends, I saw you do it." Colonel Neff and Major Holliday of the 33d Virginia were very active in getting the men up and keeping them in such order as was possible. General Winder advised Major Holliday to dismount, telling him he was exposing himself very much on horseback. "No, General," he replied in a tone which struck me by its total absence of any excitement, "I have always found I can discharge my duties very much better on horseback in a battle." Once, if not oftener, the General and his staff—I think the General went with Lieutenant Garnett and myself—went back in the swamp thicket, just behind us, to bring or drive out some of the men who were scattered through it. Force is quicker, if not more effective than persuasion in such cases and without taking time to parley, we used the flats of our swords freely, not infrequently, may be, on commissioned officers. Sometimes there would be half a dozen or more men in a long single line behind one tree, and it was comical, even in that awful time to see a shiver pass up the file when the hindmost was struck with the flat of a sword, or how the line would swing to the right or left when a shell passed by. But I wish not to do any injustice to men who were availing themselves of shelter at hand in such a trying time, and perhaps the picture I have drawn may give an exaggerated impression. Most of these men whom we got up with such scant ceremony were not cowardly skulkers, but in the rapid marching up in the dark and on such ground they had become separated from their commands and did not know which way to turn to find them. And all this while the advance was being held by men stubbornly standing under as terrific a fire as can well be imagined, and, mixed up as they were, each one sustained by his own individual courage.

About 9 o'clock the enemy's fire began to slacken and seeing that the action was nearly over, we got our men in a more orderly line along the position we were holding and extended it to the right (west). General Winder now sent me back with orders to urge any troops I might find to move up to his support. A few hundred yards— perhaps two or three or four—I came on a large body of men in the woods to the west of the road, and finding Brigadier-General George B. Anderson,[11] I stated the case to him. But he was wounded, and I think told me his command had other orders. I turned to Colonel Bradley T. Johnson, who was near by with his 1st Maryland Regiment well in hand as usual and who promptly said, "General Winder wants support, does he?" and that he would move up. I remember he was sitting on the ground at the root of a tree (but not behind it), and before rising he pulled out his pipe, filled it and struck a match and kindled a piece of paper which flared up and made a little illumination around in the dark woods. Scores, it seemed to me hundreds, of voices rang out, "Put out that light," "Kill the scoundrel," "Shoot him!" A few shells were still passing through the woods, which these outcriers foolishly imagined might be at- tracted by the glare, although they came, of course, from far off. I was apprehensive that some might be insane enough to carry out their threats and looked at Colonel Johnson in some trepidation as with perfect unconcern he continued to puff at his pipe until it was well lighted; he at length threw the burning paper on the ground, rose up and said, "Ah yes, you cowards, if you want to shoot anybody, go up to the front," then turning to his men, he said, "General Winder wants assistance, fall in." Without waiting to accompany him, I went to the front again, finding General Lawton with his Georgia brigade of our division, moving down the road towards it. Being ignorant of the ground, General

[11] General Anderson, of North Carolina and an officer of the old United States Army, was commanding a North Carolina brigade in D. H. Hill's Division.

Lawton put his men at General Winder's disposal, by whom both they and the Maryland regiment were used to extend the line to the right and forward.

All firing had ceased, and our position being now well established, General Winder rode back (with Lieutenant James M. Garnett,[12] brigade ordnance officer, and myself, Captain O'Brien,[13] the adjutant-general, having been hurt by a fall from his horse and not with us), to report to General Jackson, whom he found with General D. H. Hill some distance in the rear.   And I am half ashamed to record that Garnett and I, having lain down under an ambulance and gone to sleep while this consultation was going on, did not wake up when General Winder returned to the front (and he must have refrained from rousing us), and opened our eyes only to find broad daylight had come.   When we then went up to the front line, there was no enemy to be seen, and orders soon came to move back a mile or two and bivouac.

And so was fought, on our part of the field and in our time of participation in it, the battle of Malvern Hill, in which it appeared to us that the Confederates were marched up against a strong position and one very strongly held by artillery and infantry, without concert, and by successive attacks unsupported, or inadequately supported, by artillery.

A drizzly rain had set in this morning (after the battle), Wednesday, July 2, making things very uncomfortable both overhead and under foot, and I do not recollect any other particulars about the day.[14]

Next day, Thursday, we marched back towards the

[12] Lieutenant James Mercer Garnett, one of the most capable staff officers on a battlefield I have known, is a Virginian, but now (1913) living in Baltimore.

[13] Captain O'Brien died a few years ago in Tennessee, Memphis or Nashville.

[14] This rain is cited among the instances to prove that heavy battles cause a rainfall, but I do not think there is anything in the theory.

Chickahominy, but did not make much distance.   On
Friday, July 4, we bent around to the right (east and
southeast), until it was evident that the army was being
directed on James River and we supposed we would again
strike the enemy there and hoped that this time it would
be to inflict a crushing blow.   Towards evening we were
nearing the river and from men coming from the front
we learned the armies would soon be face to face, as we
knew also from various familiar signs.   We finally halted
and formed line on the left (east) of the road we had been
marching on and at right angles to it.   But we presently
bivouacked.

We remained here several uneventful days.   We
understood that the army of the enemy was very close
in front, holding the edge of the high ground beyond
which was the bottom land of James River,[15] but his
line was not visible from ours, at least not from our part
of it, being screened by woods.   Some skirmshing went
on, irregularly, and there were some shells fired from the
gun boats in the river, but not coming in our neighborhood.   These shells were described to me by an artillery-
man[16] who had been under them as "big as a flour
barrel."

General Winder here caused all the regimental surgeons to report on the physical condition of the men and
sent up their reports to General Jackson with an urgent
recommendation that they be allowed a rest after the
long marching and other hardships of the last two
months.   The surgeons all stated that the feet of most
of the men were bruised and sore so as to be in a pitiable
condition and that they were well nigh broken down.   It
was said that Jackson was not well pleased with General

[15] At Harrison's Landing.
[16] Stirling Murray, of Maryland, a member of Stuart's Horse Artillery.

Winder's action in this matter, but the latter cared not for that; no consideration of favor or disfavor ever moved him in the discharge of what he deemed to be a duty.

After not many days[17] the Stonewall Brigade, with others, marched towards Richmond. And on the next morning I started before it, wishing to get myself a uniform, for so far I had worn only a plain grey coat, with no marks of rank except the epaulets which had been sewed on the shoulders by Mrs. Kennedy of "Cassilis" during our brief occupation of Charlestown in the Valley campaign.

[17] It appears to have been on July 10.

CHAPTER XVII

RICHMOND—ORANGE AND LOUISA COUNTIES

I found the Confederate capital full of officers and soldiers, some on various duties and some, like myself, on leave for proper purposes, but many evidently not having any sufficient reason for being there. And the next day I saw Colonel Lay (or Colonel Deas?) of the adjutant general's office, going about the streets and verbally, in the name of the commander-in-chief, ordering all officers to rejoin their commands; I fear that most, like myself, gave little more than a respectful hearing to his good humored notification. I think I was only two days in Richmond, however, and rejoined the brigade which was now up and in camp on the Mechanicsville Turnpike Road—a few miles out northeast from the city. Here we remained some days, enjoying a well earned repose. My uniform being made, in the pride of my heart I had my picture taken to be sent home—an ambrotype coupled with one of Captain William H. Murray, my old company commander in the 1st Maryland; mine was somewhat marred, however, by a temporary swelling of the lower jaw. (Frontispiece.)

I remember one morning, while sitting on a camp stool in front of our tent engaged in some staff business, an officer rode up whom I saluted in our customary careless fashion without rising. Without response, he dismounted, grasped his bridle at the bit and stood erect at his horses' head, with his heels brought together, and looking at me gravely, slowly saluted in a most formal military manner and in broken English asked me for

159

some direction—to General Jackson's headquarters perhaps. Observing his fine physical appearance—over six feet in height and very robust—and the quaint formality of his manner, and never having seen him, or any one like him, before, I enquired about him afterwards and learned he was a German named Von Borcke, who had come over to serve our cause.[1]

In less than a week the division, composed now of the 1st or Stonewall Brigade, under General Winder, the 2d Brigade, commanded at this time by some regimental commander I think, the 3d Brigade under Brigadier-General William B. Taliaferro—all Virginia troops—and the 4th, or Georgia Brigade under Brigadier-General Alexander R. Lawton—but still having no Division commander under Jackson—was ordered to Gordonsville.[2] I think we marched the first day to Hanover Junction and remained there the next day. Here the Virginia Central Railroad, going to Gordonsville and beyond, and the Richmond and Fredericksburg Railroad cross, and in the fork south of the junction lived Mr. Theodore S. Garnett, father of Lieutenant Garnett, our brigade ordinance officer, and by him the General and staff were entertained with a hospitality for which we

---

[1] Major Heros Von Borcke, of Prussia, soon became well known to the Army of Northern Virginia as a very brave and popular officer of General "Jeb" Stuart's staff. He was badly wounded in the throat in a cavalry engagement at Upperville on June 19, 1863, and incapacitated for further service. After his slow convalescence he had to wear a silver tube in his windpipe and, I understood, for the rest of his life. But I believe he served in the Prussian-Austrian War. And I heard also that he flew a Confederate flag at his castle in Prussia and that once when the "Red Prince," the distinguished Prussian cavalry general, came to visit him and was shown his picture hanging above that of Jeb Stuart, he remarked that he had only one fault to find—his picture ought to be below Stuart's, not above it. Major Von Borcke paid a visit, about twenty years ago, to the scene of his former exploits and services and had a warm reception in Baltimore, as well as in Virginia. He died soon afterwards.

[2] It seems to have been on July 17.

felt very grateful. It was the first time since the war began that I found myself at a home with a filled ice house and I well remember after 50 years the mint juleps in tumblers filled with crushed ice. In the evening a cousin of Mr. Garnett came over a near by river to whom we were introduced as "Mr. R. M. T. Hunter."[3] Leaving this place with regret, I think we took the cars at the Junction and my recollection is that we moved by rail as far as Louisa Court House and then marched by Trevilian's Station to Gordonsville, near which we camped.

After staying here only a day or two the division moved back some miles south, through Gordonsville, to the edge of the rich "Green Spring" oasis in Louisa County and went into camp near a little place—it could hardly be called a village—named Mechanicsville. Having the promise, or expectation, of being there some time, drills were established and camp life was put on a more regular footing than for a long time back. But in about a week we broke up here, and, passing through Gordonsville again, which is in Orange County but close to where Louisa and Albemarle Counties corner with it, we took the Liberty Mill or Madison Court House road over Haxall's Mountain of the South West range. About three miles from Gordonsville we diverged on a road to the left and after going another mile, we went into camp in a very favorable situation on the farm of Mr. Oliver H. P. Terrell and in a rich section of country. The five regiments and two batteries of the brigade were placed in a fine piece of woods,[4] on high, dry ground and with a good

---

[3] U. S. Senator, Confederate States Senator and Secretary of State, etc. Of Essex County, Virginia.

[4] This piece of woods, part belonging to Terrell (whose place was called "Glencoe") and part to Colonel Magruder, whose house, "Frescati," on the east side of the Liberty Mill road, was the old home of Philip Pendleton Barbour,

stream of water between it and the Liberty Mill road—a
branch of Blue Run. General Winder and his staff
pitched their tents near the house and were treated by
Mr. and Mrs. Terrell with the kindest hospitality. Here
the Stonewall Brigade enjoyed an uninterrupted rest of
between one and two weeks, the men being moderately
drilled.

At this time Major R. Snowden Andrews (of Baltimore),
recently promoted, was assigned as chief of artillery of
the division, and there being no division commander or
staff organization, he pitched his tent near by and messed
with us. He was suffering from a wound in the leg,
received in the Richmond battles, still requiring frequent
dressing, and anyone not of his temperament would
have been away in hospital or on sick leave.

We heard rumors of the enemy's being disposed to be
aggressive on the other side of the Rapidan River, which
at its nearest point, Liberty Mill, was only some three
miles distant, and were not surprised to receive orders
to move on the afternoon of August 7, no intimation
being given, however, of the object of the movement.
General Winder had been for some days in an enfeebled
condition from sickness and, the weather being very hot,
he was advised by the medical director of the brigade not
to go with the command. But "his ardent patriotism
and military pride could bear no such restraint" (General
Jackson's official report), and he directed me to ride to
Jackson's headquarters and inform him of his condition
and to ask if there would be a battle and, if so, when, and
where the army was moving to, so that he might be up in

a distinguished Virginian, was always afterwards called "the camp woods,"
and is probably so known to this day.

My impression is that we camped here on our first coming to Gordonsville
on July 19th, from Richmond, but I am not sure.

time. I remonstrated and said, "But General Jackson does not like to have such questions asked." "Go to General Jackson and ask him what I told you," he said curtly. I went on my errand with a good deal of unwillingness. Jackson's headquarters were about a couple of miles towards Gordonsville, in a strip of woods at Dr. Jones's house, east of the road, and near the foot of Haxall's Mountain. When I entered the room where he was I found him kneeling on both knees[5] stuffing some things in an old fashioned "carpet bag," with his side face to me. I said, "General, General Winder sent me to say that he is too sick to go with the command." "General Winder sick? I am sorry for that," he interrupted me in the curt, slightly muffled voice I have before described. I said "Yes, sir, and the medical director has told him he must not go with the brigade. But he sent me to ask you if there will be a battle, and if so, when and he would be up, and which way the army is going?" Still kneeling he was silent for a few moments, turning his head slightly away, but, to my relief, I saw his mouth widen a little with one of his diffident smiles. "Say to General Winder that I am truly sorry he is sick"—then after a slight pause—"that there will be a battle, but not tomorrow, and I hope he will be up; tell him the army will march to Barnet's Ford—and he can learn its further direction there."

I rode back, wondering at my escape from a sharp rebuff to myself and General Winder, to whom I reported Jackson's words. He determined to rest quietly and follow on next morning. The brigade moved off in the afternoon.

[5] Did I interrupt him at one of his prayers?

CHAPTER XVIII

BATTLE OF CEDAR RUN

The next day, Friday, August 8 (1862), General Winder, Colonel Cunningham of the 21st Virginia in the 2d Brigade, who was also on the sick list,[1] and I rode leisurely during the morning—I cannot say in the cool of the morning, for it was an excessively hot spell of weather —about ten miles to Orange Court House, and as both of them suffered from the heat in their weak condition, we stopped at Captain Erasmus Taylor's, north of that place, and (there being nobody at the house,) rested in the shade of the trees in the yard until near sundown. We then rode on slowly, crossed the Rapidan River at Barnet's Ford and about a mile beyond and shortly after dark we found the Brigade in bivouac in the woods on the left side of the road. The General laid down without giving formal notice of his arrival. Some time during the night we were awakened by an irregular firing in the rear and close at hand and a number of bullets passed overhead through the trees. Not knowing what it meant, the General directed me to order the regimental commanders to form their men. When I said to one of them, "Colonel ————, General Winder directs you to form your command," one of the sleeping soldiers raised his head from under his blanket and asked, "Has General Winder come up?" On my answering "Yes," "Thank God for that," said he in a tone of evident relief. Something of the same sort occurred a second time and I was

[1] Lieutenant Colonel Richard H. Cunningham, of Richmond, Virginia, a fine officer and much esteemed as a man, was killed next day.

struck by the sincerity of their confidence and satisfaction at his presence. Things quieted presently but a second alarm came and the General and staff then rode out to the open field in rear where the trouble seemed to be, and finding other parts of the division under arms, we were told that a body of cavalry had suddenly ridden in on a road from the Madison Court House (west) side and after a brief firing they had retired by the way they had come. I do not remember that anybody was struck on our side and on examining the ground I saw no killed or wounded of the enemy. It was a very bright moonlight night—about full moon—and the trees and fencing made deep shadows, causing firing to be wild and inaccurate. General Lawton being the senior officer present, a note was sent by him by General Winder's advice to Jackson, informing him of what had occurred and asking for instructions. Shortly after daylight General Winder received a communication from General Jackson, the original of which I still have:

Hd. Qu. V. D.
Aug. 9th, 1862.
4 a.m.

Gen.

    Gen. Taliaferro's note in reference to appearance of the enemy is received. Gen. Lawton is left a guard to the Divn. train. Gen. Jackson directs that you assume command of the three remaining brigades of the Division.

Respt.

A. S. PENDLETON.
A. A. G.

Gen. Winder
  [on the back] Gen. Winder
               Comdg. 1st Division.

The heading "V. D." in the foregoing order means "Valley District," that having been General Jackson's military department before the Richmond battles and from the command of which he had not yet been relieved. Alexander ("Sandy") S. Pendleton (son of the Reverend General William N. Pendleton, General Lee's chief of artillery), was now Jackson's principal, and most efficient, adjutant-general, for I think the Reverend Major R. L. Dabney had resigned on account of ill health after the Richmond battles.[2]

General Lawton was one of the oldest (in point of seniority of rank,) of the brigadier-generals in the service, but Winder's tried character and services under Jackson's own eye preferred him for the command, at last, of his favorite Division and I think it is certain that he would have retained it ever afterwards. I know it would have met the hearty approval of the other parts of the division, which at other times had willingly put themselves under his orders, on the march and on the field of battle.[3]

Upon receiving Jackson's order General Winder assumed command of the three brigades and moved forward on the Culpepper Court House road. The day was hot and the dust oppressive and the march was a slow one for the reason also that the road was occupied by troops in front. About midday we were nearly abreast (at the head of the column,) of Slaughter's or Cedar Mountain on our right and learned that the enemy were a short distance in front. Ewell's Division, which had been ahead of us, went off the road to the right (east) and occupied the ground to the base of

[2] In my notes written fifteen or twenty years ago I have it that General Lawton sent the note to Jackson about the appearance of the enemy's cavalry, whereas the order above speaks of one from Taliaferro, (commanding the 3d Brigade). I may be mistaken in my recollection, or both may have written to Jackson.

[3] President Jefferson Davis told me after the war that General Winder was just about to be made a major-general when he was killed. It was the common impression that his promotion had been determined on.

Slaughter's Mountain, leaving the road itself in front and the country to its left (west) to us. Our division was halted in column in the road for some time and several of our generals (including Early and Ewell or Trimble,) conversed for a while off the right of the road. I remember seeing my brother, Major Charles Howard, Early's chief commissary, a little behind them and apparently keeping out of sight, and on my asking the reason, he said that, being a Commissary, his General had ordered him to go to his proper place in the rear, which he was not minded to do. At this time there was some skirmish firing to the right oblique, in the direction of the west base of Slaughter's Mountain, a round isolated mass several hundred feet high, on the east side of which we knew was the Orange and Alexandria Railroad.

By about 2 o'clock Ewell's Division had been moved in that direction—forward and to the right—and when our division was ordered forward, we found the road and the ground on its left was unoccupied between us and the enemy, who, however, was not yet visible to us. Riding ahead with his staff, General Winder presently came to a point on the road where a fence with woods behind it ran off at right angles to the right (east), in front of which was a cleared field, the woods continuing however, to the front on the left (west) side of the road. Looking over the fence corner at the road, we saw in the distance, across the open field, the enemy's batteries directing their fire on Ewell's forces towards the mountain. The General immediately directed Major R. Snowden Andrews, chief of artillery of the division, to order up a rifled piece (or two pieces?) from the batteries of the Stonewall Brigade. Meanwhile we pulled down a section of the fence. The gun or guns soon came up and opened on the batteries of the enemy and I think one or two more were brought up. At our first shot the enemy turned his guns on us with a very heavy fire. Our position, being at the apex of a right angle of open ground with the two sides bordered by woods, gave him a fair mark for his converging fire and soon the din of bursting shells principally, we thought, shrapnel,[4] was quite appalling,

[4] The ammunition used in the field artillery of the Confederate Army of Northern Virginia (and that of the Union Army was, I believe, much the same), was of four kinds, (1) solid shot, being round iron balls, but these were not often used; (2) shrapnel or spherical case, although when shells came to be elongated in shape, the word "spherical" was inaccurate; this was a shell, not very thick, loaded with a small charge of powder and filled with lead balls of an ounce weight, among which in the shell was poured melted sulphur to keep the balls in place until the bursting; (3) ordinary shells, made thicker than shrapnel and filled with powder. Both shrapnel and common shells had fuses which were cut to make them explode in so many seconds according to the estimated distance. Such shells as we had with percussion caps on the end to make them explode on impact were mostly, if not all, captured from the enemy, who used many of foreign invention, such as the Schenkel and Scheibert shells, shaped somewhat like an old fashioned soda water bottle. (4) Canister, sometimes called—by other than artillerymen—grape; this was in shape like a tomato can, and was filled with iron balls, an inch in diameter and only kept together by sawdust, being intended for short distances and to fly apart at the mouth of the gun.

Our guns were very heterogeneous in the first part of the war, but were improved and made more uniform by importations and captures, and finally by our own manufacture. We imported early some Blakeley and Whitworth rifled pieces. The short and light Blakeley guns kicked like a mule, and for this and other reasons they gradually disappeared. The favorite guns soon came to be the 10 and 20-pound rifled Parrotts (all of which were captured from the enemy), for distant firing, and, especially, the 12-pound Napoleon howitzer, not rifled and having a smaller chamber at the bottom of the bore for the powder to be concentrated behind the ball and so to diminish the thickness and weight of the piece. These guns were designed to be made of copper or bronze, and of such we had a great many in the army which we had captured, for in the first half of the war we captured many pieces and lost very few. But the Tredegar Iron Works, of Richmond made a very good gun of this pattern of iron—copper being soon exhausted in the Confederacy.

For the corroboration of my general recollection on this subject and for the foregoing details, I am indebted to my friend Mr. Joseph Packard, formerly of Virginia and now residing in Baltimore, who was first a member of the Rockbridge Battery and afterwards lieutenant and ordnance officer with the Reserve Ordnance Train of the Army of Northern Virginia.

made more so from the splintering of tree branches overhead. A number of battery commanders and other officers had gathered here, looking on and waiting orders and there were some narrow escapes, although so far there was more noise than execution. I remember Captain Willie Caskie, of Caskie's Battery, attached to the 2d Brigade, coming up to me in a half dazed way and asking me "just to look at his back," and on looking I saw a broad dusty streak across his shoulders where a falling limb cut by a shell had struck him.

About 4 o'clock General Winder made his dispositions for a forward movement. Retaining at this point the 3d Brigade, General William B. Taliaferro, in support of the artillery and for other service, and holding the 1st (Stonewall), now under command of Colonel Ronald, of the 4th Virginia, in reserve, he directed me to order the 2d Brigade, under Lieutenant-Colonel Thomas S. Garnett of the 48th Virginia, to move to the front under cover of the woods on the left (west) side of the road until he arrived on the flank of the nearest battery, which he was then to charge. I rode back and communicated these instructions to Colonel Garnett, and as he did not know the ground, I thought it best to accompany him a part of the way. We passed up about a hundred yards inside the woods from the road, coming, however, under part of the artillery fire directed into the angle. I saw a shell explode in the column just behind me (we were marching in the usual column of fours), which killed or wounded four or five men. Getting past this point and keeping with the brigade until it was some distance to the front and, I thought, required my services as a guide no longer (I had only been told to order it up,) I was going diagonally back to the angle where I had left General Winder, when I met Major Andrews riding hastily towards the direction from which I had come, who called out to me, "Go to the General." I asked, "Has anything happened?" But he only repeated, "Go to the General," and passed on. I hurried back and across the very short distance to the angle where I found General Winder lying dreadfully wounded by a piece of shell, which had passed between his left arm and side, tearing the flesh from the inside of the arm above and below the elbow and lacerating the left side as far back as the spine. He still had the use of the arm but it was evident that the wound to the body was mortal. He had been placed on a stretcher,[5] and was not suffering as much pain as he would have suffered if the shock had not been so great. I leaned over him and asked, "General, do you know me?" Turning his eyes to my face with a look of recognition, he answered, "Oh yes" and said some words of sorrow for his wife and children. Other friends and followers were standing around, full of grief, but he paid no attention to them, his thoughts were of home and family and he turned to me as a link with those associations. Surgeons came to his side but there was not the slightest hope and all that could be done was to alleviate his sufferings in his last moments. A Chaplain bent over him and said, "General, lift up your heart to God." He replied, "I do, I do lift it up to Him." He was presently carried by men towards a place of quiet in the rear. Just as we were starting, the Stonewall Brigade filed by, moving to attack, and officers crowded around with sincere sorrow on their faces, while the men passed by in silence, taking a last look at the leader who

[5] Mr. C. A. Fonerden of Carpenter's Battery now (1913) living in Baltimore, in a little *History of Carpenter's Battery*, printed at Newmarket, Virginia, 1911, says that he and Major Andrews and one or two others placed him on the stretcher.

had so well won their confidence and attachment. Perhaps prompted by this, he asked me how the battle was going, and seemed gratified at my reply. He became quieter presently, and as I walked beside with his hand in mine, I could feel it growing colder. At a stream crossing the road about half a mile back I met a part of A. P. Hill's Division going to the west side of the road on its way to the front.

A quarter of a mile further we stopped in a grove surrounding a church or school house on the west side of the road. By this time—I suppose it was after 6 o'clock—he had become totally unconscious and at sundown, with my arm around his neck and supporting his head, he expired, so quietly that I could scarcely mark the exact time of his death.

I placed General Winder's body in an ambulance and started it back to Orange Court House.

But learning that Major R. Snowden Andrews, chief of artillery of the division, had been desperately wounded and had been carried back to the Garnett house, a short distance from the East side of the road, I rode over to see him. He was in a lower room of the house. A fragment of shell (apparently) had torn the wall and laid open the right side of the abdomen and, passing on I suppose, had cut the top of the thigh over the joint. The former wound had opened widely so that my hand would have about covered the place as it so lay open and the intestines were fully exposed. There was a surgeon or assistant surgeon, with him, also his orderly (courier). Dr. Black, senior surgeon of the brigade, stopped for a while, whom I asked if there was any hope. He said no, that the wound was not necessarily fatal as a wound but that inflammation would be certain to set in. And we were having an extremely hot spell of weather. But

Major Andrews was perfectly cool and composed, and even cheerful, and no one in the next room listening to the natural tone of his voice as he gave directions about himself could have believed that it was the wounded man who was talking. "Doctor," said he to one of the surgeons, "how many chances have I?" and receiving

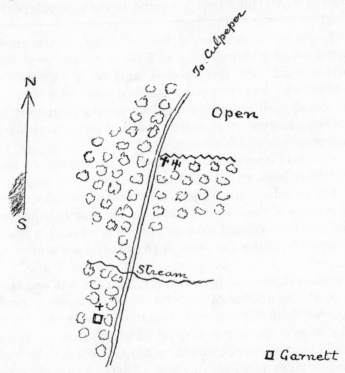

no reply, he added, "one out of ten?" (or perhaps one out of twenty.) "Not more than that," answered the surgeon gravely. "Well," said he cheerfully, "I am going to hold on to my one chance"—which the doctor had not promised him. When the wound was sewed he aided with his own hands in bringing the sides together. Most reluctantly, I left him at 10 or 11 o'clock, expecting never to see him again. Before I went he drew off and gave me his seal ring, to be given to his wife in case of a fatal result.[6]

I overtook the ambulance at no great distance, the road being much blocked by the army wagons which were coming up. From the front there had been the sound of cannon until long after nightfall. About midnight we met a body of cavalry just as it was coming into the road on a side road from the east, and I feared it might be the enemy riding in as on the night before and wondered if they would respect my sad errand and let me go on. But on parleying with the leader, I recognized the features of General J. E. B. Stuart, of the cavalry, just coming up from Richmond, who listened with interest to my account of the battle, so far as I knew about it. Captain John F. O'Brien, assistant adjutant-general, had accompanied me with the ambulance, and he now rode on ahead to make arrangements at Orange Court House, if possible, for the transportation of the General's body to Richmond. Day broke when I passed over the Rapidan at Barnett's Ford (Sunday, August 10), and I well remember the purple clouds above the rising sun and the oppressive heat even at that early hour.

Arriving at Orange Court House I found that Captain O'Brien had not been able to make any arrangements, and there being no connection, by rail or telegraph, with Gordonsville, the nearest point in communication with

[6] It was the worst wound I ever knew anyone to recover from, and I have always attributed his recovery largely to his remarkable coolness and indomitable will. I had the pleasure of restoring his ring some months afterwards. Some years after the war I asked him where *my* seal ring was, and he replied that he had lost it from his finger in a collision in the Patapsco River, when he nearly lost his life. He had to wear a silver plate over the place of the wound for the rest of his life.

Richmond, and the weather being extremely hot, I reluctantly submitted to the necessity of burying the General, temporarily at least, at this place. The Freemasons offered a lot in their part of the cemetery, situated on the Gordonsville road, half a mile south of the town. The place was full of officers, slightly wounded in the battle or going to the front, among the former Captain Joseph Carpenter[7] of Carpenter's Battery, and among the latter Colonel A. J. Grigsby of the 27th Virginia, both of the Stonewall Brigade, and most were around the tavern, and when I announced that the funeral was about to take place and invited all to join, a large number followed the coffin to the Episcopal Church, where there were many ladies and citizens of the town. Thence, after part of the burial service, a long line went to the grave, where at sunset was buried the best soldier under Lee and Jackson in the Army of Northern Virginia.[8]

[7] But Captain Carpenter's wound, in the head, thought not to be serious, unexpectedly resulted in his death.

[8] General Jackson's tribute to General Winder in his official report of the battle of Cedar Run was singularly appropriate and evidently written under sincere feeling, although eight months afterwards. He never wrote so about anyone else. It will be found in the *War of the Rebellion Records*, Series 1, volume XII, Part II, page 183: "It is difficult within the proper reserve of an official report to do justice to the merits of this accomplished officer. Urged by the medical director to take no part in the movements of the day because of the then enfeebled state of his health, his ardent patriotism and military pride could bear no such restraint. Richly endowed with those qualities of mind and person which fit an officer for command and which attract the admiration and excite the enthusiasm of troops, he was rapidly rising to the front rank of his profession. His loss has been severely felt."

In a letter to Mrs. Jackson, written two days after the battle, he says: "I can hardly think of the fall of Brigadier-General C. S. Winder without tearful eyes." *Memoirs of Stonewall Jackson*, by his widow, Mary. Anna Jackson, page 314. And I was told by one of his staff officers that some time afterwards upon some trying occasion on the march or in battle, he turned to him and said with feeling, "Now I miss Winder."

General Lee, in his official report of operations of that time *War of the Re-*

bellion Records, Series 1, volume XII, Part II, page 178, wrote: "I can add nothing to the well deserved tribute to the courage, capacity and conspicuous merit of this lamented officer by General Jackson, in whose brilliant campaign in the Valley and on the Chickahominy he bore a distinguished part."

Charles Sydney Winder, son of Captain Edward S. Winder of the United States Army, and Elizabeth Tayloe Lloyd, was born (probably in Talbot County, Maryland), on October 7, 1829. He entered West Point Military Academy 1 July, 1846, and was graduated 1 July, 1850, as brevet second-lieutenant of artillery. He was commissioned second lieutenant of the 3d Regiment of Artillery 21st July, 1851. In December, 1853, he was in charge of a party of men, with other troops, being transported from New York to the Pacific coast on the steamer *San Francisco* when that vessel was made a helpless wreck by a hurricane in the Gulf Stream. There were one or more rescues from the disabled steamer by other vessels, but he refused to leave his men. He was supposed to be lost for several weeks, but was taken, with his men, by a passing vessel to Liverpool. For his conduct he was promoted to be first lieutenant in the same regiment and on 3 March, 1855, was made captain in the 9th Infantry, being, I understood at the time, the youngest captain in the army. He was in Colonel Steptoe's disastrous campaign against the Walla Walla or Spokane Indians in Washington Territory in 1858 and in Colonel Wright's punitive expedition against the same Indians following it.

When the war broke out he was at home in Talbot County, Maryland, on leave and resigned from the army 1st April, 1861, and went to Montgomery, Alabama, then the Confederate capital, and entered the service of the Confederacy, being commissioned major of artillery in the regular army. He was present at the fall of Fort Sumpter, serving, I think, as military secretary to General Beauregard or some other general. He then ventured to return home for a brief visit, and on going back was made commandant of the South Carolina Arsenal. Early in July he was made colonel of the 6th South Carolina Regiment of Infantry and took his regiment to Virginia, arriving at Manassas on the evening of July 21st, just too late to take part in the battle. I think the occupation of Munson's or Hall's Hill in August, after a brief skirmish was made at his suggestion and was under his direction. His regiment was in the engagement at Drainesville, December 20, 1861, but Colonel Winder was not present with it, being on court martial duty. In March, 1862, he was made brigadier-general, and his subsequent career I have narrated. Had he lived he would have risen to high rank and had a distinguished career.

His widow and two sons are now living in Baltimore.

CHAPTER XIX

Orange County and the Valley

At the conclusion of the burial service, being now without rank or place in the army—for my commission as first lieutenant and aide de camp was vacated by the death of General Winder—I mounted my horse and rode over to our kind friends the Terrells whom we had left the two eventful days before. It was ten miles to the west and night soon overtook me on the way. By mistake, I turned off the Orange and Liberty Mill Plank Road too soon, just beyond Montpelier,[1] and wandered about for some hours in the hilly and wooded country back of that place, so that it was late in the night before I found myself at Terrell's house. Not wishing to rouse the family at such an hour, I turned my horse loose in the yard and crept into the covered back porch until morning, but although exhausted in body, my mental disturbance was such that I found little sleep or rest.

Here I remained for some time, considering how next to enter the service, although my kind friends urged me to stay out of it and make my home with them until the war was over. Communication with Richmond was still irregular and it was not until too late to attend that I learned from a newspaper that General Winder's body had been disinterred and was about to have a soldier's funeral there.[2]

[1] The home of President James Madison, who is buried there.

[2] He had a public military funeral and was interred in the beautiful Hollywood Cemetery, in the vault of a Mr. Davis. But in the Fall of 1865 I went to

In two or three days the Division came back from Cedar Run to its old camping ground. The Stonewall Brigade was now under Colonel William S. H. Baylor, of the 5th Virginia Regiment, who, it was expected, would be promoted to be its permanent commander. And he cordially invited me (out of respect for General Winder,) to go with him as aide de camp, but having another plan then in view, I declined.[3] The 1st Maryland Infantry had just been disbanded on the expiration of its term of service—or the term of most of the companies—and I contemplated raising a company from among the old members and men who were continually coming over from Maryland. With that object, I wrote to Richmond and received from friends there assurances of success, and I also visited Charlottesville and Staunton, going so far, I think, as to post hand bills in those two places. But after the exciting news of the Second Manassas battles, rumors came of the army having crossed the Potomac into Maryland, and when at Gordonsville one day a gentleman exhibited a flower which he said he had plucked on Maryland soil, I could stand it no longer and determined to abandon my plans in the rear and seek what service I could find at the front. I waited a few days to have the company of Surgeon David Watson of the Greenspring district in Louisa

Richmond and brought the body to Baltimore and thence to Talbot County where he was finally buried in the old Lloyd graveyard at Wye House. The grave of Admiral Franklin Buchanan—his uncle by marriage—is in the same burying ground.

Mr. Davis—a Northern man by birth—charged upwards of a hundred dollars for the occupation of the vault, which was paid by the General's family through me, at which, the Reverend Mr. Peterkin told me, Richmond people were very indignant.

[3] He gratified me by saying that the appointment would be acceptable to the Brigade (on General Winder's account, of course). Colonel Baylor was killed 30th August, in the Second Manassas battles.

County, and as soon as he came up to the house of
his brother-in-law, B. Johnson Barbour, of "Barboursville," a fine estate two miles from Terrell's, we started
off; it was about the middle of September.   We went by
the way of Madison Court House, Luray and Front-
Royal, nearly a hundred miles to Winchester, where we
arrived on the third day.

We found the army had just returned from its brief
Maryland campaign and was resting between Winchester
and the Potomac.   Brigadier-General George H. Steuart,
who was still partially disabled by a broken collar bone
at the battle of Cross Keys on June 8, was commanding
Winchester as a post, and being throughout the war a
constant and kind friend to me, and most of his staff
being old comrades, I accepted an invitation to join them,
for the present at least.   Captain George Williamson
was his adjutant-general and Lieutenant Randolph H.
McKim his aide de camp, both of my old mess in Murray's company of the 1st Maryland.   Major George H.
Kyle, also of Baltimore, was his commissary and quartermaster.   Mr. Brooke, a gentleman of Prince George's
County, Maryland, was also with him and acting as
provost marshal, and Dr. John Boyle of the same
county was a guest but giving medical services to all
Marylanders in his way.   We rented—or occupied, I
suppose the quartermaster paid rent—the small house of
a union man named Doyle or Dooley, on the street back
of the Taylor Hotel.

General Steuart soon announced me as ordnance officer
of the Maryland Line, then organizing under his command, and composed of the new 1st Maryland Infantry
(which soon changed its name to the 2d Maryland, to
distinguish it from the disbanded 1st), the 1st Maryland
Cavalry and the Baltimore Light Artillery.   It had been

published in General Orders that ordnance officers were to be appointed throughout the army after passing special examinations, but he was confident of having this requirement dispensed with in my case and discouraged my suggestions that I ought to apply for such examination.[4]

There being little to do in the way of ordnance duties, my time was fully occupied with general staff business. In particular, all soldiers leaving the army, on sick furlough or otherwise, were required to have their papers examined at our headquarters and a room—in another part of the town—was generally well filled with them, waiting their turn. Smallpox was very prevalent at this time and we were conscious of being brought into daily contact with infected papers and persons. One or more large smallpox hospitals were established in the town, around which a cordon of sentinels was maintained. Of these risks, however, we took little heed.

I became well acquainted with many of the people of this tried and true community, who were especially kind and hospitable to Marylanders. But of the house of my cousins, the Masons, where I had been welcomed in the first part of the war, literally one stone did not now stand upon another, and even the garden and grounds were but a barren waste. Mr. James M. Mason was Confederate Commissioner to England and his family were refugees in Richmond.

---

[4] I find in the *War of the Rebellion Records*, Series 1, Volume XIX, Part II, page 664, a letter from General Steuart to the Secretary of War, dated Winchester 13th October, 1862, in which he says: "I hope you received my letter . . . . also one requesting the appointment of McHenry Howard as ordnance officer on my staff, he being an officer of merit and aide de camp to the late Brigadier-General C. S. Winder." I served as ordnance officer until I left the Valley about 1st January, 1863, but the appointment was not made. However, Colonel Gorgas, chief of the Ordnance Bureau, himself certified to my pay account when I went to Richmond.

Some time in October or November a Virginia officer who had served on Jackson's staff—as he did afterwards—but who at this particular time, as I understood, had gone back to his company, of which he was a lieutenant, in the 2d Virginia Regiment in the Stonewall Brigade, went out of his way to write a long letter to General Stonewall Jackson, in which he said that the Maryland men who composed the post troops at Winchester were misconducting themselves and were obnoxious to the people of the town.   General Jackson referred the letter to General Steuart.   I took it and showed it to Mr. Robert M. Conrad, Mr. Joseph Sherrard and probably to other leading citizens, who said the statements in the letter were not true and expressed much indignation that any one should have undertaken to misrepresent the people of the town.   I believe the matter so rested.[5]

Officers going back from the army occasionally spent a day or night with us at the Dooley house.   I have a lively recollection of General Longstreet staying one night—but not lively on his part, for I do not think he spoke much more than a dozen words while with us.

Colonel Andrew Jackson Grigsby, of the 27th Virginia in the Stonewall Brigade, also came.   He had just resigned from the service because, although the senior officer, he was not promoted to the command of the brigade after the death at Second Manassas of Colonel Baylor, then about to be promoted.   Colonel Grigsby was filled with resentment against Jackson and told me that for the good of the service he would do nothing

[5] This officer was a very capable and gallant one, but certainly with a share of vanity.   During the war his associations were with Virginians and he had little partiality for Marylanders.   He was from Shepherdstown, Virginia, but after the war settled in Hagerstown and became very well known in Maryland, and I think most people would be surprised to learn that he was not a native born of the State.

while the war lasted, but that as soon as it ended he would certainly challenge Jackson.

Some thought Jackson did not promote him because he was given to swearing. But Stonewall appreciated a good soldier although a swearer. His own quartermaster had the reputation of being the hardest swearer in the army and soldiers used to say he could start a mule train a mile long by his strong language at the back end.

A curious question came up at this time about the title to my horse, which, it will be remembered, had been captured with General Reynolds at the battle of Gaines's Mill on June 27 and was turned over to me by the quartermaster in the place of my own which he had mixed with the government horses. One day my servant, Washington, came to our headquarters and reported that a Confederate officer, a surgeon, claimed the mare as his and would have taken her then and there, but Washington, of course, would not allow him. He asked Washington if she did not refuse to drink any but the purest water, which was true, for she gave me a good deal of trouble by that fastidiousness. His story was that the mare had escaped from him in the falling back from Manassas in the Spring. I did not doubt his story but maintained that when she ran into the enemy's lines, she became captured property and his ownership ceased and did not revive when she became captured Confederate property at the battle of Gaines's Mill. The question was carried up to Colonel Corley, chief quartermaster of the army, whose decision—backed by the opinion of Colonel Charles Marshall, General Lee's military secretary, and a lawyer—was in my favor. But the plaintiff, or my rival for the mare's affections, was a South Carolinian of Scotch-Irish descent, an obstinate race, and he insisted on appealing the case to Richmond; but I heard nothing more of it.   I had told the Surgeon that I would yield the mare to his prior claim if the quartermaster would furnish me another as good.

About the middle of November I heard through a man who came across the lines that one of my two younger sisters had died but was left for some time in a state of uncertainty which one it was.[6]

The last of the month General Jackson's Corps left the Valley, the rest of the army having preceded it, and we were left in occupation, with the Maryland Line and Brigadier-General William E. Jones's Cavalry command now composing the forces of the "Valley District." Winchester was now an outpost and in danger of an advance by the enemy from Harper's Ferry or Martinsburg or from Romney or Moorfield, and if from the last named place, it would probably be a movement on Strasburg, eighteen miles in our rear and so cutting us off. We were, therefore, on the alert, or at least in readiness to move at any time, trusting to Jones's cavalry for warning. I remember an alarm that the enemy were approaching on the Berryville road, but this being from the front, we went out to fight, and I remember also the fine appearance which the Marylanders made in marching out from the town, drums beating and the ladies and citizens crowding the street to encourage us, in confident expectation of a conflict.   But after waiting for some hours several miles out on the Berryville road, no enemy came and before night we returned to quarters.

In the last part of the month General Steuart, whose

[6] Elizabeth Gray Howard died on 14th November, 1862.   Her father who had been a "Prisoner of State" for nearly a year and a half, was permitted to come out of Fort Warren on parole and be at her death bed.

broken collar bone had never satisfactorily knit since the battle of Cross Keys, found it necessary to leave the field and General Jones succeeded to the command. He had thus a double set of staff officers, his regular cavalry staff and that of the Maryland Line—Captain Williamson, adjutant-general; Major Kyle; quartermaster and commissary, and myself as ordnance officer; but we were left very much to ourselves with the Line.

About the 1st of December the enemy was reported coming in strong force from Harper's Ferry and Berryville, and this time we were compelled to retire to, or near, Strasburg, but learning that they had gone back, we returned to Winchester the next day, or perhaps the day after.[7] We re-entered the town in a snow storm, and the Maryland Line Staff unceremoniously took possession of the Dooley house again.

But about a week later we were compelled, or thought it prudent, to leave Winchester again, I think because of apprehensions about our rear at Strasburg. We marched back to that place on the old Valley Pike, which had witnessed so many marches of both sides, and camped a little to the west of it—probably on the Wardensville or Moorfield road.

On a Saturday morning,[8] I think, Captain Frank P. Clark, a staff officer in Jones's command and a native of Winchester, and I thought we would like to ride to Winchester and spend Sunday, and I went to General Jones

[7] The diary of Spence M. Grayson, a private in Murray's Company of the 2d Maryland Infantry says: "1862 December 2. Left Winchester, marched eighteen miles to Strasburg vicinity and on the 3d returned to Winchester." But the Federal account in Volume XXI of the *Rebellion Record*, page 34, says they entered Winchester on 4th December and left it at 3 p.m.

[8] Although Grayson's diary says: "Dec. 19. Left Strasburg." This was Friday.

to ask permission. Just then a cavalry captain or lieutenant of his command came in to report a skirmish he had had with the enemy, advancing on the Wardensville or Moorefield road, and in which he had been worsted. When the officer described how his men had used their sabres in cutting in the hand to hand encounter Jones said in his peculiar drawling voice, "You ought to have stuck them, Captain." Like General Andrew Jackson who so doubled up his opponent with the end of a fence rail, Jones was a believer in thrusting with the sword rather than the downright blow. When I preferred my request, he simply answered, "You heard what was said, Captain." And presently he issued orders to move. We marched, or the Maryland Line at least, with which I had a wagon loaded with ordnance articles, a short distance east of Strasburg on the Front Royal road, and went into bivouac in a field, with a cold raw wind blowing. But it was early in the evening and Captain Clark and I determined to make our ride to Winchester, believing we could go and get back without being missed. Perhaps I quibbled on Jones's words, not being a direct refusal of my request.

So we recklessly rode to Winchester, which we found to be entirely outside our lines but not occupied by the enemy. We spent the next day, Sunday (or Saturday?) quietly, he with his family and I visiting friends, and in the evening I escorted one of Winchester's fairest daughters, (Miss Sallie Conrad) to the service, held at the McGill house, the Episcopal Church being closed. We saw no other Confederates in the town. Next morning we started to return. We heard some disquieting rumors before getting out of the place and soon met on the Turnpike road people straggling in who reported the enemy were between us and Strasburg. We proceeded, however, as far as Newtown—six miles—when we were convinced we might be captured at any time if we went on further. We therefore turned off from the Valley Pike to the east and rode straight across the country to Millwood, in Clarke County and near the Shenandoah River. Here, considering that we were reasonably out of immediate danger, we not only took dinner, but, I think, stopped for the night at the house of Dr. Benjamin Harrison, whose wife—a Miss Page—I believed to be one of my distant Virginia cousins. At any rate, Captain Clark knew them and they treated us hospitably. Next morning we crossed the Shenandoah (where we forded it going to Manassas in July, 1861) and turned to the south on a road going up the river to Front Royal. We were in much doubt whether we would not find that place in possession of the enemy, in which case, if we did not run into a capture, we would have to cross the Blue Ridge, and so we were on the alert and made cautious enquiries as we proceeded. But we found no enemy there and passed this last danger point and continued up the East side of the river twenty-two miles further to Luray. We must have stopped somewhere on the road one night. Relieved of fear of capture, we now speculated whether our prolonged absence had come to the knowledge of General Jones and what punishment or rebuke would be meted out for our escapade. At Luray we turned West on the Newmarket Road, and I think it was Christmas Eve when we crossed the Massanutton Mountain at this picturesque gap, the only road crossing in the fifty mile stretch of this lofty range, for I remember seeing, while climbing over the mountain pass, Captain Emack of the Maryland cavalry with a Christmas turkey hanging to his saddle. He told us where the command was in camp near Newmarket. On reaching it we were not solicitous of attracting attention to our arrival. But nothing was ever said about it by General Jones, and I don't believe he knew of our absence.[9]

[9] Captain Frank Peyton Clark removed to Baltimore after the war and went into business as an Insurance Adjuster. But at the same time he completed his law studies and soon gave himself entirely to the practice of the law, making a specialty of corporation business. He died in Baltimore 13th January, 1912.

General William E. Jones, of Washington County, Va. was an old U. S. Army Officer but had resigned in 1858. He promptly entered the Confederate service as Captain of Cavalry and became Colonel and Brigadier, distinguishing himself on many occasions. Unfortunately, he had a lasting quarrel with Gen. J. E. B. Stuart. He was killed in battle 5th June, 1864 at Piedmont, or New Hope, Augusta County.

CHAPTER XX

The Valley to Richmond and Jackson's Headquarters

I was at this time in an unsatisfactory state of health, suffering from something like scurvy or an impure condition of the blood, and partly for this reason and partly because of my unsettled military status, filling a position and yet not having received a commission for it—which seemed uncertain now on account of General Steuart's absence—I determined to leave the Valley and go to Richmond. I would have, too, the companionship of my old comrade in Murray's company, T. Harry Oliver, whose health did not permit his going into service and who, after a visit to us, was now about to leave. And I think it was on the last day of December (1862) that Harry Oliver and I left the camp near Newmarket and rode eastwardly on the road by which I had come a few days before over the Massanutton Mountain. I have before described this picturesque and lofty range, which bisects the great Valley of Virginia for 50 miles, and having an elevation in all its extent of between 2000 and 3000 feet. Some one has justly called it the glory of the Valley. But aside from its beauty as a physical feature, it played a most important part in Stonewall Jackson's operations, shielding his flank when on the defensive and both protecting and concealing his offensive movements.

The road which we took—the only one which crosses the range—goes up a small stream issuing out of the gap and then mounts to the summit by a winding or zigzag course and descends similarly on the eastern side. The scenery is beautiful and wild, the beds of streams, and often the roadside, rocky—grey in color—and the whole mountain wooded. This gap was sometimes called Fisher's Gap, but I was never satisfied that was its right name; being the only pass in the range it was not necessary to distinguish it by a name as with the Blue Ridge gaps, and we usually called it simply the Massanutton or Newmarket Gap. We passed out of the eastern mouth of this gap and presently came to the south or main fork of the Shenandoah River. But instead of fording it and keeping straight on to Luray, we turned south to the old Columbia bridge place, about six miles up. Whether we forded here or still higher up (all the bridges had been destroyed in Jackson's Valley campaign), I do not remember, but evening found us on the east side of the Luray Valley and close to the entrance of Milam's Gap of the Blue Ridge and we stopped for the night at a small tavern by the roadside, kept by a man named Newman. And among the distinct war time pictures in my mind is one of the Blue Ridge here, rising to a great elevation just in front, all wooded and dark, but with the deep blue tinge which gives this range its name, the hollows and prominences distinctly shown in the shading evening light.

Next morning we soon began to climb. This gap or pass is the highest of all in the Blue Ridge.[1] We were told that it was fourteen miles across by the road, which zigzags much more than any of the other roads, but several miles shorter to a horseman or pedestrian by taking paths from loop to loop. But these short cuts were so

[1] The government maps give an elevation of 3000 feet to the top of the road crossing against 2500 for Swift Run Gap which is fifteen miles to the southwest, and the same for Brown's Gap, twelve miles further. "Hawksbill Mountain" two miles north of the gap is 4066 feet high. Milam's Gap is sometimes called Fisher's Gap on the war maps. I do not recall that the army ever used it.

steep that we tried few, if any, of them. In descending, a raven (not a crow, but much larger,) flew into a tree about thirty yards behind me and began making its discordant noises. Turning in my saddle, I fired a shot at it with my pistol and, to my surprise and half regret, it fell dead, being struck in the head. I picked it up and carried it at my saddle nearly all day, but people stared so, perhaps wondering if soldiers were reduced to such rations, that I finally threw it away. It had beautiful glossy black plumage and a head nearly as large as a cat's. At the eastern foot of the descent the principal head stream of Robinson's River, a branch of the Rapidan, pours out, with the road, from something of a gorge dark and gloomy with arbor vitae or other fir trees, and the stream bed, much too wide for its ordinary volume of water, is filled with small boulder stones—like a street bed torn up. I augured the flood which must sometimes pour down, and when we presently came to the little hamlet of Criglersville, almost on a continuation of these rolled down stones, I thought it insecurely located.[2] I suppose we rode through Madison Court House about midday and after several hours more crossed the Rapidan at either Liberty Mill or Barboursville, and three or four miles further brought us to Terrell's, whence I had set out for the army in September before. We had made a pretty long day's ride. The next morning, while we were engaged in the very short and simple operation of Confederate dressing, Harrison,[3] or his son Robert,

[2] I read in the newspaper some years ago of its being swept away by a flood.

[3] Harrison Terrell was the valet of General Grant who was interviewed so much by reporters in the General's last illness. He died in Washington some years ago. He was an excellent man, as a slave and as a freedman. His son Robert, who was four or five years old in 1863, went to Harvard when he grew up and graduated high in his class. In 1893 when my son, Charles McHenry Howard, upon graduating at the law school in Baltimore, was, by the Judge of

brought to our room a two storey tumbler of mint julep. This is another war time moving picture fixed in my mind.

Harry Oliver and I did not stay here many days and, leaving our horses, we took the cars at Gordonsville for Richmond. Here I stayed with my brother, Lieutenant-Colonel James Howard, commanding the 18th and 20th Virginia battalions of Heavy Artillery, holding a part of the inner line of Richmond defences, with headquarters in the house of Mrs. Chevallie, opposite the Old Fair Ground or Camp of Instruction, where Murray's company was quartered at its organization—a mile north west of Richmond.

I now determined to make application for a lieutenancy in the regular army of the Confederate States, and I went to the army at Fredericksburg to ask General Jackson for a letter in aid of it. I took the train from Richmond and got off at some point—my impression has been that it was at Milford and that I rode over in a stage coach from that station two miles to Bowling Green, the court house town of Caroline County; but perhaps I had gone on to Guiney Station. But whether from Bowling Green or Guiney, I think I found a place in an ambulance or other vehicle which was going over to Moss Neck on the Rappahannock River nine miles below Fredericksburg, where General Jackson's headquarters then were. The Moss Neck house was a large one with a long front, like many Colonial or old houses in Virginia and Maryland, and all the surroundings gave evidence of the wealth and social position of the family—the Corbins. I was

the Superior Court, admitted to practice, I read in next morning's newspaper the name of Robert Terrell as one of a party who came over from Washington to be admitted at the same time. He is now (1913), I believe, at or near the head of one of the legal departments in Washington.

told that Jackson would not accept a room in the house, but established his headquarters in the southwest corner of the front yard. Here, at any rate, was a large tent, used for meals, and in which slept Dr. Hunter McGuire, medical director or chief surgeon of the corps, and perhaps other staff officers.

Towards evening three general officers came in—one, I think, was Major-General Jubal Early, another, Major-General Rodes, the third I do not recall—and they were asked to stay to dinner. A turkey—I think it was —was placed on the table in the large tent in which we were, and at this moment General Jackson went out for some purpose, possibly to say a long grace all by himself. Dr. McGuire, who had been lying down on his pallet along one side of the tent, sprang to his feet, with a suddenness which almost startled me, "Gentlemen," said he, "wouldn't you like to have a drink before dinner?" The general officers made no reply, but looked one. McGuire reached down and pulled out a canteen from under his bed and thrust it into the hands of one of the major-generals, saying, "Drink quick, the General will be back in a moment," and these three generals, high in rank, and I—longo intervallo—drank hurriedly, like schoolboys doing something wrong on the sly. McGuire hastily shoved the canteen back and we all straightened up just as Jackson reëntered, whereupon we sat down to dinner. If Stonewall smelled anything he made no sign.

The next morning "Sandy" (Alexander S.) Pendleton, his adjutant-general, gave me the letter I had asked for. I have it now—a prized possession, although I know of course, that its recommendation is formal and that the giving of it was because of his esteem for General Winder. It is all in General Jackson's own handwriting, including the indorsement, and I give it exactly here especially because, being written on Confederate paper with Confederate ink, it is becoming less distinct and moreover the margin was once slightly damaged by water trickling down the wall of my office on which it was hanging.

It will be noticed that Jackson's recommendation is for my appointment in the provisional army, that is, the temporary army organized for service during the war only, whereas my intention was to apply for a position in the regular or standing army. Jackson probably misapprehended my purpose.

This was the last time I saw Stonewall Jackson until, on the 11th of May, I looked on his face as he lay in his coffin at the Governor's house in Richmond.

I returned to Richmond, probably on the day I received his letter, which was either the 16th or 17th of January. I then wrote to General Steuart and to General Trimble and they sent me the following letters of recommendation, General Steuart's being also endorsed by General Elzey:

Savannah, Feby. 7th, 1863.

THE HON. JAS. A. SEDDON, Secretary of War.

SIR:—I have the honor to recommend to you for an appointment in the military service of the Confederate States McHenry Howard of Maryland. He is well qualified for duty as an Assistant Adjutant-General, Ordnance Officer, or in t e line of the army. At the commencement of the war he came to Virginia, went into service immediately in Company H of the 1st Md. Regt. then forming, where he was at once appointed Sergeant. He served in the 1st Md. Regt. under my command for more than nine months, in the most soldier-like, faithful and exact manner, so much so that it was my intention of endeavouring to have him promoted at the first opportunity. In March 1862 he was selected as Aid-de-Camp by the late Brig. Genl. C. S. Winder and served as such until that gallant and highly accomplished Officer was killed at the battle of Cedar Run in August last. He was at the first battle of Manassas, in those of the Valley of Virginia under Genl. Jackson, and around Richmond under Genl. Lee, and various skirmishes with the enemy. At the death of Genl. Winder his appointment as Aid-de-Camp ceased, but he was informed he would receive another appointment in the Army. He, however, lost no time in endeavoring to do all in his power to facilitate the formation of the Maryland Battalion. About that time I recommended him for the appointment of ordnance officer on my staff, and afterwards addressed several communications to the War Dept. on the subject, but he was not appointed, as I had earnestly hoped he would have been. Whilst with Gen. Winder he acquired a thorough knowledge of the duties of an assistant adjutant and inspector general. When I was commanding at Winchester last fall he not only performed the duties of ordnance officer but occasionally the above mentioned in the most satisfactory manner. I cannot in fact speak of him in too high terms, and most earnestly recommend him to your favourable consideration.

I am sir with great respect,

Yr. obt. servant

GEO. H. STEUART,
Brig. Genl. P.A.C.S.

Richmond, Va., Feb. 28, 1863.

Mr. Howard served under my command in the 1st Md. Regt. I know him to be a good soldier, and worthy of the confidence and consideration of the Government, and therefore take great pleasure in recommending him for a position in the Army.

Very respectfully

ARNOLD ELZEY,
Maj. Genl.

General Trimble's letter is as follows:

Charlottesville, Jany. 24th, 63.

HONBLE. J. A. SEDDON, Sec. of War.

SIR:—I take the liberty of bringing to your notice McHenry Howard—son of Charles Howard of Balto. who with other citizens suffered a long incarceration in Fort La Fayette for the cause of the South. Young Howard entered the Army as a private in the Maryland Regt. and encountered all the hardships of the service unflinchingly for a year, when he was appointed by the late Genl. Winder his Aid-de-Camp. After the death of that gallant officer, Howard was made the acting Ordnance Officer in Genl. Steuart's Brigade, serving as such until a short time ago. In every position occupied by young Howard in the Army he has acquitted himself with conspicuous success and merit.

After near two years experience in the Army, he now asks for a commission in the Confederate service, and it appears to me that his personal worth and high moral character, as well as his father's sacrifices in the cause of liberty and Southern rights, recommend him to the favourable notice of the Dept.

I have the honour to be respectfully,

Your obt. Sevt.

I. R. TRIMBLE,
Brig. Genl.

On February 17, I filed at the War Department my application for appointment, which I see does not say in terms in the regular army, but it was so meant and was so understood:

Near Richmond, February 17th, 1863.

HON. JAMES A. SEDDON, Secretary of War.

SIR:—I have the honor respectfully to make application for a Commission in the Military Service of the Confederate States.

On the 1st day of June 1861 I left Baltimore and entered the Army as a sergeant in the 1st Maryland Regt. and continued in that capacity until appointed Aide-de-Camp to the late Brig. Genl. Chas. S. Winder. Owing to his death at the battle of Cedar Run in August last my Commission expired, and shortly after I was nominated by Brig. Genl. Geo. H. Steuart, com'd'g. Md. Line, for the position of Ordnance Officer on his Staff. I continued to perform such duty until the 1st of January last. The appointment, however, was not made.

I respectfully refer you to the accompanying letters of recommendation from Lieut. Genl. Jackson, Major Genl. Trimble and Brig. Genl. Steuart.

I am, sir, very respectfully,

Your obt. servt.

McHENRY HOWARD.

On this application appears the following endorsement:

McHENRY HOWARD
Richmond, Feby. 17/63.

Applies for *Commission* in *C. S. Army*. Entered 1st Md. Regt. as a private, was made 1st Sgt. of Compy. H, served more than 9 months in that position when he was appointed A.D.C. to Genl. *Chas. S. Winder* and served with him until his death at *Cedar Run*. He then served on Genl. Geo. Steuart's Staff as Ordnance Officer. Is the son of Chas. Howard of Baltimore who was incarcerated in Fort La Fayette. Recommended by Lt. Genl. Jackson, Genl. Trimble and Genl. Geo. Steuart.

Recd. Feby.   1863   File.

I may add that the way I come to have this application and the letters now is that General Trimble having been very soon after his letter made a major-general and thereupon having given me a position on his staff, I withdrew them from the war office. I must have appreciated the letters, especially Jackson's, even then—I value them infinitely more now. I make no excuse for giving Stonewall Jackson's letter here—a smaller circle for whom I write my story will care to have recorded in it the other kind and partial letters.

CHAPTER XXI

RICHMOND TO MONTGOMERY SULPHUR SPRINGS AND HALIFAX COUNTY

Several times in 1863 I essayed to keep a diary and I cannot do better than to reproduce the entries here, with some omissions and immaterial changes in phraseology and with comments. The first entry is dated 21st January when I was staying with my brother near Richmond, suffering from something like scurvy, on account of which I had left active service in the Valley and which seemed to be aggravated and to be running a rather severe course.

"Richmond, Jan. 21, 1863. A windy and rainy day—such a one as we used to dread on the coast before the War, but now we hail it as a friend. May it send some of Burnside's vessels to the bottom!

"31st. Opening of Charleston Harbor! Breaking up of the blockade! Heard of the sinking of some of the enemy's gunboats and scatteration of the rest with novel sensations. We have been looking to foreign nations to break the blockade when this demonstrates that we can do it ourselves. A city possessing the necessary materials for constructing gun boats can always build them of sufficient strength to keep its harbor open.[1]

"Feb. 1st. Nothing but good news—that from the North showing the dissensions of our enemy most encour-

---

[1] This refers to an attack made on the blockading squadron on the morning of this day by Commodore Ingraham with two ironclad rams when several of the blockading vessels were injured and all were driven out of sight, so that the harbor remained open for several hours or half a day.

aging of all. May this diary of the latter part of the war be a brief one!

"February 2d. A mild, beautiful day, like Spring.

"February 3d. Ground covered with snow! One of the coldest days of the winter. Our poor soldiers!

"February 24th. A long interval, full of annoyances— snow, rain, interspersed with a few days of lovely weather. Confined to my room for almost three weeks with the most violent cold I ever had. Got some croton oil in my eye, which was consequently closed for three or four days." [The Doctor told me to rub my throat with it, which I did so plentifully, not knowing its potency, that some went up my cheek and into one eye. My brother came home in the evening and found me stumbling about the room and upsetting the chairs in the extreme pain it caused me. He went over to Camp Lee (as the Old Fair Ground or Camp of Instruction had now come to be called), and brought back Dr. John Boyle, of Maryland, who gave me a soothing lotion, but the eyeball felt as if it had a wound or scar for some time. Meanwhile my run down physical condition had not improve d. If I bent my arm the tightened skin would break in many places and sores also came on my body. For a week or two I had been living almost wholly on some arrow root which I got in Richmond and cooked with water, only sweetened with a little brown sugar.]

"Have been sick from exposure and coarse fare in the Valley for more than two months, so determined to visit the Montgomery Sulphur Springs for the water. Started from Richmond on February 21 at 5 p.m. Soon began to snow. Ran off the track at Farmville and delayed until middle of next day. Next, snowed up and train got no further than Appomattox that day. Spent the night there in the car. Next morning proceeded slowly and reached Lynchburg at 2 p.m. Had not eaten a mouthful except two or three apples since morning before.[2] Stopped at the Norvell House, where I now write, will lay over until tomorrow morning. Queer time to go to Springs, ground covered with snow!"

[When I left Richmond my brother gave me a letter to Captain Decie, an English or Irish gentleman who was staying at the Montgomery Springs in the summer of 1862 when he, my brother, was there with Major-General Gustavus W. Smith on whose staff he then was. General Smith's health had broken down after he succeeded General Joseph E. Johnston who was wounded on the first day of the battle of Seven Pines, and he went, with his personal staff, to these Springs to recuperate. Captain Decie was having his separate table at the Springs at which he hospitably entertained the General and staff, since when he had built himself a house. I now by accident found Captain Decie staying at the Norvell House and presented my letter of introducton. He told me that the Springs were closed and the buildings were used as a Confederate Hospital, but he added that I would, of course, go to his house, an invitation which he pressed and I accepted. But he requested me to wait two or three days before going, when I would find them ready to receive me there, although he would still be absent a few days].

"February 27th. Still at Lynchburg. Queer, outlandish old place—built on side of a hill, some of the streets so steep that I walked several squares before I would venture to descend to the parallel street below, the pavements being very slippery with snow. Not

[2] My experience on this trip will give an illustration of the condition of the Confederate railroad service and the inconveniences of travel. It is now about a four hours run from Richmond to Lynchburg.

nearly as pretty a place as Winchester and other Virginia towns. Altogether an unsightly place to my eyes. Paradise for small boys in winter time on account of facilities for sledding, but purgatory for everybody else. Glad to leave it tomorrow."

[My unfavorable impression of Lynchburg in my then condition of health and low spirits was much changed on my next visit.]

"March 1st. Left Lynchburg at 4 a.m. yesterday." [By the Virginia and Tennessee Railroad—now a part of the Norfolk and Western Railway system.] "Passed the Peaks of Otter at daylight. Arrived at Captain Decie's, near Montgomery Springs, at 12m. Met a most cordial reception. This morning walked over to the Springs, one and a half miles distant; am now sitting by the Spring imbibing sulphur water. Drank a bottle of claret yesterday with great satisfaction and almost forgot the war. Received also some gloves, socks, etc., from Baltimore with my initials in my dear mother's writing on a card attached to each one."

The Montgomery Sulphur Springs are in Montgomery County, Virginia, about eighty miles west from Lynchburg, in the Allegheny Mountains at an elevation of 2000 feet. The Hotel and Spring are a mile and a half north of the Railroad Station, with which it is or was connected by a tram road. But the Hotel had been closed and a Confederate Hospital was there. Captain Decie's house was on a high hill nearer to the station and east of the tram road. This house, a large two-story one with four large rooms on each floor, had just been finished before my arrival and a road to it from near the station and winding up the hill side had been graded, at the foot of which and alongside a large fish pond was being dug. All these improvements—the graded road was over half a mile long—must have cost a lot of money. Captain Decie had run the blockade into the Confederacy in his yacht, the famous *America*, which a few years before the war had made such a sensation by crossing the Atlantic from the United States and beating all the British vessels in a great boat race off the Isle of Wight. He brought his wife and children. I understood it was while attempting to run the blockade a second time and when he was not with it (being at these Springs, I think), that the *America* was captured on the southern coast and it was used by the blockading fleet.[3] His yacht library, of some eighty or one hundred volumes in pasteboard binding, with the bookcase and some other furniture, seemed to have been saved and gave me interesting reading. I understood that in connection with the running of the blockade he had rendered some services to the Confederate government, for which the authorities showed him attentions. Once when I remarked that I had made application for a commission in the regular army, "Yes," said he, "I was present when your application was laid before President Davis, and he said that no appointments in the regular army were being made." That was the reply made to me when I enquired about my application at the War Office. Noticing that in his small library there were several books about Garabaldi, I once spoke of it and Captain Decie said he was with him at Buenos Aires—or perhaps that he was at Buenos Aires when Garabaldi attempted to get up his revolution there; and he went into some details. I am not sure he did not add that he was with him, or knew him, in Italy. I also noticed an English yacht book in which Captain Decie's name appeared as a member of one of the leading

[3] After the war it was owned by General Ben Butler, of ill fame.

Clubs (the Royal Scotch?).   But he was a taciturn man and spoke very little about his own life.   While at the Springs Hotel the year before he had lost three children in quick succession by diphtheria, leaving only one or two, a calamity which had much impaired Mrs. Decie's health, so that I saw very little of her.   But she once pointed to one of several colored pictures of the Crimean war, I think the particular one was of the battle of Inkerman, and told me that her father was an English general and was killed there.   I have her visiting card, "Mrs. Decie, Phele House."   About Confederate money at least, Captain Decie was very careless.   A few days before I left he sold a number of sheep for $3500 in that currency and asked me to count the money, which I did and handed it back to him.   He rolled it up and tied a string around it and to my surprise tossed the bundle carelessly on the top of the low bookcase.   I said "Why, Captain, you were only the other day warning me not to leave anything valuable lying around as your Portuguese servant was not honest."   "Oh," said he, "a servant will never think of looking there."   When the furnishing of the Red Sulphur Springs—about forty miles across the country was sold out the year before, he had gone over and bought the entire stock of wine, which he was liberally dispensing when my brother was here. And now every day before dinner, at sunset, he would bring up from the cellar several bottles of claret which he expected me to consume before bedtime.   He was very abstemious himself and hardly tasted the claret even.

My health improved much and I would be most ungrateful if I did not always remember Captain Decie's kindness.

But to return to my diary.

"March 3d.   Am much better—attributable   to

change of climate and living. A cold, windy day. Snowflakes occasionally falling, although sky not covered with clouds.

"March 7th. Received yesterday a letter from General Trimble offering me position of A.D.C. on his Staff. Answered this morning accepting. Very pleasant position—puts me with several of my best friends on his Staff and at same time in my old Division where I have so many pleasant associations."

General Trimble's letter was as follows:

Hd. Qrs. Trimble's Div. Feby. 28th, 63.
My dear Sir:—I am able to offer you the position of Aid on my Staff, which I do with great pleasure and hope you may be able to accept it. Please write me on receipt of this.

Yours truly

I. R. TRIMBLE,

McHenry Howard.   Maj. Genl.

If you can procure the order from Adjt. Genl. do so and join me here.

My reply explained why I could not immediately join him:

Montgomery White Sulphur Springs, March 8, 1863.
GENERAL:—A copy of your letter was forwarded by my brother Jim and reached me yesterday. I accept your offer of the position of A.D.C. on your Staff with many thanks and much pleasure. It is a position singularly grateful to me, bringing into contact with yourself and so many of my friends on your Staff, and at the same time placing me again in that Division in which I have already seen so much service. Jim writes me word, however, that there seems to be some difficulty in the way as you have already nominated two Aides in Richmond. I presume this will be soon cleared up. I was quite sick in Richmond during the months of January and February, and the Doctor finally ordered me to this place to drink the Sulphur water. Under the influence of the water and a change of climate and manner of life, I am slowly but steadily getting well. I hope it will not be necessary for me to remain here more than a week or ten days longer. I am very desirous of joining you as soon as possible. . . . .

Hoping to be with you soon, I remain,

Very truly yours

McHENRY HOWARD.

Major General I. R. Trimble, Commanding Division, 2d Corps, Army No. Va.

My old messmate and friend, W. Duncan McKim, together with whom I had left Murray's company for Richmond on 26th March 1862, we receiving Staff appointments at the same time, I on Winder's and he on Trimble's, wrote to me at the same time, welcoming me to the staff.

General Trimble, on recovering from a bad wound in the leg received in the second Manassas battles, was in January 1863, nominated to be major-general and was confirmed April 23—by the Senate. Upon his nomination he was assigned by General Lee to the command of "Jackson's Old Division," sometimes called the "Stonewall Division," thus in fact succeeding Winder. The difficulty mentioned in my letter of his having already appointed two aids (a major-general was entitled to two,) was adjusted in some way; I think one of his nominees behaved badly in some manner before receiving his appointment and I was named in his stead. At any rate I received a certificate of appointment signed by Samuel W. Melton, assistant adjutant-general at Richmond, dated March 12, 1863, to rank from February 1, "subject to confirmation by the Senate at their present session," and I afterwards received a more formal notice of my appointment by the President, dated April 23 and signed by James A. Seddon, Secretary of War.

[But I go back to my diary at the Montgomery Springs —or Captain Decie's]

"March 11th 1863. Heavy fall of snow yesterday— today melting rapidly.

"12th. Snowed a little early this morning, but now sun shining brightly. A different sort of life from what I have been accustomed to the last two years. I do little but write and read novels and light literature all day. Shall I settle down into my old student life when this

HOWARD

LIEUTENANT MCHENRY HOWARD, C. S. A.
From ambrotype taken in Richmond, July, 1862

1A.

FATIGUE UNIFORM

MARYLAND GUARD HALF FATIGUE UNIFORM, 1861

MURRAY

Captain William H. Murray
Captain of Company H, 1st Maryland Infantry, C. S. A.
From ambrotype taken in Richmond, July, 1862

ASHBY

Brigadier-General Turner Ashby, C. S. A.

JACKSON

STONEWALL JACKSON
From etching of sketch from life by A. J. Volck of Baltimore

5A.

WINDER

Brigadier-General Charles S. Winder, C. S. A.

6A.

Head quarters 2d Corps A N Va
Jany 16th 1863

Hon Jas A Seddon
Secretary of War

Sir,

I respectfully recommend Mr McHenry Howard of Baltimore Md for a Lieutenancy in the Provisional Army of the Confederate States. Mr H. was for nearly twelve months a private in the 1st Maryland Regt. Subsequently he was aid de camp to Brig Genl Charles S. Winder. He continued to fill this post with marked ability until the death of Genl W at the Battle of Cedar Run. His patriotic course during the war, and the successful manner in which he has discharged his duties, entitles him to great praise and confidence.

I am Sir your Obdt servt
T J Jackson
Maj genl

JACKSON'S LETTER

PHOTOGRAPH OF JACKSON'S LETTER OF JANUARY 16, 1862

J. E. Johnston
M. Genl.

Hd. Qrs 2d Corps a.p. Va.
Jany 18th, 1863.

Recommending Mr
McHenry Howard
for a Lieutenancy
in the Engineers.

TRIMBLE

Major-General Isaac Ridgeway Trimble, C. S. A.

STEUART

BRIGADIER-GENERAL GEORGE HUME STEUART, C. S. A.

LEE

Major-General George Washington Custis Lee, C. S. A.

MONUMENT

12A.

unhappy war is over? I only know I am somewhat changed. Many of my most cherished opinions and modes of thought are altered, I now see that there are other ways of learning worldly wisdom than by books. I am uncertain whether the experience of the past two years has been more advantageous than hurtful.

"Sunday, 15th March. Very little difference between Sunday and any other day. Oh, for a quiet, peaceful Sabbath of the old time!

"March 17th. A warm most lovely day. A few more such and we shall hear of stirring news from the front.

"March 20th. A cheerless day—ground covered several inches with snow—or rather, hail. Began to rain day before yesterday evening. Yesterday morning changed to hail, which has continued at intervals ever since.

"March 23d. Continued hailing until the day before yesterday morning. Ground several inches deep with hail. Yesterday went to take the cars to go to Lynchburg but no train. Started again today. Came 10 or 12 miles when delayed by landslide and did not arrive in Lynchburg until night."

[The next entry in my diary is on June 26, but it goes back to the last above.]

"June 26th" [after some moralizing]. "Arriving in Lynchburg on March 23rd, I remained there several days with Davis Thomson.[4] Impressions of Lynchburg very different now. Received with great kindness by the G's and S's. I had a most agreeable time." [These were the Garland and Slaughter families, at whose houses, on Dr. Thomson's introduction, I spent agreeable evenings.]

[4] Surgeon Ignatius Davis Thomson, of Maryland, who had one of the Confederate military hospitals in Lynchburg.

Before I left Captain Decie's he had corresponded with Captain McCorkle, a leading business man of Lynchburg, and agreed to buy from him bonds of the Confederate States $15,000,000 Cotton Loan, as an investment of the $3500 sheep money. These bonds were considered a "gilt edge" investment, having as security the cotton bought up by the Government. I had brought with me Decie's cheque on a Blacksburg or Christiansburg Bank which I tendered to McCorkle. He wanted me to endorse it, but I said I did not like to put my name on any paper as if it lent value when my signature, as an exiled Marylander, was worth nothing. I suggested telegraphing to the bank, which he did, and the reply being satisfactory, he took the cheque and gave the bonds, which I sent to Decie. After spending several days in Lynchburg, my diary states briefly that I proceeded to Richmond and then after a few days went to Halifax County, on the North Carolina border, to see my sister-in-law, the wife of my brother Major Charles Howard, who was making a long stay with her friend Mrs. Nannie (Clark) Bruce at her place "Tarover," in a fine section of country near South Boston Depot, on the Richmond and Danville Railroad. This was a great contrast to the region in which I had been staying, being an old settled and well cultivated country, with many large plantations and fine houses. Near by was the imposing residence of Mr. James Bruce—"Berry Hill—one of the wealthiest men of Virginia, where, I was told, even some of the washbasins were of silver. Another neighbor, Mr. Claiborne, interested me (although he himself was absent in service) as being a direct descendant of William Claiborne who gave Maryland so much trouble at its settlement.

This was farther south than I had ever been before and I noticed some difference in trees and vegetation. There were also peculiarities of speech, particularly among the children and negroes, some of our usual compound words, for instance, being inverted—as peck o'wood for woodpecker. The Bruce and Howard children spoke of the "possum pan" in the kitchen, and we determined that it was, of course, the pan in which the the negroes cooked possums. But it further appeared that the pan was lined with porcelain, which they evidently corrupted to the familiar sounding name to them of "possum." I have no doubt many plausible and accepted derivations are as erroneous as our first assumption in this instance.

In this easy and luxurious life, remote from war's alarms, my health steadily improved, and I was the more willing to stay so long because General Trimble had been compelled to go away from the army on account of an attack of erysipelas—probably from his wounded leg.

My diary, still under date of June 16th, briefly says: "Remained" [at Tarover] "a month, when battles at Chancellorsville brought me to Richmond. Arrived too late to take part, so, after waiting several days to see if I could aid in removing Duncan's body and spending a week in Louisa[5] and Orange[6] Counties, my health not being completely re-established and General Trimble being still off duty sick, I determined to return to Halifax County for a week or two.

What havoc among my friends at Chancellorsville! Duncan McKim—there was no nobler man from our

[5] At Jerdone Castle, General Clayton G. Coleman's place, near Fredericks-hall.

[6] At Oliver H. P. Terrell's place, Glencoe, near Gordonsville.

State.[7] It may have been well for me that I was not in the fight, but it was a miserable feeling to think of my friends falling in discharge of their duty and I not there."

After a few more words my diary stops and is not resumed until the 28th of June. But I was in Richmond at the time of Stonewall Jackson's funeral services there, for I went to take a last look at him on the evening of May 11 when his body lay in the Governor's house, and next day I marched a part of the way in the funeral procession through the streets when his body was borne to the Capitol, claiming a place among the representatives of the Stonewall Brigade. And I think it was about May 15 when I returned to Halifax. The last of May or 1st of June I received a letter from General Trimble informing me that he was assigned to the command of the Valley District, with the Marylanders under him; that I was not to join him yet however, and would be put on the duty of going about in the army or elsewhere looking up Maryland men and facilitating their transfer to his command. And I think he added that he would send me further and specific instructions.

So I went to Richmond and waited for orders.

[7] Major William Duncan McKim, chief of staff of Trimble's Division, was killed on May 2 while riding with conspicuous gallantry along the front of the line. He was buried on the field but ten days afterwards his cousin Randolph H. McKim removed his body to Staunton. After the war his body was brought to Baltimore and finally interred in Greenmount Cemetery. .

Lieutenant Alfred Hoffman, of Baltimore, also of Trimble's staff, was twice wounded in the same battle, in the leg and foot. He was taken to Richmond, to the house of Mrs. Allan, Main and 4th (?) streets, where I saw him several times and did not suppose his wounds mortal, but after several weeks he died.

Charles Edward Grogan, of Baltimore, serving on the same staff as a volunteer, was wounded in the shoulder.

All these were serving as staff officers for Brigadier-General Raleigh T. Colston, commanding the division in General Trimble's absence.

CHAPTER XXII

RICHMOND TO MARYLAND AND PENNSYLVANIA
AND BACK TO THE POTOMAC

I do not remember hearing from General Trimble
again and I got very restive at reports of our army having
started from Fredericksburg towards Maryland once
more. I suppose the entry in my diary under June
16th was made in Richmond and that I left there immediately or soon after, going as far as Terrell's in Orange
County. But I heard such accounts of the army having
arrived in the lower valley and apparently aiming for
Maryland that I determined to wait no longer and to
put off after it, feeling sure that General Trimble would
go with it. I lingered still a day or two trying to find a
companion for the long ride of nearly a hundred miles, as
I had done the year before. Indeed the road over the
Blue Ridge was said to be not safe, from Confederate
deserters or skulkers in the mountains. But no companion turning up, I set out by myself on Sunday June 28.
And on the road I took up my diary again as follows:

"June 28th [1863]. Left Terrell's this morning at
9.30 a.m. Rainy weather, wind from the east, has been
so many days." [I had cut across the country about
three miles to Barboursville, where I had struck the
Turnpike Road from Gordonsville to Swift Run Gap and
on it had passed through Stannardsville, the county
town of Greene County, being about thirteen miles
further and three or four miles from the Gap entrance.]
"Rained but slightly until I entered Swift Run Gap
when a hard shower. Stood it for two or three mile

when compelled to take refuge in a barn. Refreshed both man and beast, the first with bread, chicken and strawberry wine, the second with a little corn, for all which thanks to forethought of Mr. and Mrs. Terrell. Am now sitting on a pile of straw in Swift Run Gap, with mountains all around. Today is Sunday. The rain shows no sign of ceasing and as I must get across the mountain before night I must start again. Sunday night. It rained all the way as I passed over the mountain and I, therefore, missed the beautiful view. However, I have seen this and others similar in the Blue Ridge before. Lost my road a mile or two. Have put up for the night at the most out of the world place imaginable, mountains all around. But my thoughts are over the hills and far away. Recognized every place this side of the Gap." [We had camped here in April, 1862]. "All reminded me of [General] C[harles] W[inder]. Yesterday was anniversary of the battle of Gaines's Mill.

"June 28th [this is an evident mistake for 30th]. Rode yesterday [i.e. June 29th] from Swift Run Gap through Luray, the county town of Page County, to within seventeen miles of Front Royal. Rain then became so heavy that, as night was not far off, concluded to stop. Both man and horse very tired. And so staid last night at the house of a Mrs. Keyser—a fine specimen of the Valley woman—a short distance east of the road. A young woman staying here whose husband was killed at Cedar Run three months after marriage. Came forty miles yesterday,[1] have to go thirty-six today to reach Winchester. Still raining. Must start again. Midday. Rained ever since I started. Have arrived at Front

---

[1] Hardly so far.

Royal [county seat of Warren County] and stopped to feed my horse. Mountain tops around are obscured by rain clouds and mist.

"July 3d. Arrived at Winchester about dark [i. e. on June 30th] and put up with the "Irish Battalion" in the fortifications.[2] Went to see my Winchester friends and concluded to lay by next day to dry after so many rainy days." [Unfortunately, or perhaps fortunately, this day's laying off, on July 1, made me miss at least the last day's battle at Gettysburg, although I was in time to be in a part of the side operations, as will be seen. But we knew little about the army and were not expecting it to have a battle just yet. I found that General Trimble had left his command of the Valley District and gone on with the army, and I determined, of course, to follow him.]

"July 1st. Spent the day at Winchester and started [on July 2] at about 11 a.m. Overtook at Bunker Hill William E. Colston [of Baltimore, who had been a comrade in Murray's company of the 1st Maryland and who was now riding on to the army as a volunteer, so went on together]. Arrived at Martinsburg that evening and took supper and put up my horse at the hotel—genuine coffee! Met Dr. Hunter and stayed with him that night. [July 3.] Left Martinsburg at 10 a.m. and arrived at Williamsport [on the Maryland side of the Potomac] at 2 p.m. Joined a body of cavalrymen and came one mile[4] when we stopped to feed, where I am now

[2] My old messmate in Murray's company, D. Giraud Wright, was a lieutenant in this command, the proper name of which was the "First Virginia Battalion of Regulars." The fortifications were on a hill on the north side of the town—having been constructed by the enemy.

[3] He afterwards joined Mosby's Partisan Rangers and was killed in an attack on Cole's cavalry camp near Harpers' Ferry on January 10, 1864.

[4] On the Williamsport and Chambersburg road.

writing. Road not safe to army and therefore glad of my company." [This body of cavalry was not a regular organization, but about thirty or forty loose men of different commands, mostly of McCausland's (?), returning to the army under charge of two officers—a captain and lieutenant—or both lieutenants].

"Exciting news from the army! Lee reported marching on Baltimore. Am on the soil of my State first time for twenty-five months.

"July 4. Rode on at dark yesterday for seven miles when we met a squad coming hastily back, reporting that they had been attacked and lost their wagon eight or nine miles ahead, so concluded to stop for the night." [In a stubble field, the wheat having been lately cut and in shocks. We fed the wheat to our horses and used sheaves for pillows, under the clear sky.] "Not an agreeable position. Started this morning" [July 4th— but I will amplify my diary a little.]

We had come to within a mile of Greencastle, in Pennsylvania, when we heard a shot in front and then met a cavalryman—an army mail carrier—galloping down the road, who reported that he had been attacked while passing through the town. We halted and our senior officer called for volunteers to form an advance party. Colston and I, a Marylander named Hack and I think another Marylander, with two or three others responded, and we went forward, the rest of the men following a hundred yards in rear. Our small party entered Greencastle, which seemed sullenly quiet, doors and windows closed and nobody on the street. We were approaching a point where the road or street appeared to branch like the letter Y, when we were suddenly fired on and cavalrymen came dashing down the forks. I heard windowpanes breaking around. We exchanged shots but our

little party soon fell back and the "Yankees" charged
after us. I stayed long enough to see forty or more and
others were still coming from the forks. We found our
main body had fled and we went on too, the enemy close
after us. So we ran for two miles. I tried to rein in my
mare several times—so much that the blanket fell out
from under the loosened saddle—but each time bullets
came pretty thick and I let her run again. But the road
was obscured by the cloud of dust we had kicked up and
the shooting was wild. The pressure behind presently
let up but it was impossible to stop the men, who kept on
at a rapid gait for another mile or two before we got into
some sort of order again, finding the enemy had discontinued the pursuit. Our two officers had disappeared,
probably mingling with the men, and abandoning the
command to me. We were going back more leisurely
when we came to a side road which came in from the
east and saw the fresh prints of horses' feet entering our
road. But I judged from the tracks that it was not a
large party and this was confirmed on questioning people
at houses that we passed. I therefore said to the men
that when we overtook them (they were going the same
way that we were—towards Williamsport) we must
immediately charge them and make our way through or
past, as our enemies in rear might come up at any moment. But most of them began to lag disgracefully behind
leaving only Colston, Hack and the other Marylander
and less than half a dozen more, to form the advance
or fighting party. We had not gone far (half an hour)
when on reaching the top of a rise in the road, we saw
them, not more than twelve or fifteen, just in front and
jogging along quietly, unconscious of our approach. We
immediately fired on and then charged them and after
returning a few shots, they broke and ran, soon turning

off the road, one after another and scampering across the fields.   Just before we charged, I had fired my pistol at a man who tumbled from his horse, but of course somebody else's bullet may have struck him.   Him we picked up and put on his horse and carried on with us, and also another whom we captured.   His wound was a furrow along the top of the head and I suppose was not a serious one.   Having thus scattered this scouting party, the main body of our men, who had been skulking behind, strung along the road, now closed up and we continued towards Williamsport.   We presently saw a solitary horseman on the brow of a rise in the road ahead who we were sure was a Confederate coming up from Williamsport, but he had heard the firing and distrusted our friendly signals and stood gazing at us until we approached when he wheeled and put spurs to his horse to the next rise, and so we chased him (if I remember right it turned out to be Major Page of the Artillery) in a ridiculous way from rise to rise, all the distance back to Williamsport—and also a squad which had gradually collected with him.   So much for my twenty hours in Maryland and Pennsylvania, and also for my only cavalry experience.   I had fired but the one shot, being busy with the men, and this one of the only two shots I fired during the war.[5]   I should add that in this little campaign we had three men captured—at Greencastle— and one wounded, who got off.   The two officers came to the front again when we neared Williamsport and resumed command.

[5] At the first battle of Manassas, being a sergeant, and therefore behind the ranks, I had stepped forward saying, "let a Sergeant take a shot," and fired my musket into the woods where the enemy were, or had just been, because I thought it might be the only battle of the war and I did not want it to end without my having fired a shot!

My diary says that having crossed the Potomac at Williamsport I was on the Virginia side at 2 p.m. (July 5) in a pouring rain and rode back 4 miles to spend the night at a house. (I think it probable that I went with Willie Colston to "Honeywood"—a Colston homestead.) I resume my diary:

"July 6th [Monday]. Yesterday morning came back to the river and found a large part of the wagon train of the army on the Maryland side, unable to cross the swollen water. It had been attacked on the road back and lost one or two hundred wagons. The army has had three days' fighting and from what I hear the enemy were not routed. Our loss heavy. Our Marylanders cut to pieces. Apprehended an attack all day—we are in a dangerous position [i.e., the wagon train]. Generals William E. Jones and Imboden command here. Served for a while on Jones's staff yesterday; he left in the evening. This morning [July 6th] no signs of river falling— hear that Lee captured 15,000 day before yesterday but that Longstreet was killed.

"July 7th. Yesterday while at dinner cannon and musketry opened on the hill above.[6] Rode up after dinner and found that the Yankees were making a brisk attack to capture our wagon train which now amounts to more than 1000 vehicles at this point. Teamsters and others armed and great confusion. We had over a dozen guns [cannon] and the firing continued until dark when the Yankees were driven back. Alarmed once or twice last night by severe picket firing. Dreamed that a great reward was offered me to leave the army. Glad to find that even in a dream had strength to refuse.

[6] Between the built up part of Williamsport, on the high ground, and the Potomac is a semicircle of low ground on which, particularly to the East, our wagon train was thickly crowded. Our line of skirmishers, teamsters and others, defended the brow of the high ground.

"July 8th. Heard yesterday morning that the road was open to Hagerstown and started to see how far I could get. Met Pickett's Division a mile from Williamsport and learned that the whole army was at Hagerstown. Pickett's Division cut up—looked like two or three regiments, and was guarding four or five thousand prisoners. Dead Yankees and horses all along the road from Williamsport to Hagerstown, even in the streets of Hagerstown.[7] Found our army [some distance north of Hagerstown] and put up for the evening and night with my brother, Surgeon Edward Lloyd Howard. Rained hard but slept with tolerable comfort under a blanket stretched on fence rails. Another great battle is expected near here. Will volunteer with General [George H.] Steuart. [I had learned that General Trimble, who had left his command of the Valley District and gone on with the army, had been severely wounded and left a prisoner at Gettysburg.][8]

"Evening [of July 8] Rode over this morning to General

[7] Stuart's cavalry had come on the rear of the cavalry force which was attacking our wagon train and scattered it.

[8] General Trimble went along with General Ewell without a command and at the successful close of the first day's action he urged Ewell to press on and occupy the Gettysburg heights (Cemetery Hill), offering to do so himself if a brigade were given him. General Ewell would not do so and, as I have heard, Trimble left him, in anger and disappointment. On July 3 General Lee placed him in command of two brigades—Lane's and Scales's—of Pender's Division who had been wounded, and he went forward in the charge, on Pickett's left and fell at or near the enemy's line with a wound in the same leg which had been struck at Second Manassas. He said to the surgeon that if he had then taken the leg off as he had told him he would not now have received this second wound. It was now amputated and he remained a prisoner until just before the close of the war, although General Lee, who had a high opinion of him, had tried to effect his exchange.

I held my rank and position as his aide-de-camp to the end of the war, while serving voluntarily with other generals, the theory being that an aide was liable to duty only with the general on whose personal staff he was.

George H. Steuart's headquarters,[9] where I met with a cordial reception from old friends—glad to find that all on his staff escaped [Captain George Williamson, Assistant Adjutant-General, first Lieutenant Randolph H. McKim, aide de camp, and Major George H. Kyle, commissary, all Marylanders]. Will probably stay with him as another fight is expected. Weather cleared off.

"July 9th. Nothing of special interest to record until night; an order has just come from Major-General Edward Johnson to hold the brigade in readiness to move at a moment's notice, as there is at least a division of the enemy at Waynesboro, Pennsylvania eight miles off, which will probably move on us at daylight. I am tired of war and long for peace, tired of it for myself, for our country and those families which lose such dear members in every battle.

"July 10th. Aroused at daylight but enemy did not come. About 11 a.m. received orders to be ready to move—enemy at Lighterstown [Leitersburg] a few miles off. We are now in readiness to move, but the little cannonading which was going on in the distance a while ago seems to have ceased.

"July 11th. Remained in readiness until near sunset yesterday when moved back two or three miles from Hagerstown [i. e. to two or 3 miles south of it, on the Williamsport road.] Not much demonstration in passing through Hagerstown. Yet it gave a peculiar sensation to march through a Maryland town. Oh, that it was Baltimore! Reached camp and had dinner or supper and went to sleep about 2 a.m. Midday. Reveille [this morning] at 4 a.m. and here we have been lying

[9] Steuart's Brigade, of Major-General Edward Johnson's Division, Ewell's (2d) Corps, was composed of the 10th, 23d and 37th Virginia, the 1st and 3d North Carolina State Troops and the 2d Maryland.

quietly ever since. I think, we are going to cross the Potomac. Alas for our hopes of redeeming our dear State. Sunset. At about 12 m. the whole army was placed in line of battle and erected breastworks[10] of fence rails, wheat straw and dirt.[11] Some cannonading from time to time at picket line, and for about ten minutes there has been sharp musketry firing with pickets on our right—going on now. July 12. Slept soundly. Yankee drums were distinctly heard a while ago and more recently cannon and musketry on picket line—battle imminent.

"July 13th. Picket firing all day yesterday—in afternoon spent more than an hour on the picket line— had a full view of half a mile of the enemy's line—moving down to our right—then drums beating and bands playing. This morning not much change. Passed half an hour at picket line—sharp firing and pickets on our right had been driven back a little. Enemy seem to be fortifying, and still moving to our right. Have the benefit of their music and drums. Vicksburg has fallen! It is very depressing. Midday. More quiet now. It is probable we will cross the river tonight. Feel very much depressed at the gloomy prospect for our State. I look around me constantly to see as much of it as I can before leaving it.

"July 15th. Moved at 10 o'clock night before last. It rained drearily and the march was a most tedious one. At daylight we reached the Potomac at Williamsport, a

[10] They were flimsy enough, the men having no implements.

[11] In the summer of 1906 or 1907 I got off the trolley car half way between Williamsport and Hagerstown to wait to take the train on the railroad from Hagerstown over to Martinsburg, which crosses the road and trolley line at this point, and recognized it at once as the place where the line of our brigade lay in line of battle in 1863—on the west side of the Hagerstown and Williamsport road—on the south side of some woods, with open country behind.

distance of only five miles. Forded the river, it being almost to the shoulders of the men—a picturesque but miserable scene."

[The place where the men waded over was just below the mouth of the Connococheague above the deeper water where the ferryboat crossed. This ferryboat had a wire cable overhead, stretching from bank to bank, on which ran two small wheels, and the stern of the flatboat being loosened so as to make the current strike the side obliquely like the wind on the sails of a vessel, the force of the current drove the boat over, like sailing on the wind. But of course a large body of troops could not be passed over in that slow way. The river had been very high, but had fallen just enough for the deep fording. It was not easy crossing on my horse.]

"And so we turned our backs on Maryland. We will in all probability never set foot on her soil again with arms in our hands. What a change in one month! Could not refrain from some bitter tears as I stood on the Virginia shore and looked back to our beloved State. Realize more than at any time before the probability of our being exiled from it forever. Last night the band played 'Sweet Home'—what a mockery to us [Marylanders]!"[12]

[12] My depression was not from any doubt of the final success of the Confederate cause, but, particularly, because of the failure of this Maryland campaign and the increased chance that the State might be ultimately lost to the Confederacy. I, and as far as my observation went the army generally, did not realize for a long time the full effect of Gettysburg. We looked on it as a drawn battle, in which the enemy made no counterstroke and after which our army remained on its ground for a day and more and then withdrew deliberately and without pursuit. And when Meade did come up after a week and confront us at Hagerstown, so far from attacking, he proceeded to entrench, and, as we now know, was supported by a full Council of War in his hesitation to attack. So far as I saw, our men were not disheartened and were as ready to fight as ever they were.

CHAPTER XXIII

Potomac River to Orange County

The next entry in my diary is under date of August 8 but it goes back to July 17. I think we bivouacked a few miles after crossing the Potomac on July 14 and resumed the march on the 15 and 16—perhaps resting on the 16th (1863).

"Marched the 17th [July], passed through Martinsburg and camped at Darkesville, the scene of our [i.e., General Steuart and two of his staff] first field experience two years ago.[1] Remained several days and then moved back to a mile northwest of Martinsburg to tear up Baltimore and Ohio Railroad track—a novel occupation. At night the light of the burning cross ties illuminated the heavens."

[The method was to detach the rails along one side of the track, then a line of men would lift up the ends of the ties on that side and overturn them—a long section at one time—to the other side. Then the detached cross ties were built up in square piles and the rails were balanced on top. When the piles were fired the intense heat caused the rails to bend in the middle and so become crooked and unserviceable.[2] Our bivouac at night was in the woods several hundred yards southwest of the railroad.]

July 21. Moved back to our camp at Darkesville.

[1] When General Joseph E. Johnston offered battle to General Patterson before marching to Manassas. It is on the Valley Pike, four miles south of Martinsburg.

[2] But we were told afterwards that Yankee ingenuity brought a machine through which the rails were rolled straight, and repaired the road in less time than it had taken us to destroy it. Later in the war the red hot softened rails were twisted around trees, which we learned from the ingenuity of our enemies.

Next morning marched to within three miles North of
Winchester. Sent out and gathered blackberries (first
mess of the season!) which, eaten with brown sugar is a
dish which a soldier only is epicure enough to appreciate.
At night went in and saw my Winchester friends.

Early next morning [July 23] marched through Winchester. Randolph McKim and I stayed in the town for
a few hours to take breakfast and bid farewell to all our
friends. Feel sad at leaving them again. They are
friends to Marylanders who will never forget them.
[McKim and I] Rode to Newtown [six miles south of
Winchester on the Valley Turnpike] and took dinner with
Mrs. Davis.[3] Saw Lyle Clarke on his way to Winchester.[4] [Left the Valley Pike and took the Front Royal
road and] Reached the brigade at sunset and found it
marching to Manassas Gap [in the Blue Ridge four
miles east of Front Royal], the Yankees having made an
attack on us there. Back to Front Royal at about 11
at night and went to sleep, while awaiting for orders,
under my horse's feet—moved a little off on waking some
time in the night and slept soundly. Started at sunrise

---

[3] Mrs. Davis, wife of Dr. ———— Davis, was a charming lady—and with a
charming daughter. She was most hospitable to all Confederate soldiers.

[4] Lieutenant Colonel J. Lyle Clarke, of Gloucester County, Virginia, was engaged in business in Baltimore when the war broke out and commanded the
"Independent Greys" Company there. He went early to Richmond and raised
a Maryland Infantry Company, as I have mentioned. But instead of going
with Dorsey's and Murray's to Winchester to assist in forming the 1st Maryland
Regiment, he took his Company to West Virginia in Colonel Gilham's 21st Virginia. Before the years term of service was out, he became commander of a
Virginia battalion of Sharp shooters. He was now on the way, with his command, from southwest Virginia to join Lee's army, with which he remained several months. Returning to service in southwest Virginia, he was again marching
to the Valley in 1864 or 1865, when one night, near Staunton, a dead branch
fell from a tree under which he was sleeping and crushed his leg so badly that
splinters of bone were coming out for years afterwards. At the close of the war
he came back to Baltimore, where he died many years ago. He had married
Miss Clark of Halifax County and left one daughter.

next morning [July 24] and marched to within four miles
of Luray. A warm, dusty and most tedious march—
also sleepy and tired. Started at usual hour next
morning [July 25] and reached a point three miles from
Luray—just where I camped fourteen months before
[where the Stonewall Brigade under General Winder
bivouacked on the night of May 22, 1862, the day before
the engagement at Front Royal]. Next day rested
[Sunday] and the next crosed the Blue Ridge at Thornton's Gap and camped at Sperryville—battle of the
rails! [This refers to an altercation I had with the men
about taking fence rails for fuel. General Lee's order
about burning rails or taking or injuring any private
property in Maryland and Pennsylvania and how the
order was obeyed are well known. On coming back
across the Potomac to Virginia we heard that some of the
men had said, "Thank God, we can now burn rails
again." Although forbidden in Virginia too, yet in fact
rails were taken, generally a few at a time. But now
when we bivoucked near Sperryville, it was in an open
green hollow, the grass fields extending, with much
fencing, up the hillsides, and the moment ranks were
broken the men went with a rush for the fences and each
one bore off a rail, pointing up to the sky. As assistant
inspector-general, for so General Steuart had announced
me, it was my duty to take particular notice of such
violation of orders and breach of discipline, and I rode
among the men peremptorily ordering them to take the
rails back, which they did, but with much grumbling and
show of angry dissatisfaction.]

"Marched next day [July 28] and camped in rain on
top of a high hill. Marched next day to Robinson River[5]

[5] One of the head streams of the Rapidan River. It rises in Milam's or
Fisher's Gap.

four miles from Madison Court House.[6] For two weeks we had been 'reveilléing' at daylight and this, with the hard marching, warm weather and rain, had been hard on officers and men. Next day [July 30] I rode ahead to Terrell's and stayed two nights and a day. Joined the brigade [August 1] on its coming up and going into camp at Montpelier."

The remaining few and (except for some moralizing) brief entries in my diary were made while in this camp and I will give them here, followed by some extracts from the diary of another, and will then write from recollection a more particular account of our life in this period of rest.

"August 9. Today is the anniversary of the battle of Cedar Run.

"August 14. Nothing of consequence since last entry. A letter this morning from my dear mother.

"August 15th. Most violent thunderstorm of the season yesterday evening.

"August 16th. Sunday. Assisted to inspect the brigade this morning which with other things, prevented my getting to church [service in camp]. Understand that Mr. Patterson [Chaplain of the 3d North Carolina], preached on the unruliness of the tongue, alluding to Christ's sighing when he cured the man who had an impediment in his speech. 'Set a guard over my lips'—'Let the words of my mouth be alway acceptable.' Rode over and dined yesterday at Terrell's.

"August 22nd. Yesterday was Fast Day. Mr. Patterson preached at our Headquarters. About a

---

[6] Many of these Virginia "Court Houses" are villages or towns of considerable size. Some of them have proper names which are seldom used and unknown to most. I think few Virginians would recognize Culpeper Court House as "Fairfax."

dozen ladies present, among them Mrs. [J. Lyle] C[larke], who came up [from Richmond] a few days ago. "August 28. Nothing new except that we are having some of the pomp and circumstance of war in the shape of reviews, brigade drills, etc. Weather getting decidedly cooler. "September 14th. Enemy reported to be advancing. We are now (the whole Division,) drawn out expecting to meet them.[7] "September 18th, 9 a.m. Raining like pitchforks— very disagreeable. Moved and seconded that somebody go and get something to eat. Regular equinoctial storm—have had nothing to eat for almost twenty-four hours. Every fire out. Kyle, Dr. Johnson, Williamson, Steuart and myself in tent together."[8]

And in this discomfort ends my diary.

Some of the foregoing entries after the army returned from Maryland having actually been made after intervals, I will here give abstracts from a diary kept by Mr. Spence M. Grayson, a private in Captain George Thomas's (formerly William H. Murray's) Company A of the 2d Maryland Battalion, in Steuart's Brigade:

1863 July 14. We made the Canal and Potomac at Wmsport and cross into Va.—up to our armpits. We camp 4½ miles from Falling Waters, having marched 9 miles.

15. March through Martinsburg, Va. and, taking the Winchester road, encamped near Darkesville. March 10 miles.

---

[7] This was the forward movement of the enemy, advancing his cavalry line of occupation from behind the Rappahannock River to the Rapidan.

[8] All of Maryland—Major George H. Kyle, of Baltimore, brigade commissary; Dr. Richard Potts Johnson, of Frederick, who had been surgeon of the 1st Maryland, I do not remember if he had any position here; Captain George Williamson, of Baltimore, assistant adjutant-general, and by "Steuart," I must have meant William Steuart of Baltimore, a younger brother of the General, if he had then come over from Maryland and was staying with his brother—as he certainly was a few months later.

16, 17, 18, 19. In camp at Darkesville.

20. Our Brigade moves a mile above Martinsburg and tear up B. & O. R. R. 8 mile march.

21. At work on the R. R. March at 3 p.m. back to Division.

22. March to Winchester, encamped near town at 2 p.m. 10 miles.

23. March from W to Front Royal 26 miles.

24. March from Front Royal on Luray road: encamp 13 miles from LR. . . . .

25. March 9 miles towards Luray. Halt at Springfield, Page Co.

27. March near Sperryville, 14 miles, over Thornton's Gap of Blue Ridge.

28. March through S. Take Madison C. H. Road—encamp on a hill—10 miles.

29. March from the hill—encamp at 2 p.m. $1\frac{1}{2}$ miles from Robinson River—about 6 miles.

30. In camp.

31. In camp till 7 p.m. when we march 3 miles beyond M.C.H.—encamp 12 midnight—7 miles march.

Aug. 1. March on the Orange Road 15 miles—3 miles from C.H. . . .

6. Move off the Orange Road—back a mile. . . . .

Sept. 5. Witnessed an execution this evening of 10 deserters from the 3d N.C. . . . .

9. Grand Review of our Corps (Ewells) by Gen. Lee 1 mile from Orange C. H.—about 5 from here.

14. . . . . Marched at daybreak 1 mile beyond Orange C. H.—remain in an open field all day and night.

15. At 3 p.m. we march back on the Madison C. H. road and cook rations.

16. Quiet in camp.

17, 18. In camp.

19. March at daybreak to near Morton's & Mitchell's Fords on the Rapidan—21 miles.

CHAPTER XXIV

CAMP ON POPLAR RUN AND MORTON'S FORD

This camp, in which Steuart's Brigade had its first long
rest since the beginning of the Gettysburg campaign,
from August 1 to September 19, deserves more notice
than has been given to it in my brief diary and that of
Mr. Grayson. It was situated between the road from
Liberty Mill to Orange Court House (on the south) and
the Rapidan River (on the north) and about three miles
westerly from the Court House. Montpelier, President
Madison's old home and a fine estate, was about a mile
to the south and sometimes gave its name to the camp,
but at our headquarters we called it "Camp on Poplar
Run," from a small tributary of the Rapidan, on or near
which, and near its mouth, our brigade was. As our
stay was prolonged, General Steuart got the ground in
better and better condition until it was made the best
ordered summer camp I ever saw in the army. It was in
woods, and from constant sweeping with brooms made of
twigs bundled together, I think several inches of the wood
mould surface were removed in the regimental grounds
until a hard dirt floor was gained. General Ewell, the
corps commander, gave it unstinted praise and often
brought over visiting ladies and others to see it. He
said he was coming to play marbles on the smooth, hard
floor. Most of the men's bunks or beds—I think every
one in Colonel E. T. H. Warren's 10th Virginia—were
raised above the ground and kept swept clean underneath. At headquarters we studied the sick reports and
found the ratio getting less and less—the 10th Virginia

having the smallest of all. We often heard of the camp
being spoken of as the model one of the army—General
Mahone's only being compared with it.

While here there was a very sad incident, alluded to in
Grayson's diary, and in which I had to take a painful
part. One day, I think the 4th of September, about
sundown, a party of 10 prisoners were brought, under
heavy guard from Richmond, to our headquarters. They
belonged to our 3d North Carolina Regiment and had
deserted, that is to say, had left to make their way back
to their homes. What made their case an unpardon-
able one was that they took their arms with them and
when intercepted in crossing James River, they had
resisted and shot the adjutant or officer commanding the
intercepting party. They had been tried by a court
martial in Richmond or somewhere and were now brought
back to receive their punishment—what it was to be
being as yet unknown. But about nine o'clock at night
came a special courier, bringing the bulky courtmartial
proceedings. I was then acting as assistant adjutant-
general in the temporary absence of Captain Williamson,
and opened and read the carefully sealed papers. Each
man was separately and successively named with the
charge—desertion—the specification giving particulars of the charge—the finding of the court, "Of the
specification, guilty; of the charge, guilty," and the
sentence, "To be shot to death by musketry at such time
as the commanding general shall appoint." And after
this ten times repeated finding and sentence was the
approval of the proceedings and order that the sentence
be carried out at 4 p.m. of the next day. With this came
a direction that the sentence should not be communicated to the prisoners until the morning of the day fixed
for the execution. I passed a wretched night, with

broken sleep and dreams that I had overslept myself and had waked to find the sun high in the heavens and that I was full of remorse at having lost the men so much of their scanty time for preparation. But although I had given the sentinel, who was always posted at head-quarters, instructions to wake me before daylight, I did not need him. I put on all my uniform, with sash and sword, and as soon as it was light enough to see to read, I went to the guard quarters and had the ten men brought out and stand in line before me and read to them all the court-martial record, with the final order that the sentence be carried into execution that day at 4 o'clock. I could not bear to look at them but I felt that no man stirred while I read. I was told that several of these men had been good soldiers and some had lately marched back from Gettysburg barefooted or nearly so. And, strangely, one of them, and said to be the ringleader, was named Barefoot. But such desertions—to the rear, not to the enemy—were increasing and it was necessary to make a stern example. And the crime of these men in going off armed, resisting and firing on the party sent to bring them back and killing the officer, was a heinous one. Before going to the guard house I had sent for the chaplain of the regiment, the Reverend George Patterson,[1] who went to the men as soon as I had finished reading and he stayed with them for the rest of their time.

---

[1] He was a native of Greece and his proper name was παφλιοθαργος, which he changed or anglicized to the nearest sounding name of Patterson. The 3d North Carolina of which he was Chaplain (Protestant Episcopalian), came largely from about Wilmington, and I heard of him there after the war. Indeed I saw him once in Baltimore. Afterwards I heard he had made a vow of poverty, even giving up his watch, and had gone to Texas and died there. With some eccentricities—perhaps it would be better to say with great simplicity of character—he was a good man and a most attentive and faithful Chaplain and I think the officers and men were much attached to him.

I think the whole division turned out at 4 o'clock to witness the execution and formed three sides of a square, facing inward. Along the fourth line was a row of ten low posts at which the condemned men knelt and to which they were bound, with bandaged eyes. There was a firing party opposite each man, half of the pieces having blank cartridges, as was customary. I will recall no further particulars. But the horrors of war should not be suppressed.[2]

My mind gladly turns to the recollection of an imposing review of the whole army by General Lee about this time, and I have a distinct mental picture of the noble figure of the General as in riding slowly down the line he passed a few paces in front of me as I sat on my horse in my proper staff place in front of the brigade and saluted with my sword.[3] The last time I had seen him so closely before was, I think, in June, 1861, when I was one of a "Committee" of three to wait on him and President Davis, to complain of the mustering in of Murray's company for the war instead of twelve months. He then had dark brown hair and moustache and no beard. Now he was grey and like the usual photographs which are so familiar.

General Steuart here practised brigade drills—a novelty I think at that time. I remember making a suggestion

[2] According to a diary quoted by Major W. W. Goldsborough in the first edition (1869) of his book "The Maryland Line C.S.A.," page 166, this execution was on September 6th, but Grayson's diary says the 5th, which I think is correct—being Friday.

[3] According to the same diary quoted from in Major Goldsborough's book, this review was on September 11th, but Spence M. Grayson's says the 9th. Perhaps it took three days. I told Chaplain Patterson, jokingly, that he would have to appear at this review and on horseback. Taking me in earnest, he said he would do so if it was his duty but must wear his surplice, as that was his uniform. I was a little alarmed lest he might so appear. A surplice on horseback would have been a strange spectacle.

that one company of each regiment should learn the artillery manual, so that captured guns might be turned on the enemy or a depleted battery be supplied; but I believe we broke camp before this was put into practice.

Lieutenant Randolph Harrison McKim, aide de camp, here left us, resigning to take a few months study before being ordained and re-entering the service as a chaplain.[4]

The last entry in my 1863 diary was made in this camp on Poplar Run on September 18 as before stated, and I think the explanation of its being interrupted on that date is that it was the next day that we broke camp and marched through Orange Court House to a position on the lower Rapidan below Morton's Ford. I remember a little incident of the march. We were going through some pine woods when a wild turkey was started up near me. These fowls do not take wing readily on level ground and this one went off running at a rapid gait. Animated by the hope of game for supper, I put spurs to my horse and chased it for a couple of hundred yards or more. It doubled several times but finally came to an old worm fence through which it stuck its head and foolishly tried to force its body between the rails. I started to dismount when the fluttering of the wings made my horse rear a little and I had to retain my seat. Just then a wretched soldier from the ranks ran by my horse's head and grabbed the prize. My memory is a photographic one, and I recall and see in my mind this chase, from start to finish, like a modern moving picture. Rations were scarce and uncertain at this time and my disappointment, for myself and the staff, was great.

Grayson's diary confirms the date of this day's move

[4] In 1911 he published a book *A Soldier's Recollections.*

and says that it was to near Morton's and Mitchell's[5] Fords on the Rapidan—twenty-one miles. During our stay of nearly three weeks here we guarded the river bank down to Sisson's Ford at the mouth of Mountain-Mine Run, and up to, or nearly, Morton's Ford. Our headquarters were at or near Gibson's house, about midway of the line and a hundred yards or so back from the high river bank. This residence had a noticeable appearance from about a dozen aspen trees in the front yard, with ghostly looking tall white trunks and the under sides of the leaves being also silvery white. The cultivated, or rather in those times of neglect the cleared farm, extended back from this high part of the river bank, from which our picket line looked down on the river at its foot and the low grounds on the other side, across which, at a considerable distance were the enemy's pickets. On these low grounds grazed a herd of cattle and some sheep, the owner of which had "refugeed" and was staying at Gibson's house. He told us that we might have some if we would get them across and save them from the enemy. General Steuart's staff determined to do so, and one night (Grayson's diary says it was September 23d), Captain Williamson, adjutant-general; Dr. Johnson, surgeon; Major Kyle, commissary, and myself, took about twenty-five men of the 23d Virginia and 2d Maryland and went over at Tobaccostick Ford— a horseback ford not far up the river from the house, guided by the cattle owner, a man with long grey hair

[5] I have never been able since the war to determine certainly what was meant by Mitchell's Ford, whether it was an unimportant crossing place below the well known Morton's Ford, or was another name for Sisson's Ford, lower down at the mouth of Mountain and Mine Runs (which unite in emptying into the Rapidan). The war maps are contradictory.

hanging down on his shoulders. To my relief and surprise, we did not encounter any pickets—which I had supposed would be advanced at night—and we brought back about forty of the cattle and sheep. Emboldened by this success, it was proposed to go back and attempt to capture a picket post. I was opposed to this as a foolish risk of life for no good purpose, and I thought the pickets must have been aroused, particularly by the splashing at the ford, across which the sheep had to be half carried by the men. But I suppose everybody was ashamed to back out when the suggestion was made. Our citizen, who was armed with a long old fashioned bell-mouthed gun, loaded with a handful of powder and shot, guided us safely a long distance back from the river and we then turned down. We were approaching a house in single file, keeping as close as we could out of the bright moonlight in the shadow of a fence, when a sentinel hailed us. We flattened ourselves to the ground, making no reply, and he fired on us, the bullet raising a little cloud of dust about three feet to my right—I was the third in line. Our citizen, who was leading, promptly returned the fire, making a bright glare and a thunderous report from his ancient piece which echoed from the wooded hills, and the sentinel cried "Murder" and made for the house, we in pursuit. Major Kyle jumped with hands and feet on the rails of the high fence around the yard and in his excitement called to the sentinel to "Stop a minute—stop a minute!" But he didn't. The reserve poured out of the house and after exchanging a few shots with them we deemed it prudent to retire. Our citizen, who knew every foot of the ground, guided us safely back to the ford by a different way. The next morning there was a body of cavalry patrolling the enemy's line, no doubt wondering what the commotion had been about. We had full rations of beef and mutton.

We remained here until early in October, when we set off in the Bristoe campaign. The weather was generally fine, the ground was very suitable for a half bivouac camp, with light duties, the constant sight of the enemy lending an interest, and I think we all enjoyed it.[6]

[6] Two or three years after the war I was staying in Orange County, at Oliver Terrell's and one day rode to the county town. In the Court House the county court was holding a session and on entering the crowded room I recognized Mr. Gibson, who had studied law after the war, in the middle of an argument, defending a negro for chicken stealing. But it seemed to me he was haranguing the crowd of spectators behind rather than addressing the judges and jury. The three Justices sat above a tribunal and the middle one I recognized as Colonel Scott, a leading man of the community. He was leaning back with his feet propped up on the tribunal and the most of him that could be seen was the soles of two boots, long and broad, for he was a tall man. Underneath the tribunal and with their backs to it sat the Jury, in a single line, the foreman in the centre. Presently I noticed the foreman, who had a long patriarchal grey beard, pull out a pipe and leisurely fill it. I supposed he thought the speech must soon be over and that he would be ready for a smoke. But he brought out an old time, big headed sulphur match, struck it on his foot and proceeded to calmly puff away, first the sulphur fumes and then the cloud of smoke rising like incense to the judges above. I thought he would be committed for contempt, or at least be rebuked, but nobody seemd to think there was any impropriety.

I remember hesitating at first in the war about smoking my pipe while reading the Bible but soon got over the feeling.

CHAPTER XXV

BRISTOE CAMPAIGN

I do not remember many of the details of this movement to get on Mead's right flank or rear and, if possible, bring him to battle in Culpeper or Fauquier County. It was somewhat like the flank march of the year before, but this time we did not keep so far to the west in the flanking or aim to get so far in the enemy's rear. And, alas, we had no Jackson to press the march, so that we only struck his rear guard—to our loss—at Bristoe Station, the main army having passed by and taken a strong position behind Bull Run, where it could not advantageously be attacked in front or be further flanked. But although no victory resulted, this aggressive movement, made only three months after Gettysburg, forced Meade back in hurried retreat over fifty miles, declining battle, and when the short campaign was over, we held for a month the advanced line of the Rappahannock, with the country behind us in which he had sat down to confront and threaten us.

I have a general impression on my mind of winding among hills or little mountains of Madison County, which adjoins Culpeper on the west, and avoiding passing across large open fields and over bare hill tops, lest the movement should be observed from the enemy's high signal stations.

For the daily marching I resort again to Mr. Grayson's diary:

[He notes on October 3, 1863, that little ginger cakes were 8 for $1, apples $1 a dozen, crackers $1 a dozen, smoking tobacco $1.50 a pound, chewing tobacco $2 a pound. He means when they could be had at all, for we had not regular army sutlers; occasionally a man would appear with a wagon containing no greater number of articles than enumerated above.]

October 8. March at about 3 p.m. from our camp on Rapidan 11 miles on Orange C. H. road and Camp at 10 p.m. . . .

9. March at 6 a.m. passing Orange C. H., fording Rapidan River and camping about 4 miles from Madison C.H.—a distance of about 21 or 22 miles. A hard day's march, over rough fields, through piney woods and vales and rocky hills. . . .

10. March at 6 a.m. passing through Madison C. H., fording the Robertson River, crossing over hard roads, flanking every prominent hill and field and camping about 8 p.m. in Culpeper Co.—a rough march, very circuitous and hard of about 15 to 18 miles. . . .

11. March at 8 a.m. through fields and country roads to Culpeper C. H. pike and march on, camping about 5½ miles from the C. H., a march so far of about 10 miles. . . . A battle imminent. . . . We intend probably to fight here should Meade not retreat to Centreville or Warrenton. . . . But we trust he will stand here . . . . We think now of the all absorbing question of Yankee haversacks full of rations and "fat" sutler stores. . . . .

12. March from C. C. H. pike at 6 a.m. fording the Hazel and crossing on a bridge the Rappahannock River into Fauquier Co. camping at night in an old Yankee camp at Warrenton Springs—15 miles march. . . .

13. March at 6 a.m. passing through. . . . . Warrenton. . . . . marched only 8 miles.

14. Marched at 5½ o'clock—after going a few miles heard fighting between Rhodes (Rodes) and the enemy . . . . continue to march for Bristow Station on the O. & A. R. R. Halted about 2 miles from there after marching about 14 or 15 miles. Have eaten all our rations—none for tomorrow. Hope for a Yankee haversack or sutler's stores.

15. Moved to adjoining woods to cook rations.

16. March down to Bristow Station, Prince William Co., to guard troops tearing up R. R. . . . .

18. At 3 a.m. we (i.e. the Maryland Battalion) recross Broad Run and join the Brigade at Bristow Station and march forward on the Culpeper R. R. halting at 3 p.m. 3 miles from Rappahannock River—a rapid march of about 20 or 22 miles.

[I remember well the fighting on the 14th of which Mr. Grayson speaks, the sound of which came from our front, or rather from our right oblique and not very distant, but we did not become engaged. We soon learned that two of A. P. Hill's Brigades—Cooke's and Kirkland's—had unexpectedly come on a strong force of the enemy's rear in a railroad cut and had been repulsed with severe loss. The value of a railroad cut for a defensive position had been demonstrated not far from here in the Second Manassas campaign the year before. Hill was much blamed for this reverse.[1] I well remember also the march back on the 18th through the level Fauquier country—along the east side of the straight railroad, where there was no regular road but the army marched easily, except for some muddy places, the country being open and all fencing gone. It was in strong contrast with our tortuous forward march through the hilly Madison County. In going through Broad Run or Kettle Run, which cross the railroad, my mare received a severe cut on one of her pasterns from a piece of old bridge iron, but I had to continue riding her back.]

Mr. Spence's diary continues:

19.   Near Rappahannock, Fauquier Co. . . . . The whole army commenced crossing at 6 A.M. and finished near 5 P.M., halting to camp on the north (?) bank of the Rappahannock, which recrossed on a pontoon bridge (just above the destroyed R. R. bridge).

20.   In camp.

21.   March down to Rappahannock to strengthen forts. . . . .

22.   Resting today. . . . .

23 . . . . March 10 miles up the R. R. beyond Brandy Station and camp.

24.   In a marshy, rainy camp.

25.   March back a mile and a half nearer Brandy Station to camp permanently. . . . .

26.   . . . . The whole Division marched across the river to protect the wagon train which went after R. R. iron. The consequence of this was a heavy skirmish lasting all day. We lost about 40 men.

27.   We are relieved this morning and hasten back to camp.

I have been under the impression that this advance of Johnson's Division across the river on October 26th was a "recognizance in force," but Grayson's account of its object—to get railroad rails—is probably correct and the presence of wagons is corroborated by a little incident: General Steuart had been planning some home industries in the brigade, to help out Government issues by repairs.   In this he was zealously seconded by Captain George Williamson, his adjutant-general.   Now Williamson observed a large pile of scraps of tin, which

[1] He frankly blames himself in his official report, *War of the Rebellion Records* Series 1, Volume XXIX, Part I, page 426.

he thought might be made useful in mending canteens, &c., and he imparted his idea to General Ewell, the corps commander, who was present, suggesting that one of the wagons might take the scrap back. "Yes," said Ewell, "a very good idea, Captain Williamson, Mrs. Ewell's bath tub wants mending." I believe Willliamson dropped the matter.[2]

Our advance was along the Railroad track about 4 miles to within a short distance of Bealeton, which we could not see because of woods in our front. Here we had some skirmishing and I saw several dead bodies but should not think we lost as many as 40. There were some artillery shots from the enemy. I do not remember or believe, that the division remained that night on the far side of the river, as might be inferred from Grayson's diary—perhaps the 2nd Maryland did—on picket.

On October 30 Mr. Grayson notes that peanuts are $1 a quart, apples $2.50 per dozen, cakes two for $1, apple and peach brandy $3 a quart.

A private's pay of $11 a month would not go far in the purchase of such luxuries—nor were there many opportunities for buying them.

And on November 3d he chronicles the departure, by train, of the 2d Maryland for Hanover Junction, near Richmond, to be part of the Maryland Line, there organizing under Colonel Bradley T. Johnson.

It was with great regret at brigade headquarters, where we were all Marylanders, that we witnessed the retirement from the command of this fine regiment. And I, always throughout the war, had a strong feeling that all Marylanders ought to be at the front of active operations,

---

[2] General Ewell's wife—when he was absent from the army after losing his leg at Second Manassas he had married the mother of his adjutant-general, Major G. Campbell Brown of Tennessee—generally stayed with or near him in the army.

and particularly Maryland organizations as there were so
few of them to represent the State in name, although
there were unknown thousands of Marylanders scattered
about in the Confederate Army.   They had a fine camp
during the winter at Hanover Junction, with the 1st
Maryland Cavalry and the Baltimore Light Artillery,
but these organizations were separated again and found
themselves at the front at the beginning of the next
campaign and each made a worthy record to the end of
the war.

Soon after the 2d Maryland left us occurred the mortifying disaster of the "téte de pont."   This little earth
work fortification was across—on the enemy's—side of
the Rappahannock, covering the approach to the river
where the railroad bridge had been and where our pontoon bridge still was.   Late in the evening the enemy
"rushed" this fortification, capturing the greater part of
Hays's Louisiana and Hoke's North Carolina Brigades.
The enemy having thus secured a foot hold on the
river—and where the ground was high at this point—
General Lee retired to the much stronger position and
true line of defence behind the Rapidan, from which he
had advanced a month before.

I have an impression of having heard of this affair from
afar, and perhaps this was the time[3] when I went to
Richmond for two or three days to be confirmed by
Bishop Johns—in St. Paul's Church.   I do not remember
if so, whether I rejoined the command just before going
back on the march, my first recollecton being that the
brigade was in camp in Orange County on the west side
of Black Walnut Run a mile or more above its emptying
into Mine Run and therefore some two miles back from

---

[3] The capture of the tete de pont was on November 7.   I think the enemy
were entitled to much credit for making the successful assault.

our former position on the Rapidan. Here we had some sort of intrenchments extending westerly or northwesterly across the wooded country, the intention apparently being to combine the defence of the Rapidan and Mine Run—on the east flank.

Whether it was at the time of the téte de pont affair or a little later that I so went to Richmond, I remember that on my return a communication came from division headquarters saying it was reported that Captain Howard had absented himself from the army and asking by what authority he had gone. I replied stating the object of my going, that I was only volunteering in my position, and, moreover, that I had first seen Colonel Charles Marshall, of General Lee's staff, who had told me that, under the circumstances, it was not necessary for me to obtain a formal leave. And I heard nothing more about the matter. But I think I ought to have applied for leave.

We began to think that we might settle in winter quarters at this place and many of the officers at least built chimneys to their tents. When a section of the canvass is partly ripped and the flap is raised and a mud fireplace is made with an outside chimney of crossed sticks daubed with mud and perhaps a barrel on top to increase the elevation and draft, a tent is very comfortable in the winter.

While here I suffered from some curious attack which made my lips turn quite white and they were so swollen and stiff that I could not open my mouth and was only able to take a little liquid food out of a teaspoon, a few drops at a time. But Captain Williamson was absent on a short leave and I was filling his place as adjutant-general, and I did not like to go off or give up my duties. This began to disappear just as the Mine Run operations came on.

CHAPTER XXVI

BATTLE OF PAYNE'S FARM OR BARTLETT'S MILL AND MINE RUN

Early in the morning of 27th November (1863).
Steuart's Brigade left its camp on Blackwalnut Run,
being the rear brigade of the division. We went down
the run and crossed Mine Run to the east at Bartlett's
Mill, which is at or very near the mouth of Blackwalnut.
We now took the rear of the artillery and ambulances of
the division—there were no wagons with us. The road[1]
now ran southeasterly and through thick woods. We had
proceeded about a mile and a half beyond Bartlett's
Mill and I was riding along the left (east) side of the
road and near the head of our brigade when I noticed one
of the men, who was plodding along just outside me,
duck his head and peer under the low tree branches up a
woods road which went off to the left. I asked him what
he was looking at and he replied that he thought he saw
a man there. We had no idea of any of the enemy being
in the vicinity, but I turned and went up the grassy road
fifty yards or so to investigate. Seeing no one, I came
back. But we had marched a very little farther when
there was a sudden commotion in the train ahead and
several of the ambulances turned and came back in
confusion, the drivers reporting that the train had been
fired on from the left. General Steuart promptly ordered
them back to their places, faced the brigade into line to
the left and deployed skirmishers to cover it and the

[1] The road to Locust Grove on the Orange and Fredericksburg Stone Road.

238

train. As soon as the line of skirmishers was formed he ordered it to advance and attack the enemy, who we supposed to be only some dismounted cavalry. But our men had scarcely advanced twenty paces in the thick woods when they encountered a strong line of infantry skirmishers and sharp firing broke out. These they drove back some distance when a solid line of the enemy was discovered, drawn up in order of battle. At this time they also opened on us with one or two pieces of artillery. Colonel Titus V. Williams, commanding the 37th Virginia, the left regiment, reporting that a body was crossing the road on his left, for the evident purpose of flanking the brigade, General Steuart ordered him to change front to rear on his first company, i.e., form his regiment at right angles to the road and so facing the threatening movement, the right of his right company still being at the road. Shortly afterwards Major-General Edward Johnson, commanding the division, arrived on this part of the field and by his order the whole brigade took up a position at right angles to its former line, the right resting on the road and connecting with the left of the Stonewall Brigade. But General Steuart was subsequently ordered to throw forward and to the right oblique his left, so as to occupy a position nearly parallel to that previously held along the road, still keeping the connection on his right with the Stonewall Brigade, so as to leave no interval open. This movement was a slow and difficult one, as it was necessary, while maintaining the connection on the right, to extend the left to prevent its being outflanked, and in the consequently increased intervals between regiments (and even between files) to stretch the line, the extraordinary density of the thicket made it impossible for the manoeuvre to be executed with regularity. Before it was completed the bri-

gade was ordered (by General Johnson) to move directly
forward. The enemy were soon encountered and were
pushed steadily back, although parts of our line, from
causes mentioned before (and others explained in the
official reports of regimental commanders,) were little
more than deployments of skirmishers. On the right and
center they were driven several hundred yards. The left
regiment, however, was under greater difficulties. Although there was a considerable interval between that
regiment—the 37th Virginia—and the 3d North Carolina
on its right and the files of the former were separated so
that it covered far more than its proper regimental front,
yet the line of the enemy extended much beyond its left
flank, and after driving the force immediately in its
front, this regiment was compelled to halt and form a
new line to repel a flank attack. The enemy presently
drove in the thin line between the 37th and the 3d and
the latter regiment, having exhausted its ammunition
(which will show how severe the fighting was), and
unable to obtain a new supply, was forced finally to
resume the position from which it had advanced. The
heavy loss sustained[2] is sufficient evidence that this
was not done until made necessary. The 37th Virginia was at one time even cut off but extricated itself
and joined the 3d North Carolina. These two regiments
were by order of Major-General Johnson, retained in
that position to guard against any further attack on that
exposed flank. Meanwhile the right regiments—10th
and 23rd Virginia and 1st North Carolina—having used
all their cartridges and the ordnance wagons not being

---

[2] The report of the corps medical director states the loss in this regiment as
seventy-two killed and wounded, but such reports generally give a smaller loss
than the official reports of regimental commanders. The list of casualties with
Colonel Thruston's report (3d North Carolina) is missing.

at hand to supply more, and deprived of support on the left, were compelled to retire a short distance, but then held a position far in advance of the line which they had previously occupied. Soon after dark, the firing having ceased, the brigade was relieved by Doles's Brigade and was ordered to form along the road.

In my foregoing account of this severe engagement I have quoted, almost literally, from General Steuart's official report, which was written for him by me—except his commendatory mention of staff officers which he added. Before this movement began, Captain George Williamson had gone off on sick leave and I was acting as assistant adjutant-general in his place, First Lieutenant James L. White (of Abingdon, Virginia), adjutant of the 37th Virginia, temporarily filling my regular position of assistant inspector-general, and he and I were the General's only two staff officers present. I made a pencil draught of the official report, to which General Steuart added in ink the mention of his staff. It is still in my possession. But having a dislike for exaggeration and high coloring in official reports, I have always thought since that I may not have done full justice to the conduct of the brigade in this battle.[3]

Our reported aggregate loss in the brigade was 233, including 22 missing but of whom many were, no doubt, killed or too badly wounded to be removed. The strength of the brigade was about 1400. Lieutenant-Colonel S. T. Walton, commanding the 23d Virginia, was killed and Colonel Hamilton A. Brown of the 1st North Carolina was wounded. Colonel Walton, of Charlotte County Virginia, was an excellent officer and a gentleman

[3] This official report will be found in the *War of the Rebellion Official Records*, Series 1, volume XXI, Part I, page 862.

of fine character. General Steuart was struck by a ball but not disabled. While we were over on the left of the brigade I heard a bullet strike his arm near the shoulder like a stone against wood. He moved the arm about and said it was nothing serious and wished to give no further attention to it. But I insisted on an examination and his (overcoat and?) coat being taken off and his shirt sleeve being rolled up it was found that only a contusion had been made—which in those few minutes time had become quite dark. We did not mind the artillery fire but the musket balls flew very thick. At one time I was riding to the front in the woods when a great many seemed to come around me and thinking I was getting on the enemy I turned back, and not very slowly either. I then came on Major-General Johnson, on foot, and that soldier of approved courage was hunching his shoulders and not disdaining the partial shelter to his broad person of a small tree—there were no large trees about there. While I stopped and talked with him the bullets coming through the switchy woods sounded somewhat like the hissing of a hail or sleet storm. Altogether, it was an interesting and in some respects a picturesque battle—the unexpected suddenness of its opening, the changes of position and encounters in the woods which covered the ground, and other features. In the first advance of our skirmishers, or in the subsequent forward movement, we had captured some prisoners and among them the adjutant of a New York regiment, from whom we learned that a corps was in our front. They had crossed the Rapidan at Germanna Ford, the next ford below the mouth of Mine Run, and were moving diagonally towards our line of march when they struck us.

Sometime after dark, being relieved by Doles's Brigade[4] as before stated, and after standing in the road for a while, we moved, following the rest of our division in a southerly direction, presently recrossing Mine Run, and before going far went into bivouac along the high ground on the west side of the wide valley of that stream.

On the morning of the 28th (November) the enemy were seen in line along the equally high ground on the opposite (east) side of the valley, at a distance, I suppose, of about 700 or 800 yards, for the valley of Mine Run is here a wide one, with the ground rising not very sharply on each side of the bottom. The positions occupied by us and by the enemy were very similar and equally strong, and either side attacking would be exposed to a murderous fire in crossing the bottom and then ascending the hill side. And neither side ventured it. During the day our men entrenched as well as they could with almost no implements, using their bayonets, tin cups, and their hands, to loosen and scoop up the dirt, which was thrown on and around the trunks of old field pine trees. But, with the shallow trench behind, it gave a pretty good protection. Where our brigade stood at least, the line was not along the crest but a little way down the hillside towards the run, and not being allowed to make large fires in such an exposure to the enemy's artillery, and the weather being keen and frosty, we suffered at night from the cold. Besides, a fire made of old field pine, which was the wood around us, is hard to kindle and equally hard to keep burning. I had only my overcoat and a very small saddle blanket (to go under the saddle on my horse's back), and I remember waking up one of these mornings with my hair white with frost. But we had got a good deal hardened to exposure. Major George H. Kyle,

[4] Of Rodes's Division, Ewell's Corps.

brigade commissary, sent from the wagons in rear some cold food for the general and staff, and also a great and most unusual treat in the shape of a small bottle of apple brandy which I suspect came from the medical stores. We did look this gift in its mouth in spite of the proverb.

I think it was on the morning of November 30, before our eyes were open, that the enemy suddenly let off his artillery on us. I saw the General, while his eyes were still shut it seemed to me, make a dive to the bottom of the "shebang"—a little pine brush shelter sloping to the ground at the back—which W. Hiter, our courier, had made. I wondered. But he was grabbing for the apple-jack bottle which he drained of the little that was in it, and then ordered the brigade into the breastworks, for protection and to be ready for the expected infantry assault. But none came, and after continuing some time the shelling ceased. I do not rembember that it caused any loss in our brigade. It seemed to be a parting salvo from General Meade, for on the morning of December 2 we saw that the enemy had disappeared from our front. Our army crossed the valley and pursued for two or three miles towards the Rapidan but found that the Union Army had all passed over it.

And so ended the Mine Run campaign, which, it seems to me, may be summed up, parodying the old nursery rhyme:

> General Meade,
> With seventy thousand men,
> Marched o'er the Rapidan,
> And marched back again.

I mean no disrepect to General Meade, however, of whom we had a good opinion. But if the movement was meant as a counterstroke to Lee's flank advance seven weeks before, it compares with it very disadvantageously. For while Lee forced him back fifty miles or more, vainly seeking to bring him to battle, Meade after placing his army on Lee's flank—which he could do at any time—was promptly confronted by Lee and offered battle which he declined, except the chance partial engagement of Payne's Farm.

My impression is that we did not return from Mine Run to our camp on Blackwalnut Run. I think that camp had been abandoned since we marched from it and our wagons had moved some distance back of our Mine Run line on the Orange and Fredericksburg Stone Road. I think we marched back on this Stone Road, on December 2 or 3, about seven miles to the neighborhood of Pisgah Church, which is a little north of the road and about seven miles east of Orange Court House. Here, a short distance north of the road, we went into a camp which proved to be our winterquarters. We gradually became convinced that such would be our stay.

The "Stone Road" is the old road, pretty straight in its course, from Orange Court House to Fredericksburg. The newer "Plank Road"—on which a few planks remained—was sometimes coincident with it, but often a mile or more to the south.

CHAPTER XXVII

Winter Quarters 1863–1864

The following account, in this and the next two chapters, of some features of life in winter quarters and the battles in the Wilderness and at Spotsylvania Court House, is reproduced, with some changes, from a paper which I wrote for the Massachusetts Military Historical Society, entitled "Notes and Recollections of the Opening of the Campaign of 1864," which I read before the Society at Boston on 16th April, 1883, and which will be found on page 83 of Volume 4 of that Society's Publications.

Lieutenant Skipwith Wilmer, the signal officer attached to Major-General Edward Johnson's Division, Ewell's Corps of General Lee's Army of Northern Virginia, had been discussing with some of the members of the Society in Boston (where he had married after the war,) the capture of the salient at Spotsylvania Court House on 12th May, 1864, the assault on which was at that time commonly supposed to have been a surprise to the Confederates, and he mentioned to them that he had recently been talking with me on the subject and that I could give some special information. They had requested him to ask me to write a paper for the Society and he told me, with some doubt whether it would be agreeable to me, that he had undertaken to promise that I would. So I wrote and sent to the Society an account of the capture of the salient. I think it was then that they honored me by making me a Corresponding Mem-

ber. Not long afterwards the Society invited me to
write another paper[1] and I suggested my enlarging the
one I had written to an account of the opening of the
campaign (as I saw it), and with some description of life
in winter quarters before. They invited me to come on
and read this completed paper myself and I did so. They
made me have a most agreeable time in Boston. At a
dinner of twenty or more which they gave me at the
Union Club I noticed only one person under the rank of
field officer, so unlike our Confederate gatherings, where
privates are usually conspicuous if not predominating.
I remember saying to them—but there was no post-
prandial speaking—that New England would at some
time have cause to regret its support of the harsh Reconstruction measures; that at present the west was ruled
largely by settlers who carried with them New England
ideas, but that the next generation would grow up with
ideas of their own and some of them radical, and at such
time when the old States ought to be found standing together in a conservative attitude, the South would be
alienated. But I remember also that at an art exhibition
and reception at the Somerset Club to which I was taken,
I was surprised by a gentleman inveighing to me but in
a voice which could be heard for some distance around
in the crowded room, against the giving of suffrage to the
negroes. He said the Southern people were right in resisting it in any way they could.

I stayed at the house of Mr. John C. Ropes, whose

---

[1] They invited me also to make an address—and in Faneuil Hall—on the
subject of "The Southern Volunteer," after Colonel Livermore had made one
on "The Northern Volunteer," but in the want then of Confederate statistics
and authorities, I did not see my way to doing so satisfactorily. At my suggestion they then invited Colonel Henry Kyd Douglas to make the address, which
I think he did.

death was so much regretted, South as well as North. He was the founder of the Society.

After Meade's demonstration at Mine Run and withdrawal to the north side of the Rapidan, in the last days of November (1863), it seemed unlikely that there would be any more active operations that year and the Army of Northern Virginia gradually settled down in winter quarters where it was, defending the line of the Rapidan. Steuart's Brigade was on a good site, for the most part wooded, on the north side of the Stone Road, six or seven miles east of Orange Court House, and the General went to work with his usual energy to clean up the ground, make the men as comfortable as possible—except by idleness—and to improve the efficiency of his command in every way. Our summer camp on Poplar Run near Montpelier, ten miles to the west, when resting from the Gettysburg campaign, had been pronounced to be a model one in the army, and he was determined that this should be its equal in every respect, while the assurance of some months' inactivity would enable him to carry out many practical measures which could not be undertaken in the uncertainty of ever continuing long in one stay in the campaigning season.

So rising ground was selected for the regimental camps and they were thoroughly "policed"² and swept, with brooms made of twigs bundled together, until several inches perhaps of the loose surface soil were removed and a hard dirt floor was gained. The men's quarters were kept clean and well ventilated and they were exhorted to have their bunks raised above the ground. The morning sick reports were carefully studied as they

² "Policing" in military language is cleaning up and doing jobs of work about the camp. Prisoners at the guard house were kept employed on this.

had been in our summer camp, when, it will be remembered, they had been found to vary according to the degree of attention which was given to such details in the several regiments and the 10th Virginia had then reduced its sick list to a lower rate than we had ever known. Now, however, to keep warm was the overruling necessity and this regulation could not be rigidly enforced, as, undoubtedly, next to the ground is the warmest way a soldier with a scanty supply of clothing and covering can sleep. Wattled cedar or pine fencing enclosed a space around the brigade guard house and the prisoners were kept employed "corduroying"[3] wet places in the roads and with other work of the sort about the camp ground and its vicinity. The orders against burning or displacing rails were strictly enforced and at the end of winter all fencing around us was in as good, if not in precisely the same condition as we had found it, some new rails having been required to be mauled I think. Even timber cut was estimated by a board of officers and certificates were given, although I cannot venture to affirm that owners were ever paid on them. The men were moderately drilled and schools of instruction were ordered for the officers. The 10th Virginia was the only regiment which had a band (I think we were getting up one in the 1st North Carolina with some instruments captured in the Gettysburg Campaign), and we utilized it to the best general advantage by having daily brigade guard mounting, with as much military pomp and circumstance as we could get up. A drum beat the hours at the brigade guard house to regulate the time of the whole camp.

A number of shoemakers in the different regiments,

---

[3] The term almost explains itself—making a bed of poles, side by side across the road and often with the addition of tough cedar brush. The soldiers' imaginations were very ready in applying old words to new processes and situations.

seventeen I think, were encouraged to send home—and in some instances were given leave to go—for their tools, and were put to work repairing shoes, being exempted from guard and other routine camp duty, but ready to fall in with their commands on any call to arms. The shoe-shops were a separate camp of tents, near brigade headquarters and under our immediate supervision, guarded by sentinels, and no person was allowed to visit them or to carry his shoes to be mended without a pass and order from his company and regimental commanders, approved by the adjutant or inspector general. A careful estimate and report of the saving of the issue of shoes to our brigade during the winter was made to the higher authorities at one time, but I am afraid to say from memory what the saving was confidently stated to have been, certainly several hundred pairs; besides, the men's feet were kept in better condition by the correction of ill fitting shoes. On the march back from Gettysburg in the summer before, the "barefooted" men of the division —not literally that except in the case of some, but those whose shoes were worn out or whose feet were sore from wearing bad shoes or other causes—were organized into a separate command, under officers, to pick their way on the grassy roadside and by easy stages on each day's march. My recollection is that this barefooted and sorefooted command sometimes numbered a fourth of the division.[4]

Having taken a sort of census of the whole brigade, we knew exactly where to look at any time for skilled workmen in different occupations. The 37th Virginia, from the mountains of the southwestern part of the State, we

[4] It seems to me now that there could hardly have been that many, although I so wrote in 1883, and certainly the number was large. I do not think they marched all the distance back in that way, but I remember officers being detailed for the duty on more than one day.

found to furnish a greater proportion of mechanics—or at least men who were used to doing jobs of handywork—the other regiments being more largely composed of men from the farming class or from sections where there were regular artizans and stores convenient. Wheelwrights were detailed to put the ambulances (this under the zealous charge of Surgeon Henkel of that regiment, senior surgeon or medical director,) and transportation generally in good order. I think log shelters were made for the horses and they were carefully looked after. General Steuart had also detailed, or meditated detailing, tinners to mend canteens, cups and other tinwork. Drummers or tanners were given a few days leave to go to their homes or places not far distant on condition of bringing back dog skins for drum heads, and although the animal's integument was tanned in a marvellously short time, it was found to answer very well.

The General was especially desirous of establishing "tailor shops" to patch and mend clothing, on a like scale with the shoe shops, or greater, and sent up urgent applications for waste odds and ends of cloth and thread at the government factories, but had received no response when the opening of the Spring campaign put a check to these and many other schemes.

In short, recognizing the straits that the Confederacy was now put to in the furnishing of supplies, we aimed to save and eke out issues in every possible way.

General Steuart also designed cloth badges (metal was not to be had), to distinguish the men of different regiments—a red cross on ground of different colors, or something that way.[5] But the failure to get the scraps

[5] I do not know whether this was an original idea with General Steuart, or whether he had heard of the admirable and picturesque system of badges of the Union Army, which we saw when we were captured two or three months later.

of cloth from the factories prevented his carrying out this project.

The physical condition of the men I do not, and did not then, consider good. Their rations had been systematically reduced to the smallest possible quantity and there was almost no variety. After an official inspection of the whole command in March or April, 1863 (I was acting assistant inspector-general and made stated inspections,[6] reports of which went up through a channel of inspectors), I had deemed it a serious duty to make it a part of my report that the sallow complexions and general appearance of the men indicated that they were insufficiently fed, and to urge that the ration should be increased. A soldier fighting for the best of causes should have, in his monotonous life, enough to eat as long as food will hold out issued in that way; he may put up with frequent irregularities, but if his ration be systematically insufficient for his appetite, his spirit and endurance must surely fail or become greatly impaired.

It is to be wished that we had statements of the rations actually issued to the men, particularly during the last two years of the war. For illustration, our meals at Brigade headquarters in this winter of 1863–64, were usually as follows: Breakfast consisted of a plate of

[6] At one of these inspections I saw an amusing instance of the difference of habits of men coming from different localities. One of the Virginia regiments was composed of companies from Louisa, Charlotte, Halifax and other tobacco counties and as I passed down the lines, which were in open order, that is, with the rear rank retired some paces from the front, there was a continuous wet line from expectoration about five feet in front of and parallel with each rank. The Colonel, who always walks with the inspecting officer, seemed to take it as a matter of course, calling for no rebuke. But when I came to the 3d North Carolina, from around Wilmington where tobacco chewing is not such a habit, the ground was all dry, and when the Colonel heard a man spit after we had passed him, he went back and in an undertone reprimanded him severely, telling him he was disgracing the whole regiment.

"corn dodgers" (corn meal cooked with water,) and mashed potatoes, the latter not issued I believe but bought at a distance. I think we had coffee also, that is to say some substitute for it, but my recollection is that there was not often a little sugar. For dinner, towards sunset, we had corn bread again and a soup made of water thickened with corn meal and mashed potatoes and cooked with a small piece of meat, which last, if salt, was taken out when the soup was done and kept to be cooked over again in the mashed potatoes for next morning's breakfast. And I suppose there was the coffee substitute again. A dog could not have lived with the mess on what was left; there was, in fact, nothing left. Officers drew one ration each, the same as the men, were prohibited from purchasing from the commissary, there were no sutlers, and as nothing could be had in the thinly settled neighborhood for love or money, we could only occasionally buy a few articles, such as apple butter, sorghum molasses, half a dozen eggs, etc., when our wagons went over to the Valley or other remote regions for supplies. But our mess at headquarters was one of Marylanders and perhaps others fared somewhat better.[7]

[7] In the spring of 1863 Major-General Trimble, then commanding this division published an order enumerating the edible wild plants, such as dandelion, poke sprouts, curly leaf dock, lambs quarter, sheep sorrel, water cresses, etc., and requiring regimental commanders to make daily details to gather them. It was said that sometimes noxious things, like plaintain, were brought in, with disagreeable results when eaten. All Confederate soldiers had long since learned the comparative merits of rye, wheat, acorns, chestnuts, sweet potatoes, dandelion, browned meal or flour, as substitutes for coffee; also sassafras, etc., for tea. I remember an alarming rumor that once spread through the army, and the country, of certain results of the use of rye coffee, bearing on the future increase of population of the Confederacy. An infusion of white oak bark was used as a tonic in place of quinine which was "contraband of war" and was, therefore, very scarce.

The men were not, therefore, to my observation, in good physical condition. Vaccination was often followed by serious consequences and this came, I think, from a low condition of the system more than from the use of impure matter. By the way, it was curious how commonly men returning from furlough reported that they had spent the first part of their leave sick at home—they were never taken sick on coming back from home to open air life in the field.

The men were often tried too by receiving letters or messages telling of dire distresses and apprehensions of worse in their families at home. These letters were constantly coming up to brigade headquarters appended to urgent applications for furloughs. They were, after proper investigation, usually, or often, forwarded approved by General Steuart, who thought they should be liberally given in such cases, both from humanity and policy. But the Confederate ranks were thin and the heavy masses of the enemy were always threatening in our front and only in extreme instances could any applications be granted.[8] But under these and many other trials and daily hardships the men bore up with a constancy that was wonderful and which can hardly be understood by the outside world.

The Rapidan River, the dividing line between the two armies, was picketed by a brigade from each division for a week at a time, and there being the usual number of four brigades in our division, the turn came to us once in every four weeks. The picket line assigned to Johnson's

[8] General D. H. Hill's ideas were more philosophic and far seeing. He once endorsed an application for furlough substantially in this way: "Respectfully forwarded approved, for the reason that if our brave soldiers are not occasionally permitted to visit their homes the next generation in the South will be composed of the descendants of skulkers and cowards."

Division was the right of the infantry line and extended from Morton's[9] Ford on the west to Sisson's Ford at the mouth of Mountain-Mine Run on the east, being the position we had held in the Fall before the Bristoe campaign. Except at one point, the river bank was high on our side, towards the right lofty, precipitous and rough, and level or gently rising on the other (Culpeper County) side, so that we were able to post our line of sentinels immediately along or overlooking the river, while those of the enemy were thrown back a couple of hundred yards or so. The exception was on our extreme right where the mouth of the Mountain-Mine Run valley made the ground low on our side while a cliff rose from the water's edge on the other side, and the vidette there posted sometimes gave us a good deal of annoyance. Our own sentinel, being almost underneath, had to fortify his position with fence rails, and it several times happened that his vis-à-vis, in a bad humor perhaps from the state of the weather or from being kept on duty over time by a negligent corporal, crept to the edge of the cliff before dawn and as soon as it was light enough to see, fired on him or on the officer of the day making his round. There were, I believe, one or two men wounded in this way during the winter. It was reported, too, that a negro soldier was often posted at this point and the rumor, although probably unfounded (I believe the colored troops were not yet at the front), produced additional irritation among our men, particularly as the usual truce between pickets was pretty well observed along the rest of the line.

[9] I wrote Mitchell's Ford in my paper for the Massachusetts Military Historical Society, but Morton's is correct. I see the war maps give different locations for a Mitchell's Ford but none that would make my former text right.

But if at a disadvantage here, we had the upper hand everywhere else. Once some North Carolinians, of our neighboring brigade I think, usually a staid set of men, undertook to vary the monotony of picket life by a practical joke, which might have had serious consequences, at Morton's Ford. At this point a strong reserve was maintained, which occupied a house[10] or yard about six hundred feet back from the crossing, while at the same distance from the north (Culpeper) bank the enemy had a like force at a house which seemed to be also the headquarters of some officer of rank. The North Carolinians had found a pair of immense wheels with a tongue attached, probably used for hauling timber, which at a distance looked not unlike a gun carriage, although it would have carried a piece of great calibre. Upon this they mounted a huge hollow log, and providing themselves with a rammer and some large round stones, they suddenly dashed out with it from the house half way to the river, wheeled into position and pointed it at the opposite house, rammed with loud words of command a stone into the log, and seemed about to knock the enemy's headquarters about their ears. For a time there was considerable commotion on the other side. The picket line hurriedly prepared for action and the house was speedily emptied, the inmates, or some of them, not standing in any order in going but making for the woods at once. The joke was presently appreciated and, with much laughter, the lines resumed their status. Such was the account at least, perhaps a little colored, which I received on riding up to Morton's Ford one day and noticing the "Quaker" piece with its rammer and pile

[10] Residence of the Hon. Jeremiah Morton, of the Virginia Legislature, and Dr. Morton, his brother.

of stones, and the picket line apparently quieting down from some excitement.

Another time we had a little alarm on our side. Early one morning a messenger came in haste to our head-quarters at Gibson's house to report that an enterprising fellow had stolen forward in the night and intrenched himself behind a heavy gatepost in such a position as to have a part of our sentinel line somewhat at his mercy—it being on higher ground but with no cover. The signal corps men stationed with us (to communicate with our principal station on Clarke's Mountain in rear,) looked through their glasses and declared they could see his shadow moving about, and on going to the river bank behind Gibson's house, we certainly saw the moving shadow plainly with the naked eye, and had no doubt it was that of the man digging to make his position behind the gatepost more secure. Expecting every moment the fellow, having established himself to his satisfaction, would pick off one of us, we were devising schemes for enfilading and dislodging him from his stronghold, if even by crossing the river at Tobaccostick Ford—a horse ford a little way to the left—and rushing him, when some one made the discovery that the shadow was simply that of the gatepost itself running up and down the bars of the gate, which, apparently closed, was imperceptibly swinging a few inches to and fro in the wind.

Another day an officer on horseback, accompanied by two Culpeper damsels, rode boldly down to the brink of the river at Tobaccostick Ford, at a bend of the stream nearly midway of our line, to propose an exchange of newspapers, as had been practised in the time of the brigade before us. We, however, were more strict in obeying orders about holding communication with the enemy, and the officer was immediately covered by a gun and bidden to come across. Naturally indignant at such a changed reception and alarmed, he attempted to explain and wished to withdraw, but our men would by no means consent, although his companions added their entreaties, almost in tears and saying that this officer had been kind to them. He was held there, with the river between, while a message was sent to our headquarters for instructions, when he was allowed to retire with an admonition to keep his distance hereafter.

Such were some of the little excitements which varied the monotony of picket life.

But there is a darker page in this account of life in winter quarters and on this picket line.

I was at the brigade guard house in camp one day in January or February (1864) when a few prisoners were brought in, under guard from division headquarters or higher up. Colonel Titus V. Williams, of the 37th Virginia, happened to be present and recognized and spoke —curtly—to one of them by his name, Rosenbaum. The Colonel told me the man was a bad soldier who had deserted, that is, had run away from his company to his mountain home in southwest Virginia, once or twice before. He had been picked up by conscript officers and was now returned to his command again under charges. In due time he was tried before the corps court martial, was found guilty of desertion and was sentenced "to be shot to death by musketry," as such sentences were worded. At that time ordinary courts martial (of officers specially detailed as occasions arose,) had been abolished, and by act of Congress each corps of the army had a standing tribunal of three appointees, who were civilians, or at any rate, appointed from outside the army; for instance, William H. Norris, a well known Baltimore lawyer, who had been compelled to become a refugee, was one such appointee, and I think a member of our corps court.

After his conviction Rosenbaum's company officers came to me and asked me so earnestly if I would not see if he could not be saved from death that I consented to examine the proceedings and see if they were in regular shape. Now by the articles of war it is absolutely necessary that in case of a capital sentence the finding should state, "Two-thirds of the court concurring," and I found that in Rosenbaum's case the proceedings said "A majority of the court." Under the old practice this would undoubtedly have made the sentence void, but in case of the new corps court a majority of three is also two-thirds. I told the officers I did not think the point was a good one, but I saw nothing else to base an appeal on, and at their request I drew up a paper making as much out of the point as I could. It was addressed to Captain H. G. Young, judge advocate-general of the Army of Northern Virginia, on General Lee's staff, and I think it was signed by Rosenbaum or his company officers. After a time a long communication came down from Captain Young, discussing the point but saying that it was a novel one and he had referred it to Richmond. But no stay of execution was ordered, the date fixed for which was about March 3. Two or three days before that Kilpatrick and Dahlgren crossed the lower Rapidan and made their cavalry raid to the neighborhood of Richmond and our brigade was sent down the Stone Road to near Chancellorsville[11] to intercept them if they returned by the same road by which they had

[11] I took advantage of being here to ride two or three miles down to Chancellorsville and went over part of the ground of Jackson's last flank attack. There were still remnants of clothing and other evidences of the battle scattered about. At the Chancellor house they gave me a graphic account of the scene there. They said it was fully believed that our army was falling back towards Gordonville or Richmond and the Union soldiers were cooking dinner and taking their ease when Jackson's line of battle came down on their flank like a thunderbolt.

gone in (but they did not). We were for two or three days stationed along the Old Stone Road, facing south and so watching what I think was the mouth of the Brock Road. A day or two before the date fixed for the execution of Rosenbaum (who had been left in camp in the Brigade guard house), I met Major E. L. Moore, of Major-General Johnson's staff—being in fact the assistant inspector-general of the division and having special charge of such matters—and I represented to him that the execution could not well be carried out while we were practically in battle array. He agreed and changed the date, to, I think, that day week. I said, "Put it in writing," and paper not being at hand, I pulled out an old letter and on the yellow Confederate envelope he wrote an order to that effect, "By command of Major-General Johnson," which I fortunately preserved. On that newly fixed date the brigade was on one of its regular tours of picket duty on the Rapidan and we had taken the condemned man, Rosenbaum, with us. On the appointed day—I think it was March 10, being Friday, on which day of the week such sentences were customarily carried out—the brigade was drawn up in the open valley of Mountain Run, a short distance back of its place of bivouac. The details were under the direction of the field officer of the day—a daily assignment by turns of one of the lieutenant-colonels or majors —but it was also one of my duties as inspector-general to see that everything was properly done. And when the man had been placed at the stake or upright piece, this officer came to me and unrolled a bushel bag and said he supposed that was to be put over the prisoner. I made him tear off a strip and bandage the man's eyes with it. He requested that several of his friends might sing a hymn while he was being shot, and the field officer referring this to me, I said I thought he might permit it—with some hesitation, however, for I was afraid it might discompose the firing party, and I am not sure it did not. As usual, one-half of the muskets were loaded with blank cartridges, to give some uncertainty to the members of the firing party by whom their comrade was shot. The prisoner prayed aloud that he might be received into that better land—

It was a gloomy, leaden evening, with a storm rapidly coming up from the west, and when the execution was over, there was scarcely time to march the men back to their bivouac, when it broke, with thunder and lightning, unusual so early in the season, and a heavy downpour of rain. That night, about one o'clock, in riding my customary round of the picket line, I went back up the valley to see if the man had been properly buried in the hurry of the storm. It was now bright moonlight and the valley with its sedge grass bottom, gloomy hillside beyond, and noise of running water, was a depressing place. He had been buried under an oak tree standing alone in the valley and whose stretched out arms, either dead or with no foliage as yet, looked ghostly in the moonlight. I own that I felt chilled and turned back with relief. Then or afterwards, I found a paper affixed to the headboard with the inscription, "murdered by usurped military authority." Some time after this, in camp, an order came from division headquarters suspending the execution. I replied that he had been executed. Back came a courier at full speed with a communication demanding by what authority the man had been shot. I sent the envelope, or a copy of it, which contained the order, both postponing the execution from the day originally fixed and naming the day on which it should be carried out—as it was. I heard nothing more on the subject.

I witnessed three executions in the army, and I believe there were not many more in the Army of Northern Virginia. The first was at Centreville in November, 1861, when two (?) of Major Robert Wheat's Battalion of Louisiana "Tigers," a very rough set requiring stern discipline, were shot for some crime, not desertion—aggravated riotous conduct I believe. The second was of the ten North Carolinians in September, 1863, of which I have given an account. And this was the third, and, from some circumstances, perhaps even more painful to me than that of the ten men. Some will say that such incidents ought to be omitted and forgotten, but, as I have said before, I do not think that the darker side of war should be hidden or suppressed.

Having the extreme right of the infantry picket line of the army and with the infantry's distrust of cavalry protection, we watched our right flank also in a measure, particularly towards the opening of Spring. During the Winter General Steuart, always active about something —or many things—had, with the assistance of Captain George Williamson, his adjutant-general, who was as zealous and indefatigable as himself, perfected a plan, according to which on a moment's notice the picket posts would deploy so as to form a connected skirmish line a mile or more long, with reserves at the more important points, and as the ground was extremely rough in places, especially on the right, and communication slow and at night difficult, this well preconcerted arrangement would have been found very effective had any attempt been made on our front. General Steuart and Captain Williamson also examined the whole river front picketed by Ewell's Corps, from Mountain-Mine Run up to Somerville's Ford and drew up an elaborate plan for guarding it, with a complete system of rules for the government

of the pickets, which was adopted by General Ewell.   It
was my practice to ride around nightly, but at uncertain
hours, to inspect our picket line, which was a work of an
hour or more.   Indeed one or two posts could not be visited after dark without dismounting and leaving my horse
some distance back from the river.   There was also the
Field Officer of the Day, and General Steuart and Captain Williamson were constantly riding about, so that
our pickets were certainly kept on the alert.   The picket

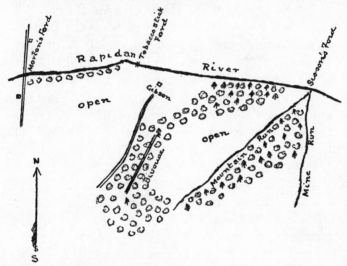

line was made up of daily details, the main body of the
Brigade being in bivouac a short distance in rear, behind
a fringe of woods.

General George Hume Steuart's (sometimes called the
3d) Brigade was composed of five regiments; 10th Virginia, Colonel E. T. H. Warren, numbering about 250
officers and men present for duty; 23d Virginia, Lieutenant-Colonel John F. Fitzgerald, about 250; 37th
Virginia, Colonel Titus V. Williams, about 300; 1st

North Carolina State Troops, Colonel Hamilton A. Brown, about 350, and 3d North Carolina State Troops, Colonel Stephen D. Thruston,[12] about 275. The North Carolina State Troops were so designated because they were two of a series of ten regiments which had been at the beginning mustered into service for the war instead of the then usual term of twelve months, and officers had been originally appointed by the governor and not elected, and continued to be nominated by him to the War Office at Richmond when there were vacancies. All of the ten that I saw during the war were the better for these distinctions and claimed something of the esprit, by some called "uppishness," of regulars. The 1st was from the central and western part of the State; the 3d was from the parts around Wilmington. The latter was certainly one of the best officered regiments I ever saw and maintained a very high state of discipline. The 10th Virginia was from the Valley, one company, however, being from Madison County on the east side of the Blue Ridge.[13] The 23d was of companies from Louisa, Charlotte, Halifax, Prince Edward and perhaps other counties and Richmond City. The 37th was from the mountainous southwestern part of the State.

General Steuart's staff was composed of Captain George Williamson, assistant-adjutant general (of Maryland); Major Tanner (of Virginia), quartermaster, and myself. I think Major George H. Kyle, of Maryland, commissary, had left us. I have before explained that I was volunteering as assistant inspector-general, and

[12] Lieutenant-Colonel Oswald M. Parsley was in command a part of the winter.

[13] I think it was to this company that Lieutenant Charles M. Crisp, after the war Speaker of the House of Representatives, belonged. He had moved to Georgia.

sometimes as assistant adjutant-general, in the captivity of my general, Major-General I. R. Trimble. General Steuart had had no aide de camp since Lieutenant Randolph H. McKim resigned to study for the ministry and reënter the service as a Chaplain.

It would be, I am satisfied, a fair estimate to say that in the Spring when the campaign opened, the effective strength of the brigade in line of battle was 1400 officers and men.

Major-General Edward Johnson's Division contained three other brigades, viz., Brigadier-General James A. Walker's (the old "Stonewall" and sometimes called the 1st Brigade), 2d, 4th, 5th, 27th (a battalion), and 33d Virginia Regiments; Brigadier-General John M. Jones's (2d Brigade), 21st, 25th, 42d, 44th, 48th and 50th Virginia; and Brigadier-General Leroy M. Stafford's, of five Louisiana regiments. I have no doubt the Division numbered closely in the neighborhood of 5200 in line of battle, Stafford's, and I think Jones's, being smaller than Steuart's and the Stonewall.

Lieutenant-General Richard S. Ewell's Corps was composed of the three Divisions of Major-Generals Edward Johnson, Jubal A. Early and Robert Rodes, numbering in all about 16,000 in battle.

Then there were Lieutenant-General Ambrose Powell Hill's Corps and two of the three Divisions of Lieutenant-General James Longstreet's Corps, the latter lately returned from hard service with the western army; and the artillery and cavalry.[14]

---

[14] Colonel Walter H. Taylor, adjutant-general of the Army of Northern Virginia, in his *Four Years With General Lee*, quoting from the official returns, except as to Longstreet's two divisions and estimating them, makes the aggregate

The men were fairly equipped as to arms—for the most part taken from the enemy—and were in light marching order, having certainly no superabundant weight of clothing and few utensils of any kind.

strength of the army, on 20th of April, 1864, 63,984 of all arms and present for duty.

Colonel Livermore, of the Union Army, in his *Numbers and Losses in the Civil War*, gives Lee 66,354 present for duty, of whom he estimates 61,025 were "effectives" (page 111), that is, after excluding non-combatants in the medical and quartermaster's departments, etc. (page 67). On muster rolls and such papers, "total" generally meant of enlisted men, "aggregate" of enlisted men and commissioned officers.

CHAPTER XXVIII

BATTLE OF THE WILDERNESS

On or about the 29th of April (1864) Steuart's Brigade left its Winter quarters near Pisgah Church and the Stone Road to perform a tour of picket duty at its usual station on the Rapidan, about six miles distant.

The face of the country had been greatly changed by the prolonged occupation of the army, fencing being gone and fields thrown open and uncultivated, and extensive forests cut down, so that we were able to pursue almost a straight course, regardless of roads, to our destination. The road, or route, led sometimes over abandoned fields, across marshy places bridged with "corduroy," and often for a long stretch through a desolate region of stumps, where the summer before had been a thick growth of oak or pine timber with luxuriant foliage. The country, thinly settled before, seemed now almost uninhabited and not even the bark of a dog or song of a bird broke the dreary silence. After a leisurely march of two or three hours we halted in a piece of woods a short distance back from the river not far from the mouth of Mountain Run and nearer to Gibson's house, which we made our headquarters, and in another hour or two the tedious operation of relieving pickets was completed and we were left in occupation.

As we were almost daily expecting the Spring campaign to open, we redoubled our vigilance on this tour and looked well to our flank, being the extreme right of the army infantry picket line. On the Culpeper County (enemy's) side the screening woods had been so thinned out in the course of the winter that several camps had come into plain view and we kept a close watch on them for any signs like breaking up. For two or three days nothing out of the way was observed but at last, about the 2d of May, an unusual quantity of smoke in the day-time and moving of lights by night gave sufficient evidence that the expected movement was about to be made. Soldiers are very apt, on breaking up camp, to make bonfires of their surplus wood and winter "fixings." On the morning of the next day (May 3d?)[1] a cloud of dust was seen floating over the woods in front and stretching in a long line parallel with and down the river, and at one exposed point the white covers of wagons and glistening muskets were visible, passing in endless succession, and there was no doubt the Union army was moving to cross one or more of the fords below, Germanna we rightly supposed. We signaled back to our principal observatory on Clark's Mountain, but were answered that they had a full view of the movement from that elevated point.

Clark's Mountain, in which the South West range, which passes through Albemarle and Orange Counties, here terminates, is a short distance in rear of the Rapidan, and commands a far and wide view of all the country in front. General Lee had his headquarters near it. All day long we watched the ominous cloud of dust hanging in the air and stream of wagons and glittering gun metal and knew that a few hours would find the two armies

---

[1] Grant's order for the movement was promulgated on May 2 and one cavalry division and a pontoon bridge train, etc., were to start on May 3 and the infantry was to begin to move at midnight of the same day. See General Humphrey's *Virginia Campaign of 1864–5*, Appendix D. I may have made an error of a day as to our observation but my recollection reduced to writing in the fall of 1883 was that wagons and troops moving down were visible on the 3d.

contending once more on a Wilderness battle ground.[2] That evening one or two deserters came over and gave confirmation, if any were needed, that Grant had put his whole army in motion.

The next morning, May 4, showed the same line of march and canopy of dust marking its course down the river. Two more deserters, one a Belgian speaking French only, came across at Morton's Ford, closely pursued and fired on to the edge of the water. In the afternoon we received orders to march, the quartermasters and men in camp being directed to pack up at winter quarters and move down the Orange and Fredericksburg Plank Road[3] to join us. About 3 p.m. we moved out under cover of the woods and took a cross road in a southerly direction towards the Wilderness, the 37th Virginia being left on the picket line with instructions to withdraw after night and overtake us. At dark we struck the Orange and Fredericksburg Stone Road, which at this point is a mile or more north of the Plank Road, and went into bivouac.

Early in the morning, May 5, Johnson's Division being now united—our 37th Virginia not being up, however— we started down the Stone Road towards Fredericksburg, but on reaching a point nearly abreast of Germanna Ford and within two miles of Wilderness Run and

[2] Colonel Warren, of the 10th Virginia, of Harrisonburg, Rockingham County in the Valley, a fine officer and a most estimable gentleman, sat with us at our headquarters in Gibson's house that night until 9 or 10 o'clock while we talked about the opening campaign. He said he was afraid Maryland could never become a part of the Confederacy but Virginia would take care of all exiled Marylanders. He added that he expected to have some influence in his county after the war and, turning to Captain Williamson, he said, "You shall be clerk of the county." Colonel Warren was slain within forty-eight hours.

[3] I wrote "Plank Road" in my published account but I should think it more probable that it was the Stone Road.

Tavern, were brought to a halt by the information that the enemy, having crossed the Rapidan at Germanna, were moving out into the country along our front. And a brisk skirmish soon began, probably with J. M. Jones's Brigade which had the advance, and turning down an old woods road which diverged from the Stone Road to the left oblique, we presently halted again and formed forward in line of battle.

We were now in the heart of "the Wilderness," a well named tract extending from the Rapidan River on the north across the Stone and Plank Roads to the south and to near Fredericksburg on the east. It is in places level and marshy, or rather with numerous wet spring heads, but for the most part rolling and sometimes rugged, with very few open fields or clearings of thin soil easily washing into gullies, and still fewer houses scattered here and there. Deer are still to be found there.[4] The woods, which seem to stretch out interminably, are in some places of pine, with low spreading branches through which a horseman cannot force his way without much turning and twisting, but generally the oak predominates. In many places the large trees had been cut down in years past—whether for the construction of plank roads or for furnaces or other purposes I do not know—and a jungle of switch, twenty or thirty feet high, more impenetrable, if possible, than the pine, had sprung up. A more difficult and disagreeable field of battle could not well be imagined. There is no room for cavalry and little range for artillery. It is an affair of musketry at close quarters, from which one combatant or the other must

---

[4] In one or more accounts of the battle of Chancellorsville I have read that Jackson's flank attack was preceded by frightened deer, rabbits and other animals.

soon recoil, if both do not construct breastworks, as they learned to do with wonderful rapidity.

Some little delay occurred in making a connected line, facing to the direction in which we had been marching, but by midday the men were lying down in position, our Brigade being nearly at right angles with the Stone Road, which was perhaps a couple of hundred yards south of our right. The skirmish firing indicated that the enemy were moving diagonally across and towards our front, and it drew closer and closer until stray bullets were cutting through the branches overhead. I was at the right of the brigade line, General Steuart being towards the centre, when Major-General Johnson rode by in some haste and called out to me,[5] that it was not intended to bring on a general engagement that day.[6] When he presently rode up a second time and called out, "Remember, Captain Howard, it is not meant to have a general engagement," I said, "But, General, it is evident that the two lines will come together in a few moments, and whether it is intended to have a general engagement or not, will it not be better for our men to have the impetus of a forward movement in the collision?" "Very well," said he, "let them go ahead a little." I looked down the line towards General Steuart (I do not remember now— 1911—whether he was in sight, but the bullets were flying thicker and the men were getting restive and the moment seemed critical), and, raising my sword, I called out "Forward!" The men responded with alacrity and almost immediately a tremendous fire rolled along the line. Battle's Brigade of Rodes's Division had just been placed

[5] Meaning it for General Steuart, of course.

[6] No doubt General Lee desired to have Longstreet's two divisions up (which having recently come from service in the west were in the rear—towards Gordonsville, I think) and the army well concentrated or connected.

behind our right and, catching the enthusiasm, it rushed forward also. We pressed right on, firing heavily and driving the enemy through the dense thicket. Large bodies were taken prisoners, one regiment, the 116th New York I think,[7] in new uniforms with heavy yellow trimmings, being captured almost as an organization—many of them, however, lay dead or wounded. For some time the woods road (I mean simply an old road through the woods, little used,) on which we had diverged from the Stone Road and across which our line extended, was blocked up by a mass of prisoners. None but our slightly wounded were allowed to guard them to the rear and they were simply directed, for the most part, to keep that road back until they would meet troops having more leisure to take charge of them. Probably many escaped.

Meanwhile we had driven the enemy through the jungle to an open field extending on both sides of the Stone Road and as they were pressed across it a destructive fire was poured into them, so that it appeared to me the ground was more thickly strewn with their dead and wounded than I had ever seen. A battery had been in the act of crossing this field, all but two pieces of which had wheeled about and gotten off, but all the horses and many of the drivers of these two had been shot down and they remained standing in the midst of the dead and wounded for the next day or two. The officer commanding the artillery, or this section, mounted on a fine Morgan horse, refused for a time to yield himself and was only saved from death by the intervention of Colonel Brown of the 1st North Carolina, who, struck with his gallantry, called out, as an inducement to surrender,

[7] Colonel Thruston, of the 3d North Carolina, says the 146th New York, commanded by Colonel Jenkins, of Elmira, New York, which seems correct from the records.

that he would give him the special honor of a commissioned officer to escort him to the rear. The Colonel
mounted his horse, however, and rode it during the rest
of the fight.[8]

At this time Major-General Johnson rode by again
and I said to him, "General, if it is not intended to have
a general engagement, the edge of the woods, with the
open space in front will be an excellent place to form our
line," and he replied, "Yes, let it be done." I communicated it to General Steuart, and it was so done.[9] About
half of our men had, however, eagerly pushed on half
way across the field and when recalled some fifteen or
twenty remained out, taking refuge in a deep gully to
avoid the stream of bullets which passed over their heads,
until able to come in under cover of night. Just before
we made our charge I had observed some confusion to
our right where J. M. Jones's Brigade[10] adjoined us, or
rather was in advance, supported by part of Battle's
(of Rodes's Division). One of Jones's best regiments,
the 25th (?) Virginia, being, unfortunately, captured
almost entire on the skirmish line and a strong attack
being made on him—which we by our forward movement
anticipated with such good result—his men gave back
and Jones himself, apparently disdaining to fly, was
killed while sitting on his horse gazing at the approaching
enemy; so his death was described to me by Captain
Cleary of his staff. A very gallant and efficient officer,
of the old regular army, his loss was severely felt, particularly at the critical moment of the assault at Spotsyl-

[8] The two guns belonged to Battery D, 1st New York, Captain Winslow.
See the *War of the Rebellion Records*.

[9] I have always since regretted having made this last suggestion.

[10] He is to be distinguished from Brigadier-General John R. Jones, who formerly (in 1862) commanded this brigade.

vania. Other troops assisted to repair this temporary
reverse and this part of the line was established and advanced with ours, or nearly.

On our left the Stonewall and Stafford's Brigades had
been and continued to be hotly engaged and, being partly
enveloped on the flank, lost heavily; General Stafford
was killed some time in the afternoon and most of his
staff were captured. The whole division finally occupied
a line extending ours on the right and left and, firing
having ceased except in a desultory way, we soon began
to construct such rude and slight breastworks as we
could without implements, and the enemy on his side
apparently busied himself in the same manner. Opposite the right of Johnson's Division, which rested near the
Stone Road, the open field separated the hostile lines by a
considerable interval, compared at least with the distance
between them on our centre and left, where the breastworks
were not more than pistol shot apart, but with a thick
jungle between. I think Steuart's Brigade now held the
right of the Division, Jones's having been much shattered.
I do not remember that a single piece of artillery had been
used on either side. The fighting had been close and the
loss in our division was heavy, including Brigadier-Generals Jones and Stafford and many officers of rank. In
Steuart's Brigade the 10th Virginia had two field officers
killed—Colonel E. T. H. Warren and Major Coffman,
both officers of unusual merit. Colonel Warren was one
of the most efficient regimental commanders in the service and a gentleman of singularly amiable character.
The other three regiments (the 37th Virginia, left on the
Rapidan on picket had not overtaken us), also suffered
severely in officers and men. It is usual to speculate on
a far greater loss on an enemy's side, but as our brigade

at least drove them across open ground, it is reasonable to suppose, and appearances indicated that in this part of the battle they lost more heavily. Certainly the field in our front was strewn very thickly with their fallen, mingled with whom were some of our own. This being now the territory of neither party, the wounded of neither could be removed or receive any attention. Several efforts were made to relieve them but the enemy opened fire whenever we exposed ourselves at the edge of the thicket and the attempts had to be abandoned.

Our picket or skirmish line had been established a few paces in advance of the breastworks—if such they could then be called—and endless alarms and exchanges of shots kept us on the alert. It was half a dozen times reported that the enemy were advancing, that the voices of their officers could be plainly heard inciting the men, but no serious attack was made for some time; and after rushing to arms more than once under the impression that a charge was imminent, we presently grew accustomed to the situation and received such alarms more stolidly.

Our 37th Virginia now came up from the rear, too late to participate in action with us, but being sent to the left to support Pegram's Brigade of Early's Division, which had been placed on the left of the Stonewall and Stafford, and where there was still desultory fighting, it soon found itself under fire and Colonel Williams was slightly wounded in the foot. Just about dark the enemy in our front made a rash charge across the corner of the open ground, apparently with the intention of recovering their two abandoned guns, but a couple of our pieces which had been posted on rising ground at the mouth of the Stone Road on our right, opened with canister and drove them back with loss. This closed the operations of the day.[11]

Shortly afterwards a number of our men came in under cover of darkness from the front, having lain in the gully for many hours—from the time when we had recalled and reformed our line within the edge of the woods.

[11] Little has been told of and justice has not been done to the strenuous and I may say successful part taken by Steuart's Brigade in this first day's battle in the Wilderness. Generals Steuart and Johnson were captured a week later and never made official reports, nor did the regimental commanders. In fact, not many Confederate reports were made from this time to the end of the war. The report of General Ewell, corps commander, *War of the Rebellion Records*, Series 1, Volume XXXVI, Part I, Serial No. 67, page 1069, is inadequate for want of information from such reports of subordinates. I did not see him on our part of the line during the battle.

Moved by this absence of recognition of the part taken by Johnson's Division, and especially Steuart's Brigade, Colonel Stephen D. Thruston of our 3d North Carolina, wrote, in 1885 or 1886, an account of the operations from May 4 to May 12, which was published in the *Southern Historical Papers*, Volume XIV, page 146. But there was not published with it a plat of the battle of May 5 which Colonel Thruston had annexed to his account, a copy of which I made and have. This plat, by a man of his superior intelligence and opportunities for information, is interesting and valuable and should be looked at by any one studying the details and result of this first day's battle of the campaign. It shows the nature of the ground (he says he made a sketch of the battlefield on May 7—when it was all accessible to us as will appear presently), and the successive positions of the Brigades of Ewell's Corps at different hours of the day; although his own observation could not have extended much beyond his own Brigade and that or those immediately on his right, his Regiment holding the right of Steuart's Brigade. The topography as shown on his plat, the clearing and surrounding woods, etc., agree closely with my account and with a plat made by me in 1883, except as to the roads. Colonel Thruston takes no notice of what I called the "woods road," and this road on which I said we diverged from the Stone Road he makes the straight Stone Road itself which he says had become impassable from the gully or washout in front, and he shows a curved traveled road on the south of it all the way over the open field and so around the head of the washout. And yet my recollection seems distinct that we did so diverge on this side road, and is in a measure confirmed by war maps, which show such a road as running over and a short cut to the road leading from Germanna Ford to the Stone Road. I do not remember Colonel Thruston's curved traveled road, but I was very little, if at all, south of the straight Stone Road.

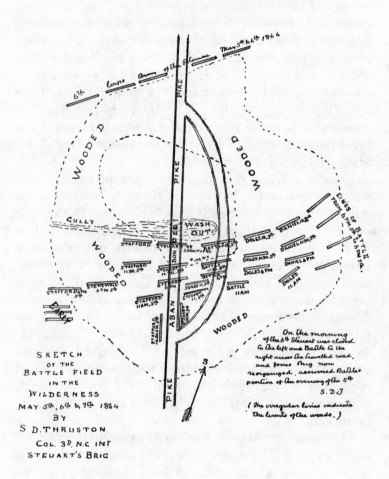

SKETCH
OF THE
BATTLE FIELD
IN THE
WILDERNESS
MAY 5ᵗʰ, 6ᵗʰ & 7ᵗʰ 1864
BY
S.D. THRUSTON
COL. 3ᴰ. N.C INf
STEUART'S BRIG

On the morning
of the 6ᵗʰ Steuart was closed
to the left and Battle to the
right across the travelled road,
and Jones Brig now
reorganized, assumed Battles
position of the evening of the 5ᵗʰ
S.D.T.

(The irregular lines indicate
the limits of the woods.)

When the enemy made their last charge at nightfall, they had passed directly over the gully and in returning several of them stopped in it for shelter from the fire of canister. These our fellows had immediately captured, finding on them some canteens of whisky, an unknown article on our side, and both parties made themselves as sociable and comfortable as their situation would permit. The senior officer of the squad, Captain DePriest of the 23d Virginia, now brought in his men and prisoners and came to me to make a voluble and unsteady report (leaning against a tree,) of what he was pleased to call his separate operations during the day.

Usually there is not much groaning or outcry from wounded men on a battlefield; they do not feel acute pain, or else bear their sufferings in silence. But on this occasion circumstances seemed to make their situation peculiarly distressing, and their moans and cries were painful to listen to. In the still night air every groan could be heard and the calls for water and entreaties to brothers and comrades by name to come and help them. Many, Federal and Confederates, lay within a dozen paces of our skirmish line, whom we found it impossible to succor, although we tried. I was myself fired on while making two separate efforts to get some in. I well remember that at midnight when I lay down to sleep, and on waking during the night, their cries were ringing in my ears.

The next day, May 6, was spent in strengthening our slight works. There was no renewal of the attack in our quarter, although the pickets fired at short range on every one who exposed himself, by which we lost two good officers, one, I think, Lieutenant Cicero Craige of the 3d North Carolina. Our men were instructed to keep a jealous watch on the two pieces of artillery which still stood outside the line to be the fruits of that side which would in the end remain masters of the field. We understood that A. P. Hill's Corps was having an engagement over to the right, but knew no particulars and I do not remember that we heard the sound of it. The heaviest firing, musketry at least, may be inaudible at a short distance, comparatively speaking, in this gloomy and tangled wilderness, although distinctly heard perhaps dozens of miles away. The dull noise of artillery will, of course go further and I have known well authenticated instances of the sound of battle being carried to the mountains of Virginia, a hundred miles or more distant, but without being heard in a part of the intervening country.[12]

A little before sunset Brigadier-General John B. Gordon (of Early's Division, Ewell's Corps), who we heard had been asking permission all day to turn the enemy's right flank, being at last accorded it, made an attack with signal success, capturing Brigadier-Generals Seymour and Shaler, with many men, and sweeping down the line for a considerable distance. We, meanwhile, stood under arms, expecting orders to carry on the movement, but it was deemed too hazardous. But it seemed to us that it might have been followed up with the promise of important results.[13]

[12] When trout fishing after the war at the head of Dry Fork of Cheat River in Randolph County, West Virginia, in the Alleghenies, I was assured that the sound of some of the battles in eastern Virginia had been heard although much more than a hundred miles away and with several mountain ranges between. At Wye House in Talbot County, Maryland, the 9 o'clock evening gun at Annapolis, twenty-odd miles distant is usually heard, even in a close room in winter. And yet I have never heard in the middle of Baltimore the sunset gun at Fort McHenry, not two miles off.

[13] Major-General Johnson told me a few days afterwards when we were prisoners together that the adjutant-general of the Union Army stated to him that on this occasion the army (that part of it?) had been doubled on its center and its

At any rate we found the enemy gone from our front
the next morning, May 7, and sallied out to examine the
ground, pushing our skirmishers forward who finally
came upon the enemy in position a long way back—I
think a mile.[14] We now hauled in our two captured
guns,[15] removed the surviving wounded, who had been
lying unsuccored for two days, and buried as many of the
dead as we could. The brush had caught fire and the
creeping flames were burning up many of the latter and,
no doubt, some of the wounded. The pioneer corps of
our division, I heard, reported having buried 582 of the
enemy in front of our (Ewell's) Corps and many were

safety seemed to be endangered. In conversation with General Collis after the
war, he informed me that he was with General Grant at the time when General
Meade rode up and reported the situation to be serious, but General Grant remarked with an impatient gesture (pushing up the front of his cap), that Burn-
sides' Corps had not been put in action and could be used if necessary. But see
note at end of this chapter.

[14] General Ewell, in his report referred to before, says the enemy drew back
their line so that Germanna Ford was entirely given up.

[15] But Colonel Thruston's account says that they were brought in on the night
of May 5. And Captain Randolph Barton, adjutant-general of the Stonewall
Brigade, now living in Baltimore, tells me that the late Eugene Blackford (who
died near Sudbrook in Baltimore County a few years ago), major of the 4th
Alabama and commanding the skirmishers of Rodes's Division, informed him
that the two guns were dragged in after dark by means of a large rope which
some courageous men had fastened to them, and probably on the night of the
6th. I suppose my recollection was a little at fault and that they had been
brought in on the night of the 5th or 6th, most likely the latter. I remember
going on the 7th to the position where they had been but do not recall then seeing them, although I think we found there, with dead men and horses, one or
more still living wounded. Whenever they were brought in, I remember the
indignation of our men at some one's having chalked on the guns "captured by
Battle's Brigade," or to that effect. They were certainly fairly taken by Steuart's Brigade. This is not only confirmed by what I have narrated about
Colonel Browne and the officer commanding the section, but Colonel Thruston
gives other particulars, among other that Captain Cantwell, Lieutenant Lyon
and Adjutant James (who lost an arm), all of the 3d North Carolina, turned the
guns on the enemy but could find no ammunition to fire them.

left uninterred for want of time.[16] The enemy's line gave evidences of having been abandoned in much haste, knapsacks, haversacks, rations, etc., lying strewn around, which were eagerly gathered by our men. About midday the enemy advanced in our front and our pickets gradually fell back, but not to their original line on the left, in the thicket. For the rest of the day there was frequent firing between the pickets or skirmishers[17] but without much damage done. At our right, near the Stone Road, there was a loss sustained, however, in the death of

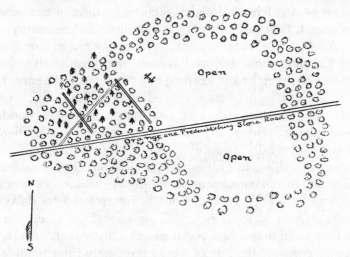

Colonel J. Thompson Brown,[18] commanding the reserve artillery of Ewell's Corps, who was shot through the

[16] General Ewell's report says that the burial parties of two of his divisions reported having interred over 1100 of the enemy and the third and larger made no report.

[17] At this time and thenceforward to the end of the war the two armies were so close that a picket line was very likely to be a skirmish line and the two terms came to be used interchangeably.

[18] Major Blackford told Captain Randolph Barton that Colonel Brown had dismounted and come through the woods to where he was and that he was endeavoring to point out a Union skirmisher to Brown, who was standing immediately behind him, when a ball struck a limb near by and, glancing, struck Brown mortally.

head by a stray bullet as he rode behind the breastworks.
One of the enemy, having climbed a tree opposite the
same point, annoyed us by attempting to pick off our
men across the open, but he was either shot down or
made too uncomfortable on his perch.

Towards dark we were notified there would be a movement by the right flank along the line of works and were
ordered to watch the troops with whom we there made
connection and follow them. So the men were kept
under arms and strictly prohibited from making fires or
noise or any unusual signs, such as rattling of canteens
or metal, that might betray our motions to the enemy.

About 9 o'clock, p.m., our neighbors began to move off
by the right flank and we followed, the skirmish line also
facing to the right and keeping between us and the enemy.
The line of breastworks, immediately behind which we
marched, ran for the most part through rugged woods
and the night being very dark, horsemen and foot soldiers
were continually stumbling over stumps, running into
trees, or falling in gullies with which the easily washed
thin soil of the country abounded. We seldom went one
or two hundred yards without being arrested by delays
in front, nor were those halts long enough or of any certainty so that the men could snatch a little rest. So the
night wore on, the line of works seemingly interminable,
up and down hill and winding about in the desolate Wilderness region. About half an hour before dawn there
was a longer halt and the men lay down in their places
and took a brief repose.

At 6 or 7 o'clock, May 8, we resumed the march, striking off from the works to the right oblique, and presently
found ourselves on a road which led in the direction of
Spotsylvania Court House. The troops we had been
keeping in touch with during the night had disappeared
while we were resting. For a couple of miles we were

compelled to pass through burning woods, the smoke and heat of which were very distressing, particularly as there was a scarcity of water, this being the ridge between the waters of the Rapidan and the Mattapony. By midday we were becoming much exhausted and the rearguard had a difficult and most disagreeable duty to perform in keeping the men from falling out. The dust, too, was very annoying and the day was hot. But at such a time the plea of physical exhaustion had to be disregarded and stragglers were urged and made to move on by persuasion and almost by force. Later in the day we struck across the country and got into another road leading to Spotsylvania Court House.[19]

[19] When my paper on the opening of the campaign was sent to the Massachusetts Military Historical Society in 1882 or 1883, Mr. John C. Ropes, founder of the Society, sent it to Colonel Lyman, of General Meade's staff, who returned it to him with a letter from which the following is an extract:

"My dear Ropes: . . . . I lent the Wilderness part to Gen. Pierson who was Lt. Col. of the 39th Mass. and in the Brigade whose fire stopped the pursuit across the 'open space' and compelled the enemy to retire to the opposite edge of the woods. He says the account (for the time he was on the field) is very accurate. What is curious is that he too remembers the cries of the wounded. Several times he essayed, with volunteers, to go out with stretchers to bring them in, but was received with such a fire as compelled him to retreat. Only in the footnote on page 10 of the Wilderness (page 278 note 13) do I observe an inaccuracy. Gen. Edward Johnson must have misunderstood Gen. Seth Williams (who gave him a good breakfast on May 12th). The army after the evening attack on the 6th Corps was not 'doubled on the centre,' but the right was swung back. If the Gen. Collis there mentioned was Col. of the 114th Penna., I think his memory must deceive him. . . . . Moreover, I rode with Gen. Meade on that occasion and heard what was said and have no recollection of seeing Gen. Collis there. Gen. Grant could not have 'pushed up the front of his cap,' for he never wore a cap. Gen. Grant seemed a little worried, but Gen. Meade was as cool as possible. He said to me 'Nonsense! It they *have* broken our line, they can do nothing more tonight,' or words to that effect; and he treated two officers of the 6th Corps who rode in with panicky reports to very sarcastic remarks. He told Grant he had ordered the Pennsylvania Reserves to the right and that was enough. Neither before nor after did I know of so profound and uncalled for a panic as this one of a portion of the 6th Corps. . . .   "Truly yours,
                                        "THEODORE LYMAN."

CHAPTER XXIX

BATTLE OF SPOTSYLVANIA COURT HOUSE

About an hour before sunset, May 8 (1864), Steuart's Brigade, in the lead of Johnson's Division, was within two miles of Spotsylvania Court House,[1] and the tired men had just been cheered by an assurance passed down the column that they were presently going into camp when firing was heard to the left oblique and news came that Rodes's Division, which preceded us, had found itself in collision with the enemy. Our column was turned in that direction[2] and soon faced to the left in line of battle a hundred yards or so in rear of Rodes, a good many bullets meant for his men passing over and striking about us.

I was here placed for a while in a very uncomfortable situation. I met General Ewell, who was alone, and he directed me to ride back and order Jones's Brigade to come up. I did so and came back with it myself—probably because, Jones having been killed, a regimental officer was in command of it, in whom I did not feel confidence—and, finding General Ewell and Major-General Johnson together, I reported to the former, "General, I have brought up Jones's Brigade as you ordered." General Ewell said, "I gave you no such order, Sir." And General Johnson broke out on me violently, "No, that brigade is in my division and moves only by my

---

[1] I think we were on the Shady Grove Church Road just before it strikes the Brock Road, a mile west of the Court House.

[2] Or moved forward across the Brock Road instead of turning to the right (east) on it.

order." I said to Ewell, "Why, General, you did order me to do it." But he again denied it, and General Johnson continued to speak to me very roughly. I felt much alarmed until General Ewell presently said, "Stop, stop, General Johnson, I did give Captain Howard the order—it was an emergency." I was greatly relieved, for my word might have availed little against General Ewell's. While leading the brigade up a bullet or something had struck my sword and a piece of stone had flown up from the ground and hit me on the breast but doing no harm. The rear of a line of battle in action is not a comfortable place unless there is some intervening high ground.

About dark the firing gradually ceased, both sides apparently holding their own, and our division was faced to the right, from line into column, and moved forward so as to extend the line from Rodes's right. By 10 o'clock the whole division was stretched out in some fashion and was ordered to rectify the alignment and throw up breastworks, but the ground was thickly wooded and on the right, which was held by Steuart's Brigade, was covered with a growth of low spreading pine trees or bushes, absolutely without any spaces between them often; so that after moving backwards and forwards and closing up to the left and to the right, we got very much tangled and the prospect of making a straight or well connected line in the worn out condition of the men became worse and worse. The voices of Generals Johnson and Steuart were heard for some time in the night, but in the thicket and darkness the men could not see them, nor could they see each other, and staff officers could not well ride through, so that, tired, hungry and sleepy, they finally sank down where each one happened to find himself.

At daylight, May 9, the line was rectified and the men went to work intrenching, without any proper implements. The enemy soon opened an artillery fire from opposite the left of the division, which, enfilading us on its right in a measure, annoyed us a good deal, although we were not visible to them. When the breastworks of Steuart's Brigade, which were nearly a continuation of the line on the left, were half made the engineer officers of the army came along and ordered us to destroy them and construct a new line. About fifty or seventy-five yards to the front of the left of the line we had been making the ground rose to a point or ridge off which there was some open country, giving a good range for artillery, and this was made a part of the new line, Jones's Brigade, or its right, being advanced a little I suppose, so as to connect with it. But the new line of Steuart's Brigade, instead of being a continuation of that of Jones and the rest of the division, and so parallel with and in advance of our old line, turned back from this elevated point or ridge at a right angle with Jones, thus making a salient in the works. I asked the engineers if our first half constructed breastwork could not remain as it could do no harm, being completely enfiladed by our new line, and might be of service, but they said no, it must be demolished, and so we half levelled it. At the point of the angle were placed six or eight pieces of artillery. The picket line off the angle was divided, of course, between us and Jones. (I keep the designation of the brigade although Jones had been killed on the 5th.) In our new position we were exposed more than before to the fire of the enemy's artillery, which now, passing over the brigades on our left for whom it was intended, took us in flank and rear, so that it was only in the intervals when the fire slackened that we were able to do much work. When completed, therefore, our intrenchments were constructed for protection from side and behind quite as much as for defence in front and consisted of a chain or series of deep square or rectangular pits, end to end. We also cleared away the small pines and brush for a space in front and made a very tolerable abatis with the interlaced branches outwards. Having few tools, the labor was tedious and it was not until the middle of the next day that the works were sufficient for protection. Meanwhile details were sent back to the wagons who brought up cooked rations, consisting in the main of cold corn bread.

Towards evening on May 10 there was some sharp firing on the skirmish line on the left of the angle and the enemy's artillery reopened with such violence as to cause us much inconvenience, although, I believe, with little or no loss of life in our command. A little before sunset I was a short distance out in front of our right, intending to find out what connection we had on our skirmish line there, for there were no troops visible on our flank, when I saw or heard some commotion back in our line and, hastening there, found a message had come that a part of the line of Rodes's Division, on Johnson's left[3] had been captured by a sudden rush and ordering our brigade to his support in all possible haste. The distance by a straight line across the angle was only a few hundred yards, but the emergency seemed so great that the head of our column was pushed on at a double quick, leaving the rear to follow as best it could, so that the men reached the scene of action with a good deal of ardor but much exhausted and strung out.[4] Several dead bodies in blue

[3] The part of Rodes's line captured was in front of the McCool house.

[4] It is better to lose a little time to preserve order. And it is extremely difficult to teach soldiers the proper double quick step, which with the shoulders and weight of the body thrown back, is not fatiguing for short distances, whereas a run is very soon exhausting.

uniform were passed, one or two hundred yards inside the line, showing, apparently, that the enemy had penetrated thus far; but they were now limiting themselves, or limited, to holding some two hundred yards—as I supposed—of the works, from which they poured a destructive fire to their front and down the line. Without waiting for the rear, our advance was formed and pushed forward along the line, but being only a few hundred men up, we were not strong enough to retake the ground, or much of it. The greater part of these bore to the right and reaching the works about where the enemy's left was, made an attempt to charge down the line. But the fire—perhaps some of it coming from our own friends on the other side of the gap—was so withering that the men recoiled from each charge, or at least made little progress and could only hold their own, or what little they had retaken.

I saw many instances of conspicuous gallantry on the part of individuals under these trying circumstances. William Steuart, the General's younger brother, who had just been appointed, or rather, determined on as aide de camp, for I do not think his appointment had been received, certainly had not been announced, and who was in black citizen's dress, attracted my attention by the very daring manner in which he headed these charges, first attempting to lead the men forward down the inside of the line, then jumping upon and walking along the top of the breastwork itself, and finally leaping upon the outer side and endeavoring to induce the men to sweep down the enemy's own side.[5] Captain Williamson, assistant adjutant-general, I saw exposing himself to an equal degree. Lieutenant Robert H. Lyon, of the 3d

[5] He was mortally wounded, either on May 12 or a few days later. He is buried in the Steuart vault in Greenmount Cemetery, Baltimore.

North Carolina, seized the regimental colors, and, calling on the men to follow, rushed with the flag so far in advance that he appeared in imminent danger of being shot down by our own fire, if not by the enemy. Captain John Badger Brown,[6] of the same regiment, one of our best officers, fell near me badly wounded, and many other officers[7] and men were killed or disabled. We regained only a part of the works and it became evident that the entire recapture should be made by a fresh body of troops marching squarely up to the gap. General Steuart so stated to General Johnson who accordingly rode off in search of such assistance, while we desisted from further attempts and confined ourselves to holding what we had. We lay down behind the breastworks, receiving in silence the enfilading fire which continued to come down them, whether from foe or friend, and watching to repel any attack that might be made in front. Several times it was reported that such an attack was being made or threatened and some of the men rose up and fired, but in the dusk which had come on I could see nothing. A more disagreeable half hour, with a bullet striking a man lying on the ground every now and then, could not well have been spent. Presently Captain Williamson passed along and informed me that General Steuart was about to reform the brigade about a hundred yards in rear, expressing a quite alarming hope that I would not be shot down in crossing over there! Here

[6] He established himself in business in Baltimore after the war and died ten or twelve years ago.

[7] I don't think I knew until afterwards that Colonel Thruston of the same regiment, which seems to have borne the brunt, was also seriously wounded. Fortunately, Lieutenant-Colonel Oswald M. Parsley, of Wilmington, was another very efficient officer of this unusually well-officered regiment. Colonel Thruston died in Texas many years ago. Lieutenant-Colonel Parsley was killed about April 6, 1865, at or near Appomattox.

about one-fourth were got together and the General, learning that other troops were passing up and not liking the idea of failing to participate with them, led his command forward.   But when we reached the works the last enemy had been driven out, or more probably were withdrawn, and about 10 o'clock we returned to our own position which had all the while been bare of defenders except the skirmish line and artillery.[8]

This affair impressed us with the necessity of strengthening our line and next morning, May 11, the men fell to work with increased energy, particularly on the abatis, the importance of which in detaining and throwing into confusion an enemy within point-blank range, they now fully appreciated.   It is a mistake made by non-combatants only to suppose that a slight field breastwork is any material obstacle of itself to a charging enemy, it being a covering only to the men behind it.   Indeed, with all its advantages in economizing life, fighting behind such fieldworks has some disadvantages also.   Give a man protection for his body and the temptation is very strong to put his head under cover too.   My observation during this campaign was that behind works not a few men will crouch down doing nothing, that many will fire

[8] Colonel Theodore Lyman, of General Meade's staff, says in the letter from which I have quoted, "The capture of a part of the line on May 10th was the assault by Upton's brigade of the 6th Corps.   By gross neglect *somewhere* that beautiful attack was unsupported.   If it had been, the whole salient would have been captured.   Upton withdrew unmolested at dark, and took nearly 1000 prisoners.   Going over that front in the Spring of 1866 I found it thickly strewn with sabots from the enemy's batteries."   (These sabots, i.e. wooden shoes of shells, were no doubt from the firing on the 12th.)   Captain Randolph Barton adjutant-general of the Stonewall Brigade, tells me he suggested to General Johnson the ordering up of Steuart's Brigade and bore himself the message from him to the brigade.   He also says that about one-third of the Stonewall Brigade was swung back from the works to face towards Upton.

Colonel Thruston complains that Ewell's report makes no mention of the part taken by Steuart's Brigade in this affair.

above the heads of their assailants, sometimes at a high angle, and few, comparatively, will raise their heads and shoulders fairly above the rampart and level their pieces with effect. When the enemy reaches the other side of the work, in perhaps five cases out of six it is carried. Whereas the object and advantage of an abatis is to detain and disorder the assailants, while the defenders, although not firing with accuracy perhaps, yet inflict loss and suffer comparatively little. But, generally speaking, the result, however favorable to those behind the works, is only a repulse, if a bloody one, and is not followed up with consequences such as attend a victory in the open field. Jackson used no field works in his Valley campaign and I think he preferred to be "foot-loose." But perhaps he would have used them in this stage of the war, although I believe he would always have made flank or other offensive movements. I may here say that I have always been an advocate of arming company officers with carbines; the fire of twenty or thirty additional pieces in a regiment, presumably in the hands of the best men, at critical times, outweighing other considerations in my opinion.

During the morning I rode over to our field hospital, about two miles distant, to see how the wounded of the evening before were getting on. Two of our best company commanders, Captain Brown and another, were among them, but doing well. The sergeant-major of the 3d North Carolina, a boy who was a favorite with all, was fast sinking, attended by his father, a surgeon in another regiment. In his last conscious moments he was thinking and talking of his mother, whose only son I was told he was. Our senior surgeon gave me a most refreshing cup of hot tea, the taste of which had been long unknown, and I also had the luxury of a change of underclothing, having been marching and lying in or near the trenches with the same clothing on for a week. Riding back, I saw General Lee examining the rear of that part of Rodes's line which had been broken the day before.[9]

Before giving an account of the disaster of the following morning it will be well to describe briefly the character of our part of the line and the disposition of the troops behind—even with some repetition.

Of the four brigades of Johnson's Division, Walker's (the Stonewall) was on the left, connecting with Rodes's Division—Doles's Brigade I think—next to which was Stafford's (Louisiana), then Jones's, and Steuart's held the right. Generals Stafford and Jones, two very gallant men, had been killed in the first day's battle, May 5, and a part of the brigade of the latter was said to be a good deal disheartened by its losses and for want of such a commander as Jones had been. All four had suffered heavily since the fighting began and I do not think they now averaged 1000 behind the works, more probably less, for besides the killed, wounded and prisoners, not a few must have fallen out from sickness or under the hardships. The three brigades first named held a continuation from the left of the main army line and running easterly,[10] but Steuart's turned back at nearly a right angle from Jones's right. There was no immediate support[11] or continuation of the line from Steuart's right (except pickets?), there being an interval—one mile we supposed at the time—between us and a part of A. P.

---

[9] I did not know then, but a new line was being constructed or laid out across the salient.

[10] In my account written for the Massachusetts Military Historical Society, I said "northerly," but I see now it ran more easterly.

[11] I did not know in 1865, nor even in 1882, that an interior line was being made across the salient and that General Gordon was getting behind it.

Hill's Corps, now commanded by Major-General Jubal A. Early. In Steuart's front the ground was densely wooded with oak and pine (except that there was a narrow half open strip off our center and right), with many small ravines and spring-heads, and we had our skirmishers well out without having felt an enemy, except on the left off the angle. The line of the other three brigades ran through oaks principally and a short distance in front the ground was partly wooded and partly open, but always rather rough. The point of the angle was on elevated ground, both open—except to its right—and sloping towards the enemy giving the only good position for artillery along the line, and both for this reason and because a heavy infantry fire could not be directed out from the angle, this salient was occupied by six or eight pieces. There were also two guns in Steuart's center, and probably others along the left of the division. Behind the three left brigades the ground was wooded, but directly in rear of Steuart it was less so, but with some bushes. In the rear of Doles (the adjoining brigade of Rodes's Division,) there was a considerable clearing— around the McCoull house.

There had been several showers during the day and towards evening the air was damp and heavy and began to be foggy. A little before sunset (May 11), we were surprised to notice all the artillery in the salient and on our center, limber up and move to the rear; and asking an officer what this meant, he replied he did not know, except that they were ordered back to camp. At our headquarters we discussed this movement with some uneasiness, but supposed other batteries would come to relieve them.[12]

[12] In the first year of the war, and part of the second, batteries were attached to and integral parts of brigades, but after that had been detached and organ-

Some time after dark[13] a message came in from our skirmish line off the angle that there was a steady rumbling in front, indicating that a large force was being massed in front or passing around to our right. General Steuart had been very active during the day and was asleep, and Captain Williamson and I, the only two staff officers present, immediately walked out some distance and afterwards stood for half an hour on the breastwork, listening to the subdued roar or noise, plainly audible in the still, heavy night air, like distant falling water or machinery. If night has the advantage of covering a military movement to the eye, it nevertheless often betrays it to the ear. Convinced that an important movement was on foot, and believing that it portended an attack on our weak angle in the morning (and I have an indistinct recollection that a deserter had gone over to the enemy who, we apprehended, might have disclosed its condition,) we reported to General Steuart who signed a dispatch to Major-General Johnson, which was written by Captain Williamson and was to this effect:

MAJOR R. W. HUNTER, Assistant Adjutant-General;

Major:—The enemy is moving and probably massing in our front and we expect to be attacked at daylight. The artillery along our front has been withdrawn, by whose orders I know not and I beg that it be sent back immediately.

GEORGE H. STEUART,
Brigadier-General commanding.[14]

---

ized into artillery battalions and with their own line of commanding officers. I do not think that even corps commanders controlled their movements and dispositions much except, I suppose, on a field of battle; Division commanders had little, if any, authority, and brigade commanders none.

[13] In my published paper I said "shortly after dark," but the Union accounts state that the movement was begun later.

[14] The next day, when we were prisoners together, and often afterwards, General Johnson informed me that on receiving this dispatch he immediately sent it or one similar to General Ewell, commanding the Corps, urgently requesting that the artillery be returned. And General Ewell or his assistant

A circular[15] was then sent around to our regimental commanders warning them that we would probably be attacked in the morning and ordering them to have their men in the works half an hour before daylight.

On the 12th our men were in readiness (but I did not walk along the line to see), and so early that one company commander—I think it was Captain Cantwell of the 3d North Carolina—afterwards told me he made his men draw their loads and clean their guns while waiting. Owing to the fog day was late in breaking and even then there was no sign for a while of an attack, which I began to believe would not be made. But presently there came the sound of a distant cheer just off the angle, followed as suddenly by a deep silence, the suspense of which was most trying, especially as we now eagerly looked and wished for our artillery, which should have been there to open in the direction of the cheering. Then in a few moments there were shots from that part of our picket line which was off the salient and growing heavier, marking the direction and progress of the attacking column.

adjutant-general told me after my exchange from prison the following winter, that he received and forwarded such a dispatch to General Lee, whose headquarters were not far distant. Mentioning these facts after the war to Colonel Charles Marshall, General Lee's Military Secretary, he said he well remembered the circumstances and that General Lee on receiving the dispatch, remarked to his staff, "See, gentlemen, how difficult it is to have certain information or how to determine what to do. Here is a dispatch from General Johnson stating that the enemy are massing in his front, and at the same time I am informed by General Early that they are moving around our left. Which am I to believe?"—that, however, General Lee ordered the artillery to be back at daylight. See a late publication, *Lieutenant-General Jubal A. Early C.S.A., Autobiographical Sketch and Narrative of the War between the States*, pages 354–355. General Early speaks of his unique position in commanding both flanks of the army at the same time, his corps being divided.

[15] A circular was a written order sent around by a courier which each regimental commander read and endorsed with his name in acknowledgment of having received it.

Presently a body of men in blue appeared in our front, to the right of the salient, and our men of Steuart's Brigade delivered a volley, perhaps more, which caused it to disappear. I do not think this was a considerable force and it seems probable that it was one which missed the point of the angle and was passing down in front of the works of our brigade, inside our picket line, about at the abatis.[16]

About this time our artillery came up, rather slowly I thought,[17] and unlimbered but had not time to fire a shot before being overwhelmed, except the two pieces in our center, which were discharged once—maybe twice. Musketry firing was now very heavy where Jones's Brigade adjoined us on our left and soon a crowd of fugitives came pouring down our line of works from the angle, showing that something must have gone wrong in that quarter. I was at this time, and had been from the beginning, at our center. The two pieces of artillery there now or shortly before fired their round—of canister as I imagined from the sound—but the six or eight guns in the angle had been overwhelmed as soon as unlimbered.[18] I saw Captain Williamson pass by from that direction and knew from the expression of his face that something momentous had happened there but had no time to stop or question him. Soon a cloud of blue uniforms came pressing down from our left, along our works, in front of them, and, by far the greater number, completely filling

[16] At the time we were captured our pickets, I was told, were bringing in some prisoners from our front, with a result very much like the scene between the policemen and the pirates in the opera of the "Pirates of Penzance."

[17] General Humphries in his *Virginia Campaign of 1864–5*, page 95, misquotes me as saying that it came up "at a gallop."

[18] A captain in the 1st North Carolina, which was on our left, afterwards told me that, seeing the guns in possession of the enemy, he ordered his men to shoot at the horses—to prevent their being taken off.

the space within the angle and so directly in our rear. The pits in our center and right being, as I have described, deep and with traverses (side walls), available for defence in front, flank and rear, I thought they might be held or the enemy might be checked until reinforcements came up, as on the evening of the 10th; and, therefore, standing on the brink of one of them, I pushed passing fugitives into it until it was full and then jumped in. I remember a Federal soldier striding down the top of the embankment, foremost of his comrades, shouting and brandishing his gun above his head, and I called out to fire and a man—I think it was Bragonier, of the 10th Virginia—did so, and my impression is, with effect. And I also remember very vividly how the smoke of the discharge seemed as if it would never dissipate or float away from the spot in the heavy air and my apprehension that we would be made to pay a penalty for our temerity in firing when we were practically captured; for in a moment the edge of our pit (nearly shoulder deep), was surrounded on all sides. And I thought my apprehension was about to be realized when the Union soldiers brought their bayonets down with a threatening appearance, but it was only for the purpose of sweeping aside the bayonets of our men which were resting on the top, and we were ordered to scramble out. I retained my sword in my hand, after some hesitation whether or not to throw it away or stick it in the ground. One man took it out of my hand and another came up while he was doing so and drawing a large clasp knife from his pocket and opening it (I wondered if he was going to stab me), he cut the scabbard from my leather belt, and they went their several ways with their trophies. We were ordered to their rear and in going I passed up the breastwork and out at the angle. In front of this and on my left as I went back the ground was open and was crowded with a dense mass streaming up and I thought that if our artillery had been in position at the angle it would have inflicted a terrible loss and perhaps have checked the assault. I never saw an occasion when artillery would have done such execution.[19] We were squeezed between this column of attack and the woods on our right and two or three times I tried to sidle into the thicket with a view to escaping, but each time was gruffly admonished to keep to the left in the open.

This assault was well planned and executed, but it is a mistake to suppose, as sometimes stated, that the Confederate infantry were taken by surprise. The sound of the cheering, and even the picket firing, would have given time enough to get into the trenches, but in fact we were (in Steuart's Brigade at least,) sufficiently prepared, as above shown. It may be that some were interrupted at their breakfasts, as that meal was then a scanty one, perhaps little, if anything, but corn bread and water, and often dispatched while waiting for action with little or no derangement. (Details of men were from time to time sent back to the wagons who brought back the slim cooked rations swung in blankets.)

Holding a salient in the shape of a right angle and with a thin line and no close at hand reserve, and no support even on our immediate right, the absence of the artillery was fatal—if the disaster could at all have been averted against so strong an attack.

The line was broken on the left of the angle and Steuart's Brigade was thus taken in rear and flank.

[19] General Barlow, who commanded the Division which struck the angle, says in a paper read before the Massachusetts Historical Society, 13th January, 1879, Volume 4, page 245, that his attack was made in close column, but the spaces between the lines disappeared as soon as they got into motion and the Division became a solid mass. So I saw it.

The long struggle afterwards for the possession of this coveted corner of ground, perhaps the bloodiest scene of the war, in which oak trees were cut down by musket balls and splintered into "basket stuff" and bodies of the wounded and dead were mangled by the ceaseless storm of bullets, has been often described—it was not my fortune to be an eye witness.

I add a plat made by me in 1882 or 1883 for my paper read before the Massachusetts Military Historical Society. There were no publications at that time with which to compare my recollection. But the plat seems to be in substantial accord with published accounts since, except as to the points of tle compass (the top of the plat is nearer east than north.) Captain Randolph Barton, adjutant-general of the Stonewall Brigade, says that it agrees exactly with his recollection.

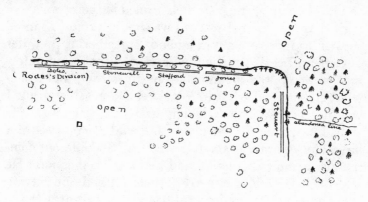

CHAPTER XXX

SPOTSYLVANIA COURT HOUSE TO FORT DELAWARE

I was conducted back about a mile, where, in an open field, the prisoners were gathered together, being most of Steuart's and Jones's Brigades and many, if not most, of Stafford's (Louisiana,) and the Stonewall—less of these because they were furthest from the salient. General Patrick, provost marshal of the Army of the Potomac, presently rode up and I asked him that I might be permitted to join General Steuart on whose staff I was. He said I could after a while when he came on the field. "But," he added, "Captain, if you are a staff officer, you can help me by getting the men formed in their respective regiments." Partly because I was not in a frame of mind to wish to facilitate anything and remembering an order of General Lee about communicating to the enemy information about the organization of the army, and somewhat embarassed what to say, I replied evasively that I was not accustomed to doing staff duty on foot. He smiled in quite a fatherly way and said, "You need not have any hesitation about giving out the different commands, I know them all," and he mentioned some. He added, "My object in getting them formed and having them numbered is to draw rations and as this attack was made so early in the morning I don't suppose your men have had their breakfasts." "Oh," I said, "if that is your object, General, I will help to get the men in their regiments," and I passed the word for the officers to collect the men. But seeing General Steuart appear in a corner of the field, about a hundred yards off I started to go to him. We were surrounded by a cordon of mounted men and when I was passing out by one of them, he angrily ordered me back. I said, "I am going to join General Steuart over yonder, as General Patrick told me I could." "I have a great mind to shoot you down," said he and pointed his pistol, the bore of which looked the usual size in the like described cases, at my head. I started to go back. But General Patrick, who was with Steuart, saw the altercation and sent over a courier who conducted me—past the same horseman and with some surly triumph on my part—across the field to my General. Of course, I had behaved foolishly, but I was chagrined at having been captured and felt the new experience as something of a disgrace.

After half an hour General Steuart and I, with our courier, Heiter (of Louisa County, detailed from the 23d Virginia,) were taken to General Patrick's headquarters, where we were given a tent. Major-General Edward Johnson, our division commander, soon joined us, coming from General Hancock's, who had given him breakfast. General Steuart had declined to shake hands with Hancock, and so had been turned over to the provost marshal with scant ceremony. General Johnson was never particular about his dress—I have told of his having been jeered at as a common cavalryman or farmer by a passing regiment before the battle of McDowell. At this time his appearance was rough indeed, some of his rather scanty, sandy colored hair sticking through a rent in his old slouch hat. He was belaboring the men behind the works with a stick, so I was told, to make them stand up when captured and came near being killed by paying no heed to calls to surrender.

He told me that on receiving our communication the night before about the probability of an attack and the departure of the artillery, he had immediately forwarded it to Lieutenant-General Ewell, commanding the corps, with an urgent request for the return of the artillery.

We stood before a fire in front of the tent, listening to the sound of the cannon and musketry and trying to determine whether the Union attack was continuing to be successful or not. Presently Captain ————, of Carlisle or some other Pennsylvania town, of the U. S. regular army, rode up to ask if we could give any information about the death of General Wadsworth, of western New York, who had been killed in the first or second day's battle in the Wilderness—over to our right.[1] I was able to confirm the fact of his death and gave him some particulars I had heard. He rode off and soon an orderly came back bringing a bottle of whiskey with the Captain's compliments. It was very acceptable, the day continuing damp or rainy, adding to our depression. While standing before the fire I heard some one say behind my back, "Why, I was at Princeton College with that fellow!" I did not turn to see who it was and he made no advances.

The next morning, May 13, Generals Johnson and Steuart and I were conducted over to where the body of prisoners was, in an open field. They were in line and in order, most of the regiments having rude poles, with designations of commands on them. And General Steuart here did a very opportune thing. Our little group was about fifty yards in front of the line, with a squad of cavalry prepared to guard us separately to the rear. He stepped forward some paces and said, "Men, keep up your spirits. You will hear all sorts of reports but do not believe them or be discouraged by anything. Remember

---

[1] Brigadier-General James S. Wadsworth, a very wealthy and well known man, of the Genesee Valley, I believe. He was mortally wounded on May 6, fell into our hands and soon died.

always that you are Confederate soldiers." Our escort looked uncomfortable during his brief address and as if they would like to stop it. The men cheered. Our escort was commanded by a major who had been a sergeant of cavalry in the old United States Army, and who knew General Steuart, who had been a captain in one of the cavalry regiments; he offered him a drink (taking one himself,) which was declined.

Three horses were brought for the two generals and myself. I did not know what General Steuart's thoughts were but I was still feeling the mortification of having been captured and intended to escape if I could, and I therefore picked out the best looking horse. After we started I found he was in good and fresh condition and ready to go forward whenever I loosened the rein. I was in doubt whether to run over open ground where I could go faster but would be fired on longer or through woods. Presently we passed through some thin woods and I made up my mind to try. I had gathered up the reins and was on the point of darting off to the left when the major in front happened to look back and must have divined my purpose from my excited face. He stopped and looked at me and called out, "Sergeant, put out a flanker about fifty yards on each side." And soon after when we made a halt of ten or fifteen minutes he made some excuse for not being able to mount me again, and I followed Generals Johnson and Steuart on foot. I next remember our being at the head of our column of prisoners and being guarded by infantry, but do not recall when the change was made. I remember this from an incident. We passed some fresh troops, in new uniforms, coming from the North to the front, and the band or drums of one regiment which had halted on the roadside to let us go by, struck up the "Rogues March." But the veterans who were guarding us called out angrily,

"Stop that—smash those instruments," and the music abruptly ceased.[2]

We must, of course, have gone through Fredericksburg and crossed the Rappahannock, but I do not recall them, and I think it was on the evening of the same day, May 13—perhaps we spent a night somewhere on the road and it was May 14—that we arrived at Belle Plain on the Potomac River (some miles below Acquia Creek), which was then a dépot of supplies for the Army of the Potomac. Here we were crowded on a river steamboat— perhaps only the officers. On the gang plank I recognized in a Federal surgeon looking on, Dr. Thomas Mackenzie, of Baltimore, an old schoolmate, but if he knew me he did not speak.

The generals and I established ourselves in a corner of the upper (main) saloon. Two or three members of the Union Christian Relief Association, or whatever its exact name was, and among them I think Mr. George H. Stuart, of Philadelphia, its head, came to the generals with a vague enquiry whether they could serve them. Colonel Hoffman, commissary-general of prisoners, also came up and looked at General Johnson, whom he had known in the old army, but, although he stood directly in front, he did not speak to him and after a few silent seconds he turned away.

We steamed down the Potomac to its mouth—I do not remember whether we stopped at Point Lookout, a Confederate prison—passed down the Chesapeake Bay and up the coast and Delaware Bay to Fort Delaware.[3]

[2] They were of Burnside's Corps, I think. I felt some gratification in reading in the newspapers afterwards that these uncivil new troops suffered a heavy loss in their first battle. With the exception of this incident we were treated with courtesy all the way back.

[3] The Rev. Isaac W. K. Handy, who was confined at Fort Delaware from July 21, 1863, to October 13, 1864, notes in his diary our arrival there as on Tuesday, May 17. See his book *United States Bonds*, page 426.

CHAPTER XXXI

Fort Delaware

Fort Delaware is built on a small flat island, of a few acres, in the middle of the river or bay, about thirty or forty miles below Philadelphia and opposite the town of Salem, New Jersey, on the east side and Delaware "City" —so pretentiously called—at the mouth of the Chesapeake and Delaware Canal, connecting the two bays, on the west side. And perhaps the island may be more properly said to be in the upper part of the bay, for the water is two or more miles wide and brackish, particularly on flood tides, which push up this far. It is called Pea Patch Island, and a doubtful story was that it was originally formed by the sinking of a vessel loaded with peas which germinated and caused an accumulation of mud and sand. Probably this is one of those fictions which are so often invented to account for natural phenomena.

The fort itself, situated on the lower end of the island, is one of those high stone structures of which so many were built before the war and which were supposed to be impregnable to an attack by vessels of war until the day of ironclads. It was perhaps an octagon in shape, at any rate many sided, and one section of the upper casemates, without guns, was used as rooms, divided by thick partition walls of brick and opening at the back on connecting passages. These were occupied during about half of the time that I was there as quarters for Confederate officers of higher rank and other somewhat favored prisoners, and life in them was more comfortable and had some special privileges and advantages. I suppose the walls of the fort enclosed an area of between one and two acres and the interior space was open.

Separated from the fort by some distance was the "pen" or quarters for the many thousand prisoners, the part for the officers and the part for the enlisted men having a fence between, twelve or fifteen feet high, with a narrow platform on the top, patrolled by sentinels, and no communication between officers and men was allowed. I therefore never saw the interior of the men's pen, of that of the officers I will speak more particularly later—after I came to be an inhabitant.

Disembarking—I think it was about the middle of the day—we were marched to the center of the island where we were halted and searched, but not roughly. I wore on a strap around my neck General Charles S. Winder's field glass, which was dented on the side when he fell at Cedar Mountain, August 9, 1862. They were about to confiscate this, but on my representing that it was of little value and explaining why I prized it, I was allowed to retain it.[1] I had nothing else of any value. Major-General Edward Johnson, Brigadier-General George H. Steuart and I—if another, it was Hiter, General Steuart's orderly—were then taken to the fort and introduced into the casemates. Here we found twenty or thirty, among them Major-General Gardner and Brigadier-Generals Archer[2] and M. Jeff. Thompson.[3] The others were all,

[1] I lost it, unfortunately, the Fall after the war at Norfolk, Virginia, when a bag was stolen on the wharf in changing steamboats while returning from Cobb's Island to Baltimore.

[2] Major-General Franklin Gardner was commander of Port Hudson on the Mississippi when it was surrendered on July 9, 1863, after the fall of Vicksburg. Brigadier-General James J. Archer, of Harford County, Maryland, was wounded and captured at Gettysburg, commanding a Tennessee brigade. Both were of the old U. S. Army.

[3] He was of Missouri but born in Virginia. I do not remember where he was captured, but it was somewhere in the Mississippi River States.

I think, of Brigadier-General John H. Morgan's well
known command and, having been captured in Morgan's
raid into Ohio, had been confined in the State peniten-
tiary until removed to this prison. They struck me as
an unusually educated and intelligent set of men, mostly
from Kentucky. Among them I remember Colonel
Richard C. Morgan and Captain Charlton H. Morgan—
brothers of the General—Colonel Basil W. Duke (both
of whose names indicate a Calvert County, Maryland,
ancestry), his brother-in-law and successor in the command after Morgan was killed; Colonel J. B. McCreary,[4]
Colonel Cicero Coleman, Colonel Tucker (I think he was
a native of Massachusetts), Colonel Ward (of Tennessee),
Captain Hart Gibson, and others. We took our meals
in a lower room, which were cooked for us by an enlisted
Federal soldier (I think he was such, perhaps some sort
of a prisoner), and I well remember my sensations the
first time I went down and saw the spread table—with
genuine coffee and condensed milk—my first acquaintance with it—to go in the coffee, but I also ate many a
spoonful, and even ice cream for dessert, which I had not
seen during the war. The service was not neat, but that
first meal seemed to me one of the finest feasts I had ever
sat down to. The water was full of "wiggle waggles,"
and large ones, being the product of the Jersey mosquito
but they were harmless, and moreover were killed by a
mixture of whiskey or brandy, which we were allowed to
get from the sutler. And to have a bottle on the shelf
in our room from which we could partake whenever, as
Sairey Gamp said, we felt "dispoged" during the day
seemed incredible.

I think we were half on parole in this first part of my
stay in the casemates and were for a while permitted to

[4] After the war Governor of Kentucky, United States Senator, etc.

go out at a certain hour on the lower end of the island, not singly but in a body and attended by two or three guards. "Jeff." Thompson was a man of a great flow of language and quaint wit and he was very popular with the garrison soldiers and it was amusing to see how our guards or attendants would sidle up as close as they could get to him to catch every word of his odd stories and sayings.

The commander of the Fort and island was Brigadier-General Albin Schoepf, a Hungarian or Austrian who had come over and entered the Union service, like many other Germans. I had heard that he had somewhat distinguished himself in the western army[5] and was surprised to find him in this semi retirement. But probably he had no friends to push or sustain him; it was said also he had married a Southern woman, or there may have been some other reason unknown to us for his being taken from the field and shelved here. In all my intercourse with him I found him a very intelligent man and courteous gentleman. Every two or three days, while our generals were there at least, he came over from his quarters to visit us in an informal and quite social way, always knocking at the door or entrance to a casemate room before coming in. We talked freely about the war and when we declared that the South could never be conquered he listened courteously but said, "Gentlemen, I think you are mistaken and underrate the determination and resources of the North."

The garrison of the island and guard over the prisoners at this first part of my imprisonment was the 5th Maryland Infantry Regiment, commanded by Colonel William Louis Schley; and I suppose there were also artillerists for the fort guns, some of which were trained to

[5] About the time of the engagement at Fisher's Creek, Kentucky, in January, 1862, when the Confederate General Zollickoffer was killed.

bear on the prison pens—very properly of course. Of the behavior of the officers and men of this regiment towards us I have nothing to record that is unfavorable— and that fact is favorable—except in the case of Colonel Schley, one of whose acts, about which I will speak presently, concerned me personally and injuriously.

But there were several others having special relations with the prisoners whom I remember very well and unfavorably; they were not of the Maryland regiment but were a part of the machinery of the post. The first of these, and the best—or worst—remembered, was Captain George W. Ahl, adjutant-general of the post. In all his intercourse with us there was never an indication of a desire to treat us, or that we should be treated, with any consideration. It was believed among the prisoners that our occasional ill usage, and failure at all times to be better treated, was, if not owing to him, at least with his approval and willing coöperation. It was the impression that he was a restraint on General Schoepf's kindly impulses, who, if he could have had his way, would have treated us as European prisoners of war are treated. It was thought that the General himself had reason to be in some fear of his influence—to his injury or danger— at Washington. It was known that complaints of "too lenient treatment of rebels" were going up from the island to the authorities at Washington and it was believed that Ahl was in sympathy at least with them. If any injustice was done to Captain Ahl in attributing to him more than he did or felt, he had only himself to blame for it, for his manner and conduct towards the prisoners certainly justified a bad impression of him and the dislike of him was universal.[6]

[6] I heard after the war that he came South representing some Pittsburgh or other Northern firm, but was warned decisively that he could not successfully transact any business in the South.

The other two who seemed to have special charge over us were Lieutenant Wolf, or Wolff, who was called assistant-commissary of prisoners, and (his?) sergeant, Cunningham. I have no special recollection of any malign feeling or conduct on their part towards us like Ahl's; they were sometimes disagreeably familiar and patronizing—especially Wolf.

I was at this time in the first room—nearest the head of the steps and whose window looked straight across the middle of the fort enclosure, but happened to be one morning in the next room, occupied by the Morgans and others when a gray haired old man (school teacher, we understood,) with a bevy of young girls unceremoniously came inside the door and coolly looked us over. When they left, passing on to the next room I was expressing my indignation when Captain Ahl appeared at the door and looked at me enquiringly. I said, "Captain Ahl, we are glad at any time to give any Northern people information about friends in the South or any other proper information, but we protest against being exhibited like wild animals." His face flushed but he withdrew without making any reply. "Dick," Morgan said to me, "You have made an enemy of Ahl and will have cause to be sorry for it." I refused to be sorry but experienced his mean enmity soon afterwards.

In the latter part of June an order came from Washington that a certain number of general and field officers[7] should be sent to Morris Island in Charleston Harbor, to be exposed under fire for the alleged placing under fire of Union officers in Charleston. But there was great envy on our part of those who were selected to go, for we

---

[7] The field officers of a regiment are the colonel, lieutenant-colonel and major. I do not think that staff officers of those ranks were properly called field officers.

did not believe or were careless about the being placed under fire and did believe that the party would be exchanged or would be nearest in the way for the first exchange. All our generals, Gardner, Johnson, Archer, Steuart and Jeff. Thompson—except Vance,[8] whose name I forgot to mention—were to go and most of the Morgan field officers. The number was made up of others in the pen or barracks, and we in the casemates who were not going were sent down there temporarily, so that the whole party might be collected in the fort. After they had been sent off,[9] General Vance was requested to furnish a list of those who were to go back to the casemates. He did so, with my name, of course, in the number. The list was sent back to him with my name erased, or with a line drawn through it. It was returned by him with my name restored and an explanation that I was one of those who had been there. But General Vance received a message to put some one in my place. And so I quickly realized the consequence of having offended Captain Ahl.[10]

Thus began my first experience in the barracks or pen. I was assigned to one of the large subdivisions of the long side of the barrack building and I think it was Division

[8] Brigadier-General Robert B. Vance was a brother of Zebulon Vance, Governor of North Carolina, and had been captured 14th January, 1864, at Cosby Creek in that State. He wrote verses fluently and gave one or more addresses or lectures in the pen. He died some years after the war, having been a Representative in Congress.

[9] Dr. Handy, in his book, *United States Bonds*, to which I before referred, records in his diary, page 454, that they were about to go June 24th; and in *The Immortal Six Hundred*, by Major J. Ogden Murray, Roanoke, Virginia, 1911, on page 40 is a list of names of the party, in number fifty.

They were not placed under fire, explanations having been made, and about 1st August (1864), were exchanged for the Union officers who had been reported under fire in Charleston and others in that department.

[10] According to Dr. Handy we were moved down from the fort to the pen on 24th June and the party, without me, was taken back to the fort on 28th June.

No. 28, along the two sides of which were two tiers of bunks or staging, holding perhaps 'fifty men. The underneath, level with the floor of the middle passage or space, was also utilized and here was my particular sleeping place at what I suppose was the southwest corner of the division. I give a sketch from memory of the officers' quarters, which I suppose covered about two acres:

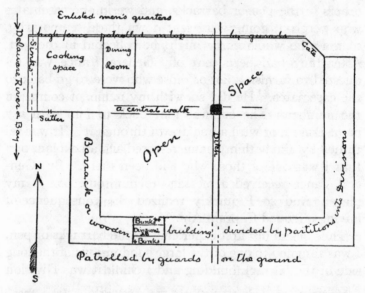

But this plat is not to be relied on for any scale nor for the exact points of the compass or other details. The cross + mark shows where I was located in this my first stay in the pen. The double cross + + shows my place on the top staging or line of bunks in my later sojourn. Windows were in the outward side of the divisions, but it was not allowed to put one's face close to them—there might be a shot or bayonet thrust from the outside patrolling sentinel. I remember once when I had my face near a window seeing out of the corner of my eye the sentinel lower the bayonet end of his gun and creep up along the outside wall; I withdrew. But this was in the time of the next regiment of guards, of which I will speak presently.

At first I went to the general dining or mess room, where the rations were placed in a double row on a long table or tables. I think there were two meals a day and that we had for breakfast a tin cup of coffee and hunk of bread, perhaps something more, and for dinner the same cup—of the usual pint size—of soup, thickened with some vegetables, and, besides the bread, a hunk of meat. Many of the prisoners took out, uneaten, their meat and cooked it over with little fires, made of pieces of boxes, etc., in tomato or other tins, in what I have designated on my plat as the "cooking space." But I soon ceased to go there and relied partly on things sent from home, and partly on the sutler at such times as he was permitted to deal with us.

We were compelled to do our washing in the ditch running through the middle of the enclosure as shown on my plat; that is to say, the ditch ran as the common expression goes, but the water was almost stagnant, moving with a slight current on ebb tides, and scummy and repulsive. The consequence was I did not do much washing at all. Drinking water was brought once or twice a week in a water boat and was supposed to be from the Brandywine River or Creek (which had an agreeable sound), but several times the boat apparently did not go high enough up, for the water was distinctly brackish and even coffee made with it had a sickening taste, for coffee does not disguise brackish water.

Boxes from home (speaking as a Marylander) or from friends or sympathizers, and communication with the post sutler were from time to time restricted or cut off, it seemed in response to waves of indignation that passed over the Northern people, or at least the press, from reports of ill treatment of Union prisoners of war. And yet I remember once when a letter from a Southern prison was published in a New York paper in which the writer said, "Let the people of the North understand what ration is issued to us"—and went on to describe it, it was pretty much the same which was being issued to the Confederate soldiers in the field when I left it. The people of the North did not understand to what a condition our resources had fallen.[11] And not only were our privileges restricted or cut off at times, which I felt, but I believe the ration issued varied for the worse, of which, however, my private resources made me more or less independent. I am not a good authority on the question of how far the Confederate prisoners were made to feel the pangs of hunger, but I can testify that my comrades—officers—were certainly poorly fed. Some of them ate rats, and even small fish caught from the Delaware River at the sinks, and it will be hardly supposed that this was from choice.

Most of them were natives of the interior country and here saw some things that were novel to them. I remember once seeing a crowd around a poor little ghost white crab on the bank of the ditch and when it would make a feeble motion towards them they gave way in alarm, reminding me of the four and twenty tailors that durst not touch a snail.

From the time I first reached Fort Delaware I had been sending to Baltimore lists of names of men—officers and soldiers, and particularly of Steuart's Brigade and,

[11] I understood that even at the close of the war a section of the Richmond and Danville Railroad, the main communication between Richmond and the South had merely strap iron rails, laid on wood. But that was one of the least of our difficulties, the greater being the want of supplies to be hauled.

more widely, of Johnson's (Army) Division—and of articles of clothing which they needed, and there were generous responses. Sometimes these supplies were sent through me and at others to the men direct, with whom a correspondence would thereafter often be kept up. Often boxes of eatables were sent to me personally and my practice was to turn over one half to the officers of the regiments of Steuart's Brigade in rotation and to keep one half for my own individual mess. I divided money sent in the same way. Of that mess of five or six I can recall at this moment only the names of Lieutenant Andrews, of Alabama and Captain Polk, of Tennessee. I think I was exempted, because of my supplies, from such slight mess duties as there were and spent my time in elegant leisure, corresponding, reading, etc. But prison life is irksome at best, as only those who have had to endure it know. Correspondence, whether via flag of truce with Confederate relatives and friends or through the regular Northern mails was restricted to purely domestic matters and letters must be of one page only. I think at one time they could only be of a certain number of lines and correspondence could only be with near relatives. These letters, to and from, were required to be unsealed and to pass inspection. The quality of the writing paper and envelopes from across the lines might have given a hint of the low ebb of Confederate resources, although I think our Southern friends used the best they had in communicating with us through the "Yankees." Several envelopes used now lie before me. Of one that came to me at Fort Delaware through the flag of truce channel I here give a copy, as a specimen of that style of correspondence:

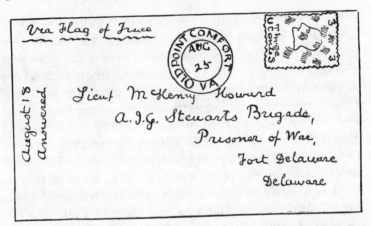

Another envelope is made out of an old half printed blank form and contains a letter written by Lieutenant James L. White, adjutant of the 37th Virginia, and who escaped capture at Spotsylvania, to my brother, Surgeon E. Lloyd Howard, and describing how the field was searched for my dead or wounded body after the battle.

Very few books were published in the Confederacy, and some of them were curiosities, being printed on coarse waste paper—even wall paper. The greatest favorite of these books was a translation of Victor Hugo's *Les Miserables*, which the soldiers humorously dubbed "Lee's Miserables." But to return to Fort Delaware from which I escaped for a time—in the foregoing digression.

Some time in May or June my father and mother and three sisters, having some reason to believe, or hope, that they would be permitted to see me, came on to Delaware City, just opposite the fort. And next morning my father crossed over in the boat which plied between. But unfortunately Colonel Schley who commanded the 5th Maryland Regiment which garrisoned the island, was in General Schoepf's office when my father entered. He

looked at my father and, taking the General aside, asked
him if he was going to allow that man to see his son, that
he was the most obnoxious man in the State of Maryland
and he protested against it.[12] So the General handed, or
caused to be handed a printed oath of allegiance to my
father who indignantly asked, if that was the condition
on which he could see his son. The General replied that
such were his orders. My father turned and left the
office and crossing back to Delaware City, the party went
disappointed home again.

But a change was much for the worse when this Maryland regiment went to the front and was succeeded by a
fifty day's regiment from Ohio, that is, one enlisted for
only fifty days service.[13] The conduct of these new men

[12] My father—Charles Howard—was President of the Board of Police of
Baltimore City when the war broke out and was arrested on 1st July, 1861, and
held as a "State Prisoner," together with my oldest brother, Frank Key Howard,
Editor of the *Baltimore Gazette* (who was arrested 13th September, 1861), in
Fort Warren and other Northern prisons until November, 1862. My other four
brothers were in the Confederate army. Colonel Schley might have added that
my mother and sisters too were "obnoxious" from his point of view, for they
spent most of their time during the war in giving aid and comfort to Confederate
prisoners.

[13] Since writing the text, I have found after discovered evidence, as the lawyers say, that this attempted visit of my family and change in our guards were
when I was still in the fort. The *War of the Rebellion—Official Records of the
Union and Confederate Armies*, Series 1, Volume XXXVII, Part I, Serial No. 70,
page 590, gives an order from Washington to Major-General Wallace at Baltimore, dated 4th June, 1864, to send a regiment of Ohio 100 days men to Fort
Delaware to relieve the 5th Maryland, followed by the detailing of the 157th
Regiment Ohio National Guard, Colonel George W. McCook, for that duty, and
its order to go on 5th June. And Volume XL, Part II, Serial No. 81, page 48,
shows that the 5th Maryland was sent to the front not later than the 15th of
June.

It does not follow that the 157th Ohio was not a *50* days regiment, as we understood at Fort Delaware that it was.

Veterans almost invariably treated prisoners of war well; with militia or half
militia like this Ohio Home Guard Regiment, or others who had not been at the
front, the rule was just the reverse.

towards the prisoners was atrocious, devilish in the apparent desire to insult and practice small cruelties.   The sentinels along the top of the fence and sinks seldom spoke to us without a curse, and they so spoke very often and without the slightest reason.   They seemed to take the greatest satisfaction in doing so, as if they thought they were sent there to abuse and tyrannize over us.   It was almost the constant practice whenever they saw a man with a penknife at the cooking place to make him come to the bottom of the fence and hand it up.   Finally, one evening about 9 o'clock, I had gone to the sink and was returning when the sentinel on the fence ordered me, with a curse, to double quick.   I did not do so, but had a feeling in my back of half expectation of a bullet but luckily had not many steps to go before I turned a corner of the dining house.   I said when I got back to the front of my division that that man would shoot somebody before the night was over.   While I was speaking a shot rang out in that direction and word came that the sentinel had shot down a Lieutenant-Colonel Jones, of Essex or Middlesex County, Virginia.   He was returning from the sink when the sentinel ordered him to double quick and on his not doing so, shot him.   Colonel Jones was only an officer of the Home Guard of his County, and he was crippled by some disability in his legs.   The gate of the prison was presently thrown open and General Schoepf came in with a surgeon and body of men, I think also Captain Ahl.   I walked over to the middle of the enclosure as they came back bearing the mortally wounded man and I heard him say, "General, what did he shoot me for?   I was not doing anything and did not even know that he was speaking to me."   He died the next day or day after.[14]   There were rumors that the man who

[14] Dr. Handy records that he was shot on 7th July and died on the night of the 9th and that the man who shot him was called Bill Douglas.

shot him was made a corporal, which I am slow to credit, although some declared they saw him as one.

The commander of this regiment was a Colonel McCook, of the well known Ohio family, and he must be held accountable for the brutal conduct of the men under him all the time his regiment was at Fort Delaware, and therefore in part for this murder.[15]

About this time my money remittances from home were stolen by somebody in the distributing department to the prisoners and I suffered a good deal of discomfort, particularly as the drinking water was now several times coming brackish and, moreover, the weather was very warm. My father wrote in strong remonstrance to General Schoepf, who sent for me to come out to his office. I went with an orderly, and I remember well the pleasure of being outside the enclosure and being able to see a distant horizon instead of the view being bounded by high plank fences and barracks. The General spoke with considerable frankness of the difficulty of his position—that he had spies around him and was constantly being complained of to Washington. He regretted not having been able to let my family see me when they came on, and I think he explained the circumstances. He told me to have money sent in future to or through him and I could come to his office to receive it. This arrangement I gladly accepted, particularly because of the relief of getting out of the confines of the pen and having a distant view, if only for a while. And he asked me if I would not like to be back in the fort, and I need not say what my reply was. So I picked up my few belongings and back

[15]My ill opinion of him was confirmed after the war when my aunt, Mrs. George H. Pendleton, told me she heard him say at a dinner that it was true the Confederate prisoners ate rats, but that it was from preference and when rations were being issued in abundance.

to the fort interior I went. This was about the middle of July.

Here I found almost a new set of companions, who were in the place of our generals and field officers who had been sent, as I have narrated, to be put under fire in Charleston Harbor. Captain Charlton H. Morgan[16] is the only one of the old set that I can now recall, but I suppose General Robert Vance was there and some others. Of the new set I became best acquainted with Captain C. B. Kilgore, assistant adjutant-general of Ector's Brigade in the western army,[17] Captain Henry Buist, of Charleston, South Carolina, Colonel Folk of North Carolina, and Major Thomas S. Mills of Chester, South Carolina, assistant adjutant-general of Major-General Richard Anderson's[18] Division in General Lee's army.

Captain Buist was a Mason of high standing—of the 33d degree. One day a large square missive was brought in to him and delivered with some formality. It proved to be a communication from the highest Masons of Massachusetts, reciting their recollection and appreciation of a Masonic address made by him before the war,

[16] He was a brother of General John H. Morgan, the well known cavalry leader and after the war married my sister and died in Lexington, Kentucky in 1912.

[17] We called the army which operated west of the Atlantic States the Western Army although it had long since been forced back from Kentucky and Tennessee to the more Southern States. Captain Kilgore was from Texas and was in Congress after the war. He died 12 or 15 years ago. He was the one who kicked open the door of the House when it was closed by order of Czar Reid.

[18] It is particularly interesting to me that General Anderson, of South Carolina, was a grandson of Captain Richard Anderson of Maryland who had a Maryland company under Colonel John Eager Howard at the battle of Cowpens in the Revolutionary War, and who, my grandfather records, in friendly rivalry with another captain for the capture of a piece of artillery put the end of his spontoon (a long stick which company officers then carried), on the ground and made a long leap which landed him on the gun and so won him the prize—See the *National Portrait Gallery*, Volume 2. See also the *Baltimore Gazette* and *Daily Advertiser* May 25, 1827, for an interview with him.

and expressing their sympathy and willingness to serve
him in any way in their power.   We prognosticated that
he would soon be exchanged, and he was shortly after
put in a movement which we believed was in the direction
of an exchange, as will be told presently.

Major Mills also had a communication of a very
different sort.   One day General Schoepf's orderly came
over bringing an open telegram from Colonel William
Hoffman, commissary-general of prisoners, that is to
say, at the head of the department at Washington which
had all matters relating to prisoners of war in its charge,
to General Schoepf, and asking simply, "How is Major
Mills's health?"   Now Mills had some particular relations with some one—I think it was with a Major Judd
of the United States Army who visited the fort once or
twice, and I think too that the connection extended
somehow to Colonel Hoffman.   Certainly Major Judd
was interested in one or two of the South Carolinians and
I remember Major Mills, although surprised, was not
altogether at a loss for a manifestation of interest in him.
At any rate, the telegram came and General Schoepf,
who may or may not have known what prompted it,
apparently thought the best way was to let Mills answer
for himself.   And he did, endorsing on the telegram,
"Never was better in my life."   Presently a message
came from General Schoepf to pack up his things and
come to his office.   The Major was jubilant and we all
sympathized in his good fortune and hastily wrote letters
for him to carry South on his impending exchange.
From a window which looked out over the fort enclosure
we enviously watched him as he crossed, with his head
up, to the office and after a brief interval came out again
and marched, but with his head dejected, straight over
to the mouth of the dungeon and into it.   The explana-

tion soon came. A Major Elliott had been put in solitary confinement in retaliation for an alleged similar treatment of a Federal officer. His health had given way under the hardship and the surgeon had reported that he could not stand it longer. So Colonel Hoffman selected Major Mills to be put in Elliott's place but first telegraphed to ascertain if his health would qualify him to be a successor. And Mills, thinking it a kindly, if surprising, interest on Hoffman's part and meant if he was well enough for exchange, so answered it to his own condemnation. And every day when we were taken for our walk out of the fort we saw Mills crouching at the door of his dungeon, which was next to the sally port and seemed to be very narrow, low and dark, and, it seemed to us, with no ventilation except by the small door which was kept open. We could only look sympathizingly at him—we were not permitted to speak.

For at that time we were taken out every morning under several guards to the river side and permitted to have a swim or bath, the drawback being, however, that the water was much polluted at this place, which was just below the prison pen. I remember a Colonel Abraham Fulkerson, although one of the thinest men I ever knew, floated like a cork. He was colonel of a Tennessee regiment, while his brother Samuel V. Fulkerson[19] was colonel of the 37th Virginia Infantry and had been known to me as colonel commanding one of Jackson's brigades in the Valley campaign. They were from Bristol where the dividing line between Virginia and Tennessee runs through the middle of the town. Colonel "Abe" Fulkerson would lie motionless on his back in the water it seemed to me for ten or fifteen minutes and be carried out a long way by the current until the guard would get

[19] He had been killed on 27th June, 1862, at Gaines's Mill or first Cold Harbor.

in a highly nervous state, thinking he was meditating an escape.

At this time Major-General Early was making his invasion of Maryland and from the scared accounts which we read in the Northern papers it looked as if he might overrun the State to the Chesapeake Bay. Now the sally port or entrance to the fort was a covered way extending from the inner wall and enclosure, perhaps for the length of fifty feet to the outer wall and along one of its sides were stacked the muskets of the daily guard detail—about a company in size. It occurred to me that as we were being marched out (we were not then on any parole), and were fairly opposite the line of stacks from end to end, we could on a given signal seize these guns and overpower the reserve guard, close the gate and take possession of the fort and with the guns mounted on the walls command the garrison of the island and release the body of prisoners, officers and men, thousands in number. My idea was that we could then get across the river, using the heavy guns of the fort, if necessary, to keep off any small vessels which in the limited time might be brought to interfere with us, and then strike across the country to Early, having a large number of our men armed with muskets of the garrison and others found in the fort. But I considered that this plan could be carried into execution on a short notice and meanwhile had better not be talked about, and so I said nothing to any one and watched the newspapers for the development of Early's movements. One day Colonel Folk took me aside and communicated to me the same plan which was working in his mind. I begged him to say nothing to anyone as the thing required no long planning and if talked about might be discovered or even betrayed. But I heard and saw him discussing it with others. Now there was one room, the nearest end one and the same I had been in during my former stay, the occupants of which lived very much to themselves and had little to do with the occupants of the other four or five rooms. We heard, too, frequent heated discussions in there but out of our hearing—or most of it, for we did hear from members of this mess expressions which made us doubt the Confederate loyalty of some of them. One of them, Colonel John A. Baker of North Carolina, made visits, I think several, to General Schoepf's headquarters which we distrusted, and the discussions in the room seemed to be with several of his room mates who were defending him. This may have had something to do with the failure to make the attempt to capture the fort and I have an impression that our daily walks outside the fort were discontinued and the opportunities thus taken away.

About the middle of August it was reported that 600 more officers were to be sent to Charleston Harbor, some for exchange and others said, and I think we in the fort understood, to be put under fire. But none had any apprehensions on that score and all were anxious to get on the list. We had heard that the first party, of generals and field officers, had been exchanged and it was believed that this second party, perhaps after a time, would have the same happy deliverance. Captain Buist, the Mason, and other favored ones, therefore were gladly numbered with the lot, and we heard that others bribed their way to places on the list. As before, we in the fort who were not to go were sent down to the barracks to be out of the way—but we never saw the interior of the fort again. I think the day we were sent down, or the next when the 600 went,[20] mail for the

[20] Dr. Handy says they left on 20th August; so too Murray's *The Immortal Six Hundred*.

prisoners who had been in the fort was delivered in a bundle, probably to General Vance, for distribution. In it were two letters for Colonel Baker, who with all or most of his mess, was of the 600, and having strong suspicions about him we did not scruple to read them. Both were from Washington. One was from a man named Goldsmith—a jeweller I think—who wrote in substance, but somewhat illiterately, "we know you were forced to go into the army" and told him to be of good courage and something would be done soon for his relief. The other was from the well known publicist Dr. Francis Lieber,[21] a long letter very much to the same effect. Believing that Colonel Baker would be speedily exchanged, and apprehending that he might play the part of a Benedict Arnold, for we understood that he commanded an important part of the cavalry line when captured, General Vance and some of us consulted how we could get a warning to Richmond. I said I had had letters, and particularly from my brother Colonel James Howard at Richmond, stating that Colonel Ould, the Confederate commissioner or agent for exchange of prisoners, would be asked to endeavor to have me specially exchanged; that I had replied discouraging the effort as unjust to so many who had been suffering captivity much longer, but I might now write urging that I be exchanged as soon as possible. And I added that I had sent a message to my brother to be sure to hold all my letters to the heat of a fire to bring out any secret writing and I could now so write a brief warning about Colonel Baker. It was

[21] Dr. Francis Lieber, a native of Prussia, came to the United States in 1827. From 1835 to 1856 he was Professor of History and Political Economy at the University of South Carolina at Columbia, after which he lived in the North. During the war he was adviser to the government at Washington on matters of international law and civil polity. He died 2d October, 1872. He had two sons in the Federal army and another was killed in the Confederate army.

agreed that these suggestions seemed the best that could be done. So I wrote stating my changed desire about a special exchange and adding a line or two written with wet starch to tell the authorities at Richmond to look out for Colonel Baker.[22]

About the time of my coming from the fort to the barracks and the departure of the 600, that is, towards the latter part of August,[23] the time of service of the 157th Ohio expired or at any rate the 6th Massachusetts Infantry came to relieve it, and it was a relief to us also, as it was like the difference between bad and good weather. The new comers had a special interest for Marylanders, for the "6th Massachusetts" was the regiment which marched, or attempted to march through Baltimore on the memorable 19th of April, 1861, and had such a rough reception. This was a reënlistment since 1861 under the name of that regiment, but I was informed that there were many of the old soldiers in it and it looked and behaved like a veteran organization, as in fact it was. The cursing and other abusive conduct, taking of penknives and other property, etc., immediately stopped, and they

[22] My brother either never received my message about hidden writing in letters or forgot about it and I "developed" this one after I was finally exchanged and got back to Richmond. Colonel John A. Baker, of Wilmington, North Carolina, of the 3d North Carolina Cavalry, took the oath of allegiance, according to Murray's *The Immortal Six Hundred*, page 331, at Fort Pulaski in March, 1865. I have been told that he went to the West Indies and never returned home, and died after the war. It is possible that he was deceiving his Union friends and he may not have had any idea of committing active treason against the Confederacy, further than by taking the oath; but we were justified in being apprehensive of him. The 600, or some of them, were placed under fire only for a short time, but experienced another and a worse sort of "retaliation." For alleged ill treatment of Union prisoners, they were put, and for a long time kept, on almost slow starvation rations at Fort Pulaski on the Savannah River and Hilton Head at its mouth. For particulars see *The Immortal Six Hundred*. Captain Henry Buist, the high Mason, was exchanged.

[23] Dr. Handy says the date was August 24.

behaved to us in a soldier-like and I may say gentlemanly
manner. The men often spoke contemptuously of the
actions of their predecessors. We were fortunate in having no other change of guard during my stay at Fort
Delaware.

In September I was grieved to hear of the death on the
morning of the 22d at Fisher's Hill, in the Valley of Virginia of my friend and fellow staff officer Captain George
Williamson and had to communicate by letter the distressing intelligence to his father.[24]

And in October I heard by letters and in the newspapers of the death, on the 14th of Chief Justice Roger
B. Taney, whose wife was my mother's aunt and whom
I had often seen in my life. But I now recalled particularly the last time I saw him at the house of his daughter,
Mrs. James Mason Campbell on Franklin Street, Baltimore, next to the Presbyterian Church, just before, I
think the evening before, I went South. When I told
him of my intention he said, "The circumstances under
which you are going are much like those under which
your grandfather went into the Revolutionary War."[25]
His wife was, as I have indicated, the sister of Francis
Scott Key, author of "The Star Spangled Banner," and
this reminds me that about this time I was amused to
read in a New York newspaper an advertisement of an
offer by some of the rich men of that city of $10,000 for

[24] Captain George Williamson, son of George W. Williamson of Baltimore,
was assistant adjutant-general of Steuart's Brigade but escaped capture at
Spottsylvania on May 12. He was one of the most cultured and in every way
one of the best of the Marylanders who went South. I have recently written
a brief memoir of him, a copy of which has been placed in the Maryland room of
the Confederate Museum at Richmond.

[25] The bronze sitting statue of him at Annapolis and a copy of which is in
Mount Vernon Place, Baltimore, is an excellent likeness, although the sculptor,
Reinhard, had only a portrait to make it from.

a new national song. The poem was not forthcoming
under the cash inspiration. Whatever criticism may be
made, and has been made, by some of our (perhaps
envious) Northern literary people, "The Star Spangled
Banner" is the only nation's song ever composed in time
of actual battle. I am one of only two now living who
saw the author on his deathbed and can recall his personal
appearance in life (1913). He died in 1843.

I think it was in the latter part of October that there
came the most memorable day of my prison life. My
family in Baltimore received an intimation that if they
came on quietly to Fort Delaware they would now be
permitted to see me. And they came, my father and
mother and two of my three sisters—the oldest, Mrs.
Edward Lloyd of Wye House on the Eastern Shore, perhaps being too far off to be communicated with in time.
They spent the day at General Schoepf's house, who had
them to dinner and treated them with every other courtesy. Although I was marched back to the pen while
they took dinner, I was permitted to be with them for
several hours, and I need not say how the privilege was
enjoyed, not having seen any of them for nearly three
and a half years. But my youngest sister was missing,
and missed, she having died in November, 1862. Besides some clothing and a gold piece of money, I think
they took advantage of the opportunity to give me the
onyx seal ring which I wear and a silver watch which I
still have and use occasionally; I did not want a gold one
because of the vicissitudes of a soldier's life. At any
rate I received both ring and watch while at Fort Delaware.

About a week before this Dr. Handy was released, to
the great loss of the prison life. As long as a Fort Delaware prisoner survives, he will be remembered with at

least respect, even by those whose characters and practices were not in accord with his example and precepts. With untiring energy although almost broken down by his long imprisonment, he established and conducted Sunday schools, Bible classes, religious services, and in every way ministered to his fellow prisoners, although more than once it was intimated to him that in making himself conspicuous he was also making himself obnoxious and prolonging his own imprisonment. While a decided Presbyterian, Dr. Handy was undenominational in his work here, and several ministers of other branches of the church who were brought to Fort Delaware for "disloyalty" during the summer and fall, worked with him in perfect harmony. In short, as I have always said, he labored like an apostle and his influence went far to counteract the evil tendencies of prolonged prison life. For this monotonous and tedious life is demoralizing in many ways.[26]

One Sunday after he left I was requested by some Episcopalians to ask a minister of that church who was there to read the Episcopal service in one of the divisions. He said at first that it was in the diocese of the bishop of Delaware and he did not know that he could officiate without his sanction. I replied that I had never heard of the bishop of Delaware visiting that part of his diocese and rather thought it was a missionary field, if not a piece of the Confederacy. He then said he had been told that if he kept quiet it might shorten his imprisonment. I thought of Dr. Handy but said nothing. How-

[26] Dr. Isaack W. K. Handy, a native of the lower counties of the Eastern Shore of Maryland, and of the well known family of that name, had a church in Portsmouth, Virginia, and while on a visit to Delaware was arrested on a charge of "disloyalty" and confined in Fort Delaware from June, 1863, to October, 1864, He died after 1874. His book, *United States Bonds*, Turnbull Brothers, Baltimore, 1874, with illustrations, is a faithful diary of prison life.

ever, he consented to read the service. When he came to the prayer for the President, he used the equivocal words "Our President," instead of "The President of the Confederate States," which I thought was, in that congregation, an improper change of the Confederate Prayer Book and an inexcusable timidity. But he was a good man and my ideas may have been too extreme.[27]

Many of the prisoners occupied their spare time—and they had a plenty of that—in making "Confederate Jewelry," and particularly rings out of jet or some black material. Some of these were quite elaborately carved or chased and inlaid with silver or mother of pearl in the shape of crosses, stars, etc. They were sometimes sent to the ladies who furnished them with food, clothing and money, or who kept up their spirits by correspond-ence, mostly from Maryland, whose women were untir-ing in this work. Sometimes they were sent to wives and sweethearts in the South. But the jewelry was also sold and brought in a helpful amount of money to the artificers.[28]

There were attempts to escape but I believe few if any succeeded, the wide water being a greater difficulty than getting out of the pen. I heard of life preservers being made out of tomato cans or other tins. And a tempting way of exit was at the sinks, which were half over the water, where, however, the guards kept a close watch. I believe one party got out by creeping in the ditch pass-ing through the enclosure, probably tearing up the floor of the barrack under which it flowed. But they were

[27] But on this point I had the courage of my convictions, for I openly prayed for him by his full official title in reading the service in the Old Capitol prison in Washington on the Sunday after Lincoln's assassination, and when a mob was on the outside.

[28] I have a few pieces still, some of which had been sent to members of my family.

recaptured. I had my doubts whether these attempts ought to be made, because of the increased restrictions they brought on us to prevent them.

There was no communication allowed between the officers and the enlisted men but only a high board fence, patrolled along the top by the guard, seemed to separate them. Some time in October the men were stirred by some particular grievance—about food I think—and sent their complaints to the officers by notes tied to pieces of coal or stone and hurled over the fence. In the dusk of evening was the favorite time for this kind of mail communication. But the sentinels were on the alert to watch for these missiles passing over and often intercepted them before they could be picked up.

During October there had been repeated "grapes"[29] about the exchange of sick and wounded prisoners, and I think one small party was sent off. But early in November it became known as a fact that 10,000 sick and wounded from the Northern prisons were to be exchanged at Savannah for a like number of Federals and there was great excitement and various preparations made for it. I heard that some got themselves placed on the list of the Fort Delaware contingent by bribes of gold watches, etc. Others by careful treatment made old wounds look like new. One even who had been wounded in the leg in the far back Mexican war shaved off the hair which had grown over it and by judicious treatment developed a bad—or good—sore. Another, I think it was Foster, of Alabama, who had never used tobacco, chewed violently and went before the Board of Medical Examiners with such a face of pallor and thumping heart that it looked as if he would not live long enough to be dumped on the Confederacy to die. Not being an adept in sinful

[29] Distorted news via the "grapevine telegraph," see page 58.

games, I did not see any prospect for myself in this exchange. But on the last day of the sitting of the Board it happened that I was sent for to come to General Schoepf's office to receive some money, transmitted from home under the arrangement I have spoken of. The General presently asked me if I would not like to be exchanged. I said I would if it did not prevent some sick or wounded man from going. He said it would not. I then remembered our anxiety that intelligence of Colonel Baker's disloyalty should get to Richmond and said that I would like very much to be exchanged. He asked, "What have you got—rheumatism?" I replied, "No, but I have a slight sore throat." He said "Rheumatism is the best thing." I said I thought I might make it on my throat. But when I left him it was with his parting injunction that "rheumatism was the best thing." On getting back to the pen I found that the Medical Board of Examiners had finished their work and finally adjourned. I wrote a letter of pretended complaint to General Schoepf stating that owing to my being at his headquarters I had been unable to go before the Board and asking that I might have a special examination and be found a suitable subject for exchange. And doubting if this would ever reach him by the regular channel through Captain Ahl, I bribed an orderly with a greenback[30] to give it to him. I then made a strong mixture of vinegar, red pepper and salt and waited. I had a large white silk handkerchief and the extraordinary luxury, perhaps single in the prison, of a small pillow with a white pillow-case—or which had started white, for I doubt if it ever had a washing—and these I put convenient for ready use. About 9 o'clock next morning my name was called out at the gate and vociferated through the prison like the

[30] A dollar note, perhaps more.

call for Sam Weller in the Fleet prison. I promptly
seized my mixture and gargled my throat until the tears
streamed from my eyes to the astonishment of my
neighbors. I tied the large white handkerchief around
my head and face (like little Tommy Grace with a pain
in his face in "Mother Goose"), and holding the white
pillow to my cheek, I went to the gate, and with a dozen
others, out of it. We were drawn up in a line and I
supposed the "special examination" would begin. But
Captain Ahl only looked at me sourly and said gruffly,
"Your name's down for exchange." So I went back,
threw my mixture away and packed up. This was not
easy, for I had accumulated what passed for a good deal
of clothing in those days. I had a gray cloth suit[31] (without any "rebel" adornment—it was not permitted to
receive any), and a gray officer's overcoat, that is, one
with a detachable long cape reaching to my wrist. This
last I think must have been brought by my family on
their visit, for it would scarcely have passed examination
if sent in one of the usual boxes. However, I put on a
double set of underclothing and what else I could, packed
a valise, and I think made up a bundle besides. I think
it was the afternoon of the same day that we whose
names were called went out to the ground in front of
General Schoepf's office. The General came out and
circulated among us and, observing my padded and
plethoric appearance, took me aside and said "This will
never do; there will be no inspection here, but there may
be at Point Lookout and half your things may be confiscated. Now there's a fellow"—and he pointed to
Captain Frank Cheatham, a nephew of Major-General

---

[31] I wore it during the rest of the war, and have the coat yet, in the camphor
wood chest—if moths have not corrupted it—if thieves broke through they
would not steal.

B. F. Cheatham of the western army—"who has very little. Give the cape of your overcoat to him and scatter your other things among those other fellows to take through for you." This good and kindly advice I followed.

And so with my disjecta membra of baggage I went aboard the boat.

CHAPTER XXXII

FORT DELAWARE TO SAVANNAH AND RICHMOND

We left Fort Delaware in the first or second week of November (1864). Going on a small steamboat—of the sort that passes through the Canal, a single deck propeller used for freight, not the passenger variety with state-rooms—we were packed below on some straw covering coal. Crossing over the half of the river to Delaware City at the mouth of the Chesapeake and Delaware Canal, just opposite the fort, we steamed through. My place was under the open hatchway, but I could not see out and all the view I had of the State of Delaware and the Eastern Shore of Maryland was an overhanging branch under which we once passed. We were packed so close that I hardly turned over in my recumbent position the whole time I was on the boat. And being just under the open hatch and in a cramped position, I think this gave me the attack of rheumatism of which I will speak presently. We then turned down the Chesapeake Bay to the Confederate prison at Point Lookout at the mouth of the Potomac River and on its north side. I do not remember exactly when we reached this place, but probably it was some time in the morning of the day after leaving Fort Delaware. I believe we were put ashore and remained there a day, hearing many stories of the eccentricities of the black sentinels by whom the prisoners were guarded. It was here, I think, that, in leaving, I was put on Colonel Mulford's (United States Exchange Commissioner) fine steamboat, the *City of New York*, and I would have enjoyed, doubtless, this part of the trip

335

had it not been that after going on board I had an attack of something like rheumatism—which, it will be remembered, General Schoepf had recommended to me as the best thing to get exchanged on, but which I had disclaimed having. It gave me no pain whatever, but after I got into a berth in one of the staterooms I could not turn over except by using my hands as if to another person. The surgeon came and prescribed for me a milk punch which I enjoyed very much. By the time we arrived at Old Point Comfort I was all right again. Here I was transferred to the old ocean steamer *Illinois*, which I believe had been of the line between New York and England but was now used, in its old age as an army transport along the Atlantic coast for such purposes as the present. That evening or the next we put to sea. For supper there was given to each of us a cube shaped piece of pork, already cooked. It was all, or nearly all, fat, but we were not fastidious and enjoyed it, with ship biscuit I think. The sea, or mouth of the bay, was smooth for sometime and there was much singing on the deck, especially of maritime songs, "A life on the ocean wave," "A wet sheet and a flowing sail," and others expressive of the joy of being on the ocean. But next morning I seemed to be the only one not down with sea-sickness and the hunks of meat were lying around disregarded and I "wittled free." There was no more singing on that trip. Having the liberty of the deck and plenty of room I enjoyed this my first experience of being well out on the ocean and watched the frequent taking the temperature of the water, sounding (so my recollection seems to be,) and everything novel to be seen, with interest. We heard that one vessel ran aground at Cape Hatteras and that one officer escaped ashore.[1]

[1] I was about to omit this as absurd and my seeming recollection as playing me a trick, but I find there was such an impression both among us and the officers

We finally entered Port Royal Harbor in South Carolina and anchored on what I thought was one of the most beautiful evenings I had ever seen, the air mild and balmy red clouds in the west, light waves dancing on the water, the ανηριθμον γελασμα of the Grecian sea, and the surrounding land looking attractive. Probably the next day I was transferred from the big *Illinois*—big for those days—to the river or bay steamboat *George Leary* and proceeded to the mouth of the Savannah River. This we ascended, passing by Fort Pulaski on the south side of the mouth, which had been captured a year or two before.[2] The appearance of this southern river was strange to me. The shores were low lying, with extensive level tracts to the woods some distance back, covered with a tall sedgelike growth which I took to be wild rice. The water seemed to go down deep at the very edge of the black mud bank, for sometimes we went along so close to it that our side paddle wheel boxes brushed the sedge. Before dusk we rejoiced to see the poor little Confederate boat or boats steaming slowly down from Savannah to meet us.[3] It was dark when one of them

of the vessel. Major Ogden Murray in his *The Immortal Six Hundred* says that one of the prisoners disappeared when the vessel struck and was thought to have escaped, but was secreted in the hold by a friendly seaman and fed there until the ship returned to New York. (But I have not Major Murray's book by me and perhaps he tells the incident as an escape of one of the Six Hundred, and we may have heard of it and my recollection may be so far off.)

[2] It was taken by the Federals in April 1862.

[3] The Baltimore *American and Commercial Advertiser* newspaper of Monday, 21st November, 1864, says that the flag of truce fleet of Lieutenant-Colonel John E. Mulford, (U. S. Agent or Commissioner for exchange of prisoners), on Tuesday, 8th November, steamed out of Hampton Roads, and that the fleet consisted of . . . . the *Illinois* . . . . *George Leary* . . . . ; That the flagship, the *New York*, was the first to drop anchor in Port Royal Harbor on Thursday evening (10th November) and at an early hour on Friday morning (11th November) Colonel Mulford proceeded on it to a point up the Savannah River about midway between Fort Pulaski and Savannah, where the

ranged alongside, but as I looked down on it—for it was much lower on the water than ours—I thought I recognized a voice and called out, "Is that you, Elliott?" He answered "Yes." It was Lieutenant or Captain Robert Elliott, with whom I had had a slight acquaintance in the Richmond campaign of 1862, when I think he was on the staff of General Lawton. I had not seen him since and had no reason to suppose he was in this part of the Confederate world. But I have always had a peculiar faculty for remembering voices. He seemed to be present here as a staff officer or one of a party from Savannah aiding the flag of truce people in receiving us.[4]

We were soon transferred to the Confederate vessel or vessels and steamed at a snail's pace a few miles up to Savannah. Landing, I, with others who had money enough, made my way to the Pulaski House, the principal hotel. I remember on coming down, rather late, to breakfast next morning wondering at the red piles at the sides of the plates where persons had eaten—looking like bits of lobster shells; they were shrimps, my first experience of that article of semi-tropical food.

I think it was in the course of the same day, Sunday, 13th November, that Mr. William Habersham, an old

steamer *Beauregard* of the Rebel fleet was met and arrangements were made for the transfer of the Confederate prisoners on Saturday—they having in the meantime arrived at Port Royal, to the number of about 3200, that, accordingly on the following afternoon (12th November) the steamers *Herman Livingston* and *George Leary*, with prisoners, accompanied by the *New York*, repaired to the same point in the Savannah River, where they were met by the Confederate steamers (of which the letter to the *American* gives a humorous description), and at nightfall the prisoners were transferred and taken to Savannah.

It is probable from this account that I had left Fort Delaware on the 5th or 6th of November.

The *George Leary* was used as a bay boat at Baltimore for many years after the war and I traveled on it often.

[4] After the war he became a minister in the Protestant Episcopal Church and finally was bishop of Texas, where he died many years ago.

friend of my father and mother, to whose house he often came when stopping in Baltimore in his annual visits to the North, hearing of my arrival, sought me out and made me straightway move from the hotel to his town house at the corner of Barnard and Harris streets. He took me to several houses in the city—among others to that of "his favorite cousins" the Elliott ladies, one of whom I remember was Miss Phoebe Elliott, cousins or sisters of Captain "Bob" Elliott; also I think to the house of Commodore Huger or his family. He was a brother of General Huger who was living next door to us in Baltimore when the war broke out. At this house I one day enjoyed some very fine old Madeira wine, although they said it might have an earthy taste from having been buried some time before during a scare that the "Yankees" were coming.[5]

Looking around Savannah, I noticed semi-tropical vegetation new to me, and especially an occasional banana plant showing its long and broad green leaves (but I saw no fruit) above a garden wall. But what interested me most was a visit to the riverside and seeing the unhulled rice taken from the boats into the mills which stood on the high river bank. A sort of trough, two feet or so wide, ran slantingly up, the flooring being either compartments or simply a long roll of cloth or other material and this flooring, on which measures of rice were poured at the boat, went up on perpetual mo-

[5] It happened a few years after the war that I was dining one day at the house, on Courtland Street, Baltimore, of Mr. Charles Nephew West, who had come from Georgia to Baltimore to practice law, when some old Madeira was produced and I was asked what I thought of it. "Well," I said, "it tastes like some I drank during the war at Commodore Huger's in Savannah." "Why," said he, "this is some of the same wine and Mrs. Huger is in the next room now." He must have formed a high opinion of my judgment of old Madeira from my somewhat chance remark.

tion, like an endless chain or long treadmill, to the top
story of the mill, from which the rice descended from floor
to floor undergoing several processes until it arrived at
the bottom in marketable condition. The hull is much
more close fitting to the grain than the chaff of wheat.

After several days, on Saturday afternoon I think,
Mr. Habersham took me to his rice plantation on the
Ogeechee River. We went by railroad some fifteen or
eighteen miles south from Savannah to a road-crossing
station and then drove a few miles easterly to his place,
which had on it a comfortable house with an interesting
flower garden. Here I found Bishop Elliott, of Georgia,
and his wife, one of the two being a near relative of Mr.
Habersham and the Bishop being, I think, the father
of Captain "Bob" Elliott. I noticed in how many, and
novel, ways rice was served in this rice district, one dish
especially being like a Virginia deep corn meal pone but
of rice instead of corn meal, with chicken legs, wings,
breast, etc., through it. The garden interested me, with
large rose bushes in full bloom, and particularly the camellias,[6] which, unlike our old time small hot house
bushes in Baltimore, were here almost trees and growing
in the open air. They were full of flowers, mostly buds.
Candles were made of the wax boiled out of myrtle-
berries and gave out a slight perfume.

One day we took a rowboat and descended the Ogeechee River some distance, stopping for a while at a plan-

[6] About 1845–1855 every young lady going to a party wore as a matter of
course in her hair, on the (right?) side of the head, a Camellia—or Japonnica as
it was then always called. The only question was whether it should be red or
white, and whether a full bloom flower or a half open bud. Feast was then the
only, and sufficient florist of the city. Mr. Habersham's Camellias therefore
called up old memories. I think this fashion had rather gone out before the
beginning of the war. The Camellia is seldom seen now and I believe few young
ladies of today would even recognize this much prized adornment of their
grandmothers.

tation called "Pinkie House." Here I was astonished
to find a cousin, Ellen Buchanan, daughter of Admiral
Franklin Buchanan, now Mrs. George P. Screven. I
remember seeing him in Baltimore when he came on
from Georgia to be married, keeping himself half concealed, or very quiet, and under an assumed name, I
think, while in the city, for it was more than a month
after the fall of Fort Sumter.[7]

Another day we rode (on the hardy yellow clay colored
horses which I was told were best for common use in that
climate,) over the rice fields, or rather around them for
they were low lying with embankments surrounding
them, on the top of which we rode. Twice, I was told,
the field has to be flooded from the neighboring river—
after the planting and when the stalks are about a foot
high. After the second flooding and the drawing off of
the water, the plants fall down flat in the mud, but soon
stand up straight again when dried by the hot sun. But
there was nothing of rice cultivation—at least of rice
growing—to be seen at this season. Although in the
beginning of winter, the sun with the stagnant air over
these low levels was rather oppressive and I could well
understand that the white people (of the gentry) could
not endure it in the summer and moved up to the pine
woods country or went elsewhere.

And on another day we rode or drove to the house of
Mr. (Duncan?) Heyward, a neighbor two or three miles
off. Mr. Habersham said Mr. Heyward was absent
and the house was closed, and I thought it odd we should
be going there. On the way he muttered some cabalistic
words several times and desired me to remember them.
Arriving and entering the empty house, Mr. Habersham
went into the dining room and it appeared that the cab-

[7] They were married in Talbot County, Maryland, on 5th June, 1861.

alistic words gave the key to the lock of the sideboard or buffet in which was some liquor which was the motive for the visit. The house was of bungalow fashion, a low structure raised above the ground and open underneath and with a wide porch. Such is the structure of many of the plantation houses in the far South. On the way over and back we passed an attractive looking country house which I was told was the residence of Dr. Cheves (Chev'-es) a son or descendant of Langdon Cheves, of whom I knew as a Representative in Congress from South Carolina in the days of Calhoun, Webster and Clay. And all these families, Habersham, Elliott, Heyward, Cheves, with many others, were properly, or formerly, of South Carolina descent, having drifted across the Savannah River. I remember particularly in passing Dr. Cheves's the large number of the strange looking palmetto trees and thinking of the account in my old school history of the defense, in the Revolutionary War, of Fort Moultrie, which was built of palmetto logs in the spongy tissue of which the cannon balls from the British fleet sank without splintering or doing any harm. I never heard of their efficacy in that way in our war— perhaps because modern guns shoot so much stronger. All this rice section was an unbroken level, the Eastern Shore of Maryland is a rolling country compared with it.

After a few days we returned to Mr. Habersham's house in Savannah—I should have mentioned that he was a bachelor.

Now I was only half exchanged, being supposed to be on parole until the authorities would announce the exchange of the 10,000 fully effective, and as I could not perform any military service, I was intending to make some stay in the southern part of the Confederacy where the half tropical country was so new and interesting to me. I even meditated going as far south as Florida.[8] But I was alarmed by the approach which General Sherman was making to the Atlantic seaboard and afraid of being cut off from Richmond. So in a day or two I took the train over to Charleston.

I had met in Savannah Major Henry Myers, a paymaster in the Army (or Navy?), who had been in Fort Warren prison, Boston Harbor, with my father and oldest brother, Frank Key Howard,[9] and on his invitation I stayed in Charleston in a small house on a cross street which was occupied by several of General Beauregard's staff, among whom I remember Col. John R. Waddy who was from the Eastern Shore of Virginia. We were in the upper part of the city and beyond the range of the big guns (one of which was known as the "Swamp Angel",) from which the enemy kept up a slow fire on it, but I could hear occasionally the explosion of the shells falling in the lower part. I walked down to the Battery—so long before called and situated like the New York Battery, but with fine dwelling houses fronting the street along the water—from which Fort Sumter and all the Harbor mouth were in plain view. And one day I dined with some officers in a large house which the family had vacated (Mrs. Foster?) situated on a large and (otherwise) unimproved tract of ground, a little way back from the Battery. Every twenty minutes or so we

[8] If I had done so, I would, after all, have been taking, in a measure, the advice which General James A. Walker of the Stonewall Brigade used to give me in the winter of 1863–64. He said, "You have the best position in the army. Belonging to the personal staff of General Trimble who is a prisoner, you are not liable to duty and can draw your pay and travel all over the Confederacy if you like. You are a fool to be volunteering in active service here and you may get yourself killed where you have no business to be."

[9] See his two pamphlets "Fourteen Months in American Bastiles" and "The Southern Rights and Union Parties in Maryland Contrasted."

heard the sound of the enemy's big guns but nobody seemed to pay any attention to it, although I had seen in walking across the common several large holes in the ground where these huge shells had fallen and exploded.

On Saturday (November), Major Waddy took me (by the Wilmington Railroad?) to Colonel Ferguson's, about eighteen or twenty miles north of Charleston and near the upper part of Cooper River. Colonel Ferguson was a gentleman of the finest old school, now eighty years of age and totally blind. He had several sons in the army.[10] He had been a great lover of horses before the war and I think prided himself, more than on anything else, on having raised a horse (Albina?) which beat the famous northern racer Planet in one of the great races. I think I fell in his estimation when I once spoke of trotting matches, for which he expressed great contempt.[11] He pleased me very much when, on my introduction, he said that my grandfather's services in South Carolina in the Revolutionary War were not forgotten in the State.[12] On the next day, Sunday, I was driven over to some old residence, which I wish I could identify, to dinner. We presently crossed the Cooper River—or perhaps one of its branches—to its east side where a church stood on the top of the high bank, surrounded by fine large live oak trees. Leaving the church on our left, we went some distance (easterly?) and presently passed through an avenue of beautiful live oaks, some of

[10] One of them was Brigadier-General Samuel Ferguson of the western army and another Major J. Duguè Ferguson, of Brigadier-General Fitzhugh Lee's staff, and who since the war has resided in Baltimore.

[11] But I still think that trotting races, while less exciting are not to be despised, being in the way of developing the most useful gait of the horse—other than the draft horse.

[12] Colonel John Eager Howard, at Camden, Cowpens, Hobkirks Hill, Eutaw Springs, etc. The Legislature of South Carolina passed resolutions of condolence on his death, 12th October, 1827.

the large lower branches of which bent down nearly to the ground. The house had, with its wings or side additions to the main central building, a long front something like the old colonial Ridout house in Annapolis, and at the extremities the walls seemed pierced in narrow loophole fashion, as if for defense. And I think I was told the house was of colonial build and was supposed to have been constructed with that in view. The central front door opened immediately into a large saloon or drawing room, on the right hand side of which was the dining room and there we found several gentlemen at dinner and drinking old Madeira, as if no war was raging in the land. On Monday morning we returned from Colonel Ferguson's to Charleston.

A day or two afterwards Lieutenant Albert White, whom I had known in Fort Delaware and who was, I think, one of the exchanged prisoners, took me to his father's country place. This was on the railroad which ran northwesterly from Charleston and I suppose eighteen or twenty miles from it. I knew that his father was a wealthy man, having made, and at that time still making, a great deal of money in the blockade running business, but I was astonished at the lavish display on the dinner table on our arrival in the evening—not only a variety of eatables but an extensive array of china and glass, with several wine glasses at each plate for the liquors, sherry, Madeira, brandy, Scotch whisky, etc. I had seen nothing approaching it since before the war and did not know that such style was kept up at any house in the South. The next day Albert White and I wandered around casting a circular handthrowing net in a bayou, etc. He showed me a place grown with tall switches like our ailanthus, where he said some well known old South Carolinian—I think he said General

Moultrie—was buried.[13] Mr. White's house was, however, as I recollect it, not an old one. I believe I stayed
only one day, possibly two, and returned to Charleston.[14]

I was planning to spend a night and a day at Fort
Sumter, for one could only go and return after dark;
but I was now seriously alarmed at the progress Sherman
was making towards the seaboard and thought I had better lose no more time in getting northward. So on the
29th or 30th November or 1st December I took the train
from Charleston going northwesterly. It was not known
exactly how far Sherman had got in marching through
Georgia, or whether he might not cross the Savannah
River into South Carolina, and I was relieved when we
passed Branchville, which is nearly opposite to Augusta,
Georgia, and turned from northwest to north and so
directly away from the line of operations. But feeling
now safe from danger of being cut off, I was minded to
make one more stop and got off at Charlotte, North Carolina, where I knew that Surgeon I. Davis Thomson, of
Maryland, was in charge of a hospital. I have narrated
how I had stayed with him in Lynchburg in the spring of
1863. I think I spent only one or two days with him.
When I left he said he would introduce me to the conductor and also furnish me with a bottle of brandy (from
the hospital stores), and on the introduction and an invitation to partake from the bottle the conductor would put
me in the ladies' car, which in those days only men accompanying ladies were permitted to enter and which
was cleaner and more comfortable than the other cars,
crowded with soldiers. So when we went to the station

[13] Not General Moultrie, who is buried in Charleston; perhaps a Middleton.

[14] Alas, the end of the war brought ruin and the family was reduced to straits.
I heard some years afterwards that the daughter of the house, a very pretty young
girl when I was there, was teaching, her father having died.

to take the train about 9 o'clock at night and he introduced me, I quickly put in, "I have a bottle of brandy
and will be glad if you will take a drink with me after I
am in the car." He said he would take the drink then
and there. But I pretended it was not convenient until
I was on the train and he put me in the ladies' car. As
soon as we started, he lost no time in coming for his extra
fare. And so I traveled more comfortably during the
night ride to Danville, Virginia. Here we changed
trains at 8 or 9 o'clock in the morning. It being now a
daylight ride to Richmond, I did not care to manoeuvre
for the ladies' car again and went into one of the common
coaches. I suppose it took nearly all of the daylight—
I was told that part of the track had only strap iron rails
—to get to Richmond; this was probably the 3d, 4th or
5th of December (1864). I think I went to the Spotswood Hotel on Main Street.

CHAPTER XXXIII

RICHMOND, ORANGE COUNTY AND CHAFFIN'S BLUFF

Within a few days after my getting back from Fort Delaware to Richmond, I suppose about the second week in December (1864) three of my four brothers in the army appointed to meet me one evening to hear the news I had to tell of home. The place of meeting was somewhere east of Richmond; either my brother Lieutenant-Colonel James Howard, on the near approach of Grant's army, had been ordered from his old headquarters at Mrs. Chevaillie's house on the northwest side of the city, or it was at the quarters of one of my other brothers, and the four of us who met were myself and Colonel Howard and, I think, Surgeon E. Lloyd Howard and Captain John E. Howard. To celebrate the occasion we had procured some apple brandy, sugar and two or three eggs and proposed to make eggnog or Tom and Jerry in a milk crock— I suppose it was the best we could do for a suggestion of milk. We heated or warmed the crock and broke the eggs into it, when to our dismay they were promptly cooked and when stirred became like scrambled eggs. But we could not afford to waste anything and so mixed in the brandy and sugar and drank or ate the result. I called for the letter in which I had written with wet starch in Fort Delaware about Colonel Baker's disloyalty and which my brother had failed to develop, either from not having received a previous message to look out for such secret writing or having forgotten it. On being now produced, the letter appeared as innocent as it had looked to the Yankee official who had examined and passed it for transmission by the flag of truce, as with all prisoners' letters. But on holding it to the heat of the fire now, my concealed warning came out distinctly. The next day I took the letter and gave a full account to the War Office at Richmond and they said they would look out for Colonel Baker, who had not yet come through.

About the middle of December (1864), not being yet declared exchanged and unable, therefore, to perform any military service, I went to pass the time at Oliver Terrell's, on the upper part of Blue Run in Orange County, half-way between Gordonsville and Liberty Mill on the Rapidan River.

On December 22 we heard that a force of the enemy's cavalry was moving from the North towards the bridge over the Rapidan at Liberty Mill, our cavalry falling back before it, and Terrell and I rode there to investigate. (My servant, Washington, had brought and left my horse here when I was taken prisoner at Spotsylvania Court House on May 12.) Soon after we started we heard the sound of artillery in that direction and when about a mile from the bridge we saw thick black smoke rising and floating away, and, nearer, we saw the flames from the burning structure, which our men, after crossing to the south (Orange County) side had fired. It was an old fashioned covered bridge and the long seasoned timbers burned fiercely. We found Major-General Lomax[1] on the west side of the Turnpike road, on the high ground overlooking the bridge and some hundreds of yards from it, watching his dismounted cavalrymen skirmishing with the enemy across the river. Being on parole, I could only be a spectator. Concluding that

---

[1] Lunsford Lindsay Lomax, of Virginia, an officer of the old U. S. Army. He died in Washington a year or two ago.

the enemy would get across, Terrell and I presently rode back to the house and he set to work moving his hams and bacon and such like stores which an enemy would be most apt to take. They were loaded in wagons which were driven back into the recesses of Campbell's Mountain, which rises just behind his farm. This took a good part of the night, and after the work was done and the wagons had driven off, Terrell and I were afraid to sleep, apprehending that the enemy might come down on us, and we frequently went out of the house, listening in the still, frosty air for the sound of horses' feet. I wondered how I would be treated if taken, being already on a sort of parole, but I did not want to take any chances. At daylight, or just before, we got on our horses and, crossing his farm, ascended Campbell's Mountain, an elevation of the South West range. On the wooded top, or high up, we rode a mile or two towards Gordonsville until we came to where the ground suddenly descended to our front and left and this descent being cleared land, we had a view of a mile of the Liberty Mill and Gordonsville road in the bottom two or three hundred feet below us, until it ascended the wooded Haxall's Mountain, which in our front crossed the road at right angles and a mile on the further side of which was Gordonsville. We had been having sleety weather and every branch and twig of every tree on our mountain, as well as the bushes, weeds and grass, had a thick casing of clear ice, and it was the most beautiful scene of the kind I ever saw, especially when the sun rose and its level beams were refracted from the ice in all imaginable colors. Fairyland could not produce such a spectacle.

We presently saw the enemy's column of cavalry come along the road from Liberty Mill, on which we looked down, and watched it as it got to the foot of Haxall's

Mountain and deployed on both sides of the road. Shifting our position more to the south end of the mountain we were on, we found ourselves directly in the rear of the center of this deployed line, which soon began to skirmish with our men who were stationed along the wooded Haxall's Mountain and not visible to us. It was a novel experience thus to witness fighting from behind the backs of the enemy with nothing but open, cultivated ground between. We must have been plainly visible to them as we sat on our horses well outside the woods behind us and within distant carbine range, but they paid no attention to our presence. The frequent sound of locomotives at Gordonsville was telling of the arrival of reinforcements from Richmond,[2] and about midday the enemy called in his skirmishers and returned by the same road. We went back some distance keeping to our mountain or ridge top to watch them as they passed along beneath us. As we stood out on our horses in the open ground near the edge of the woods at one point, some of them halted in the road and one (or two?) took a shot at us with his carbine or rifle. I suppose the distance was four or five hundred yards and we were about two hundred feet above them. We retired into the edge of the woods and Terrell wanted to stop there, but I had observed several leave the road, to get behind us I apprehended, and I insisted on going in to a safe distance. Towards sundown, believing the enemy must be back across the Rapidan, we cautiously returned to the house, which we found had not been visited, the side road to it from the main road being about a mile long.

In January or February, 1865, I and the other prison-

---

[2] Colonel Thomas S. Rhett's command, of the Richmond defences, came and perhaps other troops. But I believe there was much whistling purposely done to make the enemy think large reinforcements were arriving.

ers who had come from Fort Delaware were declared fully exchanged and no longer on parole,[3] and, if not already in Richmond, I went there to determine where to reënter active service—General Trimble still being in captivity. I was sure that General George H. Steuart, who now had a brigade in Pickett's Division of Anderson's Corps, along the line in front of Petersburg, would welcome me to his staff again and was probably expecting me to join him. But my brother Lieutenant-Colonel James Howard, whose command the 18th and 20th Virginia Battalions, of the Richmond Defences, was now at the front, occupying a part of the line of works extending north from Chaffin's Bluff on James River, and in the recently formed Division of Major-General G. W. Custis Lee, brought me an invitation from that general to serve on his staff as acting assistant inspector-general, and, to be with my brother, I determined to accept it. However, I thought it proper first to make a visit to General Steuart, and took the train from Richmond to Petersburg. On the way I sat behind two men of his brigade, one of whom was returning from a long absence. Said the other, "Bill, we have the most cur'ous man for a commander you ever saw. When you are on the picket line he doesn't come like other officers, but comes a bustin' through the bushes where you least expect him and you have to be on the lookout all the time." And he proceeded to pour out a tale of other eccentric doings showing to me that the general in his new command was still up to his old activities. Remembering the first year of the war when Colonel Steuart was disciplining the 1st Maryland and would sometimes break into the camp sentinel line with the cry of "Indians!"—I would

[3] *Pay*role many of the soldiers pronounced it, with unconscious, or perhaps conscious, humor. There were more paroles than pay rolls in those days.

have now recognized him if his name had not been mentioned.

General Steuart received me with open arms—literally, for he put them around my neck, and I felt much compunction in telling him I was not coming back to him; but he agreed it was natural I should wish to be with my brother. I spent the night with him and we had some interesting conversation about the army and Confederate matters. I remember one thing he said struck me, being both characteristic of him and true. I had remarked that if the absentees from the army would come back, we could defeat the enemy yet (meaning at that time, for I did not doubt our ultimate success down to the very end). "Yes," said he, "Mr. Howard, but if every man would do his duty with his whole heart and strength, we could defeat them with the men we have here present."

General Steuart gave his own services to that high degree all through the war.

I suppose it was in February that I went to (the neighborhood of) Chaffin's Bluff, seven miles below Richmond, to take my new position on General Custis Lee's staff. It was a volunteer service, for I still held my place as aide-de-camp to Major-General Trimble, the theory being that aides were on active duty only with their generals, as I have said. But I always thought that Marylanders in particular ought to be at the front and not be seen loafing in the rear, and I had been therefore volunteering to fill positions with other Generals during Trimble's long captivity since Gettysburg. I messed with my brother and slept in his tent, which was a very little way in rear of the fortified line and on the north side of the (Osborne?) road; General Custis Lee's headquarters were some distance back on the same road.

George Washington Custis Lee, the eldest son of General Robert E. Lee, had been retained during the war by President Davis on his staff but had been lately promoted to be major-general and given this new and curiously made up division. It was organized as two Brigades, the one under Brigadier-General Seth M. Barton and the other under Colonel Stapleton Crutchfield. I did not hold my position long enough to know much about the command of General Barton, an officer of the old United States Army and who had been transferred to this from another brigade in the Army of Northern Virginia.[4] My impression is that he had here some veteran regiments and some of the Richmond Reserves or Defences, which I suppose had duties in Richmond when not called out to the trenches. Colonel Crutchfield I had known as Stonewall Jackson's chief of artillery and he was recovering from a wound received when that hero so unhappily fell.[5] His command here was a lately organized brigade composed of six—I think there were six—battalions of heavy artillery but armed with muskets. The brigade organization was different from the usual one. There were the 10th and 19th Virginia Battalions, each under a major and with Lieutenant-Colonel John W. Atkinson[6] over both, and the 18th and 20th Virginia, under Majors M. B. Hardin and James Robertson, respectively, with my brother, Lieutenant-Colonel James Howard over both. These four were heavy artillery by enlistment and had been manning the

[4] He had been transferred for some reason from the brigade now commanded by General George H. Steuart.

[5] The sense of Jackson's loss in the army, and outside, is illustrated by an address, made by a Catholic priest, I believe, at New Orleans some years ago. He said that in 1863 Providence, having determined that the Confederacy should not succeed, *found it necessary to remove its servant Stonewall Jackson from the field.*

[6] He was half a Marylander, being a son of Bishop Atkinson of North Carolina who had been long rector of Grace Church in Baltimore. He died in Wilmington, North Carolina a few years ago.

earth defence works, with heavy guns, around Richmond until recently brought to the front on its east side; they were now, if not before, armed with muskets. The 5th Battalion was the 18th Georgia, enlisted as heavy artillery but also with muskets. I remember it very well because I inspected it one day and being struck by its soldierly appearance, I enquired about its history and was told by its commander, Major Basinger, with some pride, of its past services. I think it had only three or four companies. I do not remember much about the 6th Battalion as a battalion organization but it was composed of several companies serving at Chaffin's Bluff. Some of these were light artillery and one was even a cavalry company by enlistment, but all, while serving as heavy artillery I believe, had muskets. Colonel Crutchfield's command thus anomalously composed and organized, was commonly known as the Heavy Artillery Brigade.

General Custis Lee had also under him several organizations of Richmond local defence troops, but I do not recall anything about them particularly and suppose they were of uncertain strength, being composed of government employees in the departments at Richmond, the Tredegar Iron Works, etc., or other half exempts; perhaps they were the same as those I spoke of as part of Barton's Brigade.

The part of the line of works of the Army of Northern Virginia which was held by Custis Lee's Division extended from Chaffin's Bluff, or from a point on James River a short distance below it, northerly about a mile to the front of Fort Harrison, or Fort Burnham as the Federals had renamed it after its capture from us some time before. And the taking and holding of it had caused a new location of our line, of which it had formerly been a part. But our new works were not more than a few hundred yards distant at the nearest point and the Fort was in plain view across the open country. The Federals had greatly strengthened it and it looked like a complete separate fortification, difficult to be recaptured and from which a destructive fire would be opened when fighting began. But we had at intervals behind our works little mortars, singly and in groups of two or three, trained on the fort, and we trusted to make it a hot place to hold or do any fighting from. These works of ours were something new to me who had seen only field breastworks, hastily constructed. And I was curious— but not desirous—to see what mortar shell fighting would be like. After being so long used to the horizontal battlefield firing, it gave me something of a feeling of unfairness to think of bombshells dropping vertically on our heads. But we had what were supposed to be bombproof shelters, partly excavated and with roofs of earth and timber, in which the men could go when the firing was only from that artillery. Outside the works and only a few yards in front was a row of upright rods—iron I think—two or three feet apart with patches of red flannel or cloth on them; these indicated a line of torpedoes planted just under the surface, but *not* exactly at the flags—meant to blow up a charging line of infantry. And I did hear that their efficacy was proved by the destruction of one or two grazing horses or cows (but I doubt cows being in that neighborhood). These torpedoes had been planted under the direction of General Gabriel Rains, who, in Richmond, was at the head of the Confederate torpedo bureau, and of whose constructive and destructive abilities in that line of business we had a good opinion.[7]

[7] In these days of flying through the air I have often thought of the proposition of a man in Richmond in the winter of 1864–65, to construct what he called an artisavis or avisartis (bird of art) with which he would hover over the enemy

Nearer the river from Fort Harrison-Burnham the enemy's works were not in view, but the picket lines were sometimes quite close. And I remember one day visiting our pickets there and leisurely scanning those of the enemy to see if I could recognize any of my old acquaintances from Wye, the home of my brother-in-law, Colonel Edward Lloyd, in Talbot County, Maryland; for at this point we had negro troops opposite to us. Some were probably there but the distance was a little too far for recognition. The ground where their sentinels walked their posts was covered with stumps of cut down trees and I was amused to see the officer of the guard come along and with the flat of his sword beat unmercifully several who, true to their nature, had sat down on the stumps and gone to sleep. At another point our sentinel or picket and one of the enemy's tramped along the top of an old breastwork (our old line abandoned when Fort Harrison was taken), to and from each other, with a log thrown across to mark their respective territories. As I approached our picket he turned his back on his enemy and came to meet me. I said "Are you not afraid that man will shoot you when you turn your back to him?" "Oh no, sir," he replied, "there's no danger." "Well," said I, "suppose you should cross that log?" "Why then he would shoot me." "And suppose he crossed it?" "I would shoot him." I did not wear an elaborate Confederate uniform at that time, such things not being allowed to be sent from Baltimore to Fort Delaware from which I had lately come, but my dress sufficiently showed that I was an officer. But the Federal soldier paid no particular attention to me, although

and drop down explosives. The newspapers made fun of it, but the man was only fifty years ahead of the time. It has been done in Tunis and Turkey (1912-1913).

in his walking to and fro he came quite close.[8] This truce of the pickets was a remarkable feature in the last half of the war and when and where it prevailed could be relied on as implicitly as a safe conduct from Grant and Lee. Sometimes it existed along certain parts of the line while constant popping at any exposure was going on elsewhere. I have heard that when orders came down to open fire, the etiquette was to give notice before beginning. But the truce between pickets prevailed all along our line while I was at Chaffin's.

Kershaw's Division joined us on our left and next to that was Field's, beyond which cavalry guarded the flank.

In my curiosity about the novelty to me of mortar firing, I one day stood and watched General E. P. Alexander, Longstreet's chief of artillery, as he, for some purpose in the way of practice, fired several large bombshells from the high river bluff near Chaffin's directly across the river. I could plainly see the shells on leaving the mortar mount to a high elevation and descend in the woods a mile or more distant. It was an interesting sight, but I thought he was very reckless about where he was dropping his shells—which were as large as an iron pot. I supposed, however, he knew his business.

I often rode up to Richmond with my brother, particularly on Sunday to attend service at St. Paul's Church, under the popular Dr. Minnegerode, who was, I believe, a cousin of Count Bismarck, and who never lost a slight German accent. We generally took dinner at the house

[8] Major Robert Stiles, who commanded the Chaffin's Bluff Battalion at this time, in his *Four Years under Marse Robert*, says that he placed a billet of wood across the work to prevent encroachment and ordered our picket to shoot the enemy's if he crossed it. I have been surprised as I have written these "Recollections" to find so many and such curiously exact confirmations of my statements.

on 7th (?) Street, north of Main, of the family of ex-Senator James Murray Mason,[9] then Confederate Min-inister or Commissioner to England. The family was "refugeeing" in Richmond, their home in Winchester having been totally demolished by the Federals so that there was not left one stone on another and the shrubbery so destroyed that the site was a waste place. Mr. Mason instructed his family to keep an open house for Confederates in Richmond, and they did. On one of these times I met there General Trimble, just returned from his long captivity in the north, but either he was not yet declared exchanged or, at any rate, was not assigned to a command and I kept my position at the front.

My pay of $135 a month had accumulated during my imprisonment, and I remember drawing it from Major John Ambler,[10] a paymaster in Richmond, and spending several hundred dollars on Governor Street for a pair of high cavalry boots. Such was the value, or want of value, of Confederate money at this time, when it was said a man would go to market with a market basket to hold his money and would bring home his purchases in his hand.

There was a mild day in the last of March when overhead an immense number of wild geese were winging their way to the North, showing that Spring and the opening of the campaign were at hand. And I was much scandalized, being an inspector and concerned about

[9] Mrs. Mason was a granddaughter of Chief Justice Benjamin Chew, of Germantown, Pennsylvania, and so a first cousin of my father.

[10] Mrs. Ambler was a daughter of James M. Mason; she had lately died. Major John Ambler was a good man, deservedly liked by all and especially popular with Marylanders. After the war he was first a lay reader and then took orders in the Protestant Episcopal Church and for some time went about like a missionary in West Virginia. He died many years ago. Judge James M. Ambler of Baltimore is one of his children.

breaches of discipline, by much popping of guns at them. But the temptation was very great. When I was a boy in Baltimore at the opening of every Spring flocks of wild geese and swans were to be seen passing over the city in their wedge shaped formations and looking by turns lead colored and then snowy white as the light was reflected from them.[11]

[11] The *War of the Rebellion—Official Records of the Union and Confederate Armies*, Series 1, Volume XLVI, Part II, Serial No. 96, page 1025, gives a Special Order from General Robert E. Lee, dated 9th January, 1865, organizing the 40th, 47th and 55th Regiments and the 22nd and 25th Battalions, Virginia Infantry, into a brigade under Brigadier-General Seth M. Barton; and the 1st, 2d, 3d and 4th Battalions of Virginia Reserves, and the 10th, 19th, 18th and 20th Virginia Battalions of Heavy Artillery, and the Battalion of five companies serving at Chaffin's Bluff, into another brigade, to which also was temporarily attached the 18th Battalion of Georgia Heavy Artillery. And these two brigades and the brigade of Local Defense Troops, consisting of the 2d and 3d Regiments and the 1st, 4th and 5th Battalions Local Defense Troops, were constituted a division, to the command of which Major-General G. W. Custis Lee was assigned.

This appears a large command on paper but it was nothing like as large in reality, the "Reserves" and "Local Defense Troop" being, I think, somewhat skeleton organizations—at least as serving in the field. I suppose most of the men—and officers—were occupied with their duties in Richmond. All these troops were under—indeed they constituted almost the entire force of—Lieutenant-General Richard S. Ewell as commander of the Department of Richmond, to the local defence of which these regiments and battalions particularly belonged although now holding a part of the general line of the Army of Northern Virginia. But I do not reconcile exactly this Special Order with General Ewell's tri-monthly returns afterwards, which will be found on pages 1274 and 1275 of the same Serial, and page 1331 of Part III, Serial No. 97. But it is not easy to understand about the Virginia Reserves, the Local Defence Troops, etc. For some account of them see also the *Confederate Military History*, Volume III, Virginia, page 558 et seq. And for Major Basinger's 18th Georgia Battalion see the same *History*, Volume VI, Georgia, page 144. The 9th Georgia Battalion of Ewell's tri-monthly returns is not, I think, an error for the 18th, and it and the "Artillery Defenses" were probably manning the earthworks on other sides of Richmond.

On the day of the writing of these last two pages, 19 February 1913, I read in the newspapers of the death of General George Washington Custis Lee at his home, "Ravensworth," near Alexandria, Virginia, on 18th February.

CHAPTER XXXIV

RETREAT FROM RICHMOND AND BATTLE OF SAILOR'S CREEK

Between 10 and 11 o'clock at night, Saturday, April 1 (1865), just as I was falling asleep in the tent on the lines a little north of Chaffin's Bluff on the north side of James River, a faint red glare illuminated the canvas, followed by a low muttering like distant thunder. The night was dark and cloudy, the atmosphere damp and heavy, and at another time·I might have found it hard to determine whether the sound was the distant roll of musketry or the rumbling of an approaching storm, but under the circumstances there was short doubt about it. Flash after flash shone through the canvas and the muttering became presently almost continuous although very little louder. There was something particularly awful in the half suppressed but deadly signs of a far off struggle contrasted with the perfect tranquillity immediately around us. Dressing ourselves and mounting the works we watched and listened for half an hour, but the battle was across the James and away over to our right, all continued quiet along our part of the line and the "Richmond Defences" soon came to the conclusion that so far it was no affair of theirs and, like true soldiers, went to sleep as fast as they could, to make the most of their present exemption.

Sunday morning was cloudless and lovely, and everything continuing quiet in our front and not the slightest intimation of any change in the condition of affairs being received at division heaquarters, I saw no reason why

I should not ride back to Richmond for the purpose of attending church. On reaching the city I was not a little astonished to find it in great commotion. Field's Division, which had formed the left of the line of three divisions on the north side of James River, had been withdrawn and marched through the city early in the morning, being called away in haste to reinforce the south side where heavy fighting, it was said, had been and was still going on. Matters were reported to be in a critical condition there; but there were also cheering rumors that General Joe Johnston had eluded Sherman and was within a few hours march of Grant's left flank, and many were buoyant with the expectation that the day would witness a repetition of the scenes of 1862, when Stonewall Jackson came down on McClellan's right.

At St. Paul's Church, at the 11 o'clock service, I sat in a pew on the left hand side near the back, and saw President Davis and, one after another, the principal Government officers and leading men mysteriously summoned away in the middle of the service. Many persons somewhat tumultuously, got up and left the church and for a while there was a good deal of confusion among those who remained, but order was presently restored, and, being Communion Sunday, the services were conducted to the conclusion without further interruption and with unusual solemnity.[1]

When I left the church, before 2 o'clock, I found the Spotswood Hotel, corner of Main and 7th Streets, and General Ewell's Headquarters (commanding the Depart-

---

[1] It so happened that the disorder was at its greatest just before the time for taking up the usual collection and I afterwards read an account of a Northern newspaper correspondent which related how the rector, recognizing the impending end of all things, with happy presence of mind, seized the occasion for reaping a last harvest from his scattering congregation!

ment of Richmond) at the northwest corner of Franklin and 7th Streets, were points of greatest interest, and here large crowds blocked the pavements, discussing the rumors, which hourly became more exciting and took more definite shape. It seemed certain that there had been heavy fighting the day before on our extreme right, in which the Confederates had been unable to withstand the pressure of overwhelming numbers. I saw Captain W. Stuart Symington[2] (of Maryland), of Major-General George E. Pickett's staff, who, reaching Richmond by railroad after passing all the way around by Burkesville Junction, reported that that general's command was cut off and in a critical situation and it was ascertained that the firing which we had listened to the night before was an attack made on the center of our line, half way between Chaffin's and Petersburg, where, owing to Pickett's Division having been drawn off to re-inforce the extreme right, the works were left defended by less than a skirmish line.

This attack had resulted in the capture of the works, a gap was thus made in our center through which the Federals poured their troops and massed them preparatory to sweeping down the line. It had been reported early in the day that General Ewell had received orders from General Lee to evacuate Richmond and the story had been twenty times repeated and denied. By 4 o'clock, however, the belief was common that the capital of the Confederacy must be abandoned, causing a general activity, though more settled gloom. The scenes of that afternoon will never be forgotten. Bundles, trunks and boxes were brought out of houses for transportation from the city or to be conveyed to places within it which were fancied to be more secure. Vehicles of every

[2] He died 9th June, 1912.

sort and description and a continuous stream of pedestrians with knapsacks or bundles filled the streets which led out from the western side of Richmond, while the forms of a few wounded officers, brought home from the battlefields, were borne along the pavements on litters, their calm, pallid faces in strange contrast with the busy ones around. Ladies stood in their doorways or wandered restlessly about the streets, interrogating every passer by for the latest news. All formality was laid aside in this supreme calamity; all felt the more closely drawn together because so soon to be separated. I did not, however, witness the last and saddest hours of the evacuation, for learning that movements would soon take place in my own command, I mounted at sundown and galloped back to Chaffin's Farm.

Here I found none of the confusion which I had left in Richmond, but there was only instead the unnatural stillness of stealthy preparation. Orders had been received at division headquarters to move out as soon as the moon went down, which would be at 2 a.m. The hostile lines were very close, Fort Harrison (Fort Burnham, as the Federals had re-christened it after their capture of it,) not being more than a few hundred yards from "Elliott's Hill" in our line, and in plain view, while the pickets were, of course, much nearer. The country for about half a mile in rear of this part of our works was open, so that the enemy could in daylight observe our slightest movement, or even any unusual activity of staff officers or couriers. We had, therefore, to exercise the very greatest circumspection. So, while at the different headquarters active but quiet preparations were in progress, every effort was made to preserve along the line its wonted aspect of apathy and Sunday rest. But as soon as we had the friendly cover of night, the work of packing and breaking up camp was begun in earnest. Unfortunately, owing to the fact that the greater part of Custis Lee's Division had been persistently regarded as fixed to the Richmond defences, it had never been equipped like the rest of the army and now at this crisis found itself utterly deficient in means of transportation. The few wretched teams were driven down as close to the line as was prudent and the men carried the cooking utensils, baggage and ordnance on their backs to meet them. Although all the wagons were loaded almost beyond the ability of the miserable animals to start them, still piles of baggage remained lying by the wayside.[3] There was no help for it, and little time for selection even, and many an officer and man found himself about to start on an indefinite campaign without a single article except what he wore upon his back, and with a very dim prospect indeed of being able to get a new supply. I took some comfort in the reflection that I was tolerably well shod at least, having invested eight hundred dollars—about six months' pay—in the purchase of a pair of high boots a few days before in Richmond. But all minor griefs were absorbed in the one great disaster to the cause and, according to their different temperaments, officers and men resigned themselves to their private destitution with cheerful resignation or the apathy of despair.

[3] In 1875 I received a letter from a gentleman in Boston stating that the writer had picked up in Richmond in 1865 a couple of books, Virgil and the Tragedies of Aeschylus, with my name and rank, "Aide de Camp to Maj.-Genl. Trimble, Richmond, January 1864," which he would like to restore to me. In reply, I asked him to write on the fly leaf of each how he had obtained and was now returning them. He did so in the following words:

"When in Richmond in the spring of 1865 as surgeon in the Army, I bought this volume at a trifling price of a negro, and am much pleased now with the opportunity of restoring it to the owner.

SAMUEL A. GREENE, M.D.,
Boston, Oct. 27, 1875."

If night has the effect of covering a military movement to the eye, its stillness nevertheless brings the disadvantage of discovering it to the ear, and although the greatest possible silence was enjoined, it was strange that, from the creaking of wagons and noise of removing guns—of which there were about twenty along our front (not to speak of some twenty four mortars and twenty heavy pieces at Chaffin's, etc., all which were abandoned) —the enemy did not get an intimation of what we were about. Besides, either from the proverbial carelessness of soldiers or from accident, every now and then a hut or pile of brush at the Bluff or in the woods in our rear, would blaze up, throwing a lurid glare far and wide, and although I gallopped from spot to spot and endeavored to impress on the men the imminent danger of drawing the enemy's fire, it was impossible to keep these blazes down.

Shortly after midnight all was ready for the final and delicate operation of withdrawing the troops. Field's Division, as before narrated, had been already taken away and there were now but two divisions on the north side of the James—except the cavalry, of the movements, of which I am wholly ignorant. Custis Lee's command included and stretched one mile from Chaffin's Bluff, and was then joined by Kershaw's Division which extended away to the left. Kershaw had already moved out and, marching diagonally from the line and across our rear, had passed the river at Wilton Bridge, a pontoon bridge some two miles above Chaffin's. Custis Lee's command now took up the movement, commencing on the left. Generally the companies were marched by the right or left of companies to the rear, and there converging to form their respective battalions, these in turn concentrated still further to the rear into brigades, which finally formed the division line of march. The pickets were left out with orders to withdraw just before day and rapidly overtake the main body. To the relief of all, no notice seemed to be taken of our movement by the enemy; it would have produced a fearful scene of confusion had his batteries been opened on us at such a time. The different columns united with tolerable regularity and the division followed the route in rear of Kershaw's across Wilton Bridge. The wagon train meanwhile had gone through Richmond to cross the James at one of the upper fords and meet the troops somewhere towards Farmville—we never saw it again.

By daylight we had made several miles on the Amelia Court House road. In the early gray of morning, while the command was resting for a few minutes, a sudden bright light drew the attention of everyone to the direction of Drewry's Bluff, our main defence with the Confederate flotilla there, of James River, about a mile above Chaffin's and on the south bank. A magnificent pyramid of fire, shooting hundreds of feet into the dusky air, and a dull explosion, told the tale of the destruction, by its own men, of the last of the Confederate Navy— except the *Shenandoah*, still cruising on the Ocean.[4]

Custis Lee's Division was now for the first time displayed as a command, in two brigades, Barton's, numbering about 1300 men, and Crutchfield's, or the Heavy Artillery brigade, about 1400; I do not remember any other troops with it. The heavy artillery men having been stationary around Richmond had been able to keep their uniforms in better plight, and their scarlet

---

[4] It kept on cruising in the remote northern Pacific Ocean, capturing and destroying vessels until 2d August, 1865, when its commander, Captain James I. Waddell, learning of the fall of the Confederacy, took his vessel back to England and handed it over to the British authorities.

caps and trimmings (artillery color,) made them present a distinctive appearance in the army, of which they were now a regular part.

After proceeding a short distance General Custis Lee sent me back to look for our pickets, which, it will be remembered were not to withdraw from the front of our lines until just before dawn. My recollection is that before getting to the river I met them coming back. I must have lingered for some reason, for I presently rode alone to overtake the command. I had gone a short distance when I heard a shot ahead of me and soon, to my surprise, came to the dead body of a soldier in the road who had evidently just been killed by the shot I heard. While wondering, I heard a clamor at a house a short way off the east (or south?) side of the road ahead, and rode over to investigate. The people were in great perturbation—all women or children I think—and told me that a Confederate officer had come there and threatened to shoot them and acted strangely and violently. Riding on to overtake and arrest him, I soon found a soldier trudging along the road who said the man had just passed and had been near shooting him. Believing that the officer had either become insane or was crazy drunk and was running "amuck," I borrowed this soldier's gun and hurried on, intending to shoot him down if necessary to protect myself in arresting him—if he did not first shoot me. Not overtaking him presently, I returned the musket to the soldier and went on until I suddenly came on the division, which was halted, having crossed the Richmond and Petersburg Railroad about 6 o'clock in the morning and proceeded some distance beyond. I began to tell General Custis Lee about the apparently crazy man and his actions when he stopped me and said he was already in arrest. He directed me to return and take the depositions of the people of the house, which I did.[5]

The division remained halted at this point about two hours. We had gone through woods and often passing over bottoms ankle deep in mud and water, to the great discomfort of the men, but here it was more open. A dense black volume of smoke was observed to rise and hang like a huge pall over the country in the direction of Richmond, some twelve miles distant, and several officers who now joined us, among them Lieutenant Robert Goldsborough,[6] aide de camp to General Custis Lee, gave us an account of the sad circumstances attending the final abandonment of the city.

Marching slowly on, and with frequent vexatious halts caused by the road being blocked in front by batteries and other obstacles in the woods and marshy places, we reached the ————— House, said to have been before the war a favorite resort of fast teams and men from Richmond, which was fifteen miles distant by an excellent straight road. Here the Major-General and staff managed to get a bread and meat dinner, or supper, which, being almost the first mouthful one of them at least had eaten—except hard raw corn—since dinner the day before, was extremely acceptable. Our horses were equally glad to get some fodder and straw. By this time the sun had set and we galloped to overtake the division. We lost ourselves and got entangled among strange troops for several hours (and no situation is more

---

[5] These depositions I took down, in pencil, in a small black blank book which I still have somewhere but cannot now lay my hands on (not the one from which I have quoted in the early part of this narrative). I never heard any explanation of this strange episode. I omitted it from my published account of this retreat at the request of Dr. J. Hand Browne seconded by the advice of Major Thomas W. Hall.

[6] Of Talbot County, Maryland. He was killed at Sailor's Creek, 6th April.

bewildering at night), but at last, striking across the country by a pocket map, we came upon the right road and found our command in bivouac near Tomahawk Church.[7] It was now past 12 o'clock and after wandering about, perfectly bewildered among the many camp fires, a half smothered bark of recognition from under a little mound of blanket fortunately guided my brother and myself (for I stayed with him at night,) to our proper place, and at 2 a.m. I wrapped myself in my saddle blanket for a couple of hours sleep.[8]

Just before dawn, 4th April, a drizzling rain began to fall and the morning broke dismally enough. Soon after daylight the division was formed along the road—there being no breakfast, little preparation was required—and, disentangling ourselves from the artillery and other troops which moved out at the same time, we succeeded in gaining a clear road. The men were cheered with the information that there was a possibility of finding provisions at Matoaca Station[9] but on striking the Richmond

[7] In the *Atlas to accompany the Official Records of the Union and Confederate Armies*, Part XVI, Plate LXXVIII, No. 1, will be found a map of "Routes from Petersburg, Chester Station and Manchester to Amelia Court House," made by order of Colonel T. M. R. Talcott, commanding the engineer troops of the Army of Northern Virginia. It was probably prepared for the impending retreat. On page 118 of volume 1 of the *Transactions of the Southern Historical Society 1874*, is General Custis Lee's report of this retreat, dated 25th April, 1865, in which he says he crossed at Wilton Bridge and moved to Branch Church and thence by Gregory's to the Genito road and camped half a mile beyond Tomahawk Church. Branch's Church may be where the Richmond refugees joined us and Gregory's where we had supper, but their distances from Richmond are less than I have given.

[8] "Bounce," my brother's pointer dog, slept under the blanket of one of us like a gentleman. We lost him at Sailor's Creek, and although advertisement was made in the newspapers afterwards, we never heard of him again, and the supposition is not so improbable that in those starvation times the dog fell a victim to the necessities of the courier who had him in special charge or of others.

[9] Colonel Talcott's map puts "Mattoax" Station at the railroad crossing of the Appomattox River, as do some other maps. If so, we struck the railroad at

and Danville Railroad at that point, they met with a disappointment. However, an hour's halt was made, in the middle of the day, as well for rest as to give those few who were so provident as to have saved a little meat or flour an opportunity to cook.

So far we had been pursuing the road which crossed the Appomattox over Genito Bridge,[11] but owing to the failure of "some one" to have the pontoons laid at that point, or have a proper crossing, we were compelled to strike more to the south and, with other troops, pass over on the railroad bridge. By 4 o'clock we were within one mile of this point, but as some flooring had to be laid or put in order and after that a large train of artillery was to pass over before us, we halted and cooked a scanty supply of flour which one or two of our wagons had luckily brought us. At dark we commenced to file by twos across the bridge, the men being cautioned to march in the very middle of the flooring, between the rails, as otherwise it might turn over. It was a long time before the rear guard had passed over, and taking a circuitous route through woods and fields to find a suitable camping ground, we finally came to a halt a little after midnight.[11] The men were exhausted from hunger and the wearisome march and, throwing themselves down under the nearest trees, were soon asleep.

some other station, for it was several miles east of the river. And it was not Chula, as suggested with a query in my published account, for that appears to have been west of the Appomattox.

[10] In my published account I said we had been pursuing the road to Goode's Bridge, which is several miles *south* of the railroad bridge. But General Custis Lee in his report before referred to, says we were aiming to cross the Genito Bridge, and I see now from the maps that our route was towards it—two or three miles *above* the railroad. I have here, therefore, changed Goode's to Genito Bridge.

[11] General Custis Lee says that after crossing the railroad bridge at Mattoax Station, we went into camp on the hills beyond the river, and next morning burned the bridge behind us.

A little before dawn, April 5, we were roused again and speedily took the road, moving parallel with and near the railroad. I was so fortunate as to get a slice of raw ham during the morning and presently not only got another but found time to broil it. After this I had nothing but hard corn, and a very insufficient supply of that. And I suppose everybody else fared about as ill—certainly all within my observation did.

When about two miles from Amelia Court House we were astonished to receive a report that the enemy's cavalry were on our right flank and destroying the wagon train, which had been moving on a parallel road a short distance in that direction. We had been under the impression that after having placed the Appomattox in our rear we were secure from close pursuit, but our eyes were now opened to a real understanding of the situation. The troops of Ewell's Corps—Custis Lee's Division and Kershaw's Division—were massed and Kershaw's was sent to the reported scene of action; but it appearing that there was no enemy near enough to interfere with our march, the column was moved on. A short distance from Amelia Court House, however, we halted again for a considerable time while the whole order of march was re-arranged and the column disposed as if moving through a hostile country. Here we learned that a large portion of our wagon train had really been captured, and that the enemy in heavy force menaced our flank and front. Much of the artillery, ambulances, etc., in our line turned back to take a different road.

At Amelia Court House our division received an efficient accession, but one which also added yet more to its heterogeneous character. This consisted, in the first place, of the so-called "Naval Brigade" or Battalion, formed of the officers and men manning the batteries at

Drewry's Bluff now organized into something like a regiment, the tars being armed with Minie muskets. They numbered about 400[12] and were commanded by Commodore J. Randolph Tucker. There were also four or five companies of "Richmond Locals," which were incorporated with or were already a part of Barton's Brigade (see page 354), and two or three companies of light artillery, armed with muskets, which were added to the Heavy Artillery brigade. Infantry, cavalry, light and heavy artillery and sailors, we had thus in our small division all the elements of a complete army and navy, and with the Richmond Locals and Defences some material for civil government besides.

During the entire day the army retreat had been conducted with an absence of order which caused endless delays and irregularities. Immediately after leaving Amelia Court House one of these halts occurred which made an unnecessary detention of an hour or two and is an example of what was frequently taking place, day and night. Riding ahead, with great difficulty, to ascertain the cause, I found a long train of artillery and wagons almost inextricably entangled, closed up in some places three abreast in the road so that a horseman even could not pass by. There seemed to be no one present exercising any authority, and the teamsters appeared to be waiting stolidly for Jove to help them out. Had there been an officer of sufficient authority present, or had the quartermasters to whom this train belonged had their hearts in the discharge of their duties at such a crisis,

[12] In my published account I said "about 1500 (?)," but Mr. Bartlett S. Johnson, formerly of North Carolina but since the war a well known resident of Baltimore, who was a midshipman in the command, says about 400. They certainly could not have been anything like 1500. Perhaps 1500 in my account was a misprint or slip of the pen for 500. There can be no question of its being a gross error.

these and many other instances of disorder and loss of precious time might have been avoided. Never, I thought, was the necessity of a well organized corps of inspectors, with high rank and well defined authority, so apparent as in this retreat.[13]

Shortly after we had managed to get by this obstruction and obtained a tolerably clear road, the enemy were reported on our left flank and skirmishers were thrown out, but no demonstration was made against our line of march. The men were now becoming exhausted and falling out in numbers, but not a ration could be anywhere procured, nor could a halt be made to give them rest and sleep. Night came and found us toiling on at a snail's pace. Nothing is so fatiguing and demoralizing to soldiers on a march as an irregular step and uncertain halts—even without the extraordinary conditions of hardship under which we were suffering.

At about 9 o'clock p.m. just as the head of the division was bending to the left and crossing the Richmond and Danville Railroad through a deep cut and with a wood in front, the column was suddenly fired into. A scene of the most painful confusion ensued. Most of the men along there became panic struck, gave way to the right and sought cover behind the fence or trees, while not a few skulked to the rear. They began to discharge their pieces at random, in many instances shooting their own comrades no doubt, and bullets were flying in every direction. I happened to be a little way down from the head of the column and about at the scene of the greatest confusion. This lasted for some time and all efforts to restore order were unavailing, only exposing those who made such attempts to imminent danger of

[13] Perhaps I have been too harsh in my criticism, under the conditions of this retreat.

being shot down. Finally the men were induced to cease their wild firing and partially reform the column in the road. It was believed that a small scouting party of the enemy fired into the head of the column and then hastily retired, but we were by no means certain that the panic did not wholly originate among ourselves and that the head of the column with its changed direction was not mistaken by those behind for an enemy.[14] Just as the line was reformed and I was riding along it my horse started violently at seeing Major Frank Smith's dead horse in the road and backed or sidled among the men and causing them to give place, and this brought a renewal of the panic along that part of the column. Warned by what had occurred before, the officers cried out earnestly, "Don't shoot, don't shoot, men," but some fifty or a hundred guns were fired, particularly from the side fence to which the men had melted back. My own predicament was a serious one, for I could not dismount from my plunging horse and with a sickening feeling I saw in the moonlight a number of bright barrels pointed directly at me and many bullets passed close by. I was the only mounted officer along there. Finally, however, the men ceased shooting and order was restored. Some valuable lives were sacrificed in this inexcusable affair,[15] among them Major Frank Smith, of Norfolk—who commanded the artillery companies (armed with muskets) which had lately joined us—Harry C. Pennington, of Baltimore, and three or four others killed (or mortally wounded), and half a dozen wounded. The latter had to be carried in ambulances until a house was reached,

[14] Many years ago I read—I think in a Baltimore County newspaper—an account of one of a scouting party of the enemy which left no doubt in my mind that it was this party which fired on us. I have the slip somewhere.

[15] But the condition of the men must be remembered—affecting both body and mind.

where their wounds were dressed and the poor fellows were then left to the care of the enemy. I saw Pennington, who lived near me in Baltimore and whom I had known all my life, in the ambulance, with another who was groaning a good deal. Pennington knew his wound was probably mortal but was quite composed and said to the groaning man, "My friend, I am worse wounded than you."[16] The whole division was disheartened by this unhappy occurrence and for some time the men marched on discussing it in subdued but eager tones, presently relapsing into a gloomy silence.

We plodded on through the night, the men becoming more and more faint from fatigue, want of sleep and hunger, particularly the latter. Every expedient was resorted to in order to obtain something to eat, however scanty, with a total disregard of the ordinary rules of discipline and respect for private property. The regimental and battalion commanders were instructed to send out small detachments to scour the thinly settled country on either flank to bring in whatever they could lay their hands on, if only a pig, a chicken or a quart of meal. Very little, however, was procured in this way, the detachments either returning empty handed or failing to rejoin the column at all. At about an hour before dawn the troops were halted in a dense thicket of old field pine. Most of the men immediately dropped down in their places and sank to sleep, while some few—a very few—parched corn or cooked any little provision they were so lucky as to have. Hunger being most pressing in my own case, I first parched a handful of corn—sharing with my horse—in a frying pan borrowed with some difficulty, and was

[16] He died at Amelia Springs within one or two days. I think his body was afterwards brought to Baltimore and placed in the Pennington vault or lot in Greenmount Cemetery.

then preparing for a nap, when the drum beat the assembly and we took the road once more.

The morning, 6th April, was damp and the ground was in bad condition for marching. In disentangling the division from various other commands which blocked the road, the artillery battalion (with muskets), lately commanded by Major Frank Smith became separated and did not join us again. We presently got ahead of the other troops, but the road was occupied by an immense train of wagons, ambulances, &c. and so we marched outside of it.

By this time the command was fearfully reduced in numbers and men were falling out continually. They were allowed to shoot from their places in the ranks pigs, chickens or whatever of the sort came in their way, commanding officers and inspectors looking on, or looking aside, without rebuke. It was, perhaps, the only instance in my experience during the war, and I had seen some hard times, when the plea of military, or rather of human, necessity imperatively overruled all consideration due to private property and military discipline. The present situation was distressing and the prospect alarming, apart from any thought of a threatening enemy. I did not see how the men could be held together much longer without food, or where the scantiest supply could be obtained or where they could get enough if they scattered in such a country. Barton's Brigade now showed not more than five hundred men in line, the Heavy Artillery but few more, and the naval battalion was much reduced—perhaps to 300.[17] But

[17] I said in my original narrative, written in October 1865, that Barton's Brigade now showed not more than 500 in line, the heavy artillery but few more and that the naval brigade was reduced to not over 600. But see a previous note about my gross overestimate of the naval battalion, which I saw only on the two days, April 5 and 6. However, the men of this battalion, being, like all

when all the circumstances are taken into consideration, never was exhibited more patient fortitude and fidelity than in this wreck of the Confederacy.

During the morning, at 10 or 11 o'clock, I fell in with an old Baltimore friend, C. Gratiot Thompson, who was, I think, in some artillery command.[18]   He asked me how I was getting along, and on my replying, badly enough, and giving some details, he said, after a little hesitation, "Well old fellow, I have fared better, having spent last night with my wagons.   And I have some apple brandy in my canteen which I will divide with you."   I had no canteen, for I never liked wearing anything around my shoulder.   I tried to borrow one, but being unsuccessful, said to him, "Grash, I will ride along with you and take my half as we go."   And so it happened that I got half a mile or so in advance of the division and came to where the enemy's cavalry suddenly appeared on the left flank and made an effort to strike the wagon train there filing by.   On riding to the spot I found quite a warm skirmish going on.   The remnant of Pickett's Division and a portion of Bushrod Johnson's[19] here formed in line and threw out skirmishers who kept the enemy back without much difficulty.   Just at this point[20] the road

sailors, more attached to or dependent on their officers, no doubt straggled off less than the others.   Once during the morning I saw two or three trying to get water at a wet place by the road side and on my asking what command they belonged to, one of the tars straightened up and said, "To the navy, by gosh, and a bully work it has done."   He would not have known what esprit de corps meant, but he had it.

[18] He died some years ago in Massachusetts.   He was here second-lieutenant and ordnance officer of McGowan's Brigade.

[19] Bushrod Johnson's and Pickett's Divisions were two of the three divisions of Lieutenant-General R. H. Anderson's Corps.

[20] Union accounts to call this locality "Hott's house" and say it is one mile to Sailor's Creek.   The left-hand road goes to Rice's Station on the Southside Railroad, i.e., the Petersburg and Lynchburg Railroad.

forked, one branch keeping a little to the left, the other at the same angle to the right. The wagon train was pursuing the right hand branch, while the troops were taking the left and so covering the train from the enemy. Custis Lee's Division soon same up—it was now a little after midday—and took position just at the fork facing to the left, connecting on our now right with Wise's Brigade of Bushrod Johnson's command and with Kershaw's Division on our left. Still further to the left, or in our late rear, was Gordon,[21] who sent several messages that he was being severely pressed in his task of bringing up the rear of the army. Having been at this point already some time before our division came up, I informed my general (Custis Lee,) that I had distinctly seen large bodies of the enemy mount, after skirmishing, and pass on to our right, i.e., as we faced easterly, with the evident intention of gaining a position across the road in front of our line of march, while a force remained to threaten and delay us, and asked if we could not destroy or abandon the rest of the wagon train and push by that right hand road ourselves. But he said his orders required him to wait for the passing of the train and to guard it afterwards by taking the left hand road; and I think I remember his receiving renewed orders to the same effect just at this time. The enemy now opened on us with two pieces of artillery, shelling the wagon train more particularly, which was hurried by as fast as possible; but about two hours were so consumed before the last wagon passed. Finally Bushrod Johnson moved on and Custis Lee and Kershaw followed. Gordon must have taken the right hand road with the wagons, as we heard nothing more of him.

[21] Lieutenant-General (better known as Major-General) John B. Gordon.

We passed through some woods at first and then came out on open ground with the depressed and rather wide valley of Sailor's Creek in front. We passed over this, a sluggish stream with bushes along it, about 3 o'clock and began to ascend the opposite slope, at first over open ground or with a low and scattered growth, which soon became larger pine woods. Just then a sharp skirmish fire was heard directly in front, followed by the roar of artillery, and word came back to our dismay, but what we ought to have expected, that Pickett[22] had encountered a heavy force of the enemy drawn up across the road immediately before him. Custis Lee's and Kershaw's Divisions were, therefore, massed on the hillside, waiting anxiously for the front to be forced. In a short time we were disturbed to observe a body of men emerge directly in our rear, and deliberately occupy a position two or three hundred yards back from Sailor's Creek, in the very road on which we had just been marching. We had some lingering doubts at first whether they were friends or foes, but all uncertainty was soon rudely dispelled. As we gazed through our glasses we saw them coolly drag out two pieces of artillery in position on the opposite hill, which opened on our unprotected masses from the rear. Under this fire the two divisions were formed in line of battle facing to the rear, with Kershaw on the (now) right of the road and Custis Lee on the left or west side. In Custis Lee's Division Lieutenant-Colonel John Atkinson's two battalions—the 10th and 19th Virginia—the Chaffin's Bluff Battalion and the 18th Georgia, Major Bassinger (all of the Heavy Artillery brigade, with muskets), were on the right and a little

---

[22] It seems that the troops in front of us were Bushrod R. Johnson's Division and what was left of Pickett's Division, all commanded by Lieutenant-General Richard H. Anderson.

thrown forward (to our late rear) on account of the nature of the ground. Next on the left was the Naval Battalion under Commodore Tucker, then Barton's Brigade, and finally Lieutenant-Colonel James Howard's command, 18th and 20th Virginia, Majors M. B. Hardin and James E. Robertson, being the rest of the heavy artillery brigade, held the extreme left. By the time this disposition was effected the enemy's fire had become very rapid and severe, being principally spherical case. On our side we were compelled to receive it in silence, not having a single piece of artillery to make reply.

The situation was now desperate, as we were entirely surrounded and reinforcements were continually pouring in to the enemy before our eyes. We were fighting back to back with Anderson's men and although the latter, or a part of them, presently succeeded (we heard afterwards,) in forcing their way through, we were not informed, and if we had been, were too hard pressed to be able to follow. Meanwhile our line began to suffer considerably under the enemy's deliberate fire. Almost all of Custis Lee's command were inexperienced in battle and the shot, sometimes plowing the gound, sometimes crashing through the trees, and not infrequently striking in the line, killing two or more at once, might well have demoralized the oldest veterans. But although surrounded by such trying circumstances—and there is no test which tries a soldier's fortitude so severely as to stand exposed to fire without the ability to return it— yet they acquitted themselves with a steadiness which could not have been more than equalled by the most seasoned troops of the Army of Northern Virginia, and as I passed along the line in rear I found scarcely a single straggler or skulker to order back.

After shelling us with impunity at easy range as long

as they pleased, the Federals advanced and engaged us with musketry, their cavalry being armed with the repeating carbine, that is, firing a number of shots[23] in succession without reloading. Thinking to overwhelm us by numbers, they made a charge which resulted in some close fighting, particularly at the road. Here some of Custis Lee's command—I believe the Chaffin's Bluff and Bassinger's Georgia Battalions—had a desperate hand to hand encounter with them, in which the Federals were worsted. The assailants thus met with a much more stubborn resistance than they anticipated and were everywhere driven back in confusion, leaving many dead and wounded on the ground. A spirited counter charge was even made—I believe by the two battalions above named and Colonel Atkinson's command and probably others—as far as the creek, driving the enemy sheer across. It was here that Colonel Stapleton Crutchfield, commanding the heavy artillery brigade, and formerly chief of artillery to Stonewall Jackson fell, shot through the head. His inspector, Captain O'Brien, had been previously wounded; that officer, said to be a nephew of the Irish patriot, Smith O'Brien, had, I understood, lately resigned from the English Army in India and come over to serve our cause.[24] I have used expressions implying a want of certainty in my own knowledge of the identity of the particular troops which had this hand to hand fighting and went as far as the creek in the counter charge,[25] because in this fighting my horse was struck

[23] Sixteen I understood.

[24] In the following Fall O'Brien wrote from New York to my brother that he had had a hard time since he was released from prison and was then shovelling in coal and doing such odd jobs as he could find, although spitting blood from his wound. I think we wrote him to come to our house but received no reply, and feared he had died.

[25] See Major Bassinger's report or account in Volume XXV, page 38, of the *Southern Historical Papers* and other references at the end of this chapter.

behind the saddle by a musket ball which sounded like a stone thrown against a fence. I was at the time with General Custis Lee and his staff on the road and, I think, with the front line. I had ridden this horse—or mare rather—ever since the battle of Gaines's Mill in 1862 where we captured General John F. Reynolds, to whom she was said to belong. My horse appearing to be mortally, or badly, wounded, I took her back fifty or a hundred yards and left her tied to a tree.

When I got back our troops which had gone forward had returned, or were returning, to their original position and both artillery and musketry opened a deadly fire on us again. I was struck by a nearly spent ball, on the shoulder[26] and another had passed through my coat, and I had also been struck but not hurt by splinters in the face; at least I thought they were such, but passing my hand over my face I found no harm done, and if "splinters" they must have been very soft ones. By this time our killed and wounded were many—among the former one of General Custis Lee's aides, the gallant and amiable Robert Goldsborough (of "Myrtle Grove," Talbot County, Maryland). There were no facilities for taking off the wounded, and indeed we had no rear to carry them to, so they were directed, when able, to crawl behind trees and into gullies. It is probable that many were shot a second time, or oftener, while so lying on the exposed hill side, sloping towards the enemy. The appeals of some of the poor fellows to their comrades and officers to put them in a place of safety were affecting, especially in the Naval Brigade where the sailors seemed to look up to their officers like children, and one such scene in particular between a wounded man and the Commodore who spoke some words of sympathy to him,

[26] A small bruise remained for some time afterwards.

still dwells vividly and painfully in my memory (October, 1865). The Heavy Artillery Brigade had not a medical officer present, and there were not more than two or three in the whole division.

My observation of the latter part of the battle, after the shooting of my horse prevented my getting about well, was chiefly limited to the center of the line—on the left (west) of the road. I noticed the naval brigade, which had been standing firm as a rock, apparently beginning to fall back but in a perfectly regular formation and I hurried over and asked Commodore Tucker the cause. He said he understood they were ordered to take a new position in rear. I told him I was sure it was a mistake for we had no place in rear to retire to. "Very well," said he, "if you say so I will move back again." I expressed a doubt if he could do so. "Oh yes," he said, "I can, but it is very different from handling men on shipboard." They had hardly gone a few steps, and he halted and faced them about and marched them back to their original position without a single skulker remaining behind. I have seldom, if ever, seen this done as well during the war. When men are once started to the rear under heavy fire, it is difficult to halt and bring them all back again.

I presently saw a number of men in blue uniform where Kershaw's line was, or had been, but supposing them be to prisoners, no attention was paid to their appearance; I presume now they were engaged in receiving the surrender of his men. Along Custis Lee's line the firing was still continued and we had no idea the battle was so nearly ended. I thought we were endeavoring to hold our ground until night might enable us to draw off, but from what I saw afterwards, we were so surrounded that escape was impossible and to have prolonged the contest would have been a useless sacrifice oi life. There being an intermission in the fire presently, I passed along the line toward the left to inspect the condition of affairs. The line was at every point unbroken and the men in excellent spirits, exulting in their success so far and confident of their ability to hold out. But, alas! there was nothing to hold out for.

It was now reported in one of Barton's regiments that we had surrendered, and although this was contradicted at first and refused to be credited, still so many and such various rumors passed along the line that the men soon were uncertain what to think. Many of them continued to reject the report with indignation and, almost with tears in their eyes, protested their ability to whip the enemy yet. Some supposed there was only a truce for the purpose of removing the wounded who lay between the hostile lines. At this moment it was observed that the enemy was advancing again in our front and we were just discussing the propriety of reopening fire when about half a dozen of them came riding in on our left rear. I walked over to them and one said, "Well you've surrendered." I denied it, and he said, "Why your Generals are prisoners and you are surrounded and the artillery of the — Corps is in position on your flank and would sweep you off the field." I finally accepted this statement as true, supported as it was by the cessation of firing all over the field and other signs. I have no doubt this was the last part of the line to give up the contest. One of my captors asked for my spurs—I had no arms whatever. In the sore feeling of the moment I asked if he demanded them as a right; he civilly replied, "Oh no, but you will have no further use for them and I would like to have them as souvenirs," so I took them off and gave them, one I think to one and one to another.

It was now a little after sunset and by the time the prisoners were gathered together in a field near General Custer's headquarters darkness had set in. The men were depressed but consoled themselves with the consciousness of having made a good fight. Our two divisions did not number more than 4000[27] in line and we had not a single piece of artillery, while particularly exposed to the deliberate fire of that of the enemy. Our loss in killed and wounded was heavy but cannot be correctly estimated. Generals Wright, Sheridan and Custer (I was told,) and others passed the warmest encomiums upon the obstinate valor of the Confederates and treated our higher officers at their headquarters with soldierlike courtesy. The Union soldiers were greatly astonished at the miscellaneous uniforms in our small division and under other circumstances we would have found amusement in listening to their comments. One of them pointed out an officer in a naval uniform with

[27] General Humphreys (commanding the 2d Corps of the Army of the Potomac) in his *History of the Virginia Campaign of 1864–1865*, page 383, puts Ewell's strength on the ground (being Custis Lee's and Kershaw's Divisions), at about 3600. And he estimates, taking my published account of 1865, Custis Lee's Division at about 1600. But I undoubtedly overestimated the naval battalion, as explained hereinbefore.

In my published account I said that against us (meaning both Ewell and Anderson,) were the Cavalry Corps and the 6th and 2d Infantry Corps and the 5th Corps or some of its artillery, and that when we surrendered we must have been surrounded by not less than 40,000 men although of course only a portion of these were actively engaged. I said also that Generals Sheridan and Custer stated that about 1000 cavalrymen were killed or wounded and that General Wright (commanding the 6th Corps,) had put the whole loss at about 6000. I wish to withdraw these statements. I have always deprecated such estimates of strength and of losses on the "other side," and this is an example which has come home to myself. Those generals could hardly have said what I heard (next morning, for I was not taken to their headquarters), for these numbers are excessive. I should have limited myself to the safe statement that we were surrounded by vastly superior numbers and inflicted (and sustained) heavy losses.

wide gold lace on it and asked me who he was. When I told him that he belonged to the navy, his jaw dropped and he said. "Good Heaven, have you gunboats way up here too?" I might have answered, as some one said earlier in the war, that we had them wherever there was a little dew on the grass had I not been in too serious a frame of mind.

This may be looked on as the last regular battle of the Army of Northern Virginia, and in it the Confederates, although at the point of physical exhaustion, conducted themselves in a manner that would have reflected honor on any troops on any former field.

I spent the night with the mass of prisoners. I saw some fellows of the baser sort worming about among our men and taking their watches and other valuables, but I kept a wary eye on them and escaped any such plundering.[28]

[28] The Federal official reports of the battle of Sailor's Creek are unusually eulogistic in speaking of the conduct of their enemy on this field, and I quote from some of them.

In the *War of the Rebellion—Official Records of the Union and Confederate Armies*, Series 1, volume XLVI, Part I, Reports, Serial No. 95, on page 906 et seq., is the report of Major-General H. G. Wright, commanding the 6th Army Corps, in which he says:

". . . . The 1st and 3d Divisions charged the enemy's position, carrying it handsomely except at a point on our right of the road crossing the creek, where a column said to be composed exclusively of the Marine Brigade and other troops which had held the lines of Richmond previous to the evacuation, made a countercharge upon that part of our lines in their front. I was never more astonished. These men were surrounded—the 1st and 3d Divisions of the Corps were on either flank, my artillery and a fresh division in their front and some three divisions of Major-General Sheridan's cavalry in their rear. Looking upon them as already our prisoners, I had ordered the artillery to cease firing as a dictate of humanity; my surprise therefore was extreme when this force charged upon our front, but the fire of our infantry which had already gained their flanks, the capture of their superior officers, already in our hands, the concentrated and murderous fire of six batteries of our artillery within effective range, brought them promptly to a surrender."

Page 946, report of Captain A. Hopkins, commanding the 37th Massachusetts

A full share of the eulogistic language in the reports about the "marine battalion" and "marine brigade" should be given to the heavy artillery brigade. (I cannot say whether Barton's brigade took part in the countercharge, as owing to my horse being shot I was not on that part of the line throughout the countercharge, but I am sure it did whatever it had any opportunity to do.) In fact it is evident to me that the fresher and variegated caps and uniforms of the heavy artillery men made the enemy suppose they belonged to the "navy brigade" or battalion, which they knew was on the ground and a distinctive feature of Custis Lee's command.

Major Bassinger made a quasi official report to General Custis Lee, dated 3d March, 1866, which was published in the *Southern Historical Papers*, volume XXV, page 38. In it he gives an account, more particularly, of his 18th Georgia Battalion and the Chaffin's Bluff Battalion under

Volunteers. ". . . . and a desperate hand to hand fight with swords, pistols and bayonets ensued.   Several men were wounded with the bayonet . . . ."
Page 952, report of Lieutenant-Colonel E. H. Rhodes, commanding the 2d Rhode Island Volunteers, ". . . . We pressed the enemy back to the woods in our front and when within a distance of about thirty yards received a charge of the enemy, both in front and on my left, which caused my men after a time to retire in some confusion.   Every effort was made to rally them without crossing the swamp. . . . At this point my regiment was somewhat scattered. . . . ."
Page 980, report of Brigadier-General T. Seymour, commanding the 3d Division, 6th Corps, ". . . . The contest was then very severe. The Confederate marine battalion fought with peculiar obstinancy, and our lines, somewhat disordered by crossing the Creek, were repulsed in the first onset. . . . ."
Page 998, report of Brigadier-General J. Warren Keifer, commanding the 2d Brigade, 3d Division, 6th Corps, ". . . . A number of men were bayoneted on both sides. The enemy had a heavy column massed in the rear of his centre with which he charged upon our troops. Owing to the fact that our troops could only be fought in one line, the enemy succeeded in breaking through the centre and gaining a momentary success. . . . . The rebel Marine Brigade fought with most extraordinary courage. . . . ."

Major Robert Stiles. See also page 139 of the same volume for an account by an officer of the 10th Virginia Battalion, which gives a list of the officers captured; also page 250 of Volume XXIV. Generals Ewell, Kershaw and Custis Lee also gave post bellum reports or accounts, in 1865, which will be found printed in the *Transactions of the Southern Historical Society* Volume I, pages 101 and 118 (*Southern Magazine.*)

CHAPTER XXXV

SAILOR'S CREEK TO WASHINGTON—OLD CAPITOL PRISON

On the morning of April 7 (1865), General Custer, easily recognized by his long yellow hair which he wore at that time falling down on his shoulders, rode past the body of Sailor's Creek prisoners with about thirty couriers behind him each bearing a captured Confederate battle flag. It was a painful sight, but it consoled us somewhat to know that we had been taken not by his cavalry alone or principally but by an overwhelming force of infantry, with artillery of which we had none, together with dismounted cavalry. Later, our generals, with their staffs and higher officers, were taken across the country to General Grant's headquarters.[1] Here there were several tents and a fire was burning in front. General (Colonel?) Badeau, Grant's military secretary, came out, rubbing his hands together, and said he was sorry the General was not there. He had camp stools brought and we, or most of us, for we were thirty or more, sat or stood for an hour or more in melancholy silence, in a large semicircle in front of the fire. I thought that to our old Indian fighters, Ewell and others, it must have been like an Indian council fire sitting. Later we were marched over to a house which was occupied as headquarters by some Pennsylvania general.[2] Here we were rather crowded in one or two rooms, and the general's cook kindly gave us some soup—I did not think it was a

[1] His headquarters were at or near Burkeville Junction.
[2] Badeau says by Colonel Sharpe, provost marshal.

ration ordered; my impression was that the cook did it out of his own kindness of heart.

A certain man from Texas (Thomas P. Ochiltree) who afterwards figured in New York and elsewhere as a wit, club man and diner out, at first claimed to be of our staff —to justify his being in that select company—and on being denied, claimed to be of General Ewell's and then of somebody else's. I don't remember if he finally succeeded in locating himself. He had been in Richmond and did not belong to the army, but may have been a clerk in one of the government departments.

I think it was the next day, May 9, that we started for Petersburg, the generals, Lieutenant-General Richard S. Ewell, Major-Generals Kershaw and Custis Lee and Brigadier-Generals Hunton and Corse (and I think there were one or two more,) being put in ambulances at the head of the column, which I think was now composed of our party and the body of prisoners—perhaps only the officers—captured at Sailor's Creek. The first day at least, we were guarded by the 2d Maryland Regiment, under Lieutenant-Colonel Benjamin F. Taylor. Just before the column began its march Colonel Taylor rode up to the head and said, "I hear there is some Marylanders, is there any Marylanders here?" He was just to my left and I answered, "Yes, I am from Baltimore." He looked at me and said, "I don't remember your face in Baltimore." I asked, "Colonel, from what part of Baltimore do you come?" He answered, "From the eastern part," and I said I lived in another part. Just then an orderly came up, reporting the column ready to move and the Colonel rode off saying, "Rectus in curio." General Kershaw and others rallied me very much on not being recognized by my fellow townsman. But Colonel Taylor and his men treated us very well and that evening he had my brother and some others at his head-quarters and gave them a plenty to eat—and to drink too, for one of them coming back stumbled over my little shelter ropes or strings and nearly knocked it down. I think it was at the end of the second day's march that we got—bought, my impression is, and by prisoners individually, not as a body—some of the toughest meat I ever tried to eat, and we believed it to be not even horse flesh, but mule meat.

Once in going through the almost interminable Chesterfield County woods we passed by the mouth of a side farm road where two or three women had come out to see us go by, and one of them in a thin piping voice said, "Men, they say we have peace, is it so?" Colonel Flowerree said "Yes, ma'am," and there was a laugh, but I noticed there was a rather sombre silence afterwards and I know that the spoken words struck something like a chill to my own heart, suggesting as they did that Lee's surrender meant also the collapse of the Confederacy. We had been told of Lee's surrender but had been slow to believe it; having been a prisoner once before, I told of the false rumors we heard on that former march back. But by this time we had been compelled to believe that there was no doubt of the main fact of the surrender.

It must have taken us three or four days to make the march of about fifty miles to Petersburg. The day before we got there some Union general met us on the road (I think it was Major-General Hartranft), and taking General Custis Lee aside, had a short conversation with him. I was told that he asked him abruptly if he knew that his mother was dead. At any rate, there was an erroneous report that she had died, and Custis Lee was permitted to leave us here and go to Richmond.

After our long march, added to our previous hardships, we were a sorry spectacle in going through Petersburg. But Major Costin (of the Eastern Shore of Virginia.) of Major-General Kershaw's staff, was determined to keep up such dignity as he could and while he marched through the streets with bursted shoes, he wore on his hands an old pair of white kid gloves, soiled and torn. And so we came from near the head of the Appomattox to City Point at its mouth on the James.   I suppose we arrived there on April 13—it may have been April 12. Here we—or a party of us, for I think our generals had left us, probably at Petersburg, and the main body of prisoners went elsewhere—were put on a steamboat and carried to Washington.

In the afternoon of Good Friday, April 14, we left the steamboat and marched to the provost marshall's office on Pennsylvania Avenue, where I suppose our sorts and conditions were noted down.   While there one of General Grant's staff officers—as I recollect it was General Ingalls—came in and spoke cordially to my brother (Lieutenant-Colonel James Howard), who had known him very well in the old U. S. Army on the Pacific Coast before the war.   He said to my brother, "Of course you will all receive the same terms that were given at Appomattox.   And when you get through here, you and your brother will go with the others to the Old Capitol Prison, but after a while I will have you out and you will come to my house and you can either take supper and spend the night, or take the train for Baltimore as you prefer."   So after we had been marched up to the Old Capitol and with our comrades were turned into the herd of prisoners already there—about sunset— while the others looked about for the softer places in the brick yard to locate themselves for the night, we walked up and down expecting our promised release. But dark came and hour after hour passed and we waited with more and more surprise and presently indignation, until at 10.30 or 11 o'clock we gave up expectation and laid down on the bricks to sleep. The next morning we heard of Lincoln's assassination. It was fortunate for us and for our family that we had not been released and gone home the evening before.

All day, Saturday, April 15, there was a mob before the prison, demanding to get at the inmates. About midday, looking out of one of the front windows, for I had found quarters in one of the upper rooms, I saw a carriage rapidly drive up out of which got General William H. F. Payne, of Warrenton, Virginia of the cavalry, and who was hurried through the door from the angry mob. He had been on his parole in the city but it became necessary to take refuge in the prison. The next day, Sunday, April 16, Colonel Flowerree, of Fauquier or Loudon County, Virginia, but who, I think had been living in Mississippi, a somewhat reckless young fellow, came to me in the morning and asked if I would read the Episcopal service. Surprised at the request from one who was well known for a good deal of levity of character, I said I would if he could not find a more suitable person. He professed that he couldn't. So I read the morning service in a large upper room and with a good sized congregation. Just before I came to the prayer for all persons in authority four or five Union officers had come up the passage, with rattling sabres or swords and stood at the door. There was a deep expectant silence. When I read out the words "Thy servant the President of the Confederate States," the officers hurriedly withdrew, their swords clanking down the passage, When the service was over Flowerree said to me "Well, old fellow, I'm sorry I got you into such a scrape." "What's the matter?" I asked. "Why" said he, "You'll be in the dungeon in five minutes." But nothing occurred. I suppose it was one of the last times that the President of the Confederacy was openly prayed for by title North of James River—certainly, I think, the last time in the Capital of the Union.

I think it was on the 17th that our party, or a party of about fifty, were taken out of the Old Capitol Prison for transfer to Johnson's Island in Lake Erie, near Sandusky, Ohio. There were still angry men loitering in front of the prison, and, while we were halted for some time on a vacant piece of ground near the Baltimore and Ohio depot in particular, we were treated to a good deal of abuse and threatening remarks. We were presently put in a passenger car or cars and carried to Camden Station, Baltimore. We then marched up Howard Street (and Park or Liberty Street and College Alley) and Cathedral Street to what was then known as the Outer Depot or Bolton Depot of the Northern Central Railroad—about where the present Mt. Royal Avenue crosses Cathedral Street. And we so passed right by our home on Cathedral Street, next to Emmanuel Church, on the site of which now stands the parish building. My brother and I had not seen it for nearly four years. We were afraid there would be trouble if recognized from the house and therefore held up the capes of our overcoats to shield our faces as we passed; it was getting dark too. In the next block, between Eager and Chase Streets, we halted for some time in the middle of Cathedral Street and my brother tried to get for me a little whiskey from some house, for I had felt quite sick since leaving Washington and had to lean on his arm. But the guard would not permit. At Bolton Depot we were again put in a passenger coach, but at Pittsburgh were transferred to box freight cars in which we were jolted across the Panhandle and the State of Ohio to Sandusky, and then a little steam ferryboat took us three miles out in Lake Erie to Johnson's Island where we were turned into the prison pen. I suppose our arrival was in the afternoon of April 18—perhaps a day or two later.[3]

[3] In the Fall of the same year, 1865, I made another visit to the Old Capitol Prison but this time only to the outside, being refused admittance.

In the early Summer my father and mother looked about for some retired place where they could spend a few months in quiet with their reunited family and they fixed on Cobb's Island, ten miles out in the Atlantic off the coast of the Eastern Shore of Virginia. Shortly after our return to Baltimore, in October I think, one morning a lady, closely veiled, drove to our house on Cathedral Street and after a few minutes private conversation with my father and mother drove as mysteriously away. She had stopped on her way from Washington to New York to say that she had received private information in Washington that both Captain William Sidney Winder, a son and aide de camp of Brigadier-General John H. Winder, commandant of Confederate prisons, and Captain Richard B. Winder, a cousin and who had been quartermaster at the Andersonville prison, were to be arrested, as Captain Wirtz, commanding at Andersonville, had been. She was on her way to warn the former in New York, and as the wife of my brother Charles Howard was a sister of Captain Richard Winder, she thought we would find a way to notify him on the Eastern Shore of Virginia. I undertook to do this. I had lost a piece of baggage—an old fashioned carpet bag—in our return from Cobb's Island and I thought I could make a fair pretext for my trip in pretending to be looking it up. So I took the next Norfolk steamboat, both on it and on the wharf at Norfolk proclaiming my object, as also on the boat to which I changed to cross the Chesapeake to Cherrystone on the Eastern Shore. But on this boat I found Dr. Alex. Thom who told me I was too late, as Captain Winder had been arrested the evening before. I necessarily continued on to the Eastern Shore and I spent a day at the house of Captain Winder's sister, Mrs. Kerr, in Eastville, where he had been, and to this day I have a vivid recollection of the great variety and excellence of the figs in the large garden.

Captain Winder was brought to the Old Capitol prison and my brother determined to try to see him there. And he thought it might facilitate if I would go with him and represent myself as Captain Winder's legal counsel. (I had been admitted to the Bar just before the war began, although disqualified just now from practice under the proscriptive laws.)

We went boldly up (it is difficult to understand now the feelings of those times,) to the sentinel at the door and told him we had come to see Captain Winder. He replied that no one was allowed to see him. "But" said I, "I come as his legal counsel." I half expected the sentinel to say "Why it is not six months since you were a rebel prisoner in here yourself—Corporal of the Guard!" But he only insisted that no one could see him. At our request he called the officer of the guard, and to him also I said I had come to see Captain Winder as his counsel. And I more than half expected him to reply, "Why you are the fellow who prayed for Jeff Davis!" But he only repeated that no one could see him, adding that when he was allowed to have counsel I would be informed.

Captain Richard Winder was finally released, on the voluntary testimony of a number of Union officers of his considerate treatment of them in prison. But in the excited feelings of those days he was in serious jeopardy.

CHAPTER XXXVI

Johnson's Island Prison—Home

Johnson's Island was a prison for officers only, of whom there were several thousand, and it had a single large rectangular enclosure or "pen," outside of which were the buildings for the quarters of the garrison, etc. On entering the gate a wide street or space, I suppose about 100 feet, extended from it to the other end of the pen, or nearly, on each side of which were the plank houses—called Blocks—for the prisoners, each Block being divided, I think, into two parts and containing a number of rooms. There was a high timber fence around the enclosure, the top of which was patrolled by sentinels and about ten or fifteen feet from it was the usual "dead line," anyone crossing which might be shot down by the sentinels forthwith.[1]

On our being turned into this enclosure my brother and I were promptly sought out by Captain William Randolph,[2] who had been in correspondence with our family in Baltimore and probably was told to look out for our coming. He conducted us to his quarters— Room No. 7 of Block 1. This Block was the house on the right hand side of the street nearest the gate, and the first half of it was a plague spot to the rest of the prisoners, being occupied by the "galvanized" men, that is, those who had taken the oath of allegiance—of whom I am glad to say there were very few. These were con-

---

[1] I add a sketch of the prison from the *War of the Rebellion*.

[2] He was a brother of the present Bishop Randolph of Southern Virginia, and died not many years after the war.

temptuously ignored by their former comrades and herded together, looking very uncomfortable in their isolation and degradation.

We became a part of Randolph's mess, which was a

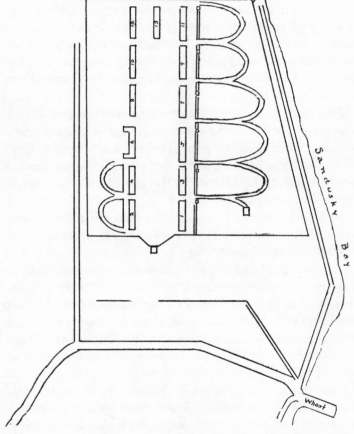

small one and composed of his room mates, for unlike Fort Delaware, where a "Division" was very large and undivided, here the "Block" was cut up into a number of small rooms, probably because of the severe winter climate—at least our room was small. I only recall one other roommate, a Captain Dyes (Deese) of Hamburg, Germany, who, we understood, was of a good family there. I had brought with me from Fort Delaware and carefully preserved a gold piece, $5, or $10, which supported us in this mess until we received money from home, for we employed a man (one of the prisoners,) to do our cooking and lived lazily. I do not remember anything about the issue of rations; probably our cook attended to it for us. We ate our meals in a shelter of some kind in rear of the Block.

The climate was the most variable I ever knew; a morning might be bright and warm even to being uncomfortable, when suddenly a piercing wind would come across the Lake from Canada, perhaps with snow, and a good fire had to be kindled in the stove, and so it would be changing during the day.

We heard many stories about the past life in the prison, many of the officers having been there a long time. Major-General Trimble had been one of the prisoners and was at the head of an organization which planned to seize the island and escape with the whole body of prisoners to Canada on a steamer which was to be fitted out there under Confederate naval officers. But the scheme which came near being carried into effect, was either discovered or was thwarted in some way and the rising never took place.

There was, I believe, some tunnelling to escape but none that was successful. There were also attempts by individuals, of which I remember one which was successful and one which deserved to be but was not. Charles E. Grogan, of Baltimore, went outside with a party to bring in hay for bedding. He kicked together a small pile and crept under it when the guard was not looking, warning his comrades when they came near not to disturb his covering. After they had gone back with their loads he remained so concealed until dark. He then wandered around the island, looking for some means of getting over to the main land and finally set about the construction of a small raft. I think he even started on this but found it unseaworthy and had to put back. Daylight was then coming on and he had to seek some other way of getting off the island and he turned to the simplest. Waiting until about 9 o'clock, he walked boldly down to the wharf and asked the sentinel what time it was and when the boat would be over from Sandusky. When it came he walked aboard and was carried over and made his way to the Confederacy.[3] He had been a prisoner once before and escaped. While being marched through Baltimore after dark, he darted down a side alley and got off. I do not believe he could have been kept a prisoner—he would either have escaped or been shot in attempting to do so.

The other story was of a man who spent some time in making himself into the counterfeit of a Federal soldier. He picked up pieces of cloth here and there until he had what in the dark would pass for a blue uniform. Out of old shoes he made a belt and the semblance of a cartridge box. He made a dummy gun of wood, silvering the barrel with pieces of tobacco wrappings. Finally, when he was ready, he sent out a note to the commander of the garrison, warning him that at a certain hour next night there would be an escape through a tunnel which had been made. Just before the designated hour the gate flew open and a company marched in to seize the escapers in

[3] I tell the tale as 'twas told to me. If there is anything wrong in the details, Mr. Grogan still survives to correct them. He is a bailiff in one of the courts of Baltimore City.

the very act, and, finding it was a hoax, marched out again. The Confederate fell in at the rear. But unfortunately the officer in command halted in the gate to see his men file past and when the Confederate came along he was holding his piece badly. "Why don't you carry your gun straight?" he asked and took hold of it to make its position right. Astonished at its light weight, he said "Why, what sort of a gun is this?" And of course the escape was stopped.

On May 1 or 2 (I know the date from a book[4] sent in to me, on a fly leaf of which is written "May 2, 1865, from my traveling bag") my aunt Alice Key Pendleton, wife of Senator George H. Pendleton, Democratic candidate for the vice-presidency on the ticket with McClellan, came, with one of her children, from Cincinnati to see us. But although Colonel Hill, commanding the post, was civil to her, he said he could not possibly transgress orders by allowing an interview. He finally said he would go so far as to permit us to look at each other for a few minutes across the fence but we must not make any sign of recognition. So at an appointed hour my brother and I mounted the steps on the outside front of the quarters of the "galvanized men," being the west end of Block 1, and stood on the little platform at the second story and so overlooking the high fence near the gate. My aunt was standing, with her child, on the outside, a distance of about a hundred feet separating us, and for five minutes we solemnly gazed at each other without so so much as smiling even. We then descended wondering what our fellow prisoners thought of our going on this shunned part of the prison. We were allowed to communicate in writing, however, and my aunt advised us that the Confederate cause was hopelessly lost and we

[4] Sir Roundell Palmer's *Book of Praise*.

could properly take the oath of allegiance and return home when the authorities would permit such a course. On this question of when it would be proper to consider the war as ended and take the oath, there had been a difference of opinion and much heated discussion took place among the prisoners since our arrival. One day there would be a meeting of the Virginians to debate the matter, the next of North Carolinians, and so on. These discussions resulted in no conclusions and my impression is that they were presently discontinued as one prop after another fell from under the Confederacy in the successive surrenders of its armed forces in the field, until all were at last ready to admit that the end had come. So when in the latter part of May an order came from Washington for the special discharge from prison of my brother and myself—and Captain Randolph— we did not hesitate to accept it. I heard two or more accounts of how this favor of a release a short time before the general release came to be granted, but never investigated to find out which was correct. One was that we were indebted to Mr. Hooper, a representative in Congress from Massachusetts, at the request of Mrs. Pendleton. There may have been several influences.

The authority under which I passed out the prison gate and from the island was the following paper, which I have preserved, and which may be thought interesting to show how these final acts of the war were done.

HEADQUARTERS U.S FORCES, AT JOHNSON'S ISLAND AND SANDUSKY,
Johnson's Island, O., May 26th, 1865.

Special Orders ⎱
No. 143 ⎰ [Extract]

Pursuant to instructions from the Secretary of War, communicated through the office of the Commissary General of Prisoners, dated May 23d, 1865, Mc-Henry Howard, late 1st Lieut. and I. G. to G. W. C. Lee, prisoner of war, is discharged from the Military Prison at this Post, and set at liberty, he having taken the oath of allegiance.

The further description of the person herein discharged is as follows:

Age 26 years; height, Five feet nine inches; complexion, Dark; eyes, Blue; hair, Brown.

By command of Col. Chas. W. Hill

GEO. M. PHILLIPS.

On the back is the following:

UNITED STATES OF AMERICA

I, McHenry Howard, of the County of Baltimore, State of Maryland, do solemnly swear that I will support, protect, and defend the Constitution and Government of the United States against all enemies,whether domestic or foreign; that I will bear true faith, allegiance and loyalty to the same, any ordinance, resolution or laws of any State, Convention, or Legislature, to the contrary notwithstanding; and further, that I will faithfully perform all the duties which may be required of me by the laws of the United States; and I take this oath freely and voluntarily, without any mental reservation or evasion whatever.

McHENRY HOWARD.

Subscribed and sworn to before me at Johnsons Island, O., this Twenty-sixth day of May, A.D. 1865.

CHAS. W. HILL, Colonel comd'g.

Office Pro. Mar. 8 Al [?]

Balto. Md. May 29, '65

Reported and registered

JOHN WOOLLEY,

Lt. Col. & Pro. Mar.

It will be noticed that I was given no transportation, the reason assigned being that my release was a special favor.

It was three miles across the water in our little steam ferry boat to Sandusky, and the first use we made of our freedom was to go to the restaurant of a hotel and enjoy the long forgotten taste of regular mint juleps. It was some time before the leaving of the train and we walked about looking at the evidences of prosperity, so different from our Southern towns, and the novel architecture of light colored limestone. When we took the cars we began to realize that we were on the way home and beginning a new chapter of life. A few miles out we stopped for some time for a Cleveland train on a track which crossed ours at right angles, and on the platform a photograph was passed around representing Lincoln on Washington's bosom, which we looked at admiringly, being desirous that our status should not be known. About midnight we reached some town—I think it was Zanesville—and had to wait an hour or so to take another train. In the hotel which we loitered at we were dumbfounded by the clerk or barkeeper coming up and saying in a low voice, "Well, our cause is lost." We were taken aback by our character being recognized, and equally so by this display of sympathy in the center of Ohio, and being afraid of a trap, were not responsive. Crossing the Ohio River at Wheeling, we passed Oakland, which had been our summer resort before the war—and has been ever since—about 7 or 8 o'clock in the morning and so by daylight went over the old familiar scenery of the Baltimore and Ohio Railroad. And so we came home to Baltimore—I think it was May 27. Having left home on the first of June, 1861, I had been absent four years less four days.

I found at home the following belated notice:

To MR. McHENRY HOWARD,

You are hereby notified that you have been this day enrolled by us in the Militia Forces of the United States, in the State of Maryland, under the Act of Congress of July, 1862, in the Third Enrollment District of Baltimore County corresponding to the 3rd Election District of said County, and will hold yourself in readiness for any such Military duty as under the Laws and Constitution of the United States may be required of you.

R. S. WILLIAMSON,
JOHN S. STITCHER,
September the——1862.   Enrolling Officers.

And I was told the circumstances of its service. One day two men came to the house and after parleying with the servant insisted on seeing my mother. They said, "Madam, we are enrolling officers and have come to get the names of male members of your family—have you a husband or sons capable of bearing arms?" She said, "Yes, a husband and six sons. "Your husband, what is his name and where is he?" "Charles Howard, he is a prisoner in Fort Warren." "And your eldest son?" "Frank Key Howard, he is also in prison with his father." "And your next son?" "John Eager Howard, he is a captain in the Confederate Army." "And the next?" "Charles Howard, he is a major in the Confederate Army." "And the next?" "James Howard, he is lieutenant-colonel in the Confederate Army." "And the next?" "Edward Lloyd Howard, he is a surgeon in the Confederate Army." During this the men had become more and more flustered and faltered out, "And your youngest son?" "McHenry Howard, he is also in the Southern Army and with Stonewall Jackson and I expect he will be here soon." (It was during the invasion of Maryland by Lee and Jackson). And she shut the door in their faces. They retired to the sidewalk and after holding a consultation, filled out the above notice and shoved it under the door.

APPENDIX

ADDRESS AT THE UNVEILING OF THE MONUMENT ERECTED BY THE DAUGHTERS OF THE CONFEDERACY IN THE STATE OF MARYLAND TO THE MARYLAND CONFEDERATE SOLDIERS AND SAILORS, IN BALTIMORE, MAY 2, 1903.

The Daughters of the Confederacy, having long had it in their hearts to erect a public and lasting memorial of the sons of Maryland who fought on the side of the Confederate States of America, now present to the community their completed work.

For such a monument they have believed that the time and place are fitting. Forty-two years have passed since the people of nearly one-half of the country desired peaceably to withdraw from a Union which their fathers had had an equal share in founding, and believed they were justified in doing so. On the other side was the theory of an indissoluble Union, with the logical right of coercion. One of the greatest civil wars in history ensued. The stronger side prevailed. The mighty armies of Blue and Gray were disbanded, on one side the victorious legions, leaving behind them garrisons in the military districts which were created in the place of once equal States, marching back to their unchanged homes in the North in triumphal procession through the capital of the country, amid plaudits and with decorations and substantial rewards—how different on the other side! For weeks and months the roads and byways of the desolated South, from the Potomac to the Rio Grande, were filled with men in faded gray, gaunt from long privation, overcome by numbers and resources, but with unconquered minds and hearts, carrying with them to their saddened homes only in the parting words of their great commander—like a benediction— the satisfaction that came from the consciousness of duty faithfully performed.

"Duty faithfully performed!" They may seem cold terms of

praise to some who are fond of sounding phrases of rhetoric. But this exalted type of a soldier and a man had written years before, "Duty is the sublimest word in our language." He therefore measured the Confederate soldier by his own most exacting standard of life and he measured him up to its fullest requirement. Success or failure, victory or defeat, have nothing to do with such a standard. And, after forty years, the highest conception of this monument is that it is a deliberate re-affirmance of the summing up of the conduct of the men of 1861–65 in the Farewell Order of Appomattox—a monument to duty faithfully performed.

I have said that the place also is fitting.

Maryland was not in fact one of the Confederate States, and she was not even represented among the thirteen stars of the flag under which her sons fought in the South. When the disruption came in 1861 no Southern State was situated like her. Others, from Virginia to Texas, large commonwealths, side by side and back to back, forming together a solid section of the country, in their remoteness not under a shadow of outside opposition, could, through their Legislatures, call their Conventions of the sovereign people and deliberately and successively withdraw from the Federal Compact with the same solemn formalities with which they had entered into it—Processional and Recessional. But as long as the great intervening States of Virginia and North Carolina were in the Union, Virginia as late as April 17, 1861, and North Carolina still later, Maryland could not possibly have gone out—if down to that time it had so desired. North Carolina had refused in February to call a Convention even to consider the question of secession, and only reversed its decision in May. Even with her sister border States, Kentucky and Missouri, the conditions were widely different. They were powerful and populous States, covering great expanses of territory, and their geographical features, especially Kentucky, ranked them naturally with the South. But Maryland was small in area and population, cut in two by a wide Bay, and its only frontier line of defence—the Potomac River—was not, like the Ohio, between it and the North, but was for military operations a line of separation from the South. Moreover, the Capital of National Government was on the very middle of its Southern border and it was essential to the integrity of the Union that this should be held by the North at any cost. It was obvious, therefore, that the State must be kept in the Union, by subjection if necessary. Accordingly, under the call for 75,000 men to put down the so-called insurrection, the armed forces of the North were organized while Virginia was still deliberating in Convention and North Carolina was taking no steps to call one, and on the day after the passage of the Ordinance of Secession by Virginia, they began to pour into and across Maryland. Baltimore was soon after garrisoned, followed by the arrest of its civil authorities. The Legislature of the State was invaded by the military arm of the government at Washington and a safe number of its members were thrown into prison to prevent the possibility of a call of a Convention of the people or any revolutionary or obstructive action. The General Assembly had, however, before it was so broken up, passed Resolutions defining the attitude of the State. In eloquent words, which I wish I had time to read, they deprecated the calamities of civil war, and expressed the consent and desire of the State for an immediate recognition of the Confederacy. They declared that coercion was unconstitutional and subversive of the free principles upon which the Union was founded, and that the people of Maryland sympathized with their Southern brethren in their resistance. They concluded that, under existing circumstances, it was inexpedient to call a Sovereign Convention of the State at that time or to take any measures for the immediate organization or arming of the militia.[1] These Reso-

---

[1] The Resolutions were written by S. Teackle Wallis, who, with other leading men of Baltimore had consented to serve in the Legislature in this crisis:

"WHEREAS, in the judgment of the General Assembly of Maryland, the war now waged by the Government of the United States upon the people of the Confederate States is unconstitutional in its origin, purposes and conduct; repugnant to civilization and sound policy; subversive of the free principles upon which the Federal Union was founded, and certain to result in the hopeless and bloody overthrow of our existing institutions; and

"WHEREAS, the people of Maryland, while recognizing the obligation of their State, as a member of the Union, to submit in good faith to the exercise of all the legal and constitutional powers of the General Government, and to join as one man in fighting its authorized battles, do reverence, nevertheless, the great American principle of self-government, and sympathize deeply with their

lutions were the voice of the people of Maryland, speaking through their chosen representatives, the only voice that was permitted to be heard, and their language and spirit sanction and justify the action of her sons who went into the Southern Army and Navy.

There can be no doubt, there was no doubt at the time and I think it has passed into the made up history of that period, that if Maryland had had the opportunity of acting through a free Convention of the people, she would in her turn, after Virginia and North Carolina, have joined her sister States of the new Confederacy.   To have done so, situated as she was, in the rapid succession of events between the seceding of South Carolina, December 20, 1860, and the clash of arms in April 1861, when Virginia went out and North Carolina prepared to go, would have been both folly and futile.   After that she was in subjection.   To have turned the resistance to coercion of the 19th of April in the streets of Baltimore into a revolutionary movement to carry the State into the Confederacy without the form of law, would not only have lowered the

Southern brethren in their noble and manly determination to uphold and defend the same; and

"WHEREAS, not merely on their own account and to turn away from their own soil the calamities of civil war, but for the blessed sake of humanity, and to avoid the wanton shedding of fraternal blood in a miserable contest which can bring nothing with it but sorrow, shame and desolation, the people of Maryland are enlisted, with their whole hearts, on the side of reconciliation and peace: now, therefore it is hereby

"Resolved by the General Assembly of Maryland, That the State of Maryland owes it to her own self-respect and her respect for the Constitution, not less than to her deepest and most honorable sympathies, to register this her solemn protest against the war which the Federal Government has declared upon the Confederate States of the South and our sister and neighbor, Virginia, and to announce her resolute determination to have no part or lot, directly or indirectly, in its prosecution.

"RESOLVED, That the State of Maryland earnestly and anxiously desires the restoration of peace between the belligerent sections of the country, and the President, authorities and people of the Confederate States having, over and over again, officially and unofficially, declared that they seek only peace and self-defence, and to be let alone, and that they are willing to throw down the sword, the instant that the sword now drawn against them shall be sheathed, the Senators and Delegates of Maryland do beseech and implore the President of the United States to accept the olive branch which is thus held out to him; and

dignity of the Southern Recessional from the Union, but the attempt would have resulted in immediate suppression and worse subjugation. Neither was such a course desired by the Confederate States. I happen to have some personal knowledge that after the collision in Baltimore of April 19 Southern leaders from across the Potomac sent messages that the Confederate forces were not sufficiently organized to come over into Maryland, that any rising in the State would precipitate aggressive action on the part of the South before it was ready, and that sympathizers in Maryland would best serve the cause by patience and quiet. I think I remember that Senator James M. Mason, of Virginia, was one of those advisers.

So then, Maryland being silenced and bound to the North by force, thousands of her sons, believing that they were free to act as individuals according to their convictions, voluntarily exiled themselves from home and gave their services to the Confederacy. And they believed that they were not only taking up the sacred cause of liberty invaded, as their fathers had gone to Massachusetts after Lexington, but were in reality fighting the battle of their own State as truly as the sons of Virginia or Carolina. Like them, they loved

in the name of God and humanity to cease this unholy and most wretched and unprofitable strife, at least until the assembling of Congress in Washington shall have given time for the prevalence of cooler and better counsels.

"RESOLVED, That the State of Maryland desires the peaceful and immediate recognition of the independence of the Confederate States, and hereby gives her cordial assent thereunto as a member of the Union; entertaining the profound conviction that the willing return of the Southern people to their former Federal relations is a thing beyond hope, and that the attempt to coerce them will only add slaughter and hate to its impossibility.

"RESOLVED, That the present military occupation of Maryland, being for purposes, in the opinion of this Legislature, in flagrant violation of the Constitution, the General Assembly of the State, in the name of her people, does hereby protest against the same, and against the oppressive restrictions and illegalities with which it is attended; calling upon all good citizens, at the same time, in the most earnest and authoritative manner, to abstain from all violent and unlawful interference of every sort with the troops in transit through our territory or quartered among us, and patiently and peacefully to leave to time and reason the ultimate and certain re-establishment and vindication of the right.

"RESOLVED, That under existing circumstances, it is inexpedient to call a Sovereign Convention of the State at this time, or to take any measure for the immediate organization or arming of the militia."

their State, unlike them, they exiled themselves from it to serve it. Some went early, others lingered. I remember, in May 1861, Teackle Wallis being consulted by some who were yet in doubt whether it was not their duty to await the further progress of events at home, in case the State would need their services in the contingencies of the future. He was asked what would be the probable condition of affairs in Maryland, and his answer briefly was, "As quiet as the grave." The next day they crossed over to Virginia. And I remember also that as this little band was passing on to Richmond, at West Point a prominent citizen of Virginia[2] came to them and said, "You are Marylanders and I wish to call your attention to some stirring verses which I have read in the morning's newspaper. I wish I could repeat them, but the refrain is 'Maryland, my Maryland.' "

How many thousands went, there are no statistics to show. Marylanders have ever been characterized by a love of independent individual action. In the Revolutionary war, to give due credit to the State for its contribution in men, you must go into the history of other State military organizations largely made up of her sons. And so now, crossing the Potomac from its upper waters to its mouth, singly and in squads, under difficulties and dangers, they found a welcome everywhere in the South, they went into service where accident or inclination led them, and fought under the banners of every State from Virginia to Texas. Liable to no conscription, they were volunteers in the war. And I believe it can be safely said that in the closing dark days of the Confederacy, the time which tested the highest qualities of the soldier and the man, there were certainly as few Marylanders—comparatively—to leave the ranks or lose heart as of any other State.

But while it is to be regretted for the due credit of Maryland that all her sons in the Army did not get together into one body bearing the name of the State, she was represented, from first to last, by separate organizations which bore her flag, side by side with the Southern Cross, and upheld the ancient renown of the Maryland Line:

Ab antiqua stirpe genus novum

---

[2] Judge John S. Caskie, of Richmond.

The 1st Maryland Regiment of Infantry, under Elzey, Steuart and Johnson, took part in the turning movement which decided the day at first Manassas. Under Bradley Johnson it fought with Stonewall Jackson throughout the Valley Campaign and the Seven Days Battles in front of Richmond. The 2d Regiment, its successor, under Herbert and Goldsborough, carried the Maryland Colors a hundred yards inside the works on the heights of Gettysburg. The only Confederate monument on that field stands in the enemy's line of breastworks on the brow of Culp's Hill, side by side with the monuments of Union regiments, with a smaller stone one hundred yards beyond and inside marking the point to which the Marylanders penetrated. By a spontaneous charge by privates and officers at a critical moment, without waiting for orders, it recaptured captured works at Second Cold Harbor, and it shared in the defence of Petersburg and Richmond and the battles which were a part of it. And finally, the names of a remnant, under Captain John Torsch, will go down to history on that among the most honorable of all records—the list of the paroled at Appomattox.

Of the 1st Maryland Cavalry, under Ridgely Brown and Dorsey, I have only time to recall, but it is enough, that it rode and fought under Stuart, Fitzhugh Lee and Hampton, and refused even to accept Appomattox as final, making its way through the surrounding enemy. Nor can I do more than mention here the 2d Maryland Cavalry and its services on the frontier under the lead of Harry Gilmor.

The batteries, known by the names of the 1st Maryland Artillery, under Snowden Andrews and afterwards Dement; the 2d Maryland Artillery or Baltimore Light, under Brockenborough and later Griffin; the 4th Maryland Artillery, or the Chesapeake, under Brown and then Chew; and in the western army the 3d Maryland Artillery, under Latrobe and afterwards Claiborne, Rowan and Ritter, were certainly among the most efficient in the service. They have made their own story in the reports of battles of the war.

There were other scattered Maryland companies at different times—Lyle Clarke's in the 21st Virginia, the Lanier Guards in the 13th Virginia, the Maryland Zouaves in the 47th Virginia—all infantry—and two Washington companies; and of cavalry there were Gaither's Company K in the 1st Virginia, Sturgis Davis's Company with Imboden, Company B in Colonel Elijah White's 35th Virginia Battalion, Frank Mason's Company C in the 7th Virginia, etc. Of artillery there was the 9th Virginia or Baltimore Heavy Artillery, and probably others. There were other commands in which Marylanders so largely predominated that they might properly be claimed as Maryland organizations—such as Breathed's Horse Artillery, in which they were fully ninety per cent, and no command made a more glorious record in the war. But all this should be made the subject of a carefully prepared historical paper. I have not time to go into the details here.

But all these commands had on their muster rolls only a small part of the Marylanders in the Southern Army and Navy. They left their homes to fight in a common cause and it did not occur to them that it mattered where they fought. They stood shoulder to shoulder with the men of Virginia and other States on many a field:

> What time the foeman's line was broke
> And all the war was rolled in smoke.

And so this monument, with the typical figure of the Confederate soldier of the ranks, like the monuments to the Unknown Dead, stands for thousands whose names can never be gathered into rolls of honor and perpetuated as with their comrades who are recorded in the distinctive Maryland organizations.

On the other hand, there are bright particular names which must come up in our minds on such an occasion as this, and which will be read by posterity in every history of the war. A large percentage of Marylanders resigned from the Army and Navy of the United States and gave their services to the South. They made greater sacrifices than any others. War was their profession in life, but it was not as soldiers and sailors of fortune that they went, following the trumpet call and the rolling of the drums, but as patriot soldiers and sailors. They lost everything but honor and glory, of that they won much for themselves and for their State. You will bear with me if I dwell for a few moments on the services of two or three of them. I do so partly in justice to them and because we are proud of them, and partly because I think that in their characteristics they were but high and bright examples of the mass of the men, whether officers or privates, to whom this monument is dedicated.

There was Admiral Franklin Buchanan, the first Commander of the Naval School at Annapolis, at the head of the Confederate Navy, under whom the *Virginia* or *Merrimac*, a new and untried engine of war, with greater audacity than Nelson's at Copenhagen, attacked a fleet in Hampton Roads, and in a day revolutionized the navies of the world; and who, in the later desperate fortunes of the Confederacy, with a still greater audacity for which I find it difficult to recall a parallel in naval annals, engaged, with a single serviceable vessel, a powerful fleet in Mobile Bay, while the world wondered. His name will live forever among the heroes of naval history.

There was Charles Sydney Winder, who in the wreck by a hurricane in the Gulf Stream of the transport *San Francisco* in 1853-54 had refused to leave his men on the sinking ship and for his conduct had been promoted. He had resigned from the Army as early as April 1 to serve the Confederate cause and was at the fall of Sumpter. Selected in 1862 to command the Stonewall Brigade, under him it made its most brilliant record in the Valley and Richmond campaign; and it cheered him after every battle. I hold in my hand the order of Jackson on the morning of Winder's death on August 9, 1862, at Cedar Mountain, detaching a senior brigadier-general whose older commission stood in the way and putting Winder in command of his own old division, which it seemed he had never been willing to entrust to any one before. His commission as major-general was about to be made out.[3] Of him Stonewall Jackson wrote:

It is difficult within the proper reserve of an official report to do justice to the merits of this distinguished officer. Urged by the Medical Director to take no part in the movements of the day because of the then enfeebled state of his health, his ardent patriotism and military pride could bear no such restraint. Richly endowed with those qualities of mind and person which fit an officer for command and which attract the admiration and excite the enthusiasm of troops, he was rapidly rising to the front rank of his profession. His loss has been severely felt.

---

[3] Such was the understanding, and President Jefferson Davis told me so after the war.

He never wrote so about any one else.

And he also wrote in a private letter—to Mrs. Jackson—"I can hardly think of the fall of Brigadier-General C. S. Winder without tearful eyes." Tears from Stonewall Jackson! Such a tribute to a Maryland soldier will outlive even this work of bronze. And afterwards, upon some trying occasion on the march or in battle, he turned to his staff and said, "Now I miss Winder." I know that if he had not been cut off untimely, not one in the Army of Northern Virginia under Lee and Jackson would have risen to higher rank and fame.

And there was Trimble, veteran in years but with the fire and aggressiveness of youth, who was also called to command Jackson's old division, and who, like Winder and after the pattern of Jackson himself, was one of the few generals who were not content on the battlefield to wait for orders, but was always ready to take responsibility and act where not restrained by orders. His capture of Manassas at night in 1862 after a march of thirty-four miles without food, General Jackson pronounced the most brilliant achievement that had, to that time, come under his notice during the war. Had his urgent advice to the general then in command on the field in the first day's engagement been followed, Gettysburg might have been a different story. He wished, and was insistent, that the enemy should then be pressed and the heights taken, and offered to do so himself if a brigade were given him, and in answer to the objection that there were no orders from Lee authorizing it, he said—and it was the key to his own military character—"But, General, you have no orders not to do so." And he turned away in anger and disappointment, refusing to stay with that general longer. On the third day, being put by Lee in command of half of Pender's Division for the memorable charge, he fell maimed, leading his men on a line with Pickett's up to the works. At the time of his fall and captivity he was holding an assignment by Lee to the command of the Valley District, the gateway between South and North, with a commission to get together at this outpost not only the regular Maryland organizations, but the other Marylanders scattered throughout the Army, to be formed into one body in the name of the State. The plan was carried out in part only the next winter by the formation of the Maryland Line under Bradley Johnson at Hanover Junction, but it was broken up again in the opening of the next campaign.

These and other names on which I have not time to dwell—Elzey, Archer, Little, Tilghman, Mackall, Semmes, Marshall, the pen of Lee, author of the articles of surrender and the Farewell Order, Herbert, Andrews, Murray—I mention only those who have crossed over the river—are recalled by this monument as distinctly as if their names were written on it.[4]

I have named only the dead among the examples of distinguished Marylanders, but there are two, at least, among the living whose services were of so high an order and who were so closely identified with the Maryland commands that it would seem ingratitude to pass them by, in their absence today, without allusion. To Colonel George H. Steuart, afterwards brigadier-general, the Marylanders were indebted for that high state of organization, drill and discipline which he impressed so thoroughly on the 1st Maryland Infantry and which was handed down in other Maryland commands to the end of the war. I have spoken in other places of his services at Gettysburg and elsewhere. I speak advisedly in saying that no one in the war gave more completely and conscientiously every faculty, every energy that was in him to the Southern cause. It is not possible here to give even a sketch of the varied career of Brigadier-General Bradley T. Johnson. He left the State early, but went as short a distance as possible from it, and drew around him at Harper's Ferry the larger part of the 1st Maryland Infantry. And his face was ever afterwards towards the State and he came back to it on every one of the three occasions when Southern Armies invaded it. He served the Confederate cause, but above all his devotion was to the cause of Maryland in the Confederacy. Assigned at times to other commands, his heart was ever with the Maryland soldiers, to whom he turned and who turned to him as a leader. President both of the Society of Army and Navy of the Confed-

---

[4] In Stonewall Jackson's Valley Campaign in 1862 out of the seven infantry brigade commanders under him, four, viz: Brigadier-Generals Winder, Trimble, Arnold Elzey and George H. Steuart were Marylanders.

erate States and of the Association of the Maryland Line. only sickness makes us miss his presence here today.

There come up in my mind, and I know in yours, instances without number of subordinate officers and privates in the ranks who in their humbler stations acted their part as conscientiously as the highest—examples of which this product of the artist's genius is but an idealized representation.   I think of one whose article of faith, like Lee's, was that duty was to be followed out no matter to what it led; who said to a friend on leaving Staunton with an unhealed wound for the front in 1864, that he did not expect to return alive; that the Confederates were so hard pressed he thought every officer was called on to expose himself as an example to the men to an extent that would not be proper under other circumstances.   He went, and in a few days George Williamson, although on Gordon's staff, fell dead on the skirmish line at Fisher's Hill.   I remember another, who, when his general on July 3, 1863, within the enemy's lines at Gettysburg, called for volunteers to go back across a field raked by shot and shell for needed ammunition, prevented a response and said, "General, do not call for volunteers while you have a staff officer whose duty it is to do such things.   I will go and get the ammunition."   He went and came back, and, thank God, is here with us today.[5]

Such deeds, which to the actors are but the simple discharge of duty, the world calls heroism and honors by public monuments.

It has been well said—and the suggestion will bear fruit—that there is one monument yet to be raised in the South—to the Confederate women; although every Southern monument, like this, is a memorial of them also, for they are all, largely, the work of their hands.   History will record, as in the annals of no other war, their constancy under privations, anxieties and distresses at home, their ministrations and encouragements to their husbands, sons and brothers in the field, and in the long, bitter years of reconstruction, which to the South were a prolongation of the worst miseries of the war.   Hardest of all to bear, and they bore it with an unconquered spirit under harsh repression, was the lot of the Southern women

[5] Reverend Randolph H. McKim.

of Maryland during the four years. I am persuaded that among other inspirations there was an added inspiration to thousands in Northern prison camps and hospitals to whom the lines of the Maryland State prisoner[6] in Fort Warren were addressed:

> Will ye not think as ye wave your glad banners,
>   How the flag of old Maryland, trodden in shame,
> Lies, sullied and torn, in the dust of her highways,
>   And will ye not strike a fresh blow in her name?
> Her mothers have sent their first born to be with you,
>   Wherever with blood there were fields to be won,
> Her daughters have wept for you, nursed you and clad you,
>   Their hopes and their vows and their smiles are your own.
>   Let her cause be your cause—

I have here two or three of a series of a hundred letters written by a Southern woman,[7] now with God, from Baltimore in 1861 and 1862. They are the best illustration of the feelings and the spirit of the women of Maryland and how they occupied themselves in doing what they could for the cause. I am sure they would bring up the past better than anything to the survivors of those women here today. I will read only a few extracts; some day they may be material in writing the story of those times. They were to her husband, arbitrarily held, with others, for fifteen months a "prisoner of State"[8]—not far from Plymouth Rock and Faneuil Hall.

You are nobly doing your duties there and will have the respect of all whose respect is worth anything. You carry your reward in your own bosoms—and nothing can deprive you of it. I sit and fancy (what I am sure we will realize) a better country for us all to live in, where the principles for which you are contending will be worth something to every one, and we shall be happy in the full enjoyment of them.

The papers talk as if property was to be confiscated if the oath of allegiance is not taken, and all such things. I had rather see you driving a dray through

---

[6] Severn Teackle Wallis, "To the Exchanged Prisoners," July 31st, 1862.

[7] Elizabeth Phoebe Key Howard, daughter of Francis Scott Key, author of "The Star Spangled Banner," and wife of Charles Howard, son of Colonel John Eager Howard, to whom Congress voted one of its only eleven military medals given in the Revolutionary War. Was it not natural that with such inspirations and associations he staid in prison until unconditionally released?

[8] In Fort Warren, Boston Harbor.

these streets than walking about them released from that prison on any imposed conditions whatever. . . . . This, of course, I know you never will allow, but they may have you annoyed by asking you to make some conditions that may seem trifling and you might think that we would expect you for our sakes to make some trifling sacrifices. I assure you not one of us desires or could bear to think of it.

I am tempted to read from another, written in a lighter mood. Like Richard III before another Richmond, it raises the flap of the tent of McClellan on the Peninsula in 1862:

I heard lately why General McClellan left the Peninsula. He said he was surrounded by four swamps and the frogs were constantly saying, Bull Run, Bull Run, Bull Run, Big Bethel, Big Bethel, Big Bethel, Ball's Bluff, Ball's Bluff, Ball's Bluff, and then the little frogs took it up, Skedaddle, Skedaddle, Skedaddle, all the time, and he could not stand it.

This, of twenty-four pages, is the story of a visit of ministration to the Confederate wounded after Antietam, and this, of fourteen pages, of taking succor to the wounded and burying dead at Gettysburg. But I will only read from one of the many letters telling of the untiring work of feeding and clothing the prisoners and caring for the sick and wounded.

There was a full supply quickly provided and sent to them [the prisoners from Kernstown]. $5000 was also collected to supply their wants, I hear. . . . . As Mrs. Murdoch and myself were buying pies and cakes for them a poor girl was standing in the shop by my side, and hearing us say what we were doing, she touched me on the arm and placed a ten-cent piece and two cents in my hand saying, with so much feeling that she could scarcely speak, "Buy something with this for them, won't you?" With such hands and hearts, do you think it could take long to get up a dinner for hungry men? The girl looked very poor. I had noticed her little money tied up in a corner of a handkerchief, and how she looked at pies and cakes and only bought a loaf of bread. God bless her.

It has been the theory of many Northern writers, and more politicians, that what they are fond of calling the great crime of 1861—when certain stars shot from their spheres—was the masterful act of a ruling class of society, and some have even professed to believe that it was a plot, deliberately conceived and carried out by some political leaders. Not so. It was an uprising of the whole people, high and low, rich and poor, men and women, carrying their leaders along with them—leaders still but not masters. This is conclusively shown, if the story of the war did not show it, by the attitude of the whole Southern people in the almost half century since, standing together as the Solid South, holding their Memorial Days and building their monuments all over the land to the soldiers who were the representatives in arms of the people's sentiments.

There is one feature in the making of this Maryland Monument which must not pass unnoticed. When the war ended and her sons came back to their homes, thousands of sons and daughters of other Southern States, escaping from the persecution of Reconstruction, came with them and after them into the old Land of the Sanctuary.[9] Here they brought their disappointed but not extinguished hopes, their abiding faith in American institutions, their disciplined energies, their characters purified and ennobled by four years sacrifices. No community in all history ever gained such a valuable accession. Children of Maryland by adoption, they have been among the foremost in this work. Therefore, this Monument to the Maryland men is not only one by the native daughters of the State, but is also a tribute to them by representatives of all the Confederacy.

So then, in these last days of the generation of the actors in the war, with feelings, if softened, yet strengthened and deepened after half a century of retrospection, in the presence of the Civil Authorities of the City, of Patriotic Societies, and of the community, the Southern women have placed in the streets of Baltimore this Monument to the Maryland Confederates. A few more years and it will have been finally committed to posterity. In the ages to come men and women will pass by and will gather around it. Some will say, "It is a worthy tribute from noble women to brave men. Both were tried and true in a time of great tribulation and they came out of it as from a refiner's fire. Obloquy has failed to touch them and this Monument is in accord with history in preserving their memory from the oblivion of common things."

Others will say, "We have come from yonder Monument at the other end of this Avenue[10] and from the other patriotic Monuments.

[9] Maryland was so called in the early days of the Colony.
[10] To the Maryland soldiers and sailors in the Revolutionary war.

The men of 1776 fought together for liberty and principles of government laid down in the Declaration of Independence and embodied in the Constitution of the American Union. The men of 1861 were of a divided household. 'Many drew swords and died.' Those who are here commemorated believed that whether under that Federal Compact or in greater rights which lay back of it and outside of it, they were justified in withdrawing as their fathers had entered. History is yet debating this and that abstract theory of the Constitution. North and South are finally content to differ about the sufficiency of the causes of the great war between the States. But these men were willing to die for the faith that was in them at Gettysburg and on other fields as their fathers sacrificed themselves at Long Island and at Camden. Their Valley Forge was a four years endurance. They increased the fame of the Maryland soldier and sailor, and it is meet that there be a monument to them also on the soil of their native State—of 'Maryland, our Maryland.' "

And there will be others: They will say, "We are the sons and the daughters of the men to whom this Monument is consecrated and of the women who were its consecrators. Like themselves, we have no weak repentance for what they did and wherein they failed, and men of right minds have long ago ceased to expect or desire such an abasement. What might have been the altered future if they had succeeded in arms is a page of history never turned and there is no profit in speculation about it. The dove with the olive branch has long ago returned to the ark of the covenant in token that the angry waters of the flood have subsided. But these men took their side with the Southern people who contended for great principles of government as they had received them from their fathers, and who, when the sword was sheathed and after the miserable failure of mis-construction, themselves, unaided, reconstructed their States in the American Union. We cherish their memory and are proud to be descended from them."

In the latter days of the Confederacy it happened that a raiding hostile Army passed by the home and the grave of Stonewall Jackson. Many turned aside to the resting place of the hero, marked then by a simple flag staff, and carried away bits of wood and other mementoes. Close behind came the pursuing Confederates. As they went by, a soldier ran out from the ranks and stood for some time in the attitude of presenting arms at the grave of his great Commander.

So in the years to come, when this Monument shall be standing for a past generation, many will come in love and reverence for the men who wore the gray,—all "whose respect is worth having" with respect and honor.

NOTES

Page 10. On Apr. 19, 1861, Baltimore citizens assaulted the 6th Massachusetts as that regiment marched through town en route to Washington. Four soldiers and twelve civilians were killed in the melee, and the number of wounded ran into the dozens. See *Maryland Historical Magazine,* XIV (1919), 60-76; XLI (1946), 257-81; LVI (1961), 39-71. Cited hereafter as *MHM* . . . Charles W. Brush commanded the Maryland Guard Battalion. When Howard inquired if he had time to go home and don his uniform, the old colonel roared: "Damn your uniform!" Howard's marginal notes in a copy of *Recollections* now in the possession of C. A. Porter Hopkins, Glyndon, Md. Cited hereafter as Howard Notations.

Page 12. Howard was never certain whether Col. Huger took command of the Maryland contingent. Yet Bradley T. Johnson stated that Huger became colonel of the 53rd Maryland Militia on Saturday, Apr. 20, 1861. *Ibid.;* Clement A. Evans (ed.), *Confederate Military History* (Atlanta, 1899), II, 23. Cited hereafter as *CMH.*

Photograph 2A. This illustration is of Howard. . . . For more on young Marylanders offering their services to the Confederacy, see W. W. Goldsborough, *The Maryland Line in the Confederate States Army* (Baltimore, 1869), 6-9; U. S. War Dept. (comp.), *War of the Rebellion: A Compilation of the Official Records of the Union and Confederate Armies* (Washington, 1880-1901), Ser. I, LI, Pt. 2, 14-15. Cited hereafter as *OR;* unless otherwise stated, all references will be to Ser. I.

Page 22. The two Baltimore companies had gone to Suffolk to bolster that town's meager defenses and to present a semblance of multi-state solidarity. Richmond *Daily Dispatch,* June 1 and 5, 1861; James McHenry Howard, *Recollections and Opinions* (Baltimore, 1922), 28-29. . . . Dislike of Col. Thomas was widespread. See *MHM,* LI (1956), 158-59; LVI (1961), 63-65. . . . Noting the presence of many Maryland recruits in the capital, a Richmond newspaper editorialized: "The gallant champions of Southern rights hailing from that section will be the nest-egg from which will be hatched a brood of avengers of Maryland's insulted honor, hard to withstand—terrible to encounter." Richmond *Daily Dispatch,* June 1, 1861.

Page 23. For varying opinions on Arnold Elzey Jones (who dropped his surname after his 1837 graduation from West Point), see *OR,* II, 496; *CHM,* II, 68; John O. Casler, *Four Years in the Stonewall Brigade* (Dayton, O., 1971), 19-20; *Southern Historical Society Papers,* IX (1881), 351. Cited hereafter as *SHSP.* . . . The Richmond *Daily Dispatch,* June 10, 13, 17 and 19, 1861, contained small stories on the formation of the Maryland companies.

Page 24. Some of the "trouble" into which the Maryland volunteers got is cited in *OR,* II, 773-74, 794, 856.

Page 26. Robert F. Morriss commanded Co. I of the 1st Virginia. . . . Clarke's troops became Co. B of the 21st Virginia, and Robertson's unit became Co. I of the 1st Maryland. . . . The two Maryland companies departed for the Shenandoah Valley on the evening of June 22. Richmond *Daily Dispatch,* June 25, 1861.

Page 28. On June 27, 1861, Howard's father and several other civic leaders in Baltimore were arrested for "Southern sympathies." Another series of arrests in September included Howard's oldest brother. For more on these imprisonments, see *OR,* II, 140; John A. Marshall, *The American Bastille* (Philadelphia, 1876), 642-711; *The Public Life and Diplomatic Correspondence of James M. Mason* (Roanoke, Va., 1903), 206-7, 229, 234.

Page 30. Howard's account of the "picturesque appearance" of the ladies of Winchester as the troops passed through town is in marked contrast to the somber description given in Goldsborough, *Maryland Line,* 15. The townspeople felt that Johnston was abandoning the city and leaving it to the mercy of the Federals.

Page 35. The forced march from the railroad siding to the battlefield was six miles long and a real trial to the participants. Randolph McKim, *A Soldier's Recollections* (New York, 1910), 34; *Confederate Veteran,* VII (1899), 63.

Page 36. In leading an assault against the 14th New York Zouaves, Kirby Smith received a frightful bullet wound in the neck. . . . The other soldier whose canteen was "wounded" was Pvt. William H. Codd, who subsequently transferred to the C. S. Ordnance Department. J. Howard, *Recollections,* 36; National Archives and Records Service (comp.), "Compiled Service Records of Confederate Soldiers Who Served in Organizations from the State of Maryland" (Washington, microfilm copy, 1961), Roll 14. Cited hereafter as CSR—Maryland.

Page 37. The conduct at First Manassas of the 14th New York left much to be desired. *OR,* II, 347, 387, 403, 410. . . . Howard was slightly in error as to the hour of the day. The time was closer to 3:30 P.M. *Ibid.,* 496.

Page 38. Different versions of Elzey's directive to his aide are in *SHSP,* IX (1881), 483; *CMH,* II, 55-56. . . . The names of Nicholas Watkins and George Lemmon should be transposed in the footnote. Howard Notations.

Page 43. Sallie Brock Putnam, in *Richmond During the War* (New York, 1867), 64, stated that the all-day rain on July 22 was a downpour rather than the "steady drizzle" mentioned by Howard. Another Maryland soldier alleged that the troops had no cover from "the pitiless storm which raged" throughout the day. Goldsborough, *Maryland Line,* 25.

Page 46. The "great and unfortunate error" to which Howard referred was the Confederate army's failure to advance on Washington after the Manassas victory. Most of Johnston's men shared this sentiment. See *ibid.,* 28-29; Eppa Hunton, *Autobiography of Eppa Hunton* (Richmond, 1933), 41; *SHSP,* X, (1882), 48-49. Cf. William H. Morgan, *Personal Reminiscences of the War of 1861-5* (Lynchburg, Va., 1911), 78-80.

Page 49. Captain Goldsborough asserted that George H. Steuart "was much disliked" when he took command of the 1st Maryland. Other members of the regiment agreed. As "an old and experienced soldier," Steuart "enforced discipline to the strictest letter of the old army regulations." Hence, he "became very unpopular with many of the free American people who composed his command." Goldsborough, *Maryland Line,* 30-31; McKim, *A Soldier's Recollections,* 28, 39-42; J. Howard, *Recollections,* 33.

Page 51. Lieutenant Col. John B. Cumming of the 20th Georgia apparently provoked the skirmish described by Howard and mentioned only by Union officers in *OR,* V, 119-21. Cumming's superior—cited on p. 53—was Col. William Duncan Smith, Jr. Lillian Henderson (comp.), *Roster of the Confederate Soldiers of Georgia, 1861-1865* (Hapeville and Atlanta, Ga., 1959-1965), II,

766, 769. A slightly different account of the reconnaissance is in Goldsborough, *Maryland Line,* 33-34.

Page 59. On Dec. 9, 1861, in front of a division, two members of the "Louisiana Tigers" were shot to death by firing squads for assault on an officer and other misconduct. Richmond *Daily Dispatch,* Dec. 14, 1861; Capt. William P. Harper (7th La.) to his mother, Dec. 10, 1861, Virginia Historical Society.

Page 60. George Washington Morgan later served with distinction in the cavalry unit of a kinsman, John Hunt Morgan. . . . The only history of the Baltimore Light Artillery is in Goldsborough, *Maryland Line,* 292-330. . . . A full discussion of the highly effective Blakely gun is in Warren Ripley, *Artillery and Ammunition of the Civil War* (New York, 1970), 148-59.

Page 63. Howard later wrote of his appointment as first sergeant: "I had in fact been acting as Orderly Sergeant the most of the time since the formation of the Company and several times in the winter Captain Murray told me of his intention of appointing me 1st Sergeant in place of Sergeant Sullivan, but I had deprecated it. The present announcement was a surprise to me." Howard Notations. . . . In his annotated copies, Howard also corrected the obvious textual errors relative to Confederate insignia. A second lieutenant wore one bar; a first lieutenant, two bars; and a captain, three bars.

Page 66. The Marylanders came under attack from the 1st New York Cavalry. See James H. Stevenson, *"Boots and Saddles:" A History of the . . . First New York (Lincoln) Cavalry* (Harrisburg, Pa., 1879), 80-82.

Page 69. Steuart left the regiment on Mar. 15 and started for Richmond. Four days later, he was commissioned a brigadier general. *SHSP,* X (1882), 50.

Page 74. Christopher Columbus Baldwin was a partner in the Baltimore dry goods firm of Woodward, Baldwin & Co. . . . Baldwin's friend was probably William B. Hollingsworth, also listed in the 1860 Baltimore city directory as a merchant.

Page 77. Winder reported to Jackson on Apr. 1, and the order assigning him officially to command of the Stonewall Brigade came three days later. *SHSP,* XLIII (1920), 171. . . . In the face of a Federal advance southward after the battle of Kernstown,

Jackson withdrew his forces to Rude's Hill. There they remained unmolested for several weeks. Jedediah Hotchkiss, *Make Me a Map of the Valley* (Dallas, Tex., 1973), 16. Cited hereafter as Hotchkiss, *Journal*.

Page 78. "Captain Wingate" must have been serving in a voluntary capacity, for no such person is mentioned either in the battle reports and official correspondence for that period or in the compiled service records of Virginia soldiers. The officer was probably R. J. Wingate, who later served on the staff of Gen. A. P. Hill. See *OR*, XIX, Pt. 1, 982.

Page 80. In 1858, a severe attack of neuralgia left the hearing in Jackson's right ear permanently impaired. Thomas J. Arnold, *Early Life and Letters of General Thomas J. Jackson* (New York, 1916), 257, 264.

Page 81. For other opinions on Garnett's dismissal, see Richard Taylor, *Destruction and Reconstruction* (New York, 1879), 79, Henry Kyd Douglas, *I Rode with Stonewall* (Chapel Hill, 1940), 37; James I. Robertson, Jr., *The Stonewall Brigade* (Baton Rouge, 1963), 78. . . . J. Lyle Clarke had become a lieutenant colonel in command of the 30th Bttn., Virginia Sharpshooters. *OR*, XIX, Pt. 1, 1083.

Page 82. The 1860 census returns for the three counties in the Rude's Hill area show no resident by the name of Lincoln. However, the Union president's grandparents, Abraham and Bathsheba Lincoln, did live for a time in Rockingham County, Va. This is probably the basis for Howard's account. John W. Wayland, *Virginia Valley Records* (Strasburg, Va., 1930), 319; Carl Sandburg, *Abraham Lincoln: The Prairie Years* (New York, 1926), I, 3-6.

Page 86. "Allegheny" Johnson arrived at Jackson's headquarters on the night of Apr. 19. Hotchkiss, *Journal*, 28. For some of the many anecdotes concerning this colorful officer, see Casler, *Four Years*, 74, 163, 333.

Page 87. Colonel Allen's unhappiness at serving under Jackson stemmed largely from Garnett's dismissal from command. See Douglas, *I Rode with Stonewall*, 37; Lenoir Chambers, *Stonewall Jackson* (New York, 1959), I, 484. The best sketch of Allen is in Charles D. Walker, *Memorial, Virginia Military Institute*

(Philadelphia, 1875), 21-25. . . . Robert D. Gardner was second in command of the 4th Virginia. . . . William H. Harman retired from service at the time of the reorganization. . . . The 27th Virginia had only seven companies when, in April, 1862, it received the additions that brought its strength to regimental level. Lee A. Wallace, Jr., *A Guide to Virginia Military Organizations, 1861-1865* (Richmond, 1964), 144. . . . Colonel John Echols of the 27th Virginia received promotion to brigadier after recuperating from his Kernstown wounds.

Page 88. Contrary to Howard's statement, little or no disappointment emanated from the ranks of the 33rd Virginia at Cummings' departure. See Robertson, *Stonewall Brigade*, 83-84. . . . Edwin G. Lee became Neff's second-in-command after the reorganization of the 33rd Virginia, and Capt. Frederick W. M. Holliday of Co. D advanced to the rank of major. Wallace, *Virginia Military Organizations*, 153. . . . The other lieutenants in the Rockbridge Artillery were William M. Brown and James C. Davis. William T. Poague, *Gunner with Stonewall* (Jackson, Tenn., 1957), 21.

Page 89. William T. Lambie and Henry H. Dunott were also lieutenants in Carpenter's Battery. *OR*, XI, Pt. 2, 574; *Confederate Veteran*, XIII (1905), 365. . . . It was not until May 8 that J. M. Garnett actually joined Winder's staff. Howard Notations. . . . Dr. Harvey Black was then acting medical director of Jackson's army because of the illness of his superior, Dr. Hunter McGuire. Hotchkiss, *Journal*, 46.

Page 90. A full discussion of the Ashby-Jackson disagreement is in Douglas S. Freeman, *Lee's Lieutenants: A Study in Command* (New York, 1942-1944), I, 337-41. . . . On May 23, Ashby was promoted to brigadier. He received the commission on May 27, only ten days before his death. Frank Cunningham, *Knight of the Confederacy* (San Antonio, 1960), 158.

Page 92. On the afternoon of Apr. 30, Jackson began his famous march. George F. R. Henderson, *Stonewall Jackson and the American Civil War* (New York, 1904), I, 284. The hardships of that march are emphasized in Douglas, *I Rode with Stonewall*, 47-48; Edward A. Moore, *The Story of a Cannoneer under Stonewall Jackson* (New York, 1907), 44-45; *SHSP*, XLIII (1920),

181-82. . . . Howard seemed to have difficulty in recalling the exact itinerary of the army during the first stages of the Valley Campaign. For a precise, step-by-step chronicle of Jackson's movements, see Hotchkiss, *Journal*, 35-36.

Page 94. The VMI Corps of Cadets operated independently of Winder's command throughout the McDowell campaign. John H. Worsham, *One of Jackson's Foot Cavalry* (Jackson, Tenn., 1964), 39n. Following the battle, the chief role of the cadets was in guarding prisoners. They "were pretty much used up by the hard marches, guard duty, etc., mere boys that most of them were." Hotchkiss, *Journal*, 45.

Page 96. Jackson dispatched at least one courier to hasten Winder's brigade to the field. Then Jackson himself rode back and led the brigade into camp. *Ibid.*, 39-40.

Page 97. Simeon G. Gibbons, reputed at twenty-nine to be the youngest colonel in the Confederate army, "fell early in the action while leading and gloriously cheering his men to the fight." *OR,* XII, Pt. 1, 482. . . . Johnson was shot near the close of the battle. Disagreement prevails over the nature of his wound. Like Howard, John Worsham believed that he was shot in the foot. Worsham, *Foot Cavalry,* 40. Douglas, *I Rode with Stonewall,* 49, asserted that the wound was in the ankle. Another staff officer stated that a bullet broke one of the bones in the ankle. Robert L. Dabney, *Life and Campaigns of Lieut.-Gen. Thomas J. Jackson* (New York, 1866), 349. Johnson himself merely reported a wound "in the leg." *OR,* XII, Pt. 1, 483.

Page 98. The location of the mass burial spot is given in Hotchkiss, *Journal*, 43. . . . Federal casualties at McDowell numbered 248 men; Jackson's losses were 498 men. *OR,* XII, Pt. 1, 462, 470-71, 476.

Page 102. In his generally exaggerated memoirs, Harry Gilmor stated that he ordered his cavalry to assist Winder because Federals were giving stiff resistance at a narrow mountain gap. Harry Gilmor, *Four Years in the Saddle* (New York, 1866), 36-37. . . . On May 11, Jackson halted the pursuit of Milroy's Federal army after he realized what he called the "impracticability of capturing the defeated enemy." *OR,* XII, Pt. 1, 473.

Page 103. Jackson's congratulatory order to his brigades is in

Dabney, *Jackson*, 353. . . . Howard's wording seemed to imply that few of Jackson's regiments had chaplains. In fact, Jackson's army contained more regimental chaplains than did any other body of Confederate troops then in the field.

Page 106. The lot of Col. John R. Kenly's 1st Maryland (U. S.) at Front Royal can only be termed a disaster. Of 1,063 men in his command, Kenly suffered 904 casualties (of whom 750 were captured). Jackson's losses were thirty-six killed and wounded. *SHSP,* XLIII (1920), 211. . . . For the jubilation of the Maryland soldiers after this battle, see *ibid,* X (1882), 55; McKim, *Recollections,* 96.

Page 107. The artillery action on May 24 occurred at Newtown and is described more fully in *OR,* XII, Pt. 1, 615, 704, 726. . . . Howard was probably mistaken about seeing and hearing the odd-shaped Schenkel shells. These projectiles were primarily used on naval vessels. Ripley, *Artillery and Ammunition,* 293-95.

Page 108. Howard exaggerated the near-panic that occurred in the darkness. A group of Confederate cavalry did bolt to the rear; but Jackson gave them such a verbal lacing that the embarrassed riders wheeled their horses and returned to the front. Dabney, *Jackson*, 375. . . . The "leading regiment" supposedly put into confusion was the 33rd Virginia. Howard Notations. . . . The best account of the delaying action waged by the 2nd Massachusetts is in George H. Gordon, *Brook Farm to Cedar Mountain in the War of the Great Rebellion, 1861-62* (Boston, 1883), 219-24.

Page 112. Winder's orders from Jackson were to advance to Charlestown, not Harper's Ferry. *OR,* XII, Pt. 1, 707. Winder's report of the movement corroborates Howard's narrative. *Ibid.,* 738-39. . . . In the skirmishing at Charlestown, the Stonewall Brigade had only one man wounded by a shell. *Ibid.,* 739.

Page 115. Some doubt exists as to the truthfulness of the alleged exchange between Jackson and Elzey. Alexander R. Boteler, who was serving on Jackson's staff at the time, remembered that Jackson quietly watched the artillery duel for awhile, then dismounted from his horse and went to sleep under a nearby tree. Boteler did not recall any courier arriving with a dispatch *SHSP,* XL (1915), 164.

Page 116. On May 31, the 2nd Virginia marched a total of thirty-six miles. *OR,* XII, Pt. 1, 708. . . . . The artillery fire that Howard heard the following day was a feeble attempt by the forces of Gen. John C. Fremont to block Jackson's withdrawal southward up the Valley. McKim, *Recollections,* 107-8.

Page 119. Jackson reached Harrisonburg "at an early hour" on June 5. *OR,* XII, Pt. 1, 712. Cf. *SHSP,* XLIII (1920), 258.

Page 120. Contrasting opinions of the swashbuckling Wyndham are in Dabney, *Jackson,* 399, and Henry R. Pyne, *Ride to War: A History of the First New Jersey Cavalry* (New Brunswick, N. J., 1961), xiii-xviii. . . . The heroism of the 1st Maryland in this fight is dramatically told in *SHSP,* X (1882), 103-6. . . . Breastplates or "body armor," were never a part of a Civil War soldier's regular uniform, and the few such accoutrements used were purchased from sutlers and private dealers, Francis A. Lord, *Civil War Collector's Encyclopedia* (Harrisburg, Pa., 1963), 58-59; *SHSP,* XXXII (1904), 221-22. . . . On the subject of exploding bullets, see *ibid.,* VIII (1880), 18-28; *Confederate Veteran,* VII (1899), 156-58. . . . Richard Taylor's reference to breastplates is in his *Destruction and Reconstruction,* 55. . . . W. Stuart Symington served as chief ordnance officer under Gen. George E. Pickett. . . . W. LeRoy Brown was superintendent of the Richmond Arsenal during the war.

Page 122. Like Howard, many of Jackson's men believed that the General preferred to fight on Sunday, and they pointed to the battles of First Manassas, Kernstown and Winchester as examples. In reality, Jackson had serious reservations about doing battle on the Sabbath. Freeman, *Lee's Lieutenants,* I, 312-13, 319-20. . . . Howard and Winder agreed as to the hour when the Federal artillery opened fire. Douglas thought that the action began soon after 7 A. M., while Hotchkiss put the first shots at 10 A. M. *OR,* XII, Pt. 1, 739; Douglas, *I Rode with Stonewall,* 85; Hotchkiss, *Journal,* 53. . . . The regiment sent in support of Poague's battery was the 2nd Virginia.

Page 124. Since Ewell never reported receiving any such order from Jackson, since he never executed any movement following such guidelines, and since he possessed no cavalry, it may have been that Jackson preceded his command with the word "if." See Freeman, *Lee's Lieutenants,* I, 447n.

Page 126. Soldiers in the Stonewall Brigade were awakened at 3:45 A. M. for the march to Port Republic. *OR,* XII, Pt. 1, 740. . . . Jackson's chief of staff, not Taylor, is the source for Confederate soldiers falling from the makeshift bridge. Dabney, *Jackson,* 419-21.

Page 128. Winder dispatched Howard to secure reinforcements from Jackson. The 2nd Virginia at that time was already engaged in battle. *OR,* XII, Pt. 1, 741.

Page 133. Howard mysteriously overlooked a confrontation at this time between Winder and Jackson. When the brigadier requested permission to go to Richmond on private business and Jackson brusquely refused, Winder tendered his resignation. Fortunately, Gen. Richard Taylor interceded and restored good relations between the two officers. Taylor, *Destruction and Reconstruction,* 79. . . . On June 19, Winder's brigade boarded railroad cars at Mechum's River. Freeman, *Lee's Lieutenants,* I, 470, 493.

Page 135. The Confederates disembarked from trains at Beaver Dam Station. W. W. Scott (ed.), *Two Confederate Items* (Richmond, 1927), 13. . . . The anecdotal footnote about Jackson's secrecy is an adaptation of a story that first appeared in John Esten Cooke, *Stonewall Jackson: A Military Biography* (New York, 1876), 205.

Page 136. Lawton's 3,500 Georgians comprised the largest brigade in the Confederate army at that time. They were the last element of Jackson's forces to enter the battle of Gaines's Mill, and the men expended their ammunition before the fighting ended. *OR,* XI, Pt. 2, 580, 595-96, 603; Freeman, *Lee's Lieutenants,* I, 529.

Page 140. As his horse struggled through the mud, Howard later recalled, a foot soldier stopped directly in front of the animal and refused to move. Howard scolded the soldier and ordered him to step aside. "Well," the man replied cooly, "I will if you will take your horse's foot off my heel." Howard Notations. . . . At the height of the battle, Capt. E. P. Lawton assumed command of the 38th Georgia. *OR,* XI, Pt. 2, 570, 580. . . . Goldsborough quoted Howard as stating: "The General has observed your movements, Sir, and thinks the place too strong for you. We will therefore charge together." *Maryland Line,* 89. On the other hand, Bradley Johnson thought that Howard asserted: "General Winder thinks that you are not strong enough to take those batteries. He directs that you wait until he can bring up the Stonewall Brigade to your support." *CMH,* II, 85-86. . . . The 52nd Virginia was the regiment that Howard got untangled. Colonel Lawson Botts of the 2nd Virginia observed Howard bearing the colors and told him after the battle: "Sir, I will see that you shall be mentioned for this." Two months later, Botts fell mortally wounded at Second Manassas. *OR,* XI, Pt. 2, 555, 570, 610; Howard Notations.

Page 142. Howard later identified the triangle of dots in the drawing as a straggler in front, Howard in the lower left and Col. Holliday in the lower right. *Ibid.* . . . Garland was only thirty-one when he was killed in action at the Sept. 14, 1862, battle of South Mountain.

Page 144. Of the discussion over seniority of rank, Lawton stated in his official report: "A hasty conversation with Brigadier-General Garland satisfied me that I was the ranking officer . . . and I at once assumed command . . ." Garland made no mention of the exchange in his report. *OR,* XI, Pt. 2, 596, 642.

Page 146. Pickets of the 4th Virginia captured Gen. Reynolds and his adjutant, Capt. Charles Kingsbury. *Ibid.,* 578. . . . Colonel Robert C. Buchanan of the 4th U. S. Infantry commanded a brigade of Regulars throughout the Seven Days Campaign. His report of Gaines's Mill is in *ibid.,* 360. . . . Some difference of opinion exists over the June 29 movements of the Stonewall Brigade. Howard's statement agrees with Winder's report in *ibid.,* 571, but see Dabney, *Jackson,* 459.

Page 149. By June 30, with his advance at White Oak Swamp seemingly blocked by superior forces, Jackson gave way to the fatigue of several weeks' campaigning. Not even the afternoon nap that Howard mentioned refreshed the general. That night, dining with some of his officers, Jackson fell asleep at the table with a biscuit clinched between his teeth. *Ibid.,* 467. Cf. *SHSP,* XXX (1902), 149.

Page 150. In contrast to Howard's statement about not hearing the sounds of battle, the din from many of the engagements of this campaign carried incredible distances. See Freeman, *Lee's Lieutenants,* I, 531 and n. Bradley Johnson termed the afternoon bombardment "the most infernal fire that has ever been concentrated in America." *SHSP,* X (1882), 216.

Page 151. The regimental commander of the 5th Virginia reported that Capt. L. J. Fletcher was mortally wounded by "a Parrott shell" during a barrage that killed another soldier and wounded four men. *OR,* XI, Pt. 2, 571, 582. . . . Around 7 P. M., Winder received orders to join Harvey Hill's command. Winder stated: "I dispatched a staff officer [Howard] to a house near by to see if I could hear of General Hill's locality." The residence in question was the Crew House. *Ibid.,* 571.

Page 153. The wild firing by some members of the Stonewall Brigade may be at least partially excused, for Winder reported that the Federals "gave us the most terrific fire I have ever seen. There was a continuous stream of shot, shell, and balls for some two hours . . ." *Ibid.,* 572. For more on the confusion in the Stonewall Brigade, see Col. Neff's report in *ibid.,* 585-86.

Page 157. Jackson's chief of staff had little respect for naval shells and felt that they "had no actual influence whatever" at Malvern Hill or thereafter. Dabney, *Jackson,* 482-84. . . . Dabney also asserted that, by the end of the campaign, half of Jackson's men were "out of their ranks from death or wounds, from the necessary labors of the care of the wounded, from straggling, and from the inefficiency of their inferior officers." *Ibid.,* 477.

Page 160. The huge von Borcke was said to have carried a saber "as long as a fence rail." Colonel G. W. Dorsey of the 1st Maryland Cavalry enjoyed telling the story of the evening in May, 1863, when his troopers fired on a body of horsemen they supposed to be Federals. Suddenly from the darkness in front came von Borcke's bull-like voice: "You, Torsey! Jeb Stuart gif you hell for this!" Howard Notations. . . . On July 13, the divisions of Jackson and Ewell (minus Richard Taylor's brigade) began the march to Gordonsville. *OR,* XII, Pt. 3, 915. . . . Theodore S. Garnett was a highly successful civil engineer and also noted for a vivacious Spanish wife. A detailed sketch of his son, who served as a staff officer with Howard, is in *SHSP,* XLI (1916), 68-81.

Page 163. Howard may have been in error as to the location of Jackson's headquarters. Hotchkiss reported the command post to be at the home of Jonathan B. Magruder, *Journal,* 65. . . . Dr. John T. Jones served as army surgeon at hospitals in Warrenton, Ashland and Gordonsville. Wyndham B. Blanton, *Medicine in Virginia in the Nineteenth Century* (Richmond, 1933), 406. Howard added that Dr. Jones was a brother of Gen. John M. Jones. Howard Notations.

Page 165. Hotchkiss noted on Aug. 9 that Winder was "not well from his sickness and looked very pale and badly." Hotchkiss, *Journal,* 66. . . . Douglas, *I Rode with Stonewall,* 125, gives a more dramatic—and less accurate—account of Winder's assignment to divisional command.

Page 166. After a few months on Jackson's staff, Dabney found that "physically he was wholly unfit for such campaigning." Recurrent attacks of "camp fever" brought him "near to death's door." Accordingly, near the end of August, he officially resigned his army post. Thomas Cary Johnson, *The Life and Letters of Robert Lewis Dabney* (Richmond, 1903), 271-72. . . . Whether or not Jackson wished to avoid a conflict of rank between Lawton and Winder, he assigned the Georgia brigade of the former to guard the wagon trains. *OR,* XII, Pt. 2, 188, 215.

Page 167. One Parrott gun from Carpenter's Battery duelled with at least five Federal cannon at a range of 700 yards. *Ibid.,* 186, 215.

Page 170. Winder was shouting an order to Edward A. Moore of the Rockbridge Artillery when he was fatally struck. "He fell straight back at full length, and lay quivering on the ground." Moore, *Cannoneer,* 95. See also Daniel A. Grimsley, *Battles in Culpeper County, Virginia, 1861-1865* (Culpeper, 1900), 29. According to a newspaper correspondent on the scene, Winder lived an hour after being hit. Richmond *Daily Dispatch,* Aug. 18, 1862. . . . For contrasting sentiments among the men over Winder's death, see Casler, *Four Years,* 102, 104; Douglas, *I Rode with Stonewall,* 126.

Page 172. The surgeon who treated Andrews was Dr. Frederick Hunter, who was attached to the Maryland artillery. Tunstall Smith (ed.), *Richard Snowden Andrews* (Baltimore, 1910), 45, 65.

Page 174. Joseph Carpenter died from a head wound. *OR*, XII, Pt. 2, 193; Moore, *Cannoneer*, 95, 155-56. . . . Andrew Grigsby was slightly wounded three times during his seventeen months of service. *Confederate Veteran*, IV (1896), 69.

Page 176. Winder's remains arrived in Richmond on the afternoon of Aug. 17. That evening his body lay in state in the Capitol. At 4 P. M. the following day, the wooden casket draped with a Maryland flag was interred in Hollywood Cemetery. Richmond *Daily Dispatch*, Aug. 18-19, 1862. Winder's body was not placed in a vault, as Howard stated in the footnote. The remains were buried near the crypt of President James Monroe. J. Peterkin to James Howard, June 27, 1865, Howard Papers, Maryland Historical Society.

Page 178. B. J. Barbour, the brother-in-law of David Watson (then medical director of A. P. Hill's division), was very active in state education and politics. He was also renowned as an orator. *OR*, XI, Pt. 2, 839; W. W. Scott, *A History of Orange County, Virginia* (Richmond, 1907), 150, 181. . . . John B. Brooke, reported Steuart at that time, was responsible for "the quiet and good order" then prevailing in Winchester. *OR*, XIX, Pt. 2, 664. . . . Confederate authorities subsequently arrested William S. Dooley and confined him for a time in Libby Prison. *Ibid.*, Ser. II, VII, 6-9; Cornelia McDonald, *A Diary with Reminiscences of the War and Refugee Life in the Shenandoah Valley, 1860-1865* (Nashville, 1934), 152.

Page 180. The Virginia officer discussed here was Henry Kyd Douglas. Howard Notations.

Page 181. Howard later observed: "I think Grigsby ought to have been promoted, but his bluff manner and reckless speech were against him." *Ibid.* A Grigsby obituary stated that he resigned from the army because "he was then in feeble health and unable to endure further active service." *Confederate Veteran*, IV (1896), 69. See also Robertson, *Stonewall Brigade*, 162-64. . . . Major John A. Harman of Staunton was Jackson's famous and profane quartermaster.

Page 183. Howard was understandably confused over the date that the Confederates withdrew from Winchester because other sources disagree as well. A resident of the city recorded in her

diary that the Marylanders headed southward on Dec. 2. Yet
Federal forces did not occupy the place until two days later.
McDonald, *Diary,* 110; *OR,* XXI, 33. . . . Captain Clark is not
listed in the compiled service records of Virginia soldiers; nor did
Jones cite him in March, 1863, as a member of his staff. However,
a "Capt. F. P. Clark, assistant quartermaster," did command a
Confederate company at the 1864 battle of Piedmont—the en-
gagement in which Jones the commander was killed. *Ibid.,* XXV,
Pt. 1, 33; LI, Pt. 1, 1225.

Page 184. Sallie Conrad and Kyd Douglas were engaged to be
married for a short period. It was she who suggested that Douglas
keep a journal of his army experiences. Howard Notations; Douglas, *I Rode with Stonewall,* 353, 381.

Page 185. Dr. Harrison and his wife, the former Mattie Cary
Page, lived at "Longwood," an impressive estate on the Millwood-
Berryville road. *Proceedings of the Clarke County Historical Association,* XIV (1956-1957), 150. . . . George M. Emack was
captain of Co. B, 1st Maryland Cavalry. In battle, wrote one
historian, his "deeds of daring at times amounted to madness."
Goldsborough, *Maryland Line,* 218.

Page 188. According to the 1860 census returns for Shenandoah
County, Benjamin Newman and his family operated a tavern near
Milam's Gap.

Page 190. Howard's brother James was quartered in the home
of Mrs. E. Chevallie, on the southeast corner of Cary and Third
streets. W. Eugene Ferslew, *Second Annual Directory for the City
of Richmond . . . for 1860* (Richmond, 1860), 67.

Page 191. "Jackson seldom gave or endorsed such papers,"
Howard subsequently wrote of the letter of recommendation.
"Captain (now the Reverend) James Power Smith, of his Staff,
says that he once refused his request that he endorse such an
application for a friend, saying that he never did so when he did
not have personal knowledge." Howard Notations.

Page 197. Although Henry E. Decie claimed to be a British
lord and post-captain in the Royal Navy, in truth he was neither.
He was a yachtsman-adventurer who appeared in Savannah, Ga.,
shortly after the Civil War began. Wined and dined by the high
society of that city, Decie suddenly vanished until he turned up

in Virginia during the year that Howard met him. Decie seems to have been an entrepreneur of British shipping, but no one ever knew precisely what he was seeking in America during the years of civil war. William M. Morrison, Jr., *The Confederate Privateers* (New Haven, 1928), 331-33.

Page 199. The *America* first gained fame in the 1850s as a racing schooner. Decie somehow acquired the vessel after it was sold by her American owners. The yacht was rechristened *Camilla* and used as a Confederate dispatch boat until its spring, 1862, capture by Federal blockaders. After the war the vessel enjoyed a long racing career, and in 1921 it was presented to the U. S. Naval Academy. *Ibid.;* U. S. Navy Dept. (comp.), *Official Records of the Union and Confederate Navies in the War of the Rebellion* (Washington, 1894-1922), Ser. II, I, 34. Cited hereafter as *Navy OR.*

Page 204. Captain David A. Claiborne led the "Dan River Rifles" (Co. K) of the 14th Virginia.

Page 206. The "Chivalrous" Duncan McKim fell "while most gallantly cheering on the men." *OR*, XXV, Pt. 1, 1006, 1008. See McKim, *Recollections,* 131-32, for more on the cousin's death and funeral. . . . The "Mrs. Allan" mentioned in the footnote was probably Mrs. J. J. Allen, wife of a judge who also served on the governor's advisory council. W. Asbury Christian, *Richmond: Her Past and Present* (Richmond, 1912), 218.

Page 208. The exact location of the "C. Kayser" residence is shown in U. S. War Dept. (comp.), *Atlas to Accompany the Official Records of the Union and Confederate Armies* (Washington, 1891-1895), Plate XCIV—2. Cited hereafter as *OR Atlas.*

Page 212. Howard erred in stating that Capt. Richard C. M. Page was the officer who fled to Williamsport. Page, who commanded a battery at that time, had been wounded in action at Gettysburg. *OR,* XXVII, Pt. 2, 287, 457.

Page 213. The heavy loss of Confederate wagons occurred on July 4, when Federal cavalry attacked Ewell's trains during the Confederate retreat. Some 1300-1500 Southern soldiers were captured along with 150-300 wagons. *Ibid.,* Pt. 1, 970-71, 988, 1019; Pt. 2, 448-49. . . . Maryland units in the Gettysburg campaign suffered aggregate losses of 39 killed and 167 wounded. *Ibid.,* 331,

341; Goldsborough, *Maryland Line*, 159-63. . . . On the evening of July 5, Jones left Col. John D. Imboden in command at Williamsport and, with a handful of his men, rode through Federal lines to rejoin the main body of his troops at Leitersburg, Md. *OR*, XXVII, Pt. 2, 753-54. . . . The rumors that Howard heard relative to both Lee and Longstreet were untrue. . . . For details of Imboden's July 6 fight at Williamsport, see *ibid.*, 322, 700-1; Robert U. Johnson and C. C. Buel (eds.), *Battles and Leaders of the Civil War* (New York, 1884-1887), III, 425-29.

Page 214. Howard's brother Edward served as chief surgeon in Trimble's brigade. *OR*, Ser. II, VII, 135. . . . For details of the heated argument between Trimble and Ewell, see Freeman, *Lee's Lieutenants*, III, 93-96. . . . Testimonials of Trimble's value to the army are in *OR*, XI, Pt. 2, 570, 618.

Page 215. The Virginia-North Carolina brigade assigned to Steuart had been formed just prior to the Gettysburg campaign. The brigade, wrote Freeman, "contained some splendid troops that had not always been well led before Steuart took command of them." Yet as Howard emphasized on subsequent pages, Steuart molded the regiments into a reliable and proud brigade. Freeman, *Lee's Lieutenants*, II, 703; III, 270 and n. . . . Howard mysteriously failed to note in his July 9 entry that he spent the greater part of the day accompanying Gens. Lee, Ewell, Early and A. P. Hill on a tour of the Confederate defenses. Hotchkiss, *Journal*, 159-60.

Page 217. "Home Sweet Home," the song that Howard heard, was the all-time favorite of Civil War soldiers. For a similar expression of homesickness for Maryland at this time, see McKim, *Recollections*, 125.

Page 221. The Rev. George Patterson, discussed at length on p. 226, was one of the outstanding Episcopal chaplains in Confederate service. Excellent insights on Patterson are in *ibid.*, 139-40, 190-91; Joseph B. Cheshire, *The Church in the Confederate States* (New York, 1912), 88-89. . . . Howard was confused in his footnote on Virginia place-names. Culpeper and Fairfax are seats of two different counties.

Page 224. On Sept. 2, 1863, Lt. Green B. Samuels of the 10th Virginia in Steuart's brigade wrote home: "I wish you could see our Camp, it is the model Camp of the Army, cool, shady and perfectly clean, the water convenient and abundant . . ." Carrie E. Spencer *et al.* (comps.), *A Civil War Marriage in Virginia: Reminiscences and Letters* (Front Royal, Va., 1956), 192.

Page 225. Additional details of the Sept. 5 execution of Pvt. William Barefoot and nine other members of the 3rd North Carolina are in Richmond *Daily Dispatch,* Sept. 5 and 7, 1863; Lynchburg *Daily Virginian,* Sept. 12, 1863; Casler, *Four Years,* 189-90.

Page 229. The Gibson home was at the western edge of the Wilderness. It and the three fords over which Howard admitted some confusion are shown in *OR Atlas,* Plate XLV—1.

Page 231. John Gibson shared a large farm with his brother Robert before embarking after the Civil War on a law career. U. S. Bureau of the Census, "Eighth Census of the United States, 1860: Returns for Orange County, Virginia." . . . Garrett Scott was a presiding judge in the county for more than a quarter of a century. Scott, *Orange County,* 162.

Page 235. In the spring of 1863, Ewell had married his widowed cousin, Lizinka Campbell Brown. They became devoted to one another—even though Ewell habitually introduced her as "my wife, Mrs. Brown." John B. Gordon, *Reminiscences of the Civil War* (New York, 1903), 158.

Page 236. The "mortifying disaster" to which Howard referred occurred Nov. 7 at Kelly's Ford and Rappahannock Bridge. Successful Federal attacks, together with an almost unbroken sequence of Confederate errors, cost Lee's army 2,023 casualties. One historian of Lee's army asserted: "Every rank and grade from headquarters to guardhouse was humiliated." Freeman, *Lee's Lieutenants,* III, 264-69.

Page 240. A more recent and authorative source puts the losses in the 3rd North Carolina at ninety-nine men killed, wounded and missing. Louis H. Manarin (comp.), *North Carolina Troops, 1861-1865: A Roster* (Raleigh, 1966-   ), III, 485. One Tarheel soldier wrote of the action: "It seemed as if the enemy was throwing minnieballs upon us by the bucket-full." Walter Clark (ed.), *Histories of the Several Regiments and Battalions from North Carolina in the Great War, 1861-'65* (Goldsboro and

Raleigh, 1901), I, 198. Cited hereafter as Clark, *N. C. Regiments*.

Page 241. Steuart's praise of Howard and Lt. White in this battle is in *OR*, XXIX, Pt. 1, 864. . . . Colonel Simeon T. Walton, whom Steuart lauded as "a most accomplished officer and chivalrous gentleman," was killed "by a ball passing through his head." *Ibid.*, 864, 869. . . . Colonel Hamilton A. Brown was shot through the hand. Clark, *N. C. Regiments*, I, 149

. *Page 242*. General Edward Johnson was the hero of the Payne's Farm battle. When his horse was killed, Johnson promptly "borrowed" the mount of a courier and continued to direct the action. Howard's statement of encountering Johnson on foot leads to speculation that the second horse may have been slain. *Ibid.*, 198. . . . Howard is in error about meeting "the adjutant of a New York regiment." The official Federal casualty returns for Payne's Farm show only two New York officers captured. Both men— Lt. Carl Stutter of the 39th New York and Capt. Sidney Mead of the 111th New York—were taken prisoner Dec. 1 while on picket duty. *OR*, XXIX, Pt. 1, 678-86; Frederick Phisterer (comp.), *New York in the War of the Rebellion, 1861 to 1865* (Albany, 1912), III, 2210; IV, 3315.

Page 243. In those last days of November, both armies suffered from the weather. An officer in Steuart's brigade would recall: "The temperature was well down to zero and the biting cold was such as to chill the warmest resolution, and when both sides marched (or stole) away, each was glad." Clark, *N. C. Regiments*, I, 199.

Page 247. Boston attorney John Codman Ropes began writing Civil War history while the struggle was still in progress. His best-known works are *The Army Under Pope* (New York, 1881) and *The Story of the Civil War* (4 vols., New York, 1894-1913). . . . Thomas L. Livermore, mentioned in the footnote, commanded the 18th New Hampshire and later became that state's most prolific Civil War historian. His speech on "The Northern Volunteers" is in *Journal of the Military Service Institution of the United States*, XII, (1891), 905-37. No record exists that any comparable address by Kyd Douglas was ever published.

Page 249. Of the winter quarters near Pisgah Church, a private in the 10th Virginia wrote that the men "were comfortable and as cheerful and happy as men can be under like circumstances." James Huffman, *Ups and Downs of a Confederate Soldier* (New York, 1940), 81-82. . . . The 1st North Carolina had a band at its 1861 muster. Apparently the group disbanded that autumn but was re-instituted in the autumn of 1863. Manarin, *N. C. Troops,* III, 143, 158, 161.

Page 250. The best accounts of the Confederate retreat from Gettysburg make no mention of any independent contingent of barefooted and poorly shod men. See *OR,* XXVII, Pt. 2, 505; *Battles and Leaders,* III, 422-29; Jubal A. Early, *Autobiographical Sketch and Narrative of the War Between the States* (Philadelphia, 1912), 279-80, 283.

Page 252. On Mar. 2, 1863, Lt. Green Samuels informed his wife: "Our fare the last week or ten days has been awful. We have been drawing such miserable pork that it is impossible to eat it." In another letter, written three weeks later, Samuels commented: "I now really enjoy a meal that two years ago I would have turned away from with *loathing.*" Spencer, *Civil War Marriage,* 163, 174. . . . The regiment with the fondness for tobacco was the 23rd Virginia.

Page 256. Jeremiah Morton abandoned his homeplace in the autumn of 1863, when war engulfed his property. General and Mrs. Ewell lived in the home for much of the period prior to the Wilderness campaign. Hotchkiss, *Journal,* 183, 187; Freeman, *Lee's Lieutenants,* III, 331. . . . Huffman, *Ups and Downs,* 83 corroborated Howard's story of the fake cannon.

Page 258. Howard's account of the execution of "Rosenbaum" is strange. No personal account by any member of Steuart's brigade mentions such an execution taking place. In addition, and of the eleven men with surnames close to "Rosenbaum" in the 37th Virginia, not one was listed as a deserter or under sentence of death. Possibly the regimental records were falsified to "cover the sin" of a man being executed. If so, the only one of the eleven soldiers it could have been was Pvt. Isaac D. Rosonbalm, whose personal file ends abruptly in the spring of 1864. National Archives and Records Service (comp.), "Compiled Service Records of Confederate Soldiers Who Served in Organizations from the State of Virginia" (Washington, microfilm copy, 1961), Roll 837.

Cited hereafter as CSR—Virginia. . . . In the autumn of 1861, William H. Norris fled Baltimore while orders were being drafted for his arrest. He and a fellow Baltimorean were regarded as "offensive in their conduct and converation as secessionists." Although efforts were made to gain a parole for Norris, he preferred to remain in the South. *OR*, Ser. II, I, 618.

Page 264. Charles F. Crisp was in Co. K of the 10th Virginia when captured at Spotsylvania. He was confined at Forts Delaware and Pulaski until his June, 1865, parole. CSR—Virginia, Roll 491. . . . "Sometime in the winter," Howard later remembered, "Gen. Steuart unknown to me made application for a Captain's commission for me, but I asked my friend Col. Charles Marshall of Gen. Lee's staff to stop the forwarding of it. My reason was partly an indifference to rank—under the circumstances—and partly that I felt a reluctance to any change in my military status while Gen. Trimble was a prisoner, he having had me appointed to my present commission of 1st Lieutenant." Howard Notations.

Page 268. Grant's push southward began on May 3, when Gen. David M. Gregg's cavalry division splashed across the Rapidan River and acted as guards while pontoon bridges were laid. *OR*, XXXVI, Pt. 1, 857, 862; Stanton P. Allen, *Down in Dixie* (Boston, 1888), 209-13.

Page 269. Marching orders for the brigade came late in the morning, Col. Thruston recalled, and Steuart's men moved out "at midday." *SHSP*, XIV (1886), 147.

Page 270. Although Ewell thought that the firing began at 11 A. M., Col. Thruston was emphatic that the "brisk skirmish" commenced closer to 10:30 A. M. In any event, Gen. John M. Jones's lead brigade collided with the Federal troops of Gen. Truman Seymour. *Ibid.*, 147-48; *OR*, XXXVI, Pt. 1, 732, 1070.

Page 272. The 116th New York was then with Gen. Franz Sigel's army in the Shenandoah Valley. . . . In the fighting of May 5, Col. David T. Jenkins' veteran 146th New York suffered 312 casualties (including 225 men missing). This was one of the highest regimental losses in the campaign. *Ibid.*, 123; Minnesota Commandery, MOLLUS, *Glimpses of the Nation's Struggle*, II (1890), 9-10. . . . The abandonment of two howitzers in Capt.

George D. Winslow's battery of the 1st New York Light Artillery is told in Charles S. Wainwright, *A Diary of Battle* (New York, 1962), 350-51. . . . The artillery officer captured was Lt. William H. Shelton. Clark, *N. C. Regiments*, I, 150-51. . . . "At this time," Howard added, "the firing was severe and I remember Lieut. Charles E. Raine, Adjutant of our 23rd Va., grasping my horse's bridle on the woods road near the edge of the clearing and advising me to dismount." Howard Notations.

Page 273. A skillfully executed flank attack by the 5th Wisconsin succeeded in the capture of 300 Confederates, mostly from the 25th Virginia. *OR*, XXXVI, Pt. 1, 672. . . . Contrary to Howard's account, Ewell's report states that Jones "fell in a desperate effort to rally [his] brigade." *Ibid.*, 1070. For additional data on Jones, see Worsham, *Jackson's Foot Cavalry*, 130-31.

Page 274. Leroy A. Stafford commanded a Louisiana brigade in Edward Johnson's division. Stafford, whom Johnson praised as "the bravest man I ever saw," was killed in the late-afternoon attack. *OR*, XXXVI, Pt. 1, 1071, 1074. . . . For additional praise of Warren, see Spencer, *Civil War Marriage*, 254. . . . Major Isaac G. Coffman died five days after being wounded. *Ibid.*, 216, 255.

Page 278. Emmett E. DePriest continued as captain of Co. H, 23rd Virginia, until his May 12 capture at Spotsylvania. Following almost a year at Fort Delaware, he was shipped to Richmond and paroled a week after Lee's surrender. CSR—Virginia, Roll 663. . . . Cicero H. Craige was shot on May 10, not May 7, and he died July 9 from the effects of the wound. Manarin, *N. C. Troops*, III, 578.

Page 279. Gordon's flank attack late on May 6 broke the Federal battle line and resulted in 400 Union dead plus hundreds more captured, including Gens. Truman Seymour and Alexander Shaler. Howard gives the impression that some Confederate shortsightedness stopped Gordon from doing further damage. In reality, Gordon reported, "the approach of darkness in the dense woodland created confusion" in his ranks and forced him to halt the action. *OR*, XXXVI, Pt. 1, 1077. See also Gordon, *Reminiscences*, 250-51. . . . A soldier in Gordon's brigade saw the two captured generals that night around one of Ewell's campfires. "General

Seymour was talking to his captors as familiarly as if he had been one of them. . . . He was a tall handsome young officer with a very pleasing address. General Shaler was short and thick-set and seemed too mad to say a word . . ." *Confederate Veteran*, XXVIII (1920), 21.

Page 280. Another source stated that the two captured howitzers were removed from the field under cover of darkness on May 6—and after a mild confrontation over the spoils between the 1st North Carolina and 6th Alabama. Clark, *N. C. Regiments*, I, 151. . . . Some 200 soldiers were cremated by flames that swept through the underbrush of the Wilderness. *OR*, XXXVI, Pt. 1, 218. . . . Grant did not become unnerved by Gordon's late-afternoon attack. Colonel Charles H. T. Collis' remarks (summarized in the footnote) contained more anti-Burnside bias than substantiated fact. For Grant's reaction to Gordon's assault, see Bruce Catton, *Grant Takes Command* (Boston, 1968), 200. . . . Of the other North Carolina officers cited in the Thruston footnote, both Capt. John L. Cantwell and Lt. Robert H. Lyon were captured May 12 at Spotsylvania. Adjutant Theodore C. James served the remainder of the war in the Invalid Corps. Manarin, *N. C. Troops*, III, 488, 543, 566.

Page 281. In footnote 16, Howard misread Ewell's report. The corps commander did state that his men buried 1,100 Federals, but this figure was the total for the May 5-12 period, not merely the May 5-6 battle in the Wilderness. *OR*, XXXVI, Pt. 1, 1075. . . . General William N. Pendleton, commanding Lee's artillery, reported that Col. J. T. Brown "fell instantly killed by the bullet of a sharpshooter as he was seeking an advanced and favorable position for some of his guns." *Ibid.*, 1041.

Page 283. On May 8, the Stonewall Brigade in Johnson's division marched for over eighteen hours. *SHSP*, XXI, (1893), 232. . . . Theodore Lyman, a strongly opinionated Massachusetts staff officer, once referred to Collis as "a petty, scheming political officer." This dislike obviously continued for many years after the war. Theodore Lyman, *Meade's Headquarters, 1863-1865* (Boston, 1922), 247. Regrettably, Lyman did not record in detail his own recollections of the Wilderness fighting.

Page 284. The Spotsylvania earthworks were so strong that

Gen. James A. Walker of the Stonewall Brigade pronounced them "one of the very best lines of temporary field works I ever saw." *SHSP*, XXI (1893), 233. . . . Estimates of Rodes's losses during the fighting of May 10 vary. Ewell put the division's casualties at 650 men, including 250 captured, while Federals claimed to have captured 900-1200 Confederates. *OR*, XXXVI, Pt. 1, 191, 668, 1072. Federal losses were close to 3,000 men. These high figures in a one-day fight stemmed in great part from an "especially disastrous" assault made by the Federals in late afternoon. *Ibid.*, 67; Douglas, *I Rode with Stonewall*, 279.

Page 290. In the footnote, Col. Lyman mentioned the "gross neglect" present in the May 10 assault. This is a reference largely to Gen. Gershom Mott's division, which fell apart in the first stage of the action. See James I. Robertson, Jr. (ed.), *The Civil War Letters of General Robert McAllister* (New Brunswick, N. J., 1965), 417 and n. . . . For Capt. Barton's own account of his May 10 actions, see Randolph Barton, *Recollections, 1861-1865* (Baltimore, 1913), 51-53.

Page 291. Sergeant-Major of the 3rd North Carolina was Robert C. McRee. Wounded on May 10, he lived until June 6. Clark, *N. C. Regiments*, I, 203; Manarin, *N. C. Troops*, III, 489.

Page 292. Anchored on the left of Steuart's brigade were the Georgia regiments of Gen. George Doles. . . . John H. Worsham is the only soldier in Jones's brigade who penned detailed memoirs of Civil War service. Worsham made no mention of any despondency in the ranks at that time. . . . Howard's statement that only a picket line connected Steuart's right with the left flank of Gen. Cadmus M. Wilcox's division is not true. On the night of May 11-12, Steuart's right merged with Gen. James H. Lane's brigade —the left wing of Wilcox's division. *SHSP*, VI (1878), 73.

Page 293. One of the better Federal accounts of the May 12 fighting is in McAllister, *Civil War Letters*, 417-21. . . . Ewell's assistant adjutant general was Maj. G. Campbell Brown, his stepson. . . . Lee's definitive biographer brusquely dismissed the allegation that Lee received a dispatch from Johnson relative to the return of the artillery. Douglas S. Freeman, *R. E. Lee: A Biography* (New York, 1934-1935), III, 316n.

Page 296. The artillery that came to Johnson's aid was Maj.

Richard C. M. Page's battalion. Pendleton praised the "extraordinary speed" displayed by the gunners in moving to the front. Johnson reported that they arrived "at a gallop." *OR*, XXXVI, Pt. 1, 1044, 1080. Artillerists in Capt. William P. Carter's battery managed to unlimber one piece and fire a single shot before Federals overran the Southern lines. *SHSP*, XXI (1893), 240, 243-44. For more on the controversy surrounding the alleged slowness of the artillery in arriving at the front, see *ibid.*, VII (1879), 535-40.

Page 297. Robert C. Bragonier was twenty-three at that time. He was captured at Spotsylvania, taken to Fort Delaware, exchanged in September, but confined in a Richmond hospital for the remainder of the war. CSR—Virginia, Roll 490.

Page 300. Marsena R. Patrick reported the capture on May 12 of "some 3,000" Confederates. His diary entry for that date also reflects a sharp dislike of Gen. Steuart. Patrick boasted in his journal of knowing the various units whose members had been captured. David S. Sparks (ed.), *Inside Lincoln's Army: The Diary of General Marsena Rudolph Patrick.* . . . (New York, 1964), 372.

Page 301. At the end of the first paragraph, Howard later added: "When I came to the group where Gen. Patrtick and Gen. Steuart were, I heard a Union officer say, 'I would give .... for that fellow.' I am sorry I do not remember what my personal equation in money was. I think $100." Howard Notations. . . . Many are the stories told of "Old Allegheny" Johnson in the May 12 fighting. On foot, clothes torn, and brandishing his cane above his head as he stood defiantly atop the earthworks, he was an awesome figure until his capture. See *SHSP*, XXI (1893), 241; XXXIII (1905), 338. An amusing but unlikely story about Johnson after his capture is in Casler, *Four Years*, 217. . . . As Col. Lyman pointed out in *supra*, 283n., Johnson had breakfast that morning with Federal Gen. Seth Williams. . . . For the details of Steuart refusing the hand of a former friend, Gen. W. S. Hancock, see *OR*, XXXVI, Pt. 1, 359.

Page 303. The Union regiment that Howard and his fellow prisoners encountered was the 11th Vermont of Gen. Horatio G. Wright's VI Corps. One of the Vermont officers considered the

Confederate prisoners "resolute looking" and "defiant," and he also gave an entirely different story about the band music. See *Letters of George E. Chamberlin* (Springfield, Ill., 1883), 315-16.

Page 304. Assistant Surg. Thomas G. Mackenzie was then acting medical purveyor for the Army of the Potomac. A report of his Belle Plain activities is in *OR*, XXXVI, Pt. 1, 273-74. . . . George H. Stuart, a wealthy Philadelphia merchant, was then chairman of the U. S. Christian Commission. . . . Colonel William Hoffman was Comissary-General of Prisoners. Grant's instructions to him regarding disposition of the men captured at Spotsylvania are in *ibid.,* Pt. 2, 697-98.

Page 305. Fort Delaware was pentagonal in shape. It became a prisoner of war compound late in March, 1862, when some 250 Southerners captured at Kernstown were sent there. The prison population fluctuated during the war; yet in the autumn of 1863, it had a peak number of 12,000 inmates.

Page 306. Captured Aug. 22, 1863, and first sent to Johnson's Island, M. Jeff Thompson arrived at Fort Delaware in February, 1864, for what became a four-month stay. See Jay Monaghan, *Swamp Fox of the Confederacy* (Tuscaloosa, Ala., 1956), 63-72.

Page 308. Polish-born Albin F. Schoepf fought in two different armies during the 1848 revolutions in Europe. He then emigrated to America, obtained a brigadier's commission at the outbreak of the Civil War, and served for a year in the Western theater. Questionable conduct at the battle of Perryville caused his transfer from field command. From Apr. 23, 1863, until Jan. 1, 1866, he was commandant of Fort Delaware. Howard's comments about him parallel those of fellow prisoner J. Ogden Murray in *The Immortal Six Hundred* (Winchester, Va., 1905), 56-57. While one inmate called Schoepf "a Hessian brute," most of the prisoners came to regard him as a courteous and considerate officer. *Confederate Veteran,* XIII (1905), 107; SHSP, XXII (1894), 130; *Reminiscences of General Basil W. Duke* (Garden City, N. Y., 1911), 371; Edward R. Rich, *Comrades Four* (New York, 1907), 153; Isaac W. K. Handy, *United States Bonds* (Baltimore, 1874), 12, 28, 178-79, 316, 379-80. . . . The fort's guns were manned by a company of Delaware heavy artillery under the command of the Capt. Ahl mentioned on succeeding pages. *OR, XXIX,* Pt. 2, 135; XXXIII, 476.

Page 309. George W. Ahl was a Pennsylvanian who served as commissary of prisoners and "acting assistant adjutant general and inspecting officer" at Fort Delaware. In July, 1863, he also assumed command of an independent artillery company composed of former Confederate prisoners who had taken the oath of loyalty to the Union. *Ibid.,* Ser. II, VII, 766; W. Emerson Wilson to the editor, Jan. 9, 1974. Fort Delaware inmates unanimously agreed that Ahl was the most disliked of their captors. Prisoners accused him of being "a cold-blooded, heartless, cruel, and cowardly South-hater," as well as a man who took delight in "exercising petty tyranny" over his helpless subjects. See *SHSP,* III (1877), 44; XXII (1894), 130-31; *Confederate Veteran,* XVIII (1910), 516; Rich, *Comrades Four,* 133-34; Handy, *United States Bonds,* 26. . . . Union and Confederate physicians both praised Schoepf's attention to the prison and its inmates. *OR,* Ser. II, VI, 215-16, 281. The *Official Records* contain no hint of dissatisfaction by Washington officials of Schoepf's administration.

Page 310. Lieutenant A. G. Wolf arrived at Fort Delaware in September, 1862, as assistant commissary of prisoners. A Virginia inmate charged that Wolf was "a graduate from the slums of Philadelphia city, a coarse, brutal creature, with all the mean, cowardly, and cruel instincts of the beast from which his name was taken." Captain Robert E. Park of the 12th Alabama noted that Wolf "is generally drunk, boastful and boisterous." Park added that Wolf and Capt. Ahl "seem to delight in harassing and annoying the defenceless victims under their care and control." *Narrative of Privations and Sufferings of United States Officers and Soldiers While Prisoners of War* (Philadelphia, 1864), 214-15; Murray, *Immortal Six Hundred,* 58; *SHSP,* III (1878), 44, 56. . . . No "Sergeant Cunningham" is mentioned in the usual rosters of prison guards at Fort Delaware. For example, see Henry R. Berkeley, *Four Years in the Confederate Artillery* (Charlottesville, Va., 1961), 148. However, prisoner Isaac Handy mentioned him as a "self-important 'acting sergeant,' " a "blustering little fellow" who "seems to think he is popular . . . but many a secret dart is hurled at him, and woe to the upstart, if any of 'our boys' should meet him in Dixie." Handy, *United States Bonds*, 63, 130. The foremost authority on Fort Delaware is of the opinion that Cunningham was a former Confederate prisoner who volunteered for service in Ahl's artillery company. W. Emerson Wilson to the editor, Jan. 9, 1974.

Page 313. So bad was the food at Fort Delaware that the prisoners dubbed the eating area "Devil's Half Acre." See Clark, *N. C. Regiments*, IV, 727; Morgan, *Personal Reminiscences*, 225; Curtis C. Davis (ed.), *Belle Boyd in Camp and Prison* (South Brunswick, N. J., 1967), 338-39. . . . Of the drinking water, Howard's friend Randolph Barton wrote: "The want of pure water would have killed half of us if we had stayed at Fort Delaware a few months longer; old barrels, regardless of former contents, were filled at Brandywine Creek, I think, loaded on river craft, brought under a blazing sun to Fort Delaware and, warm and putrid, were doled out to us." Barton, *Recollections*, 35-36. Cf. *OR*, Ser. II, VI, 215. . . . Examples of unwarranted restrictions placed on the Fort Delaware inmates are in *ibid.*, VI, 625, 628; VII, 809-11.

Page 318. Lieutenant Col. E. Pope Jones of the 109th Virginia Militia was "quite lame" at the time. On the night of July 7, Pvt. William G. Douglass of the 157th Ohio (a home guard unit recruited for 100 days' service) shot Jones when the latter refused to leave the sink after being ordered three times to do so. *North Carolina Historical Review*, XXXIX (1962), 65; *OR*, Ser. II, VII, 452-54; Handy, *United States Bonds*, 473-75, 477, 481. Douglass was eighteen at the time; and contrary to rumor, he was not promoted to corporal because of his deed. *Official Roster of the State of Ohio in the War of the Rebellion, 1861-1865* (Akron and Cincinnati, 1889-1893), IX, 248.

Page 321. Henry B. Judd was then military commander of the Wilmington, Del., district. *OR*, Ser. III, IV, 1085. . . . On June 13, 1864, Gen. John Hunt Morgan's commissary officer, Maj. William P. Elliott, had been placed in solitary confinement in retaliation for alleged mistreatment at Libby Prison of Maj. Nathan Goff of the 4th West Virginia Cavalry. Elliott "having been taken sick," Maj. Mills replaced him on Aug. 30 and re-

452   RECOLLECTIONS OF A CONFEDERATE SOLDIER

mained in the dungeon until Sept. 3. *Ibid.,* Ser. II, VII, 368, 391, 626, 834.

Page 324. One or more prisoners did alert Richmond authorities of the suspected loyalties of Col. John A. Baker of the 3rd North Carolina Cavalry. On Sept. 30, 1864, Sec. of War James A. Seddon directed that if Baker's release could be effected, he was to be brought at once to Richmond "for examination or trial" because of "very serious charges" lodged against him. *Ibid.,* 899.

Page 325. According to the 1862 Washington city directory, Henry Goldsmith was a sutler operating out of the Northern capital.

Page 327. Members of the 6th Massachusetts reciprocated Howard's sentiments. "Our boys seemed to cherish not a spark of ill-will toward their captured enemies," the chaplain of the regiment observed. "The pleasantest relations existed between us, and, so far as the regulations allowed, agreeable intercourse was had." John W. Hanson, *Historical Sketch of the Old Sixth Regiment* . . . (Boston, 1866), 301. Contrary to Howard's statement, the 6th Massachusetts did not remain at Fort Delaware until the end of the war. The New Englanders embarked for home on Oct. 19, 1864, and were replaced by the 9th Delaware. *Ibid.,* 305.

Page 329. Isaac Handy had originally been arrested for derogatory remarks concerning the American flag. *United States Bonds,* 5-9. In September, 1864, Adj. Boyle of the 32nd North Carolina wrote: "This gentleman, a victim of Federal oppression, has been imprisoned here for more than 14 months for I may say *no* cause just or unjust. He has labored most faithfully and has done much good amongst his fellow prisoners. He has preached more than 300 sermons since his imprisonment." *North Carolina Historical Review,* XXXIX (1962), 68-69.

Page 331. Handy made note in his diary of a number of escape attempts. In July, 1864, one Confederate officer drowned while attempting to get to the mainland. *Ibid.,* 62. . . . A. C. Foster of the 4th Alabama was captured in November, 1863, and was one of 600 Confederates transferred to Charleston. Handy, *United States Bonds,* 641.

Page 335. The Negro sentinels were members of the 36th U. S.

Colored Infantry and had been recruited in North Carolina. Edwin W. Beitzell, *Point Lookout Prison Camp for Confederates* (Washington, 1972), 26, 36, 112; *SHSP*, VII (1879), 393-94, 489. . . . The *City of New York* made transatlantic crossings until the Civil War forced its conversion into a coastline freighter. *OR*, Ser. II, II, 451; *Navy OR*, IV, 483; VI, 88.

Page 336. Skimpy naval communiques of that period make no mention of any vessel running aground at Cape Hatteras. *Ibid.*, XVI, 47, 53, 461.

Page 338. Captain Robert W. B. Elliott served on Gen. A. R. Lawton's staff through the Gettysburg campaign. When Howard encountered him at Savannah, Elliott was assistant adjutant-general to Gen. Lafayette McLaws. *OR*, XXXVII, Pt. 2, 452; XLIV, 952. . . . Willim N. Habersham was a wealthy Savannah merchant whose principal source of income was a steam rice mill. He was an authority on both salmon fishing and Madeira wines. Josephine C. Habersham, *Ebb Tide* (Athens, Ga., 1958), 10-11.

Page 339. "Commodore Huger" was Joseph A. Huger. He was the second husband of Mary Elliott, Bishop Elliott's niece. Her first husband, Robert Habersham Elliott, was also her cousin. He died in service early in the war. Mrs. Lilla M. Hawes, Georgia Historical Society, to the editor, Jan. 16, 1974.

Page 340. The Rt. Rev. Stephen Elliott was first Episcopal bishop for the Diocese of Georgia. Robert Elliott was his son by a second marriage to Charlotte B. Barnwell, who was also the Bishop's cousin. The "near relative" to whom Howard referred was Mary Habersham, William Habersham's half-sister. Stephen B. Barnwell, *The Story of an American Family* (Marquette, Wis., 1969), 159-60, 200, 231-32; J. G. B. Bulloch, *History and Genealogy of the Habersham Family* . . . (Columbia, S. C., 1901), 16.

Page 342. Dr. Edward Cheves, son of the famous Langdon Cheves, was active early in the war in the development of balloons and torpedoes. On July 10, 1863, he was killed in action at Battery Wagner, S. C. The family owned two plantations. "The Delta," alongside the Ogeechee River, was the one that Howard visited. *Savannah Republican*, July 17, 1862; E. Porter Alexander, *Military Memoirs of a Confederate* (New York, 1907), 172-73; *South Carolina Historical Magazine*, XLV (1944), 1-11.

Page 343. Early in the war, paymaster Henry Myers of the C. S. Navy was travelling on a French ship that docked at Tangier. There he was arrested and charged with being an officer of "the rebel steamer Sumter." Myers was forcibly returned to America and imprisoned for a time at Fort Warren. *OR*, Ser. II, III, 284, 287, 477; IV, 315, 441. . . . Lieutenant Col. John R. Waddy served as Beauregard's chief of ordnance. *Ibid.*, Ser. I, XXXV, Pt. 1, 549.

Page 349. On Dec. 19, 1864, Maj. Gen. Alfred T. A. Torbert with 5,000 Federal cavalry left Winchester on an expedition into central Virginia. Torbert's men collided three days later near Gordonsville with 1,300 Southern horsemen under Maj. Gen. Lunsford Lomax. Superior Federal numbers pushed back Lomax's men, but the Confederates concentrated their forces and fought Torbert to a standstill. On Dec. 23, Gen. John Bratton's South Carolina brigade (not Rhett's troops, as Howard stated) arrived and forced Torbert's withdrawal. While Torbert reported the capture of 30 prisoners, 1,000 head of stock and 2 cannon, his command suffered 7 killed, 48 wounded and 47 missing. Lomax's total losses are unknown. *Ibid.*, XLII, Pt. 1, 882-83; XLIII, Pt. 1, 679; Pt. 2, 833, 942, 947.

Page 354. The new major-general was "a man of the highest character and an officer of the finest culture and a very high order of ability." Yet because Custis Lee had never commanded troops in the field, "every time he met one of his father's veteran fighting colonels he felt compromised at having the stars and wreath of a major-general on his collar." Robert Stiles, *Four Years under Marse Robert* (New York, 1903), 312; Freeman, *Lee's Lieutenants,* III, 685. . . . Seth M. Barton had been a brigade commander since the latter part of 1862. However, vacillation in battles at New Berne, N. C., and Drewry's Bluff, Va., led to his reassignment to the Richmond defenses. *OR*, XXXIII, 93-94; Ezra J. Warner, *Generals in Gray* (Baton Rouge, 1959), 18-19. . . . Colonel Atkinson's battalion commanders were Majs. James O. Hensley and N. Robert Cary. *OR*, XLVI, Pt. 2, 1112. . . . General Steuart had taken command of Lewis A. Armistead's old brigade of five veteran Virginia regiments. *Ibid.*, 1268.

Page 355. Major William S. Basinger's 18th Georgia Infantry

Battalion had not seen as much active duty as its members boasted. Its first battle experience occurred in May, 1864, at Charleston, S. C. That autumn the Georgians did extensive improvements on the defenses of Mattoax Station, which Howard mentioned subsequently. *Ibid.*, XL, Pt. 2, 691-92; XLII, Pt. 2, 264-65; Pt. 2, 1225, 1251; *SHSP*, XXIV (1896), 251. . . . While it is natural to think of a division in the Civil War as having 12,000-15,000 men, it should be remembered that in the last months of the war Confederate units were skeletal in size. Custis Lee's "division" numbered no more than 3,000 troops—far less than the normal strength of a brigade. Basinger's 18th Georgia Battalion consisted of precisely eighty-five men. *OR*, XLVI, Pt. 1, 1295; *SHSP*, XLII (1917), 151.

Page 356. Brigadier Gen. Rains developed land-mines during the campaigns of the 1840s against the Seminole Indians in Florida. He re-employed these novel weapons with even greater success against McClellan's army during the 1862 Peninsular Campaign. See Milton F. Perry, *Infernal Machines* (Baton Rouge, 1965), 20-27.

Page 358. E. Porter Alexander was chief of artillery for Longstreet's First Corps. What Howard beheld was Alexander testing the range and accuracy of the rapidly deteriorating Confederate guns. *OR*, XLVI, Pt. 2, 1194, 1266-67. . . . Richmond's best-known wartime minister was the Rev. Charles M. Minnegerode, rector of St. Paul's Episcopal Church. He was not related to Bismarck, but he did speak what one listener called "broken English." Charles A. Page, *Letters of a War Correspondent* (Boston, 1899), 348.

Page 362. On the afternoon of Apr. 1, Maj. Gen. Charles W. Field was ordered to transfer his division from the extreme Confederate left to the shattered right flank at Five Forks. Field's command consisted of 4,600 men—equal in number to two-thirds of the Confederates captured at Five Forks. Freeman, *Lee's Lieutenants*, III, 671, 675.

Page 363. Symington was one of Pickett's most trusted aides. At the 1862 Frayser's Farm battle, his horse received seven bullet wounds while the young officer rallied the men. LaSalle Corbett Pickett, *Pickett and His Men* (Atlanta, 1900), 189. . . . Lee's orders to Ewell for the abandonment of Richmond are in *OR,* XLVI, Pt. 3, 1380.

Page 365. Ewell, commanding the Richmond defenses, stated in his official report: "General G. W. C. Lee's division, being mostly composed of heavy artillery, was almost without transportation, which was procured by impressing all that could be found." *Ibid.,* Pt. 1, 1293. . . . Major Stiles wrote that the men of his "poor little battalion" of artillery left Chaffin's Bluff with "more baggage piled upon their backs than any one brigade, perhaps I might say division, in General Lee's army was bearing at the same moment." Yet, Stiles added, "there was no time to correct the folly." Stiles, *Marse Robert,* 322. . . . Of inflation rampant in Richmond in 1865, Capt. Thomas B. Blake of Custis Lee's command observed: "It was a joke of the day that you went to market with a basket full of money and put your marketing in your pocket." *Confederate Veteran,* XXVIII (1920), 213. . . . Dr. Samuel A. Green served successively as a surgeon in the 1st and 24th Massachusetts. After the war he was a trustee of Harvard University and vice president of the Massachusetts Historical Society. Mass. Adj. Gen. (comp.), *Massachusetts Soldiers, Sailors and Marines in the Civil War* (Norwood, Mass., 1931), I, 2; II, 776; Alfred S. Roe, *The Twenty-fourth Regiment, Massachusetts Volunteers, 1861-1866* (Worcester, Mass., 1907), 454.

Page 367. The James River squadron consisted of the ironclads *Virginia, Richmond* and *Fredericksburg,* plus five wooden gunboats. Their destruction is sadly related in Raphael Semmes, *Memoirs of Service Afloat during the War between the States* (Baltimore, 1869), 803, 810-12.

Page 370. Howard may have confused his dates. April 5, not April 4, was a day of constant rainshowers. *Contributions to a History of the Richmond Howitzer Battalion,* III (1884), 57.

Page 372. Major Basinger of the 18th Georgia Battalion later recalled: "I need not . . . enlarge on the starving condition of the troops further than to say that from the commencement of the movement to the moment of our falling into the hands of the enemy, the only stores issued were one pound of meal and one-third of a pound of bacon. These were issued on the afternoon of the 4th, and so far as I was informed, only to this brigade

. . ." *SHSP,* XXV (1897), 38-39. Major Stiles, in *Marse Robert,* 326-27, cited only one issue of rations between Petersburg and Sayler's Creek. . . . The attack that day by Federal cavalry under Gen. Henry E. Davies, Jr., resulted in the destruction of some 180 wagons that the Confederates could ill afford to lose. *OR,* XLVI, Pt. 1, 1107, 1145, 1301. . . . At times Commodore Tucker forgot and issued orders to his men in naval jargon. For more on the unique Naval Battalion, see Stiles, *Marse Robert,* 329; Ohio Commandery, MOLLUS, *Sketches of War History,* III (1890), 11-12.

Page 374. The surprise attack, Maj. Basinger believed, occurred at 10 P. M. from "what was supposed to be a small advanced party of the enemy's cavalry." *SHSP,* XXV (1897), 39. Custis Lee reported the volleys as coming from "some of the enemy's scouts." *OR,* XLVI, Pt. 1, 1296.

Page 378. By Apr. 6, the Army of Northern Virginia was falling apart. "Initiative was gone," Dr. Freeman concluded. "Dispirited movements were mechanical. Men acted as if they were in a nightmare and could not make their muscles respond." *Lee's Lieutenants,* III, 703. When a large gap subsequently developed in the Confederate line of retreat, Sheridan's Federal cavalry drove through it like a wedge. This isolated the rear third of Lee's army and led to the battle of Sayler's Creek. *SHSP,* XLII (1917), 143-44.

Page 379. Custis Lee spent the critical period 11 A. M.-2 P. M. waiting for the Confederate wagons to pass safely. In addition, Lee provided protection for Gen. John B. Gordon's men, who were bringing up the rear of the struggling Confederate army. *OR,* XLVI, Pt. 1, 1294, 1297.

Page 380. Two Federal guns initially deployed on the crest of the Hillsman farm. Other artillery quickly joined in the bombardment. Some discrepancy exists over the duration of the barrage. Stiles was of the opinion that the shelling lasted but "a few minutes;" Ewell reported that it continued "nearly half an hour;" Custis Lee, in his first major battle, was certain that the barrage lasted "an hour or more." Stiles, *Marse Robert,* 330; *OR,* XLVI, Pt. 1, 652, 1295, 1297.

Page 381. During the artillery duel, Maj. Basinger observed of

Stiles's gunners: "There was something surprising in their perfect steadiness and order," particularly since they "had never before been engaged." Stiles, naturally in a position to observe more closely, wrote: "The expression of the men's faces indicated clearly enough [the bombardment's] effect upon them. They did not appear to be hopelessly demoralized, but they did look blanched and haggard and awe-struck." *SHSP,* XXV (1897), 40; Stiles, *Marse Robert,* 330.

Page 382. The repeating rifles used in this battle were seven-shot Spencer carbines. *OR,* XLVI, Pt. 1, 942; James L. Bowen, *History of the Thirty-seventh Regiment Mass. Volunteers in the Civil War of 1861-1865* (Holyoke, Mass., 1884), 417. . . . In fighting at first reminiscent of Fredericksburg, Confederates poured volleys of musketry into the approaching lines of Federals. The bluecoats fell back—whereupon Custis Lee's green troops, caught up in the novel enthusiasm of battle, foolishly jumped from their works and made an impromptu counterattack. Soon, wrote an artillery officer, "the two lines mingled in one promiscuous and prolonged melee with clubbed muskets and bayonets, as if bent upon exterminating each other individually." Alexander, *Military Memoirs,* 596. See also *OR,* XLVI, Pt. 1, 946-47, 998, 1297; *SHSP,* XXV (1897), 40-41; Stiles, *Marse Robert,* 332-33. . . . While "gallantly leading a successful charge against the enemy," Col. Crutchfield was beheaded by a cannon shot. *OR,* XLVI, Pt. 1, 1297; Moore, *Cannoneer,* 281. . . . No "Capt. O'Brien" is listed in the major roster of Confederate officers captured at Sayler's Creek. The officer in question was probably Augustin P. O'Brien, a British soldier-of-fortune. *New York Herald,* Apr. 9, 1865.

Page 383. Howard may have been correct in asserting that some of the Confederate wounded were shot a second time during the heat of the battle. Major Basinger later wrote: "I displayed my handkerchief in token of surrender. As I did, the enemy . . . rushed into the road, and fired upon my wounded who lay in the gulley . . . It was with the greatest difficulty they could be induced to cease from this barbarity." *SHSP,* XXV (1897), 42.

Page 386. Wright's praise of Custis Lee's stand is in *supra,* 387n. . . . General Philip Sheridan, never one to commend a foe, nevertheless wrote of the "gallant resistance" waged by Lee's division; and in later years, Sheridan spoke of Lee's troops fighting with the desperation of "a tiger at bay." *OR*, XLVI, Pt. 1, 1108; *Personal Memoirs of P. H. Sheridan* (New York, 1888), II, 180, 183. General George Custer made no reference to Confederate valor in his report. *OR*, XLVI, Pt. 1, 1132.

Page 387. Major John A. Salsbury of the 10th Vermont was in charge of the guard detail for the Sayler's Creek prisoners. Presumably the Federal troops who looted the personal possessions were members of Gen. William S. Truex's brigade, which consisted of the 10th Vermont, 14th New Jersey, 87th Pennsylvania, and 106th and 151st New York. E. M. Haynes, *A History of the Tenth Regiment, Vt. Vols.* (Rutland, Vt., 1894), 371; *OR*, XLVI, Pt. 1, 572.

Page 390. After the war, Federal Gen. Hazard Stevens wrote with obvious contempt: "The next day [April 7], seeing Custer ride past, followed by an escort bearing in triumph thirty-seven captured battle-flags, an old soldier of the Sixth Corps was heard to remark, 'Oh, yes, my boy, you have picked up the apples, but the Sixth Corps shook the tree for you.'" *Papers of the Military Historical Society of Massachusetts,* VI (1907), 447. . . . Colonel Adam Badeau remembered that on Apr. 7 he was handling dispatches at Grant's Burkeville headquarters when the contingent of captured generals arrived. "It was a sorry company of tired and hungry and dejected men," Badeau stated. "I gave them some whiskey, and they warmed themselves at the campfire, and then they were locked up in a house near by, under the orders of the provost marshal, Colonel [George H.] Sharpe." Adam Badeau, *Military History of Ulysses S. Grant* (New York, 1868-1881), III, 577-78. Sharpe commandeered the Burkeville home of Withers Waller for the overnight use of the Confederate officers. Hunton, *Autobiography*, 125.

Page 391. For a photograph and biographical sketch of the colorful Thomas P. Ochiltree, see *Confederate Veteran,* IX (1901), 231. . . . The other captured generals whom Howard could not recall were Seth M. Barton and Dudley M. Du Bose.

Page 392. Twenty-two-year-old Charles C. Flowerree commanded the 7th Virginia at the time of his capture. . . . Howard's group reached Petersburg on Apr. 13. There Custis Lee received word that his mother was dying in Richmond. Lee did not wish to leave his fellow prisoners, but at their urging he did so. "It turned out that his mother was not more disposed than usual, and that [the report] was a generous device on the part of some of his old army friends and West Point classmates to avoid sending him to prison." Hunton, *Autobiography*, 128.

Page 394. General William H. F. Payne had successively led the "Black Horse Cavalry" and the 4th Virginia Cavalry. He was wounded and captured at Gettysburg. Subsequently exchanged, Payne commanded a cavalry brigade before his arrest on the night of Lincoln's assassination. "Carried into Washington the next day, he narrowly escaped violence at the hands of the populace." *CMH*, III, 647.

Page 398. William Fitzhugh Randolph, the older brother of Bishop Alfred M. Randolph, served in the 39th Virginia Cavalry. Howard probably met him in 1862, when Randolph's company served as bodyguard for Gen. R. S. Ewell. Randolph was captured in September, 1863, while on patrol in Fauquier County. CSR— Virginia, Roll 199.

Page 400. Captain Gustavus A. Dyes, a native of Hamburg, Germany, lived in St. Charles, Mo., at the outbreak of war. He served with Sterling Price's forces. McHenry Howard notebook, Howard Papers; *OR*, XXII, Pt. 1, 417. . . . Trimble's grandiose but futile escape attempt, hatched in the latter part of 1863, is described in *SHSP*, XIX (1891), 283-88; XXIII (1895), 283-90. . . . Contrary to Howard's assertion, a large number of successful escapes were made from Johnson's Island. Donald J. Breen, "The History of the Federal Military Prison on Johnson's Island, Ohio, 1862-1865" (M. A. thesis, Kent State University, 1962), 119-71. Colonel B. L. Farinholt of Baltimore, a fellow prisoner, stated that Grogan escaped "by secreting himself in some straw at the bottom of a barge which was being towed back to Sandusky . . ." *Confederate Veteran*, V (1897), 514.

Page 402. At least two earlier escape attempts using Federal uniforms were made. One was successful, *Ibid.*, XXIV (1916), 362. . . . The child accompanying Mrs. Pendleton was her daughter Jeannie, who later married Washington attorney Arthur Brice.

Howard Notations. . . . Colonel Charles W. Hill served as Adjutant General of Ohio until his appointment to command of the 128th Ohio, the regiment entrusted with the security of Johnson's Island. *Civil War History*, VIII (1962), 210. For praise of his kindness and consideration toward prisoners, see W. S. Dunlop, *Lee's Sharpshooters* (Little Rock, 1899), 322.

Photograph 12A. The Confederate monument is located in Mt. Royal Place, not Eutaw Place as stated in the caption. Howard Notations. Dedicatory ceremonies for the monument are summarized in *Confederate Veteran*, XI (1903), 268-69.

INDEX

INDEX (Continued)

INDEX (Continued)

INDEX (Continued)

INDEX (Continued)

INDEX (Continued)

INDEX (Continued)

INDEX (Continued)

470   RECOLLECTIONS OF A CONFEDERATE SOLDIER

INDEX (Continued)

INDEX (Continued)

INDEX (Continued)

INDEX (Continued)

INDEX (Continued)

INDEX (Continued)

INDEX (Continued)

INDEX (Continued)

INDEX (Continued)

INDEX (Continued)

INDEX (Continued)

INDEX (Continued)

INDEX (Continued)

INDEX (Continued)

Books Published by Morningside Bookshop

ALLAN—HOTCHKISS; History of the Campaign of Thomas J. Jackson in the Shenandoah Valley of Virginia Nov. 1861-June 1862. Maps, Dayton, 1974.   Price $15.00

ANDERSON, EPHRAIM McDOWELL, Memoirs: Historical and Personal; Including the CAMPAIGNS OF THE FIRST MISSOURI CONFEDERATE BRIGADE edited by Edwin C. Bearss, Index by Margie Riddle Bearss, with Map by Barbara Long, 616 pp, Dayton, 1972.   Price $15.00

CALDWELL, J. F. J.; The History of a Brigade of South Carolinians, known first as "Gregg's" and subsequently as "McGowan's Brigade" 249 pp, Dayton, 1974.   Paperback $7.50. Cloth Price $12.50

CASLER, JOHN O., of Co. A, 33rd Virginia Infantry, A.N.V., Four Years in the Stonewall Brigade. 362 pp. Edited by Dr. James I. Robertson. Dayton, 1971.   Price $10.00

CHAMBERLAIN, JOSHUA L., The Passing of the Armies, an account of the final Campaign of the Army of the Potomac. 392 pp, Maps, Dayton, 1974.   Price $17.50

Confederate Veteran Magazine Index, 1893-1932. An exact reprint of the indices as issued 1893-1932, 296 pp. Dayton, 1972.   Price $25.00

DACUS, DR. ROBERT H., Reminiscences of Company "H", First Arkansas Mounted Rifles, 47 pp, Dayton, 1972. Wraps Price $5.00

DICKERT, D. AUGUSTUS, History of the Kershaw Brigade. New introduction by Dr. Wm. Stanley Hoole, 583 pp, index, errata, photos, roster and biographical sketches.   Out-of-Print

DINKINS, JAMES, 1861-1865, by an Old Johnnie. Personal recollections and experiences in the Confederate Army. 280 pp. Service with Barksdale's Mississippi Brigade, and as a staff officer on Chalmers Staff, of Forrest Cavalry. Reprint of 1897 edition.   Price $15.00

FOX, WILLIAM F., Regimental Losses, 1861-1865, 595 pp. A must for every C. W. or Confederate library. Dayton, 1974.   Price $35.00

GRAINGER, GERVIS D., Co. I, 6th Kentucky Infantry, Four Years with the Boys in Gray, 45 pp, Dayton, 1972. Grainger's experiences as an escaped prisoner.   Price $5.00

HOTCHKISS, JED, Confederate Military History, Virginia Expanded Volume, 1295 pp, photos, maps. Hundreds of personal sketches of lesser known Virginia soldiers.   Price $32.50

HOWARD, McHENRY: Recollections of a Maryland Confederate Soldier and Staff Officer under Johnston, Jackson and Lee. Edited by Dr. James I. Robertson, Jr., 483 pp, photographs, map.
                                                                        Price $20.00

JONES, BENJAMIN WASHINGTON: Under Stars and Bars, a history of the Surry Light Artillery, edited by Lee A. Wallace, Jr., Photos, map, frequent observations of Richmond in wartime. Reprint of 1909 Edition with notes.   Price $20.00

JORDAN & PRYOR'S The Campaigns of Lt. Gen. Forrest and of Forrest's Cavalry. No other book written about him or his exploits carries the General's imprimatur, for every word of which he assumed responsibility. It is the most cited of all sources in biographies of Forrest. 704 pp.   Out-of-Print

LOEHR, CHARLES T., War History of the Old First Virginia Infantry Regt. Reprint of 1884 edition. Edited by Lee A. Wallace, Jr.
Out-of-Print

MINOR, KATE PLEASANTS, An Author and Subject Index to the Southern Historical Society Papers. Introduction by Ray O. Hummel, Jr., Dayton, 1970. Reprint of 1913 Edition.   Price $10.00

OATES, W. C., War Between Union and Confederacy and History of 15th Alabama, edited by Robert Krick, of Fredericksburg Battlefield, 808 pp, plus notes by Krick. A NEALE CLASSIC. Dayton, 1974.
Price $20.00

OPIE, JOHN N., 6th Virginia Cavalry, A Rebel Cavalryman with Lee, Stuart and Jackson, 336 pp, reprint of the 1899 Edition. Dayton, 1972.   Price $12.50

SMITH, G. W., The Battle of Seven Pines, 202 pp, Maps, Dayton, 1974.
Cloth   Price $15.00

STEVENS, CAPT. C. A., Berdan's United States Sharpshooters in the Army of the Potomac, 1861-1865, illustrated, 554 pp.   Price $15.00

TAYLOR, WALTER H., General Lee, his Campaigns in Virginia, 1861-1865, with personal reminiscences, nine colored folding maps, 314 pp. The most reliable of books on Campaigns of Lee by his adjutant of four years, reprint of 1906 edition.   Price $22.50

THOMPSON, ED. PORTER. History of the Orphan Brigade, new introduction by Wm. C. Davis, 1264 pp, photos, biographical sketches, rosters, index.   Price $25.00

TUCKER, GLENN, High Tide at Gettysburg, New 1974 revised edition. 462 pp, Dayton, 1974.   Price $9.00

TUNNARD, WILLIAM H., and BEARSS, EDWIN C., 3rd Louisiana Infantry, A Southern Record, The History of the Third Louisiana Infantry, 581 pp, index by Margie Riddle Bearss; notes, roster and introduction by Edwin C. Bearss, reprint of rare 1866 Edition.
Price $15.00

WYETH, JOHN ALLAN, M.D., The Life of General Nathan Bedford Forrest. Reprint of 1899 edition, with all original photographs. 656 pp.   Price $20.00

IN PREPARATION:

EDWARDS, JOHN N., Noted Guerrillas, or, the Warfare of the Border, Reprint of the 1877 Edition, 488 pp, with Introductions by Albert Castel, (Greatest Authority on the War in the West).
Price $20.00

Morningside Bookshop

Publishers and Booksellers
Post Office Box 336, Forest Park Station
Dayton, Ohio 45405